AMERICAN MINORITIES
AND ECONOMIC OPPORTUNITY

AMERICAN MINORITIES and ECONOMIC OPPORTUNITY

H. ROY KAPLAN

SUNY Buffalo and Pitzer College

F. E. PEACOCK PUBLISHERS, INC.
ITASCA, ILLINOIS 60143

Copyright © 1977
F. E. Peacock Publishers, Inc.
All rights reserved
Library of Congress
Catalog Card No. 76-41992

Contributors

Joseph Spielberg Benitez is Professor of Anthropology, Michigan State University, East Lansing.

Leonard D Cain is Professor of Sociology and Urban Studies and Director of the Institute on Aging at Portland State University.

Hilda H. Golden is Associate Professor of Sociology at the University of Massachusetts, Amherst.

Joseph G. Jorgensen is a Professor in and Director of the Program in Comparative Culture at the University of California, Irvine.

H. Roy Kaplan is Associate Professor of Sociology at the State University of New York at Buffalo.

Bart Landry is Assistant Professor of Sociology at the University of Maryland, College Park.

Adeline Levine is Associate Professor of Sociology at the State University of New York at Buffalo.

Elena Padilla is a Professor in the Graduate School of Public Administration at New York University and Director of the Health Policy, Planning and Administration Program there.

Curt Tausky is Professor of Sociology at the University of Massachusetts, Amherst.

Sidney M. Willhelm is Associate Professor of Sociology at the State University of New York at Buffalo.

Acknowledgments

I wish to thank the contributors to this book. Without their efforts this project would not have been possible. I am also indebted to Sidney Willhelm for his suggestions, which aided me in the formative stages of this work. The editorial assistance provided by Mary Connolly and Gloria Reardon is greatly appreciated. Thanks are also extended to Edna Paine, Norma Burk, Patti Skokowski, and Marie Coleman for their typing of the manuscript. Finally, I want to thank Ted Peacock for his patience and understanding during the time this book was in preparation.

Contents

Preface

Work on this book began seven years ago. Since then the United States has undergone many momentous political and economic changes—changes which have witnessed the transference of power in three presidential administrations, and wide fluctuations in our economy from record affluence to depths of unemployment, poverty, and despair surpassed only by the depression of the 1930s. Recurrent energy crises threaten to become a standard occurrence in the absence of a reasoned energy policy, sporadically plunging segments of the labor force into the ranks of the unemployed. Yet, throughout these years of recession and inflation, of good times and bad, certain economic facts of life have persisted. While some segments of the labor force have had to endure the transitory vagaries of unemployment, the disproportionate share of the misery is borne by women, the aged, and the racial and ethnic minorities discussed in this book. They are the last to benefit during periods of national recovery and the first to feel the sting of downturns. Their second-class status has been created and perpetuated by discriminatory hiring and promotional practices which continue despite legislative reform and occasional favorable judicial decisions.

During his presidential election campaign, Jimmy Carter promised to create jobs and reduce unemployment, and he received the solid backing of these minorities. Their hopes were raised with the promise of increased federal allocations for public works projects, and it appears that $4 billion will be spent on such programs in 1977. But this will not be sufficient to ameliorate the suffering and rectify the injustices which are daily perpetrated against them. Institutionalized racial, sexual and age discrimination is highly resistant to change, and the creation of thousands of dead-end jobs at subsistence wages can hardly be viewed as a panacea for the structural ills which plague our economy.

Energy shortages, technological changes in manufacturing and delivery of services, and the growing scarcity of natural resources are perpetuating high levels of unemployment. There is no instant solution to these problems. The Carter administration is now aiming for a 5 to 5½ percent unemployment rate by 1980, recognizing that we must confront chronic long-term unemployment trends. In the coming years, hard decisions must be made about the allocation of scarce resources and the appropriation of funds to train and re-train minorities, technologically displaced workers, and people who become obsolete when shortages of raw materials force curtailment of production. We are now in a period of transition. More durable goods will be produced and we will be transformed from a consumption-oriented to a low or no-growth society. Our standard of living may decline during this process, and the transition will continue to be calamitous and disorienting until long-range planning is integrated into our social system. This book presents evidence of the value and meaning of work to groups of people who have traditionally been excluded from the security, affluence, and opportunities for upward mobility in our past and present society. It is ironic that as the obstacles to their upward mobility are being removed many of the jobs which they aspired to are becoming casualties of the social, economic and technological changes of our transformation. Will they be able to overcome these impediments and progress toward equality or will others join them as we back into the future?

February 25, 1977

H. Roy Kaplan
Claremont, California

Introduction

H. Roy Kaplan

> You work that you may keep peace with
> the earth and the soul of the earth.
> —*Kahlil Gibran*
> To earn a living can be as hard as
> to part the Red Sea.
> —*Talmud*

For most people work is an indispensable part of life which integrates them into society and simultaneously meets their social and economic needs and wants. It provides opportunities for individuals to engage in stimulating activities which develop their skills and talents. Some people value work primarily as a place where they can make friends, while others view it as a source of status and prestige which result from specific occupational ranks and titles. Just as the health faddists' claim "You are what you eat" has some validity, so too does the sociologists' observation "You are what you do," for an individual's worth and social standing are often measured by his or her occupational achievement. Some people think everyone should work because it has been divinely ordained. This belief, which is common to Judeo-Christian religions, is echoed in the words of the Hebrew Pharisees: "Blessed the man who bows himself like an ox under the yoke, and like an ass to the burden," and the admonition of St. Paul to the Thessalonians, "If any would not work, neither should he eat."

These meanings and functions of work have been referred to as *expressive* values (see Figure 1), since they imply intrinsic interest in work and the social and psychological rewards derived from having a job. Work, under these circumstances, is viewed as an end in itself.

1

FIGURE 1
A Typology of Meanings of Work

I. *Expressive*

  A. *Work as an intrinsically satisfying activity.* The performance of the job itself, e.g., rendering a service to others, provides satisfaction and a sense of accomplishment. There may be a desire for new experience, to learn more, and to utilize and develop abilities in one's job; in other words, to self-actualize.

  B. *Work as a source of satisfying interpersonal experiences.* Satisfactions may be derived from associations with others during the course of one's work with clients, patrons, patients, or co-workers. The satisfactions are not from services rendered but from affiliative relations in one's job.

  C. *Work as a status and prestige-bestowing activity.* People may exhibit a desire for status achievement in monetary or social terms. A job or type of work may be valued for the prestige ascribed to the person performing such a task. Status or prestige may be sought from one's co-workers, friends, or relatives.

  D. *Work as a morally correct activity.* Work is viewed as an activity that fulfills a prescribed role in society. It has an ethical and moral connotation.

II. *Instrumental*

  A. *Work as an economic activity—a means of survival.* Work is engaged in for monetary purposes. It is prized for the opportunities it provides for obtaining satisfactions away from one's job.

  B. *Work as a scheduled or routinized activity which keeps one occupied.* It consumes time and energy, and may be viewed as a vehicle for avoiding negative consequences associated with laziness and idleness, e.g., illegal activities.

On the other hand, for some people the job itself is neither rewarding nor satisfying. For them it is merely a means to an end. People sometimes work simply to keep occupied, to eliminate the boredom in their lives, and occasionally to avoid getting into trouble. For others, the paycheck is the sole reward of the job.

These last two meanings of work, as depicted in Figure 1, can be referred to as *instrumental* value orientations. They connote an extrinsic interest in work. Work is viewed as an activity which is not satisfying but which can provide rewards away from the job.

The United States was developed through the work of oppressed religious and ethnic minorities who were reared under the ideology of a work ethic which emphasized individual initiative, industriousness, thrift, and deferred gratification (cf. Weber, 1958). This drive to succeed is imbedded in our culture, which extolls the virtues of labor for expressive rewards. From childhood we are socialized into the work world, taught it is natural and desirable to work and to take pride in doing our jobs well.

Many white middle- and working-class people doubt, however, that women and minority groups share this value system. Myths and stereotypes persist depicting them as unprofessional, lazy, and inferior workers. These negative impressions have perpetuated a system of discrimination that systematically excludes them from many of the perquisites of the affluent society. In a nation where per capita income of $5,523 is the highest of any industrialized country; where the labor force is one of the most educated and technologically sophisticated (Crittenden, 1975: 3), segments of the population are excluded from this munificence. Even prosperous times finds them living marginal existences. When cyclical downturns occur in the economy, they are driven into states of degradation and despair, as in the recession of the 1970s. Although the unemployment rate for whites rose to 6.4 percent in the fourth quarter of 1974, it soared to 12.5 percent for blacks (U.S. Department of Labor, 1975: 33). In this period, there were an additional 845,000 discouraged workers—people who wanted jobs but stopped looking for them because they lost hope. Two thirds of these discouraged workers were women, and another fifth were elderly workers and male teen-agers. We should not, however, preoccupy ourselves with these fluctuations. It is the trends which deserve our consideration. Since the midfifties, as Bart Landry shows in Chapter 2, the black unemployment rate has been twice that of the white, and since 1971 the unemployment rate for black teen-agers has *averaged more than 30 percent*—two and a half times the rate of white teen-agers (U.S. Department of Labor, 1975: 34).

One ironical effect of job discrimination is that groups victimized by discrimination are in turn stigmatized because of the effects of that same discrimination. In the case of women, as Adeline Levine shows in Chapter 6, myths and stereotypes developed which depicted their primary life role as procreation and motherhood. This belief ultimately circumscribed their opportunities in the work world, since it was assumed their allegiance was to home and family. They were therefore denied opportunities for interesting, responsible, and career-oriented jobs, reinforcing the male self-fulfilling perception of them as minimally committed workers. Yet, many women seek satisfaction from their work. Nearly 45 percent of working-age women were in the labor force in 1973. At some time during the year, 70 percent of working women have full-time jobs, and 40 percent are employed full time throughout the year (U.S. Department of Labor, 1975: 62). Furthermore, as Levine documents, women's earnings are primarily used to support themselves and their families.

Other groups are similarly victimized. Blacks are ridiculed for having lower levels of skills than whites, but, as Landry shows, this was not the case until they were systematically excluded from skilled trades in the mid-19th century. Joseph Jorgensen, in Chapter 5, indicates that external pressures have also created and perpetuated poverty among Indians. Spanish-Americans are often depicted as lazy, shiftless, and undependable, but Joseph Spielberg Benitez reveals in Chapter 3 that Mexican-Americans feel the same way about Anglos, a thought which challenges the applicability of the expressive-instrumental dichotomy to that ethnic group. In fact, the labor force participation rate of Spanish-American males aged 20 and over in 1973 was *higher* than that of white or black men (85.9%, compared to 81.6% white and 78.2% black).[1] Nevertheless, differences in labor force participation among the three groups are not significant.

These figures refute the stereotype that minorities are slothful, but official government publications and "concerned" citizen groups unwittingly perpetuate it. Minorities are often depicted as "hard-core unemployed," leading the public to believe they are also felons, drug addicts, alcoholics, and social misfits. Television commercials of the National Alliance of Businessmen continually emphasize the street-corner orientation of minorities and poor whites. This approach is counterproductive, for disadvantaged people may very well avoid rehabilitative programs because of the stigma associated with them.

Although there may be a nucleus of chronically unemployed which fits the stereotype of minority-group persons, there is no scientific or social justification for labeling the minority group in general "hard core." Most people are willing to work when they are physically able, as labor force participation rates indicate.[2]

One characteristic of the occupationally disadvantaged is their inability to gain secure positions in the labor force. They are constantly displaced by national and industrial economic fluctuations and victimized by the practice of "last hired, first fired." They are often thrust in and out of the labor force. The luxury of occupational choice is denied them because of their inferior education and skills and because of discrimination. They often drift from one job to another, taking what is available. Many disadvantaged poor become victims of occupational drift and are thrust into dead-end jobs. We miss the significance of this phenomenon, however, if we view it as volitional, for drift is not dependent upon choice as much as it results from a person's inability, indecision, or unwillingness to make a choice.

In addition to technological and structural changes in our economy, which, as Sidney Willhelm shows in Chapter 9, have catapulted the state into the preeminent position of primary employer and provider, considerable evidence exists, as H. Roy Kaplan reveals in Chapter 8, which indicates that even when government addresses the issue of discrimination in the labor force, the effort is often marred by reticence and ineptitude.

When members of these groups are employed, as most of them are, they are often forced to labor in jobs that no one else wants. Dull, dirty, often dangerous, frequently monotonous, and nearly always low-paying jobs characterize their working lives. They are frequently compelled to forego the luxury of self-fulfillment in work which minimally taps their abilities. They are chronically *underemployed.* Many of the menial jobs which are available to the minority groups provide services vital for the maintenance of the affluent lifestyle of the white middle class. They make our clothes, care for our sick and elderly, dig our ditches, type our letters (and manuscripts), harvest our food, and clean up our garbage. For this they get paid less,[3] are more likely to be laid off during recessions, receive fewer fringe benefits, are denied access to upward mobility in their organizations, and are often forced to view work in instrumental (purely economic) terms. (In the case of older workers, employers, to avoid paying them higher pensions, sometimes systematically terminate them or coerce them into early retirement, under the pretense that they are worn out or technologically obsolete.) Despite the exigencies of their lives, they realize that the key to upward social and economic mobility in our society is through work, and studies reveal some interesting similarities in the work-value orientations of minorities and the majority.

Kaplan (1971) sought to ascertain the occupational aspirations of 275 chronically unemployed blacks and Puerto Ricans in a job-training program. Less than half the respondents were looking for white-collar jobs; nearly a third sought semiskilled or unskilled positions. The preoccupation with lower-level jobs was interpreted as a realistic assessment of their employment potential. A 50-year-old Puerto Rican male put it: "I'm not sure what kind of job I most want. The only kind of job I'll ever get will be in a factory or labor cause I don't have an education." A 34-year-old black female replied, "Factory type work—that's all I'm capable of doing with my limited abilities" (Kaplan, 1971: 186). However, when respondents were asked if there was some kind of job they would like if they had the opportunity to finish high school and college, 66 percent cited *professional* white-collar occupations. In addition to frequently named jobs such as teacher, doctor, lawyer, and social worker, such divergent careers as biologist, musician, dietician, journalist, computer programmer, and psychotherapist were desired. Interestingly, 47 people could not respond to the question; 15 of them said they never thought about having any special type of job other than what they ordinarily did. As a 52-year-old white male in the program explained, "No, I never thought about having any such jobs. I was raised on a farm. I had 16 brothers and sisters and we all had to quit school and help out on the farm" (Kaplan, 1971: 192).

Only 19 percent of the respondents were confident of realizing their dreams. A 37-year-old black male who had wanted to become a doctor summed up most of their feelings by saying, "You can forget about those dreams now" (Kaplan, 1971: 192).

The study reveals that the middle-class emphasis on the attainment of white-collar professions and occupations is shared by disadvantaged individuals. Other evidence indicates that women and minority groups have as strong, and perhaps stronger, expressive orientations to work than white males. National studies of the labor force conducted by the Survey Research Center of the University of Michigan have found no significant differences between the sexes in overall job satisfaction in the last decade (Quinn, Staines, & McCullough, 1974: 10–11), but the 1969 Survey of Working Conditions and the Quality of Employment Survey of 1973 revealed that women were significantly *less* satisfied than men with the financial rewards and the *challenge* provided by their jobs (Quinn, Mangione, & DeMandilovitch, 1973: 38.)

Goodwin (1972) studied the work orientations of predominantly black welfare recipients and established that they identified their self-esteem with work as strongly as white nonpoor workers did and had similar life aspirations. One fascinating finding was that short- and long-term welfare mothers endorsed the work ethic and exerted a strong influence on the work orientations of their sons, while white middle-class parents exerted little influence on their sons' orientations.

In a study of 1,441 whites, blacks and Mexican-Americans in Houston, Texas, Davidson and Gaitz (1974) determined that poor minority-group members were *more* likely to choose work-oriented responses to social-psychological questions designed to tap their commitment to work than nonpoor whites were. The researchers also found that poor blacks and Mexican-Americans had a *greater* future orientation than white poor and working-class persons.

In their study of 275 chronically unemployed, Kaplan and Tausky (1972) found blacks and Puerto Ricans exhibited as strong a commitment to work as that reported among employed blue- and white-collar workers. Although work was prized for the economic function it performed, many respondents exhibited expressive work values.

Despite the growing body of literature indicating women and minorities are committed to work and share the expressive value orientations of the stable working and middle classes, negative stereotypes about their work orientations persist. Goodwin's (1971) study of Work Incentive Program (WIN) trainees in six cities revealed that the predominantly middle-class staff held distorted views of the importance of work to trainees. Contrary to staff predictions, trainees exhibited a strong commitment to the work ethic and identification with their work. Staff members perceived trainees as inclined toward illegal activities and assumed that trainees exhibiting high self-identification with work were confident of their abilities, but the responses of trainees indicated the opposite. Goodwin attributed these misperceptions to a middle-class inability to understand occupationally disadvantaged poor.

Misconceptions about the poor may not only impede the effectiveness of remedial programs; they can, as in the case reported by Quinn, Fine, and Levitin (1971), precipitate their collapse. In this instance, a large manufacturing firm embarked upon a program to recruit, train, and hire "hard-core" unemployed minority group members. After learning that 42 percent of the recruits left within the first six weeks of employment, the company instituted a training program to overcome supposed motivational deficiencies thought to be responsible for the high attrition. However, no significant differences were found in the retention rates between trainees and nontrainees. Interviews with recruits who quit their jobs revealed that the primary reasons for leaving were the jobs themselves and the supervisors. Thirty-five percent of the former workers had been injured during the first six weeks on the job. It was learned that supervisors were sometimes capricious and punitive; one supervisor offered to fire a worker who failed to keep an appointment for an interview, though he made no effort to determine why the interview was missed. The researchers concluded that there was no relationship between beliefs, attitudes, and other personality factors and job turnover, and efforts to improve the economic situation of disadvantaged workers should focus on improving the quality of jobs rather than modifying the behavior of individuals.

FOCUS OF THE BOOK

This book is devoted to an analysis of the labor force participation and work commitment of women, the elderly, and deprived American minorities. Although women and older workers are not cultural minorities in the sense of the ethnic groups, they have endured their share of job discrimination. This fact has been recognized and expressed in recent legislation and court decisions; therefore, references made to minorities throughout this book will include women and the aged.

Studies of these groups in relation to the labor force have generally taken the form of statistical and demographic analyses. While such analyses are necessary for the allocation of resources to aid the disadvantaged, mere numbers are an impersonal medium of communication. It is difficult for them to convey the full social and psychological impact that decades of discrimination have had on these groups. Statistical analyses also overlook the meaning and function of work for minority-group members. This book represents an attempt to set forth the significance of work in the lives of deprived minorities in an effort to develop the human side of the issue. Each chapter, with the exception of the one on American Indians, was written by a member of the minority group discussed. It was felt that their knowledge might yield interesting insights into the meaning and importance of work to the members of their subculture. Although statistics are utilized, the authors have made a conscientious effort to use them as a frame of reference from which they explore the social-psychological import of work to the groups. Despite the paucity of materials on the subject, the contributors have developed theoretical analyses of the work orientations of the groups which defy generalizations and stereotypes about them. It is hoped this book will contribute to a fuller understanding of the human side of their quest for equality in the world of work and lead to a deeper appreciation of the uniqueness and worth of all people in our society.

NOTES

1. The higher participation rate of Spanish-Americans may be attributable to high participation in the 20–24 age group, which reflects the youthfulness of their population, and the smaller number of Spanish-Americans in school at that age compared to whites (see McKay, 1974: 14). The median age of Spanish-Americans is 20.1 years, compared to 28.5 years for the total U.S. population (U.S. Bureau of the Census, 1975: 4).

2. The lower labor force participation rate of Puerto Rican men, 73% in 1972, may be the result of health problems. One fourth of all Puerto Rican males under 65 who did not participate in the labor force that year reported being disabled (Ryscavage & Mellor, 1973: 5).

3. In 1974 amendments were passed to the Fair Labor Standards Act which increased the federal minimum wage to $2.30 an hour by January 1, 1976, and increased by 7.4 million the number of nonsupervisory workers (56.8%) covered by the legislation. Newly protected workers include more public and private household workers, and workers in selected service and retail trade industries. Overtime protection was also expanded to include 8.4 million more nonsupervisory workers, bringing the total to 51 million (Elder, 1974: 35). Although this was a needed reform, the income afforded by the minimum wage is hardly a reason for jubilation.

It is noteworthy that the majority of the 9.5 million workers exempt from minimum wage provisions are in the retail trades and service industries—areas where there are heavy concentrations of women and minority groups (see Elder, 1974: Table 2, p. 35). More than 8 million of the 13 million workers not covered by the new overtime provisions (which require time and a half pay for hours in excess of the first 40 a week) are in agriculture, retail trades, and service industries (Elder, 1974: Table 3, p. 36).

REFERENCES

Crittenden, Ann. "Vital Dialogue Is Beginning between the Rich and the Poor." *The New York Times,* September 28, 1975, sect. E, p. 3.

Davidson, Chandler, and Charles M. Gaitz. "Are the Poor Different? A Comparison of Work Behavior and Attitudes among the Urban Poor and Nonpoor." *Social Problems* 22 (December 1974): 229–245.

Elder, Payton. "The 1974 Amendments to the Federal Minimum Wage Law." *Monthly Labor Review* 97 (July 1974): 33–37.

Goodwin, Leonard. "On Making Social Research Relevant to Public Policy and National Problem-Solving." *American Psychologist* 26 (1971): 431–442.

Goodwin, Leonard. *Do the Poor Want to Work?* Washington, D.C.: The Brookings Institution, 1972.

Kaplan, H. Roy. "The Meaning of Work among the Hard-Core Unemployed." Ph.D. dissertation, University of Massachusetts, Amherst, 1971.

Kaplan, H. Roy, and Curt Tausky. "Work and the Welfare Cadillac: The Function of and Commitment to Work among the Hard-Core Unemployed." *Social Problems* 19 (1972): 469–483.

McKay, Roberta V. "Employment and Unemployment among Americans of Spanish Origin." *Monthly Labor Review* 97 (1974): 12–16.

Quinn, Robert P., B. D. Fine, & Teresa Levitin. *Turnover and Training: A Social Psychological Study of Disadvantaged Workers.* National Technical Information Service, Operations Div., Doc. No. PB194775. Springfield, Va., 1971.

Quinn, Robert P., Thomas W. Mangione, & Martha S. Baldi De Mandilovitch. "Evaluating Working Conditions in America." *Monthly Labor Review* 96 (November 1973): 32–41.

Quinn, Robert P., Graham L. Staines, & Margaret R. McCullough. "Job Satisfaction: Is There A Trend?" U.S. Department of Labor, *Manpower Research Monograph,* No. 30. Washington, D.C.: U.S. Government Printing Office, 1974.

Ryscavage, Paul M., & Earl F. Mellor. "The Economic Situation of Spanish Americans." *Monthly Labor Review* 96 (April 1973): 3–9.

U.S. Bureau of the Census. "Persons of Spanish Origin in the United States: March 1974." *Current Population Reports,* Series P–20, No. 280. Washington, D.C.: U.S. Government Printing Office, 1975.

U.S. Department of Labor. *Manpower Report of the President, 1975.* Washington, D.C.: U.S. Government Printing Office, 1975.

U.S. Department of Labor. *Why Women Work.* Women's Bureau. Washington, D.C.: U.S. Government Printing Office, 1974.

Weber, Max. *The Protestant Ethic and The Spirit of Capitalism.* Trans. Talcott Parsons. New York: Charles Scribner's Sons, 1958.

CHAPTER 1

Minority groups in the world of work

Hilda H. Golden and Curt Tausky

INTRODUCTION

This chapter presents a brief, largely quantitative overview of the position of some minority groups in the American world of work. We will look at blacks, Mexican-Americans, Puerto Ricans, Indians, women, and the elderly. In the first few pages this overview provides historical and comparative materials on the American labor scene. By placing our later ttses in this broader context, we hope that the majority-minority data will gain in meaning.

It is no exaggeration to refer to changes in our economy during the past 70 years as the industrial transformation of America. Several features of this transformation are shown in Table 1.1. First, the overall industrialization of American society is apparent in the huge increase in the use of inanimate power. Second, there has been an accompanying immense increase in the labor force—from about 29 million in 1900 to more than 80 million in 1970. Third, industrialization, particularly mechanization and automation, whose impact on productivity underlay the development of a consumer-service–oriented economy, has drastically changed the type of labor performed by members of the labor force. The most striking trend is the decline in the proportion of the labor force engaged in agriculture, from more than 70% in 1820 to just under 40% in 1900, to less than 5% in 1970. Within the agricul-

TABLE 1.1
The Transformation of American Society, 1900–1970: Industrialization

Year	Horsepower per 100,000 Population[1]	Labor Force (000)	Percent Increase of Labor Force from Preceding Date	Distribution of Labor Force, by Major Occupational Groups[2] (percent)						
				Nonfarm				Farm		
				Total	White Collar	Manual	Service	Total	Owners and Managers	Laborers and Foremen
1900	86,000	29,030	—	62.4%	17.6%	35.8%	9.0%	37.6%	19.9%	17.7%
1930	1,353,000	48,686	67.7%	78.8	29.4	39.6	9.8	21.2	12.4	8.8
1960	6,145,000	67,990	39.6	93.7	42.2	39.7	11.8	6.3	3.9	2.4
1970	10,400,000	82,897	27.7	96.9	48.2	35.9	12.8	3.1	1.9	1.2

1. Adapted from "Historical Statistics of the United Stated, Colonial Times to 1957," Statistical Abstract of the United States, 1966, 1972.

2. Data from Irene B. Taeuber and Conrad Taeuber, People of the United States in the 20th Century, U.S. Bureau of the Census Monograph (Washington, D.C.: U.S. Government Printing Office, 1971), p. 182. 1970 figures adapted from U.S. Bureau of the Census, "General Social and Economic Characteristics," Census of Population: 1970, U.S. Summary, Final Report PC(1)–C1 (Washington, D.C.: U.S. Government Printing Office, 1972), Tables 78 & 91, pp. 372 & 392.

tural segment of the labor force, the decline of unskilled farm laborers preceded the decline of farm owners and managers, but the decline of the latter took place so quickly in the past few decades that currently both groups are very small—3.2% (laborers) and 1.7% (owner-managers) of the labor force. Concomitantly, other jobs have greatly expanded: The proportion of the labor force in white-collar occupations increased from 18% in 1900 to 48% in 1970, or from about 5 million workers to roughly 38 million in 70 years, while within blue-collar occupations the proportion of unskilled laborers has greatly declined.

A look at Table 1.2 shows that another feature of the transformation of

TABLE 1.2
The Transformation of American Society, 1900–1970: Urbanization

Year	Urban Population		Population in Large Urban Agglomerations	
	Number (000)	Percent of Total Population	Number (000)	Percent of Total Population
1900	30,125	39.6%	14,208	18.6%
1930	69,161	56.1	36,463	29.6
1960	125,269	69.9	91,256	50.9
1970	149,329	73.5	112,690	55.5

Source: U.S. Bureau of the Census, "Number of Inhabitants," *Census of Population: 1970, U.S. Summary,* Final Report PC (1)–A1 (Washington, D.C.: U.S. Government Printing Office, December 1971), Tables 4 & 7, pp. 43 & 47. For 1900 and 1930 the figures refer to cities 100,000 and over; 1960 and 1970 data refer to urbanized areas 100,000 and over.

the American world of work is the emergence of the modern metropolis as its site. In contrast to the compact, dense, and largely industrial cities of the turn of the century, in which jobs were concentrated at a limited number of central locations, the modern metropolis consists of a network of differentiated subareas, some of which are centers of employment, others centers of residence, and others a mixture of the two. Many participants in today's metropolitan world of work, for whom technological developments in transportation have made many locations increasingly interchangeable, can exercise choices among residential locations.

But the job dispersion which provides choices also impedes the flow of information about job opportunities to the jobless and increases the cost of searching for a job. Once it is found, a job today often requires personal consumption expenditures for transportation which place a strain on those with low incomes: According to government statistics on personal consumption expenditures, Americans today spend about as much for transportation, exclusive of business, as for housing. Many jobs are accessible only by car or require considerable expenditures of time and money if they are to be reached by public transportation; and those who lack the fare also are more likely than others to lack cars.

The increased importance of monetary income is another dimension of the long-term transformation of America. The individual American is today experiencing poverty or wealth, employment or unemployment, in a society which attaches immense importance not only to a job, particularly a job with a future, but also to the monetary income which, in a market society, means access to goods and services. As productivity has increased with industrialization, per capita income has increased, except during depression periods. In addition to the incomes which were rising until the recession of the 1970's, as seen in Table 1.3, the American labor force has reaped other fruits of

TABLE 1.3
**Median Money Income, Families and Unrelated Individuals,
1947–1975**

Year	Constant (1967) Dollars		Current Dollars	
	Families	Unrelated Individuals	Families	Unrelated Individuals
1947	$4,521	$1,499	$ 3,031	$ 980
1950	4,630	1,501	3,319	1,045
1960	6,341	2,172	6,620	1,720
1970	8,483	2,697	9,867	3,137
1975 (as of March)	8,134	2,813	12,836	4,439

Source: U.S. Bureau of the Census, "Income in 1970 of Families and Persons in the United States," *Current Population Reports*, Series P–60, No. 80 (October 4, 1971), pp. 22–23. U.S. Bureau of the Census, "Consumer Income," *Current Population Reports*, Series P–60, No. 101 (January 1976), p. 1.

increased productivity, such as reduced working hours, shorter work weeks, long weekends, and paid vacations.

Another major aspect of the transformation is the new relationship between formal education and work. The long-term rise in educational achievement, while associated with the altered demands of the changing occupational structure, also reflects the supply of increasing numbers of educated persons among each cohort of workers entering the labor force (see Table 1.4). The close connection between formal educational levels and more highly rewarded occupations probably enhanced the general com-

TABLE 1.4
Industrialization and Educational Development in the United States,
1870–1970 (percent)

Year	Decline of Agricultural Employment[1]	Decline of Illiteracy in Population 10 and Over[2]	Increase of Youths 5–20 Enrolled in School[3]
1870	47%	20.0%	40.0%
1900	62	10.7	(1920) 64.3
1930	21	4.3	69.9
1960	6	2.2	81.8
1970	3	1.0	90.5

1. See Table 1.1 above. 1870 data have been adapted from U.S. Bureau of the Census, *Historical Statistics of the United States, 1889–1945* (Washington, D.C.: U.S. Government Printing Office, 1949), p. 64.

2. Adapted from U.S. Bureau of the Census, "Illiteracy in the United States: November 1969," *Current Population Reports*, Series P–20, No. 217 (March 10, 1971). 1960 and 1970 percentages are our estimates based on surveys in 1959 and 1969.

3. *Statistical Abstract of the United States, 1966*, p. 110; *1972*, p. 105. 1870 percentage is our estimate based on data in Abbott L. Ferriss, *Indicators of Trends in American Education* (New York: Russell Sage Foundation, 1969), p. 376. 1970 percentage refers to population age 5–19.

mitment of Americans to the expansion of public education. Given changed demand and supply, educational achievements are among the credentials used for selecting among job applicants; hence, over time, the educational levels of labor force participants have increased steadily, in part as a response to the inducements of "better" employment.

In short, an important aspect of the world of work of American minority groups is their presence in a highly industrialized, urbanized, and affluent society with an extremely high per capita income (when judged from a world perspective). This broad context should be kept in mind as we present our data on specific minority groups.

BLACKS

Black people comprise 11 percent of the U.S. population. Nearly half of them now live in regions outside the South, mainly in large cities (U.S. Bureau of the Census, 1971d: 11 & 18). As will be seen, the situation of blacks in the economy shows improvement over earlier years in some respects but not in others.

If we turn first to education, a picture emerges of substantial change in the average number of years spent in school, yet there has been a persistent, though decreasing, black-white education gap. The median years of school completed was 6.8 among the black population in 1950 and 9.3 among the general population; in 1970 the medians were 9.9 and 12.2, respectively. Still comparing 1950 and 1970, but only among the younger population segment 25 through 29 years of age, the median among blacks rose from 8.6 to 12.2, while among others of the same age segment the change was from 12.1 to 12.6 (U.S. Bureau of the Census, 1972c: 109).

The whittling down, but not the elimination, of the education gap is further illustrated in Table 1.5. Between 1960 and 1973, proportions of high school graduates were increased for both black and white persons in the 20–24 age group, although a 15% gap between black and white males remained. In 1971, among 18-year-old black males, 23% had dropped out of high school, a rate almost twice that of white males. College graduates among persons aged 25–34 have increased among all races, with the greatest increase between 1960 and 1973 occurring among black males (100%) and large increases among black females (80%). Among youths 18–24, the period 1965 to 1973 showed a 73% increase in college enrollments among black males, 40% among black females, a slight decline among white males, and a slight increase among white females. The enrollment disparities along racial lines thus persisted, but at diminished rates.

The final set of data in Table 1.5 shows that in 1971, at each level of family income, white families were more likely to have an 18- to 24-year-old enrolled in college than were their black counterparts. The smallest black-white differences occurred in the middle-income categories and the largest at both ends of the income scale. The surprising feature of these data is the relatively low proportion (36%) of black families in the highest income category with youths attending college, an indication of significantly weaker transmission of status opportunities across generations among black families than among their white counterparts at this income level.[1]

As with education, income trends among the black population cannot be encapsulated under any single indicator. (See Moynihan, 1972, and Farley & Hermalin, 1972, for useful discussions of these trends.) Time-series data on black median family income as a percent of white median annual family income are shown in Table 1.6, which reveals that between 1947 and 1973 black median family income increased 7% (U.S. Bureau of the Census, 1971d: 29). However, since 1968 the black-white difference on this measure has not changed. Applying current standards of gauging poverty-level income,[2] the proportion of black families living in poverty has declined from nearly 50% in 1960 to about 30% in 1973, compared to 15% and 7% among white families over these years. For all persons, including individuals living alone, the proportions in poverty are somewhat greater, 1 out of 3 black and 1 out of 10 white persons in 1970 (U.S. Bureau of the Census, 1971d: 38).

Among the demographic-like factors reflected in these poverty rates are the following, as reported by the U.S. Bureau of the Census (1971d).

1. Many of the black families in poverty are headed by women, a critical

TABLE 1.5
Indicators of Educational Level, by Race and Sex (percent)

	Persons 20–24, H.S. Graduates			High School Dropouts, 1971, Age			Persons 25–34, College Graduates			Persons 18–24, Enrolled in College		Families with One or More Members 18–24, by College Enrollment and Family Income, 1971[1]			
	1960	1970	1973	16	17	18	1960	1970	1973	1965	1973	Under $3,000	3,000– $4,999	5,000– $9,999	Over $10,000
Black															
Male	36%	62%	70%	7%	12%	23%	4%	6%	8%	11%	19%	11%	20%	27%	36%
Female	41	67	72	4	15	21	5	6	9	10	14				
White															
Male	63	83	85	5	8	13	16	21	23	34	29	16	22	32	51
Female	65	83	85	6	11	14	8	12	16	18	21				

1. These data include college enrollment only among young persons who are not themselves heads of families. Each percent is the proportion of all families in that income and race category with at least one youth attending college full time.

Source: Adapted from U.S. Bureau of the Census, "Social and Economic Status of the Black Population in the United States, 1971," *Current Population Reports,* Series P–23, No. 42 (1972), pp. 81, 83–86, and "Social and Economic Status of the Black Population in the United States, 1973," *Current Population Reports,* Series P–23, No. 48 (1974), pp. 67 & 69.

TABLE 1.6
Annual Income among Black Families, 1947–1973
(percent; in 1970 constant dollars)

	Black Families[1]				White Families			
	1947	1960	1970	1973[2]	1947	1960	1970	1973
Under $3,000. . .	54%	36%	20%	16%	20%	13%	8%	5%
$3–4,999. . .	25	22	17	18	24	13	10	8
$5–6,999. . .	11	16	16	14	24	17	11	9
$7–9,999. . .	7	15	18	17	18	26	20	15
$10–14,999. . .⎱	4	8	17	19	⎱ 15	21	28	26
Over $15,000. . .⎰		3	11	16	⎰	10	24	38
	100%	100%	100%	100%	100%	100%	100%	100%
Median income . . .	$2,807	$4,236	$6,516	$7,269	$5,478	$7,664	$10,236	$12,595
Black median income as percent of white	51%	55%	61%	58%				
Families in poverty[3] . . .	(68%)	48%	29%	28%	(24%)	15%	8%	7%

1. Black families are reported in the source for this table as "Negro and other races," indicating nonwhites; however, 90% of the category "Negro and other races" is composed of the black population. For 1947 and 1960, black income as percent of white income is based on this somewhat larger population; for 1970 and 1973 actual black income was available.

2. Data for 1973 are in that year's current dollars.

3. The cut-off level for poverty is in 1970 constant dollars: $3,968 for a nonfarm family of four (the 1947 percentages in poverty are enclosed in parentheses and are our estimates). For 1973, adjusting for inflation, the poverty level was defined as $4,540 for a nonfarm family of four. All proportions of families in poverty are adjusted for family size.

Source: Adapted from U.S. Bureau of the Census, "Social and Economic Status of the Black Population, 1971," pp. 29–30, and "Social and Economic Status of the Black Population, 1973," pp. 19 & 30.

factor since females have lower earnings and higher unemployment rates than men, not to mention the problems associated with job seeking for mothers of young children. In 1970, 30% of black families were headed by women, over half of which were in poverty, compared to 17% for male-headed black families (p. 39).

2. The families of the poor, whether black or white, are larger than those of the nonpoor. However, among the poor, black families have the larger families, averaging one child more than their white counterparts: 4.7 children, compared to 3.6 (p. 44).

3. Historically, unemployment has averaged about twice as high among black labor force participants as among white participants (p. 53).

Table 1.7 presents family income in more detail and reveals one major

TABLE 1.7
Median Income of Husband-Wife Families
with Head under 35 Years, by Region, 1972

	North and West		South	
	Black	White	Black	White
Only husband worked	$ 7,563	$10,630	$6,375	$ 9,055
Husband and wife worked	$12,300	$12,170	$9,420	$11,228
Black income as percent of white:				
Only husband worked	71%		70%	
Husband and wife worked	101%		84%	
Percent of families in which:				
Only husband worked	31%	43%·	26%	38%
Husband and wife worked	67	55	72	61
Wife worked 50–52 weeks	54	42	50	42
Wife's earnings (full and				
part time) as percent of				
family income	36	28	32	29

Source: Adapted from U.S. Bureau of the Census, "Social and Economic Status of the Black Population, 1973," pp. 25–27.

surprise, to be noted presently. It has been seen that black median annual family income is about 60% that of white median annual family income, and we noted that half of all female-headed black families are poor. But if we focus on younger (head under 35 years old), intact black families within regions of the United States, the picture changes. First, it can be seen in Table 1.7 that in 1972 earnings in the South were less than in the North and West for all races. Outside the South, younger black families with just the husband working averaged only 71% of white income, but surprisingly, if both husband and wife worked, black families averaged slightly *larger* earnings (by 1%) than their white counterparts. It is thus the working wives that raised the family income, and the black wives accounted for 31% of the family income, whereas only 26% of family income was accounted for by the white working wives. Black wives, although earning less than their husbands, work more hours over the course of a year than white working wives and thereby average larger annual dollar contributions to the family budget.[3]

The occupations in which black persons worked are shown in Table 1.8

TABLE 1.8

Occupational Distributions of Employed Black Workers Compared to White Workers, 1940–1974 (percent)

Occupational Category	Black Workers								White Workers		Black Workers as Percent of All Workers in Each Category	
	1940		1950		1960		1970		1970		1970	1974
	Male	Female	Male	Female	Male	Female	Male	Female	Male	Female		
Professional, technical, and managerial	3.1%	5.0%	4.2%	7.0%	5.3%	8.8%	8.8%	12.8%	27.0%	20.3%	4.4%	4.6%
Clerical and sales	2.0	1.4	4.2	5.4	6.9	9.8	10.1	23.2	15.2	45.0	6.1	6.6
Skilled workers and foremen	4.5	0.2	7.8	0.6	10.7	0.7	15.3	1.4	21.6	1.9	6.3	6.7
Semiskilled workers	12.6	6.3	21.4	14.9	26.5	13.7	29.6	16.5	18.5	14.0	13.0	13.5
Nonfarm laborers	21.4	0.8	24.0	1.6	22.0	1.1	15.8	1.5	5.7	0.9	20.1	17.4
Service workers	12.2	10.4	13.5	19.1	15.2	23.1	15.6	25.5	7.3	15.3	17.1	16.5
Private household workers	2.9	59.9	1.0	42.1	0.8	38.7	0.4	17.9	0.1	2.0	53.0	37.3
Farmers and farm laborers	41.3	16.0	23.9	9.3	12.2	3.8	4.4	1.2	4.6	0.6	9.2	7.4

Source: Data for 1940, 1950, and 1960 are adapted from Daniel O. Price, Changing Characteristics of the Negro Population, U.S. Bureau of the Census Monograph (Washington, D.C.: U.S. Government Printing Office, 1969), p. 116. Data for 1970 have been adapted from U.S. Bureau of the Census, "General Social and Economic Characteristics," pp. 375 & 392. Data for 1974 adapted from U.S. Bureau of the Census, "Social and Economic Status of the Black Population in the United States, 1974," Current Population Reports, Series P–23, No. 54 (Washington, D.C.: U.S. Government Printing Office, 1975), p. 75.

(see also Ferman, Kornbluh, & Miller, 1968). For 1940, a clustering can be observed in the less rewarded occupations. If we consider white-collar and skilled manual workers as "higher level" occupations, it can be seen that about 10% of the men and 7% of the black women held such jobs, while the large remainder of black men and women were in the "lower level" jobs in 1940. By 1970 changes had occurred in these distributions, with about 34% of the men and 37% of the women in higher-level positions. These figures indicate a significant improvement, but they are still substantially different from the distributions of white job holders. This difference is clearly evident in the right-hand column of the table, which shows the 1974 proportion of black persons in each of the occupational categories. Blacks are underrepresented in higher-level jobs and overrepresented in the less rewarded jobs. The proportion of blacks in higher occupational categories is less than 10%, while they account for proportions greater than 10% in the lower occupational categories. That nearly 40% of all domestics are black women is indeed revealing, as is the low proportion (5%) of blacks in professional, technical, and managerial positions.

Inspection of the data presented in this section shows that although improvement in the situation of black persons in the economy has occurred, a very considerable gap along racial lines remains.

MEXICAN-AMERICANS

Today there are approximately 5 to 6 million Mexican-Americans in the United States (see Table 1.9), of whom about 85% live in the five Southwestern states—Arizona, California, Colorado, New Mexico, and Texas. Between 1960 and 1970 the number of Mexican-Americans increased rapidly as the result of a high rate of natural increase and immigration. Aside from affecting the size of the group, immigration has also affected the aggregate measures of material welfare, because recent immigrants generally have fewer skills, less education, and lower earnings than Mexican-Americans of native birth. For instance, median family income of Spanish-surname families in the five Southwestern states with a *native-born* head (native parentage or Mexican parentage) is much higher than for families whose head was born in Mexico.

Just as including the foreign-born in the population count affects aggregate measures, so does excluding any part of the category native-born of native parentage: For instance, enumerating Mexican-Americans as only an immigrant or foreign-stock group (persons born in Mexico or native-born of Mexican or mixed parentage; 46% of the Spanish-surname population; see Table 1.9) omits the considerable number of Mexican-Americans (54%) who are native-born of native parentage and who are more often in white-collar occupations than is the foreign-stock group. But the use of a question in which the enumerated person can designate his or her origin can

TABLE 1.9
Mexican-American Population, by Place of Birth and Parentage,
for the United States and Five Southwestern States, 1960̂1970

Mexican-American	United States		Five Southwestern States	
Population by Origin	1970	1960	1970	1960
Native-born of native parentage	54.0%	54.8%	55.3%	54.8%
Native-born of foreign or mixed parentage	31.0	30.3	28.7	29.7 ·
Foreign-born	15.0	14.9	16.0	15.5
Total Mexican-American population Percent	100.0%	100.0%	100.0%	100.0%
Number (in millions)	5.5	3.8	4.6	3.3

Source: 1970 figures are derived from U.S. Bureau of the Census, 1973d and on the basis of 1960 data. 1960 figures have been adapted from Leo Grebler, Joan Moore, and Ralph Guzman, *The Mexican-American People* (New York: Free Press, 1970), pp. 601–602; Robert D. Grove, "Vital Statistics for the Negro, Puerto Rican, and Mexican Populations . . . ," in David M. Heer (ed.), *Social Statistics and the City* (Cambridge, Mass.: Harvard University Press, 1968), p. 111; U.S. Bureau of the Census, "Characteristics of the Population," *Census of Population: 1960*, Vol. I (Washington, D.C.: U.S. Government Printing Office, 1964), Tables 162 and 163.

also produce omissions, since Spanish-surnamed persons of native parentage may choose "other Spanish" rather than "Mexican," or they may fill in "no, none of these," meaning that they are original settlers of Texas. Also, the count of the Mexican-American–origin group varies with the number of choices offered. In short, with reference to socioeconomic measures, the three enumeration procedures currently used by the Census Bureau (Spanish-surname and language, Mexican-American foreign stock, and Mexican-American origin by self-identification) produce different total counts and slightly varying results.[4]

Regardless of the means used to identify the group, there is evidence of economic progress during the sixties. The improvements can be shown most precisely by comparable data on Spanish-surname families or persons for the five Southwestern states.[5] In 1959 median income of Spanish-surname families was $4,164, or about 65% of non–Spanish-surname family income; in 1970 it was $7,077, or above 70% of non–Spanish-surname family income. Similarly, in 1960 about 35% of Spanish-surname families fell below the low-income threshold, whereas the corresponding figure for 1970 was about 23%. Both the 1970 census and the current population survey of 1973 suggest that only 24% of the families who identify themselves as Mexican have incomes below the poverty line. At the same time, the proportion of families with moderately high incomes has increased. By 1970, for instance, the proportion of all Spanish-surname families with incomes of $10,000 and over was 28.4%; in 1973 the corresponding percentage for the Mexican-origin families was 31% (Grebler, Moore, & Guzman, 1970: 181, 185, & 197; and U.S. Bureau of the Census, 1973c: 121, 1973d: 81, 1974: 25 & 27).[6]

Despite the progress made during the sixties, however, median family income of Mexican-Americans remains considerably below that of all whites and close to that of other minority groups, such as blacks and Puerto Ricans. As Table 1.10 shows, in 1970 median income of all Mexican-American families was only about 70% of the median family income of all other white families. If we compare families whose heads work full time, the relative position of Mexican-Americans vis-à-vis other white Americans looks better; but if we compare the median income per family member, their position deteriorates because Mexican-American families tend to be larger. Whatever income measure we use, we can point to the continuation of disparities in financial well-being.

One explanation for the failure of Mexican-Americans to earn as large an income as other white Americans is their fewer years of education: The median number of school years completed for persons 25 years and older is still below 9, even though there have been considerable improvements among younger Mexican-Americans. Similarly, the proportion of the Mexican-American population that has completed college is low; in 1973 the percentage was 2.4 for the Mexican-origin population, in contrast to 13.2 for the Cuban-origin population (U.S. Bureau of the Census, 1973c: 55, 1973d: 21, 1974: 24 & 25). But not all income differences can be explained by the educational gap, since at low levels of education Mexican-American males have done well in income competition (Fogel, 1967: 173; see Table 1.11).

Since income differences in favor of the majority do exist at higher levels of education, we need to consider additional factors, such as labor force participation rates, unemployment rates, and the relative distribution of the employed labor force in the occupational structure. Though in 1960 Mexican-American males participated in the labor force slightly less than other males, this difference has disappeared. In 1973, for instance, Mexican-origin males aged 16 and over had a labor force participation rate close to the national average (79%), though their unemployment rate continued to be higher than the national average. But the lower than average labor force participation rate of women, together with a high unemployment rate for those Mexican-American women in the labor force, accounts for some of the difference in family income. Yet even here some changes are taking place: Young Mexican-American women or native-born Mexican-

TABLE 1.10
Median Family Income and Median Income of Males Age 25 Years and over in 1970, by Race, Ethnic Origin, and Work Status of Head

Race or Ethnic Origin	Median Family Income				Median Income per Family Member[1]				Median Income of Males Age 25 Plus	
	All Families		Head Worked Year Round, Full Time		All Families		Head Worked Year Round, Full Time			
	Dollars	Percent of White Income	Dollars	Percent of White Income	Dollars	Percent of White Income	Dollars	Percent of White Income	Dollars	Percent of White Income
All Families	$ 9,867		$11,804		$2,763		$3,306		$7,891	
White	10,236		12,016		2,925		3,433		8,224	
Negro	6,279	61.3%	8,880	73.7%	1,513	51.7%	2,140	62.3%	5,041	61.0%
Mexican-American	7,117	69.5	8,946	78.2	1,618	55.3	2,033	59.2	6,002	72.9
Puerto-Rican	5,975	58.2	8,829	73.2	1,572	53.7	2,311	67.3	5,879	71.4

1. We arrived at these figures by dividing median family income figures by median size of family, 1970 (4.4 for Mexican-Americans, 4.15 for blacks, 3.8 for Puerto Ricans, 3.5 for whites, and 3.57 for total population). U.S. Bureau of the Census, "General Population Characteristics," Census of Population: 1970, U.S. Summary, Final Report PC(1)–B1 (January 1972), Table 54, pp. 279–280, and "Selected Characteristics of Persons and Families of Mexican, Puerto Rican, and other Spanish Origin: March 1972," Current Population Reports, Series P–20, No. 238 (July 1972), p. 4.

Source: U.S. Bureau of the Census, "Selected Characteristics of Persons and Families of Mexican, Puerto Rican and other Spanish Origin: March 1971," Current Population Reports, Series P–20, No. 224 (October 1971), pp. 5–6. In these surveys origin is determined by self-identification. The category "white" includes most persons of Mexican-American and Puerto Rican origin.

TABLE 1.11
Schooling and Income of Mexican-Americans

	Median Income of Males 25 and Over in 1971	
Years of School Completed	All Males	Mexican-Origin Males
Elementary:		
0–4	$ 2,945	$3,956
5–7	4,241	5,648
8 years	5,472	6,136
High school:		
1–3	7,571	7,132
4 years	9,091	8,421
College:		
1 or more	11,887	9,154

Source: U.S. Bureau of the Census, "Selected Characteristics of Persons and Families of Mexican, Puerto Rican, and Other Spanish Origin: March 1972," *Current Population Reports*, Series P–20, No. 238 (July 1972), p. 8. For similar data for all persons 25 years old and over, see *Current Population Reports*, Series P–20, No. 267 (July 1974), p. 6.

American women now participate in the labor force at a rate close to the average for all women, and more than 40% of the Mexican-origin and 44% of Spanish-surname employed females are now in white-collar jobs (Grebler et al., 1970: 205–209; U.S. Bureau of the Census, 1973c: 75 & 95, 1973d: 43 & 60, 1974: 24).

As the women's situation suggests, the participation of Mexican-Americans in the occupational structure has changed. In 1930 about 45% of Mexican-American employed males were farm workers (Fogel, 1967: 62–63), whereas in 1973 fewer than 10% were so employed. Today, although the Mexican-American males' share of jobs decreases sharply once the line separating white-collar from blue-collar jobs is crossed (Schmidt, 1970), their share of higher paying jobs has increased (see Table 1.12). In white-collar occupations, Mexican-American males have made slow gains. They are still concentrated in the lower paying and less prestigious white-collar jobs, less likely if professionals, for example, to be doctors than medical technicians. In blue-collar occupations, however, particularly at the higher-skill levels, their gains have been significant. According to 1973 estimates, Mexican-American males are no longer underrepresented in skilled blue-collar occupations, though they are still overrepresented in the operative category and among farm workers. Yet most Mexican-American workers are not farm laborers. According to the 1970 census there were fewer than 100,000 male workers aged 16 and over of Mexican origin engaged as farm laborers.[7]

Although there have been improvements both in absolute and relative terms, the average Mexican-American family continues to suffer from considerable disadvantages in the labor market.

PUERTO RICANS

The 2.7 million inhabitants of the Commonwealth of Puerto Rico live under harsh economic conditions. The island's median family income in 1960 was $1,268 (U.S. Bureau of the Census, 1972c: 784), and the median education was less than six years of schooling (U.S. Bureau of the Census, 1963: viii). Immigration from Puerto Rico to the United States—simplified by a law passed in 1917 conferring U.S. citizenship on all residents of Puerto Rico—gained momentum after 1945, so that approximately 1.5 million persons of Puerto Rican origin or parentage now make their homes on the U.S. mainland. Nearly 2 out of 3 of these immigrants settled in New York City, which as of 1970 had an estimated 925,000 Puerto Ricans, while the remainder located in other large cities such as Chicago, Philadelphia, and Los Angeles.

Conditions of life, though better than on the island, are difficult for a large proportion of Puerto Ricans in the United States. According to a U.S. Bureau of the Census report on persons of Spanish origin in March 1971 (1971c), the unemployment rate of Puerto Ricans is high, averaging 10% in 1971 compared to a national rate of 6% (p. 10).[8] Not surprisingly, poverty is also prevalent among them. By government income standards, 29% of all Puerto Ricans were living in poverty in 1970 (p. 7). One of the reasons for this situation is their very low average level of education—a critical factor in competing on the job market. Currently, only 20% of Puerto Ricans over 25 years of age have completed high school, whereas the total U.S. proportion is 56%. Change can be seen in that over 33% of Puerto Ricans *under 30* have completed high school, but the national rate is over 77% (p. 12). Puerto Rican poverty is also linked to traditional norms regarding working wives (p. 9). Puerto Rican women have a lower rate of participation in the labor force than other women: 29% as opposed to 49%. Additionally, Puerto Rican families tend to be large: 16% have four or more children and 33% have three or more, compared nationally to 9 and 17%, respectively (p. 14). Family income, then, reflecting the factors mentioned above, as well as language problems and a high proportion of female-headed families (34% compared to 9% nationally) (p. 14),[9] is about 58% as high as that of other families in the United States. In 1970 the median annual family income nationwide was $9,867, while for Puerto Rican families it was $5,975 (see Table 1.10 above).

TABLE 1.12
Mexican-Americans in the U.S. World of Work, 1960–1974

A. PERCENT DISTRIBUTION OF EMPLOYED SPANISH-SURNAME MALES
IN FIVE SOUTHWESTERN STATES

	1960 Total[1]	1970[2] Total	Native of Native Parentage	Mexican Parentage	Mexican Birth
Total employed Spanish-surname males 16+					
Number	n.a.	923,201	392,782	266,994	173,153
Percent	100.0%	100.0%	100.0%	100.0%	100.0%
White-collar workers .	17.1%	22.1%	24.6%	21.7%	11.3%
Professional	4.1	6.4	7.2	5.8	2.8
Managers, administrators, except farm	4.6	5.2	5.6	5.1	2.9
Sales workers	3.6	3.9	4.4	3.6	2.4
Clerical workers . . .	4.8	6.6	7.4	7.2	3.2
Blue-collar workers . .	56.0%	58.3%	57.7%	61.2%	60.0%
Craftsmen and kindred	16.8	20.8	20.5	22.4	19.1
Operatives, including transportation	24.1	25.4	25.0	26.5	26.8
Laborers, except farm	15.2	12.1	12.2	12.3	14.1
Farm workers	19.2%	9.0%	6.4%	7.8%	17.8%
Farmers and farm managers	2.4	0.9	0.8	0.6	0.7
Farm laborers and foremen	16.8	8.1	5.6	7.2	17.1
Service workers	7.5%	10.6%	11.2%	9.5%	10.8%

1. Data from Grebler et al., *Mexican-American People*, p. 209.

2. U.S. Bureau of the Census, "Persons of Spanish Surname." *Census of Population: 1970, Subject Reports*, Final Report PC(2)–ID (June 1973), Table 10, pp. 60–61. The total employed Spanish surnamed males includes males who were born outside the United States and outside Mexico or whose parents were born outside the United States or Mexico.

TABLE 1.12 (Continued)

B. PERCENT DISTRIBUTION OF EMPLOYED MEXICAN-AMERICAN MALES IN THE UNITED STATES
1970

| | | Mexican Foreign Stock | | 1974 |
	Total	Mexican Birth Only[3]	Mexican[4] Origin	Mexican[5] Origin
Employed Mexican-American Males 16+				
Number	589,208	229,110	897,080	1,344,000
Percent	100.0%	100.0%	100.0%	100.0%
White-collar workers	18.7%	12.2%	18.3%	18.6%
Professional and technical	5.5	3.5	5.3	5.2
Managers, administrators, except farm	4.4	3.0	4.0	5.7
Sales workers	3.1	2.3	3.2	2.7
Clerical workers	5.7	3.4	5.8	5.0
Blue-collar workers	60.6%	60.9%	61.4%	60.2%
Craftsmen and kindred	20.7	19.0	21.0	19.2
Operatives, including transportation	27.0	27.7	27.0	26.8
Laborers, except farm	12.9	14.2	13.4	14.2
Farm workers	10.7%	16.0%	9.8%	11.8%
Farmers and farm managers	0.6	0.6	0.6	0.4
Farm laborers and foremen	10.1	15.4	9.2	11.4
Service workers	9.9%	10.8%	10.5%	9.3%

3. U.S. Bureau of the Census, "National Origin and Language," Census of Population: 1970, Subject Reports, Final Report No. PC(2)–1A (June 1973), Table 13, p. 145.

4. U.S. Bureau of the Census, "Persons of Spanish Origin," Census of Population: 1970, Subject Reports, Final Report No. PC(2)–1C, Table 8, p. 95.

5. U.S. Bureau of the Census, "Persons of Spanish Origin in the United States: March 1974,"Current Population Reports, Series P–20, No. 267 (July 1974), p. 5.

Table 1.13 shows the occupations held by Puerto Ricans in 1970. It can readily be seen that men of Puerto Rican birth or parentage were clustered in the two least rewarded occupational categories, the semiskilled blue-collar laborer and the service worker occupations, with 60% of the Puerto Rican men in these jobs. Considering all blue-collar occupations, a highly dispro-portionate 77% of Puerto Rican men and 54% of Puerto Rican women were found in these jobs. On the upper end of the occupational ladder—the professional, technical, managerial, proprietors' and officials' jobs—we find 9% of the Puerto Rican men and women. A detailed study of employment in 100 large New York City firms found that only 3% of white-collar jobs in these firms were held by Puerto Ricans, and only 1% of the managerial positions, yet Puerto Ricans made up 10% of the city's population (U.S. Department of Labor, 1970: 103).

The occupational distributions shown on the right in Table 1.13 present a less gloomy picture, providing a glimpse at occupational change between generations. If we compare the men born in Puerto Rico with their second-generation sons, we see a substantially reduced clustering in the two lower blue-collar job categories, from 61% to 44%, and an increase in the two upper white-collar job categories, from a low 8% to 16%. Among the women, the most striking shift occurred in the semiskilled blue-collar category, which alone accounted for 47% of the Puerto Rican–born job-holding women but was reduced to 14% among their second-generation daughters. This reflects mainly the movement out of the highly seasonal New York garment industry. Also worth noting is the large increase among clerical and sales occupations, from 29% to over half of all second-generation Puerto Rican women; and the two top white-collar job categories, held by 8% of Puerto Rican–born women, accounted for 12% of their daughters' occupations. These genera-tional changes are also reflected by the income data shown in Table 1.13.

The average Puerto Rican in the United States suffers an obvious disadvantage in the labor market. Evidence is apparent in the data on education, unemployment, income, and occupation. However, the data on occupational change among the Puerto Rican–born and their sons and daughters indicate improvements from one generation to the next, and as Elena Padilla indicates in Chapter 4 below, Puerto Ricans are continuing to upgrade their occupational skills.

AMERICAN INDIANS

The nearly 800,000 American Indians make up considerably less than 1% of the current U.S. population, with a slight majority still living in rural locations—on reservations and in other rural places. Despite the sizable numbers that have recently moved to large urban centers, only the Los Angeles–Long Beach metropolitan area had more than 25,000 American

TABLE 1.13
Puerto Ricans in the U.S. World of Work, 1970 (percent)

	Puerto Rican Birth or Parentage		Men		Women	
	Men	Women	Puerto Rican Birth	Puerto Rican Parentage	Puerto Rican Birth	Puerto Rican Parentage
Professional and technical	5%	7%	4%	10%	6%	10%
Managers, proprietors and officials	4	2	4	6	2	2
Clerical and sales	15	34	13	23	29	57
Skilled blue collar	16	2	16	17	3	1
Semiskilled blue collar and laborers......	42	41	43	30	47	14
Service workers	18	13	18	14	13	15
Farmers and farm laborers	1	—	2	1	—	—
Number (000)	262	122	226	36	98	24

Median annual income of families whose head is of:
Puerto Rican parentage $7,435
Puerto Rican birth $5,987

Source: Adapted from U.S. Bureau of the Census, "Puerto Ricans in the United States, 1970," Census of Population: 1970, Subject Reports, Final Report No. PC(2)-1E (June 1973), pp. 54–55, 69–70, 89.

Indians in 1970. They are, therefore, still the most rural minority group—with 55% of their population classified as rural and 30% living in large agglomerations (U.S. Bureau of the Census, 1972a: Table 48, p. 262, Table 67, pp. 324–333).

The fact that the American Indians are a rural people is closely associated with their standing in a variety of socioeconomic measures: In 1960 and in 1970 American Indians were characterized by marginality in the world of work, by poverty, and by economic deprivation. For example, in 1970 only 63% of Indian males 16 years and older were in the labor force. The unemployment rate of Indians in 1970 (11.6%) was three times higher than the national average. Furthermore, the employed male workers were heavily concentrated in blue-collar jobs (Table 1.14). As a result of high unemploy-

TABLE 1.14
Occupational Distribution of Employed Indian Workers,
1960 and 1970 (percent)

	1960		1970	
Occupational Category	Male	Female	Male	Female
Professional, technical, and managerial	7.7%	11.1%	14.2%	13.5%
Clerical and sales	4.9	17.8	8.1	29.1
Skilled workers and foremen	15.5	1.2	22.1	2.1
Semiskilled workers	21.9	15.2	23.9	18.7
Nonfarm laborers	20.2	1.7	13.2	1.3
Service workers	6.0	25.8	10.3	2.3
Private household workers .	.3	16.8	.1	26.3
Farmers and farm laborers .	23.5	10.5	8.0	6.7
Median income of Indians with income	$1,792	below $1,000	$3,509	$1,697
Median income of urban Indians with income			$4,568	$2,023

Source: Adapted from U.S. Bureau of the Census, "Nonwhite Population by Race," *U.S. Census of Population: 1960, Subject Reports,* Final Report PC (2)–1C (Washington, D.C.: U.S. Government Printing Office, 1963), Table 33, p. 104; U.S. Bureau of the Census, "American Indians," *Census of Population: 1970, Subject Reports,* Final Report PC (2)–1F (Washington, D.C.: U.S. Government Printing Office, 1973), Tables 6 & 7, pp. 61 & 87.

ment and disadvantaged location in the occupational structure, the 1969 median income of employed males was $3,509, and for employed females it was $1,697 (U.S. Bureau of the Census, 1973a, p. 27).[10]

However, between 1960 and 1970 there have been some improvements in the socioeconomic position of the Indian minority. The employment situation improved somewhat in line with overall trends, and as can be seen from Table 1.14, employed Indian workers have become less heavily concentrated in the semiskilled and unskilled occupations. By 1970 more than one fifth of the employed male labor force and more than two fifths of the employed female labor force were in white-collar occupations. Also, the income gap between Indian workers and other workers has narrowed slightly.

Despite these gains, American Indians continue to be the most disadvantaged minority group in the American world of work. For example, although their families are large, their median family income continues to be less than 50% of white family income and even below that of other poor minority groups: in 1969, Puerto Rican families had a median family income of $6,119, while the corresponding figure for American Indians was $5,832. The American Indians' marginality in the world of work, their poverty and economic deprivation, can also be shown by the high proportion of individuals and families that were classed in 1969 as being below the poverty level—nearly 40% of individuals and 33% of families. Rural American Indians suffer especially from lack of gainful employment: the median family income for rural Indian families in 1969 was $4,691 for nonfarm families and $4,319 for farm families. In the much more favorably situated urban families, the adult male members were more likely to be employed and therefore had higher incomes, with median family income for urban families being $7,323 (U.S. Bureau of the Census, 1973a).

In summation, as American Indians become more urbanized, they may well experience improvements in their relative standing in the occupational structure, but given the economic fluctuations of the urban labor market and the obstacles to entering white-collar occupations as Joseph Jorgensen indicates in Chapter 5, the improvements are likely to be quite slow.

WOMEN

Approximately 36 million women were in the civilian labor force in 1974 (U.S. Department of Labor, 1975: 203), nearly a sevenfold increase since the turn of the century (U.S. Department of Labor, n.d.), from approximately 18% of the American labor force in 1900 to about 40% at present. Most of the increase has taken place since 1940 (Table 1.15).[11] About 8 million women entered the labor force during the sixties alone, with the result that there are now about 40% of all females 14 years and older in the labor force. Among those aged 20–24, labor force participation reaches 56%, and the proportion rises to 60% among black women aged 35 to 44 (U.S. Bureau of the Census, 1972b: 390 & 505).

TABLE 1.15
Women Age 14 Years and Older in the Labor Force, by Employment Status, Age, and Race, 1940–1970

	1940	1950	1960	1970	Black Women, 1970
Number (000)	12,887	16,564	22,410	30,821	3,617
Percent in labor force	25.4%	29.0%	34.5%	39.6%	44.5%
Percent unemployed	13.3	4.6	5.4	5.2	7.8
Participation rates by age					
14–17	18.0	11.5	14.0	14.7	9.1
18–24	45.0	43.2	45.3	53.4	50.4
25–34	33.3	31.8	35.3	44.9	58.9
35–44	27.2	35.0	42.7	50.3	60.4
45–54	22.5	32.9	46.6	54.0	} 52.3
55–64	16.8	23.4	35.0	43.0	
65 and older	6.1	7.8	10.3	10.0	13.2
Participation rates by marital status					
Single	45.5	46.3	42.9	53.0	45.4
Married, with husband present	13.8	21.6	30.6	39.2	50.7
Divorced or separated	} 33.7	} 35.5	} 38.7	62.0	} 43.1
Widowed				26.0	

Source: Adapted from U.S. Bureau of the Census, "General Social and Economic Characteristics," pp. 349–350, 371–372, 390, 505; Valerie K. Oppenheimer, The Female Labor Force in the United States, Population Monograph Series, No. 5 (Berkeley, Calif.: University of California Press, 1970), pp. 8–11; U.S. Department of Labor, Women's Bureau, Women Workers Today (Washington, D.C.: U.S. Government Printing Office, 1971), p. 2, and Facts on Women Workers of Minority Races (Washington, D.C.: U.S. Government Printing Office, 1972), p. 3.

It can be seen in Table 1.15 that the steepest rise in labor force participation rates was experienced by women who are now aged 45 to 54 and who probably had their first labor force experience during World War II. In 1950, when these women were between 25 and 34, they had a labor force participation rate of 31.8%; in 1970 their labor force participation rate was 54%.

Even more remarkable than the overall rapid increase of the female labor force is the sharp break with the tradition of married women staying in the home. Until 1940 most working women were single or, to a lesser extent, divorced, separated, or widowed; but married women today constitute close to 60% of the total female labor force (U.S. Department of Labor, 1972b: 1). One significant new pattern was the entry, or reentry, into the labor market of older women—most of whom were married (see Table 1.16). By 1970

TABLE 1.16
Married Women in Labor Force, by Age of Own Children and by Race, 1970 (percent)

	Labor Force Participation Rates			
Marital Status, Age of Children	All Women	White Women	Black Women	Spanish Heritage Women
All women 16 and over	41.4%	40.6%	47.5%	38.1%
Married women, husband present	39.2	38.2	50.7	34.9
With own children under 6 ...	28.2	26.1	48.1	27.2
With own children 6–17	47.1	46.2	58.4	41.4
Other women	44.6	44.5	44.9	43.0

Source: U.S. Bureau of the Census, "General Social and Economic Characteristics," pp. 350, 390, & 407. The category "Other Women" includes separated, divorced, and widowed women. In the 1970 Census the category of Spanish heritage includes both persons of Puerto Rican and Mexican-American background. For a detailed description of the enumeration procedures, see U.S. Bureau of the Census, *1970 Census Users' Guide* (Washington, D.C.: U.S. Government Printing Office, 1970), Part 1, p. 97.

married women without preschool children, but with children between 6 and 17 years of age, had a work rate close to that of single women (47% vs. 53%). This change has been much more marked among white than black women, since married black women already had a moderately high work rate by 1940, but it has noticeably affected black women, too.[12] Today, black women with husband present, without preschool children but with children 6 to 17 years of age, have a work rate considerably above that of single black women—58% vs. 45% (Tables 1.15 and 1.16).

The data in Table 1.16 suggest another trend which characterizes both black and white women and apparently started in the 1950s: by 1970, married women with preschool children were increasingly combining the social roles of wife, mother, and worker (Oppenheimer, 1973: 947). Whereas in 1950 the work rate for women with preschool children was less than 12%, today it is 30%—about 26% for white women and 48% for black women (U.S. Bureau of the Census, 1973e: 220).

The societal transformation which accompanied the increased demand for female labor did not take place in a random fashion. The newly created opportunities for women to enter the labor force came at *particular points* (Ferriss, 1971: 85–88), namely at locations in the occupational structure where increasing demand met jobs already labeled as female. At the turn of the century, specific occupations such as teacher, nurse, stenographer, and certain types of operatives were largely female, and these occupations expanded enormously during the next 70 years (Oppenheimer, 1972: 136–145). The already existing sexual segregation of the labor market was linked with an increased demand for female labor, but the demand was patterned according to skill, education, age, and martial status.

As the demand for female labor in certain occupations increased, employers adjusted to the changing availability of particular categories of women. Those women who used to be the main element of the female labor force—the young and unmarried—became less available, particularly after 1940, because of their increasing participation in secondary and higher education and because of the declining marriage age. Increasingly, employers used categories of women who had often been discriminated against in the past (Oppenheimer, 1970: 35–52 & 127–139).

Employers could shift their specific demands because the female-labeled occupations, though they varied in the level of education required, usually did not require much prior career experience for entry.[13] Furthermore, employers' altered demands were met by a responsive change in the supply: sex labeling of occupations affected the supply of women for female occupations because women were able to prepare themselves for these predictably available occupations. Increasingly, married women, for a variety of reasons—their work experience as single women, their education, changes in norms, and housekeeping technology—were willing and able to respond to a demand for their labor.

The interaction of demand and supply factors has also affected the labor force participation rate of black women. Since 1950, the black female labor force increased from about 1.9 million to 3.6 million (U.S. Bureau of the Census, 1972b: 371). Today, black married women with husband present have a higher work rate than either black single women or the combined category of separated, divorced, and widowed women (U.S. Bureau of the Census, 1972b: 350 & 407; U.S. Department of Labor, 1972a: 3). Furthermore, supply and demand have made the female labor force predominantly white-collar: as Table 1.17 shows, about 62% in 1970 compared to 18% in

TABLE 1.17
Occupational Distribution of Women, 1900–1970 (percent)

Occupational Category	1900	1930	1960	1970
All occupational groups	100%	100%	100%	100%
White-collar workers	17.9%	44.2%	56.3%	62.2%
Professional, technical, kindred	8.2	13.8	13.3	15.9
Managers, officials, proprietors	1.4	2.7	3.8	3.7
Clerical and kindred	4.0	20.9	30.9	35.2
Sales workers	4.3	6.8	8.3	7.4
Manual and service workers	63.3%	47.4%	41.9%	37.1%
Craftsmen, foremen, and kindred	1.4	1.0	1.3	1.8
Operatives and kindred	23.8	17.4	17.2	14.1
Laborers, except farm	2.6	1.5	0.6	1.0
Private household workers	28.7	17.8	8.4	3.9
Service other than private	6.8	9.7	14.4	16.3
Farm workers	19.0%	8.4%	1.9%	0.7%
Farmers and farm managers ..	5.9	2.4	0.6	0.2
Farm laborers and foremen ...	13.1	6.0	1.3	0.5

Source: Adapted from Taueber and Taueber, *People of the United States in the 20th Century*, pp. 182–183. U.S. Bureau of the Census, "General Social and Economic Characteristics," p. 375.

1900. Women of minority groups have also answered the growing demand for white-collar workers, though to a lesser degree. For example, in 1970 about 36% of black employed women and about 48% of Spanish-heritage females were in white-collar occupations (U.S. Bureau of the Census, 1972b: 392 & 430). The growing demand for women in white-collar occupations corresponded (on the supply side) to an upgrading in educational achievement; as Table 1.18 shows, each cohort of women aged 20–24 and 25–29 completed high school in larger proportions than the preceding cohort.

Although more highly concentrated in white-collar occupations than men, women in these occupations are more likely to hold the less prestigious, less skilled, non–career-type jobs. Within the broad white-collar category, women are most heavily concentrated in clerical or similar occupations, and within the narrower category of professional, technical, and kindred work-

TABLE 1.18
Women Aged 20–24 and 25–29 with Four Years of
High School or More, by Color (percent)

	White		Nonwhite	
	20–24	25–29	20–24	25–29
1947	62.1%	56.8%	24.5%	24.6%
1957	66.9	66.1	41.5	35.2
1967	78.8	75.3	59.3	55.4

Source: Ferriss, *Indicators of Trends in the Status of American Women* (1971 ed.), p. 319.

ers, women are more likely to be nurses than doctors or elementary and secondary school teachers than college professors. In general, women still tend to be concentrated in predominantly female occupations. For example, nearly 13% of the 1970 female labor force consisted of secretaries, stenographers, and typists; of the slightly more than 3.8 million employees in this occupational category, 97% were female (U.S. Bureau of the Census, 1972b: 392). Evidently, as Table 1.19 shows, the level of sex segregation that prevailed between 1900 and 1960 did not decline during the past decade (Gross, 1972: 344 & 346). Furthermore, in compiling Table 1.19 we found

TABLE 1.19
Sexual Segregation of Occupations, 1950–1970

	Index of Dissimilarity	
Year	Based on Detailed Classification	Based on Broad Classification
1950	65.6	41.8
1960	68.4	44.2
1970	66.0	39.2
White males/white females only		41.8
White males/black males		32.4
Black males/black females		52.5
White females/black females		29.8

Note: Indices may be read as percentages of females (or males) who would have to change occupations in order that the distribution of sexes in occupations would be the same. The index ranges from 0 to 100: the lower the index, the more equal the two distributions being compared.

Source: The indices based on detailed occupational classifications were taken from Edward Gross, "Plus Ca Change . . .? The Sexual Structure of Occupations Over Time," *Social Problems,* 16 (Fall 1968), p. 202, and from Daphne Spain, "Sex-Segregation in the Occupational Structure: 1950-1970," M.A. thesis, University of Massachusetts, 1974, p. 27. Indices for 1950 and 1960 based on only the major occupational categories were taken from Ferriss, *Indicators of Trends in the Status of Women,* p. 379. 1970 indices were computed from 1970 census data, U.S Bureau of the Census, 1971b.

more segregation based on sex rather than on race in the occupational structure, even though we used only broad occupational classifications. Whereas the index of dissimilarity turned out to be relatively low for male workers of both races (32.4) and for female workers of both races (29.8), it was quite high for sexual segregation *within* each race—41.8 for whites and 52.5 for blacks—reflecting some ways in which labor markets have become organized.

The existence of separate female and male occupational worlds is reflected in a number of other ways. For example, women have persistently had a higher unemployment rate than men, even if comparison is restricted to full-time year-round workers (Ferriss, 1971: 121–136). Separate labor markets make it difficult for women to earn as much as men for similar occupational achievements. Income, to be sure, is affected by numerous factors, such as the length of work experience, full or part-time employment, and the skill or educational requirements of the job, so the extent of the differences between male and female earnings cannot be readily attributed to one factor alone. But even controlling for these factors, we still find a considerable gap (Suter & Miller, 1973: 971).

Though the median annual income of women workers has increased, the increases have not been sufficient to equalize female and male income, even among workers fully employed year round. In 1970, women's median earnings were 59% those of men—$5,323 vs. $8,966, whereas in 1955 they were 64%. There is, then, evidence of a slight widening of the earnings gap between men and women (U.S. Department of Labor, 1971: 1).

Table 1.20 shows that the widening disparity of earnings is not characteristic of all broad occupational groups but stems from the proportionate increase of female clerical workers. Thus the change in the aggregate income ratio is the result of the simultaneous operation of income and occupational trends, both within and between broad occupational categories. Overall, the income gap is both an indication and a product of the separateness of labor markets.[14]

Though the earnings of year-round full-time black female workers are also lower than the earnings of year-round full-time black male workers, the 29% gap is considerably less than the 41% gap among whites (U.S. Department of Labor, 1972a: 9). Because black women's earnings are much closer to black men's incomes, the contribution that black married women make to family income is extremely important in lifting most families with employed husbands and wives above the poverty line (see the section above on blacks). More specifically, the importance of the black working wife's contribution to family income can be seen in the fact that black wives' earnings account for 31% of family income, while white wives' earnings account for only 26%.[15]

To summarize, although the female labor force has grown rapidly and has achieved a considerable upgrading, it has remained to a substantial

TABLE 1.20
Median Wage or Salary Income of Full-Time Year-Round Workers, by Sex and Selected Major Occupation Group, 1955 and 1970

| | Median Wage or Salary Income | | | | Women's Median Wage or Salary Income as Percent of Men's | |
| | Women | | Men | | | |
	1955	1970	1955	1970	1955	1970
Professional and technical workers	$3,559	$7,878	$5,668	$11,806	62.7%	66.7%
Nonfarm managers, officials, and proprietors	2,851	6,834	5,477	12,117	52.0	56.4
Clerical workers	3,109	5,551	4,248	8,617	73.2	64.4
Sales workers	2,165	4,188	5,194	9,790	41.7	42.8
Operatives	2,532	4,510	4,117	7,623	61.5	59.2
Service workers, except private household	1,767	3,953	3,674	6,955	48.1	56.8
All workers	2,719	5,323	4,252	8,966	63.9	59.4

Source: U.S. Bureau of the Census, "Consumer Income: Income Growth Rates in 1939 to 1968 for Persons by Occupations and Industry Groups," for the United States, "Current Population Reports, Series P–60, No. 69 (April 6, 1970), p. 83; U.S. Department of Labor, Women's Bureau, Fact Sheet on the Earnings Gap (Washington, D.C.: U.S. Government Printing Office, 1971), p. 2.

degree sexually segregated in the occupational structure. Furthermore, the existence of separate labor markets for men and women is manifested, on the negative side, in higher unemployment rates for women and in lower earnings, and on the positive side, in the concentration of women in white-collar occupations and in the contribution that women, particularly minority women, make to family income. To judge by the data summarized here, the labor of the typical female worker outside the home is still used to support the family in its traditional social and economic role. But these data also suggest that women's increasing labor force experience may help to broaden the structure of the female labor market.

THE ELDERLY

The elderly—a vague term pointing to a social category with no specific age boundaries—comprised approximately 10% of the U.S. population, or nearly 20 million persons in 1970, if the age boundary defining elderly is located at age 65. (This is awkward, since some students of aging predicted it would not be until 1980 that the 10% proportion might be reached [Kreps, 1963: 6], which underscores that projections are hazardous.) Because women tend to outlive men, our elderly population includes more women than men.

Among the persons aged 65 and older, 52% are living as married couples, with the remainder widowed (38%), divorced (2%), or single (8%). Within this latter category of single, widowed, or divorced elderly, 46% are living with kin. Combining the number of elderly living as couples with the number of elderly living with a family member reveals that slightly under 70% of all elderly persons live in a family.[16]

Elderly people are now much less likely than formerly to be in the labor force, for a variety of reasons, including employers' disinclination to hire the elderly, the great increase in pension plans sponsored by the federal government and states, private industrial retirement plans, and individual insurance programs. Some private pension programs, such as that negotiated in 1964 by the United Auto Workers (and recently proposed social security changes), allow for early retirement—although with reduced benefits—at age 60. This sort of arrangement may become more pervasive and thus increase the proportion of persons in retirement. The indications are that earlier retirement is favorably viewed by potential retirees.[17] Not surprisingly, the most significant obstacle to early retirement appears to be insufficient retirement income.[18]

Table 1.21 provides an overview of changes in labor force participation among the elderly. It can be seen that from 1890 to 1971 there has been slight change in total labor force participation rates among males, remaining at 80% or so, while the rate for females has more than doubled, to over 43%.

TABLE 1.21
Labor Force Participation Rates, 1890–1971 (percent)

	Total Labor Force		All Persons 65 or Older		Nonwhites 65 or Older	
	Male	Female	Male	Female	Male	Female
1890	84.3%	18.2%	68.3%	7.6%	—	—
1900	85.7	20.0	63.1	8.3	—	—
1920	84.6	22.7	55.6	7.3	—	—
1948	86.8	31.8	46.8	9.1	50.3%	17.5%
1955	86.2	35.7	39.6	10.6	40.1	12.1
1971	80.6	43.4	26.8	9.7	27.4	12.2

Source: Data for 1890–1920 were adapted from U.S. Bureau of the Census, *Historical Statistics of the United States, Colonial Times to 1957* (Washington, D.C.: U.S. Government Printing Office) (1960), p. 71. For 1948 and later, adapted from U.S. Department of Labor, *Handbook of Labor Statistics, 1971,* pp. 29–30. Data for nonwhites are drawn from U.S. Department of Labor, *Manpower Report of the President,* 1970, p. 162, and *Manpower Report of the President,* 1972, p. 193.

But among elderly men, the rate has decreased by more than half, to 26%, although among elderly women little change is evident, with the rates fluctuating between 7% and 10%. Moreover, the percentage of elderly full-time workers is about half of the proportion of working elderly men and women. For the most part, then, the elderly in our society today, in contrast to earlier eras, no longer work.

When queried about not working by Bureau of the Census interviewers, a large majority of elderly women (85%) said that responsibilities around the home precluded work, while 3 out of 4 elderly men said they were pensioners. Health-related reasons were given by 17% of the men and 8% of the women (U.S. Department of Labor, 1971: 41). It appears that not working is satisfying, according to 73% of the retirees in a recent national survey (Barfield & Morgan, 1969: 66), which revealed the proportions of persons satisfied with retirement increased as retirement income increased: with family income $6,000 or more, 85% of the retirees were satisfied, but even in the lowest income category ($2,000 or less), 65% enjoyed retirement (Barfield & Morgan, 1969: 68).

The pleasures of retirement are less enticing, however, to persons who have had comparatively lengthy educations, especially to men, as is evident in Table 1.22. Thus, among men with a grade-school education, less than 10% are full-time workers, compared to more than 1 out of 4 male college graduates. It is, of course, also true that a job is less readily obtained with a limited education, and the type of work which might be available is less

TABLE 1.22
Employment and Median Annual Income in 1970 of Persons 65 and Older, by Education

Elderly Income Recipient	Education				
	8 Years or Less	Some High School	High School Graduate	Some College	College Graduate
Male					
Number (000)	4,902	1,075	1,075	446	667
Median income	$2,542	$3,500	$4,035	$4,811	$6,535
Percent of full-time workers	9.6%	14.6%	20.0%	19.4%	27.7%
Median income of elderly full-time workers	$5,477	$7,043	$7,638	$7,909	$9,991
Female					
Number (000)	5,003	1,370	1,746	671	547
Median income	$1,338	$1,648	$1,832	$2,151	$3,784
Percent of full-time workers	2.2%	6.0%	6.3%	7.9%	12.3%
Median income of elderly full-time workers	$3,749	$4,536	$5,141	$6,769	

Source: U.S. Bureau of the Census, "Consumer Income," *Current Population Reports*, Series P–60, No. 80 (October 1971), pp. 104 & 108.

intrinsically satisfying. The especially interesting feature of these data is the influence of education on the income of the elderly; the presence or absence of a college degree persists in impact over the whole life-span.[19] Among both men and women each increment in education is accompanied by an income increment, because retirement pensions are tied to prior work income, which in turn is linked to formal educational achievement. If elderly people are still working, their incomes are on the average higher at each level of education, for example ranging among the male elderly full-time workers from a median of $5,477 for those with a grade school education or less to a median of $9,991 among male college graduates.

The 1970 median annual income of elderly persons with diverse living arrangements is shown in Table 1.23. While incomes of married couples were higher in 1970 than those of other elderly persons, it must be borne in mind that two people must live on this income. In a per capita sense (the median

TABLE 1.23
Living Arrangements of Elderly Persons, by Income and Race, 1970

	All Elderly		Black Elderly	
	Number (000)	Median Income	Number (000)	Median Income
Married couples				
Age 65–72	3,664	$5,196	258	$3,381
73+	2,420	3,865	149	2,695
Single, widowed, or divorced, living with kin				
Male				
Age 65–72	339	2,268	19	—
73+	472	1,777	63	—
Female				
Age 65–72	997	1,604	133	1,264
73+	1,683	1,285	164	1,098
Not living with kin				
Male				
Age 65–72	660	2,543	66	—
73+	751	2,156	68	—
Female				
Age 65–72	2,002	2,126	145	1,477
73+	2,396	1,758	162	1,276

Source: Adapted from U.S. Bureau of the Census, "Consumer Income" (October 1971), pp. 97 & 98.

income divided by two), the elderly couples aged 65–72 do not fare much better than the others, except for the females living with children or other kin. As is evident among all categories of elderly persons, income decreases with age, and the couples age 73 and over are not exempt. These couples are only slightly better off per capita than their single age counterparts. It can be seen that elderly men are in better financial shape than elderly women, and that there is little income difference among the elderly associated with living or not living in a family.

Racial variations in income are readily apparent. In all comparisons shown in Table 1.23, elderly black persons fare less well. Black married couples, in per capita terms, are only slightly better off than other black persons, although it should be noted that it costs a little less per person for two people residing together than for a single person living alone.

A different way of describing income among the elderly is shown in Table 1.24, which presents income distributions. It may be of help in interpreting this table to note that according to 1971 government standards of poverty among nonfarm persons, a married couple age 65 or over requires about $2,450 a year and a single person $1,950, based on the Social Security

TABLE 1.24
Annual Income of Elderly Families and Unrelated Individuals, 1971 (percent)

Income	Families		Unrelated Individuals	
	All Families	Head 65 or over	All Persons	Persons 65 or over
Under $1,999	4.1%	8.0%	31.3%	44.2%
$2,000—2,999	4.2	11.9	13.1	23.9
$3,000—3,999	4.8	13.0	10.2	11.2
$4,000—4,999	5.4	12.6	8.1	6.8
$5,000—5,999	5.7	10.1	6.5	3.1
$6,000—7,999	11.7	13.6	11.0	4.3
$8,000—9,999	12.3	8.7	7.2	2.5
$10,000 and over	50.7	22.2	10.6	3.9
Total	100%	100%	100%	100%
Number (000)	53,296	7,478	16,311	6,060
Median income	$10,285	$5,453	$3,316	$2,199
Blacks' median income	6,279	3,282	2,117	1,443

Source: U.S. Bureau of the Census, "Consumer Income," *Current Population Reports*, Series P–60, No. 83 (July 1972), p. 4. Black income data are from "Consumer Income" (October 1971), pp. 37 & 39.

Administration's "economy food plan."[20] It can be seen that 20% of the elderly families, those with incomes of $3,000 or less, are below or close to this minimum subsistence level, and another 13% are in the adjacent income range ($3,000–3,999). However, fully 44% of the unrelated individuals 65 and over are in the income range which defines the poverty level, and their median income of $2,199 is barely higher. The median income of unrelated elderly black persons is below the poverty level, although the median income of elderly black married couples is somewhat higher than the poverty standard.

Our rough estimates, based on the rather minimal standards of the economy food plan, indicate that 29% of the white elderly, 48% of the black elderly, and 31% of all elderly are very close to or in poverty. For many persons, then, the condition of being elderly is accompanied by an unenviable economic situation.[21]

CONCLUSION

In examining the general economic situation of American minority groups, particularly their position in the labor force, we have shown a moderately strong relationship between the continuing transformation of American society and the improvements for minority groups. But some minority groups have made much more progress than others, and for no group have all aspects of the economic and social situation improved in identical fashion. Three main points are suggested by these loose rather than determinate relationships.

First, for all minority groups, income levels have risen; the type of labor that they perform has, in an aggregate sense, changed in the direction of more skilled and higher-paying jobs. Furthermore, their range of possible alternatives in the job market has increased. In general, then, minority groups have made some significant gains, though we must emphasize that our conclusion is based on the analysis of *statistical* indicators and not on an examination of psychological feelings and responses.

Second, the progress has not been sufficiently great to close the gap between minority and majority groups, or even among minority groups. Table 1.25, for example, shows that 1970 median family income ranged for "ethnic origin" groups from a high of $11,619 to a low of $5,975, and for racial groups it ranged from $10,236 to about $5,832, and that elderly couples had a median family income of only $4,965.

Third, improvements in the general economic situation of minority groups have not meant an end to segregation in the labor market. Improvements do not necessarily bring about equal distributions or integration within occupations. The female labor force, for example, remains to a considerable degree in female-labeled occupations. But our data suggest

TABLE 1.25

Population and Median Family Income, by Ethnic Origin, Race, or Minority Group Status, 1970

Race, Ethnic Origin, or Minority Group	Population (000,000)	Rank	Median Family Income (dollars)	Rank
White	178	1	$10,236	3
Negro	23	2	6,279	7
Elderly	20	3	4,965	10
Irish	16	4	9,964	4
Italian	9	5	11,619	2
Mexican-American	5	6	7,117	·6
Polish	5	7	11,619	1
Puerto Rican	1.5	8	5,975	8
American Indian	0.8	9	5,832	9
All families			9,867	5

Source: Adapted from 1970 U.S. Census data and *Current Population Reports*, Series P–60, No. 80, and Series P–20, Nos. 249 and 250.

that sex labeling may be of some economic advantage to minority-group women: as Table 1.8 shows, the upgrading of the black female labor force has been spectacular—from 6.4% in white-collar occupations in 1940 to 36% in 1970—and the occupational distribution of Spanish-heritage women workers is very close to that of the total white female labor force.

In sum, in a changing and increasingly affluent society, minority-group membership remains an important factor in determining people's general economic situations and the types of jobs in which they characteristically engage.

NOTES

1. A similar conclusion is discussed in fuller detail by Duncan (1969).

2. For a family of four, poverty was defined in the 1970 census as income of $3,968 or less; among farm families, the poverty level was defined as 85% of the nonfarm poverty-level income. The comparisons over time are shown in constant 1970 dollars (U.S. Bureau of the Census, 1971d: 38).

3. The mean earnings of black wives in the North and West in 1970 were $3,903, compared to white wives' earnings of $3,008 (U.S. Bureau of the Census, 1971d: 36). Unfortunately, the mean rather than the median was reported in this important source of data.

4. As part of its overall tabulation on country of origin, the Bureau of the Census tabulated those persons who responded that they were born in Mexico or had one or both parents who were born there. This provided for 1970 a count of 2.3 million

persons of Mexican foreign stock. For the five Southwestern states the Bureau counted both persons with Spanish surnames and persons of Spanish-speaking background. The census surname count came to 4.6 million people, of whom 4.1 million both had a Spanish surname and came from a Spanish-speaking background. The Bureau also tabulated the results of the self-identification question; this provided a count of 4.5 million Mexican-Americans in the United States. As part of the current population survey, March 1973, the Bureau again asked a self-identification question. This survey provided an estimate of 6.2 million Mexican-Americans. See U.S. Bureau of the Census (1973b, 1973c, 1973d, 1974) and U.S. Commission on Civil Rights (1974: 56–86).

5. Most of our information for 1960 is derived from Grebler, Moore, and Guzman (1970: 142–247). We have also used many reports from the Mexican-American Study Project at the University of California, Los Angeles.

6. The low-income threshold for 1959 was $2,793, and for 1972, $4,275 for a nonfarm family of four. U.S. Bureau of the Census, 1973f, p. 141.

7. For a discussion of the slow improvements prior to 1960, see Grebler, Moore, and Guzman (1970: 209–226); and U.S. Bureau of the Census (1973c: 95, 1973d: 60).

8. Also see, for general discussion, Senior (1961) and Padilla (1968).

9. The national percent does not include black families.

10. For comparative information on other minority groups, see "American Indians," Census of Population: 1970, Subject Reports, Final Reports PC(2)–1A through 1G.

11. In her detailed study (1970), Oppenheimer points out that "because of inconsistent efforts to count hard-to-enumerate workers . . . there is a possibility that the 1900–1940 five-percentage increase in the female work rate is little more than artifact of the data-collecting process" and that increases in work participation rates for adult women were closely balanced by decreasing rates for young, single girls ages 14 to 19. For an excellent discussion of historical data, see The Female Labor Force in the United States.

12. According to Durand (1948: 51 & 216–217) nonwhite married women had a work participation rate of 32.2% in 1940, as compared to 13.9% for married native-born white women and 11.7% for married foreign-born white women.

13. For an excellent discussion of the components of labor force change, see Jaffe and Carleton (1954: 19 ff).

14. A government survey conducted in November 1970 strongly suggests the existence of separate but overlapping labor markets for male and female college graduates, with different salaries associated with the jobs (U.S. Department of Labor, 1971: 5).

15. According to a report by the U.S. Department of Labor (1972c), there is now a positive relationship between husband's income and the probability of a wife working. Of married women, husband present, about 50% were married to men whose income in 1970 was above $7,000. These women constituted also the largest segment of the female labor force, i.e., 35% (p. 1; also see U.S. Bureau of the Census, 1972c: 1–2).

16. Calculated from U.S. Bureau of the Census (1972c: 32 and 1971a: 97). It may be of interest that our calculations show the proportion of elderly black persons living with kin to be nearly identical to the national proportion.

17. For a discussion of the UAW situation, see Barfield and Morgan (1969). This report shows that 2 out of 3 persons affected by the program already have or will opt for early retirement (p. 6).

18. Barfield and Morgan (1969: 3). A national survey supplementing the UAW interviews suggests a similar conclusion.

19. These data do not support the thesis that the impact of education on income (and occupation) is weak, as argued in the widely publicized article by Bane and Jenks (1972: 37 ff., especially 40–41).

20. Based on 1969 "economy food plan" dollar requirements adjusted to 1971; for 1969 see U.S. Bureau of the Census (1972c: 321).

21. For 1969 proportions of elderly in poverty, which turn out to differ little from our 1971 estimates, see U.S. Bureau of the Census (1972c: 324).

REFERENCES

Bane, Mary Jo, & Christopher Jencks. "The School and Equal Opportunity." *Saturday Review of Education,* October 1972, p. 37 ff.

Barfield, Richard, & James Morgan. *Early Retirement.* Ann Arbor, Mich.: Institute for Social Research, Survey Research Center, 1969.

Duncan, Otis D. "Inheritance of Poverty or Inheritance of Race?" In Daniel P. Moynihan (ed.), *On Understanding Poverty.* New York: Basic Books, 1969.

Durand, John D. *The Labor Force in the United States.* New York: Social Science Research Council, 1948.

Farley, Reynolds, & Albert Hermalin. "The 1960's: A Decade of Progress for Blacks?" *Demography* 9 (August 1972): 353–370.

Ferman, Louis, Joyce L. Kornbluh, & J. A. Miller. *Negroes and Jobs.* Ann Arbor: University of Michigan Press, 1968.

Ferriss, Abbot L. *Indicators of Trends in the Status of American Women.* New York: Russell Sage Foundation, 1971.

Fogel, Walter. *Mexican-Americans in the Southwest Labor Markets.* Los Angeles: University of California Press, 1967.

Grebler, Leo, Joan W. Moore, & Ralph C. Guzman. *The Mexican-American People.* New York: Free Press, 1970.

Gross, Edward. "Plus Ca Change . . . ? The Sexual Structure of Occupations Over Time." In Ronald M. Pavalko (ed.), *Sociological Perspectives on Occupations.* Itasca, Ill.: F. E. Peacock Publishers, 1972.

Jaffe, A. J., and R. O. Carleton. *Occupational Mobility in the United States, 1930–1960.* New York: King's Crown Press, 1954.

Kreps, Juanita (ed). *Employment, Income and Retirement Problems of the Aged.* Durham, N.C.: Duke University Press, 1963.

Moynihan, Daniel P. "The Schism in Black America." *The Public Interest* 27 (Spring 1972): 3–24.

Oppenheimer, Valerie Kincade. *The Female Labor Force in the United States.* Berkeley: University of California, Institute of International Studies, 1970.

Oppenheimer, Valerie Kincade. "The Sex Labeling of Jobs." In William Peterson (ed.), *Readings in Population.* New York: Macmillan, 1972.

Oppenheimer, Valerie Kincade. "Demographic Influence on Female Employment and the Status of Women." *American Journal of Sociology* 78 (January 1973): 946–961.

Padilla, Elena. *Up from Puerto Rico.* New York: Columbia University Press, 1968.

Schmidt, Fred H. *Spanish Surnamed American Employment in the Southwest.* Washington, D.C.: U.S. Government Printing Office, 1970.

Senior, Clarence. *The Puerto Ricans—Strangers, Then Neighbors.* Chicago: Quadrangle Books, 1961.

Suter, Larry E., & Herman P. Miller. "Income Differences Between Men and Career Women." *American Journal of Sociology* 78 (1973): 962–974.

U.S. Bureau of the Census. "Puerto Ricans in the United States." *Census of Population: 1960, Subject Reports.* Final Report PC(2)–1D. Washington, D.C.: U.S. Government Printing Office, 1963.

U.S. Bureau of the Census. "Consumer Income." *Current Population Reports,* Series P–60, No. 80. Washington, D.C.: U.S. Government Printing Office, 1971. (a)

U.S. Bureau of the Census. "Differences between Incomes of White and Negro Families by Work Experience of Wife and Region. 1970, 1969, and 1959." *Current Population Reports,* Series P–23, No. 39. Washington, D.C.: U.S. Government Printing Office, 1971. (b)

U.S. Bureau of the Census. "Selected Characteristics of Persons and Families of Mexican, Puerto Rican, and Other Spanish Origin: March 1971." *Current Population Reports,* Series P–20, No. 224. Washington, D.C.: U.S. Government Printing Office, 1971. (c)

· U.S. Bureau of the Census. "The Social and Economic Status of the Black Population in the United States." *Current Population Reports,* Series P–23, No. 42. Washington, D.C.: U.S. Government Printing Office, 1971. (d)

U.S. Bureau of the Census. "General Population Characteristics." *Census of Population: 1970, U.S. Summary.* Final Report PC(1)–B1. Washington, D.C.: U.S. Government Printing Office, 1972. (a)

U.S. Bureau of the Census. "General Social and Economic Characteristics." *Census of Population: 1970, U.S. Summary.* Final Report PC(1)–C1. Washington, D.C.: U.S. Government Printing Office, 1972. (b)

U.S. Bureau of the Census. *Statistical Abstract of the United States, 1971.* Washington, D.C.: U.S. Government Printing Office, 1972. (c)

U.S. Bureau of the Census. "American Indians." *Census of Population: 1970, Subject Reports.* Final Report PC(2)–1F. Washington, D.C.: U.S. Government Printing Office, 1973. (a)

U.S. Bureau of the Census. "National Origin and Language." *Census of Popula-*

tion: 1970, Subject Reports. Final Report PC(2)–1A. Washington, D.C.: U.S. Government Printing Office, 1973. (b)

U.S. Bureau of the Census. "Persons of Spanish Origin." *Census of Population: 1970, Subject Reports.* Final Report PC(2)–1C. Washington, D.C.: U.S. Government Printing Office, 1973. (c)

U.S. Bureau of the Census. "Persons of Spanish Surname." *Census of Population: 1970, Subject Reports.* Final Report PC(2)–1D. Washington, D.C.: U.S. Government Printing Office, 1973. (d)

U.S. Bureau of the Census. *Statistical Abstract of the United States, 1972.* Washington, D.C.: U.S. Government Printing Office, 1973. (e)

U.S. Bureau of the Census. "Characteristics of the Low Income Population," *Current Population Reports,* Series P–60, No. 91. Washington, D.C.: U.S. Government Printing Office, 1973. (f)

U.S. Bureau of the Census. "Persons of Spanish Origin in the United States: March 1973." *Current Population Reports,* Series P–20, No. 264. Washington, D.C.: U.S. Government Printing Office, 1974.

U.S. Bureau of the Census. "Money Income in 1974 of Families and Persons in the United States," *Current Population Reports,* P–60, No. 101. Washington, D.C.: U.S. Government Printing Office, 1976.

U.S. Commission on Civil Rights. *Counting the Forgotten.* Washington, D.C.: U.S. Government Printing Office, 1974.

U.S. Department of Labor. *Manpower Report of the President.* Washington, D.C.: U.S. Government Printing Office, 1970.

U.S. Department of Labor. *Fact Sheet on the Earnings Gap.* Women's Bureau. Washington, D.C.: U.S. Government Printing Office, 1971.

U.S. Department of Labor. *Handbook of Labor Statistics, 1971.* Bureau of Labor Statistics, Bull. No. 1705. Washington, D.C.: U.S. Government Printing Office, 1971.

U.S. Department of Labor. *Facts on Women Workers of Minority Races.* Women's Bureau. Washington, D.C.: U.S. Government Printing Office, 1972. (a)

U.S. Department of Labor. *Why Women Work.* Women's Bureau. Washington, D.C.: U.S. Government Printing Office, 1972. (b)

U.S. Department of Labor. *Manpower Report of the President.* Washington, D.C.: U.S. Government Printing Office, 1975.

U.S. Department of Labor. *Women as Workers.* Women's Bureau. Washington, D.C.: U.S. Government Printing Office, n.d.

CHAPTER 2

The economic position
of black Americans

Bart Landry

Any discussion of the position of blacks in the economy of the United States can be approached through one of two viewpoints. The first, and by far the most common approach—while acknowledging lingering inequalities in economic well-being—stresses the progress made by blacks over the past half century. The second approach emphasizes the past and present disparity between blacks and whites in the economy. Writers leaning toward this second approach are more likely to subscribe to the "internal colonialism" model, which sees the conditions of society operating to maintain blacks in positions of dependency (See Blauner, 1972; Ferman, Kornbluth, & Miller, 1968: 1–8; Tabb, 1970). While we are inclined toward the second position, the issue is by no means settled.

Considerable economic and sociological literature exists on the economic position of blacks in the United States. Most of it, however, focuses on one or two of the principal components of black economic status and, to some extent, on the determinants of these components. Furthermore, very little analysis of the 1960s has been done. In the following pages we will first attempt to develop a comprehensive picture of the occupational distribution, employment status and income of blacks in the U.S. economy, and then try to draw some conclusions about the factors responsible for those conditions. Attention will be given primarily to the decades of the 20th century, with emphasis placed upon the changes in the economic status of blacks, their position relative to whites, and the factors related to both. Although our concern is primarily with the 20th century, as Killingsworth emphasizes, "the present economic status of American Negroes can be understood only by understanding the nature and consequences of slavery" (Killingsworth, 1968: 6). Consequently, we begin our analysis with a brief review of conditions during the 19th century.

CHANGES IN THE POSITION OF BLACKS IN THE U.S. ECONOMY

The 19th Century

The general patterns of black occupational distribution, as well as some of the factors responsible for the occupational disparity between blacks and whites, date back to the decades before and after 1865. Prior to Emancipation, most blacks were engaged in agricultural labor or domestic service in the households of whites. This was particularly true in the South, where almost all blacks resided, most of them as slaves. A small number of slaves were trained as skilled laborers, either to meet the needs of the plantation or to be hired out in towns as blacksmiths, carpenters, masons, bricklayers, painters, shoemakers, harness makers, or mechanics. The use of slaves for skilled labor, especially in towns, placed white workers at some competitive disadvantage, as is indicated by the fact that in 1865 5 out of 6 mechanics in the South were black (Ross, 1967: 8). As mining and manufacturing developed, slaves came to be used in these occupations as well. On the railroads and steamboats, slaves worked at almost every job except as conductors and pilots (Ross, 1967: 8).

Free blacks, both North and South, found themselves concentrated in the ranks of the unskilled laborers, though here again a small number of them became skilled artisans or entrepreneurs. The latter were concentrated in the service industries and catered mainly to well-to-do whites. Included in these occupations were hackmen, owners of livery stables, fashionable tailors, restauranteurs and caterers, and proprietors of coal and lumber yards. Blacks dominated "the fashionable catering business" in Philadelphia until the end of the 19th century, and in Charleston, South Carolina, and a few other southern cities, "free Blacks monopolized barbering, practically controlled the building trades, and were prominent among the shoemakers and butchers" (Meier & Rudwick, 1970: 99). To this small group of black artisans and entrepreneurs can be added an even smaller number of black professionals: physicians, lawyers, teachers, and clergymen.

While these black artisans were able to hold their own in Southern cities and towns for a time, their position became eroded even before 1865 as white workers strove to eliminate them from the better paying jobs. In a number of places they succeeded in obtaining legislation barring both slaves and free blacks from some or all of the skilled trades (Franklin, 1967: 594; Meier & Rudwick, 1970: 100). Blacks fared even worse in the North because of severe competition from white immigrants. Blacks trained in the trades frequently were forced to accept unskilled labor to avoid unemployment. As the number of unskilled immigrants increased (especially the Irish), black men and women found themselves being pushed out of even the most undesirable jobs, such as porters, bootblacks, maids, cooks, and washerwomen. So severe was the situation that Frederick Douglass wrote in the early 1850s, "Every hour sees the black man elbowed out of employment by some newly arrived emigrant whose hunger and whose color are thought to give him a better title to the place" (Meier & Rudwick, 1970: 100).

The economically disadvantaged position of free blacks in the antebellum years is reflected in two facts: the internal stratification of the black community, and the hiring practices of white employers. So extensive was discrimination in the hiring of blacks in any but menial capacities that even leading white abolitionists failed to hire blacks in the antislavery offices and in their places of business (Meier & Rudwick, 1970: 118–19). This pervasive occupational discrimination resulted in a black class structure that diverged markedly from that of whites. Not only were the majority of free blacks unskilled laborers, but so thin were the ranks of the skilled worker and of professionals that among the "upper stratum" of the black community were included barbers, caterers, and even the domestics of the most socially prominent white families in the North (Meier & Rudwick, 1970: 101).

The effect of Emancipation on the occupational distribution of blacks was mixed. Some old and some new forces were at work during the next 35 years. By 1900 their combined negative and positive effects had allowed blacks only a slight increase in occupational diversification. The bulk of blacks, now legally free, still found themselves concentrated in the least profitable occupations: agriculture and domestic service (see Ross, 1967: Tables 1 & 2, pp. 4 & 7). Emancipation itself had little effect on the occupations of blacks. The immediate economic result of emancipation was the beginning of a struggle between blacks and whites to determine the new economic structure of the South. In the ensuing decades blacks fought for a modicum of economic independence, while white landowners tried to convert freed slaves into a class of cheap labor. Economic independence would come, blacks hoped, through the acquisition of their own land, the much talked about "forty acres and a mule." Whites struck back with the Black Codes, which, in a variety of ways, attempted to restrict the mobility and freedom of choice of freedmen, thus ensuring a continuation of cheap farm labor. When these laws were struck down, white planters continued their attempt to create a dependent agricultural labor force.

While some freedmen were successful in acquiring land for themselves, most did not do so. The majority of blacks were eventually forced to return to the plantations in some employee capacity, as most of the confiscated lands that had been leased to blacks were returned to white planters by President Andrew Johnson (Quarles, 1969: 149). Experimentation on a number of work arrangements was conducted in the wake of Emancipation: day labor, share tenants, gang labor, wage earners under contract, and sharecropping. The gang labor system was the least popular among blacks because it was reminiscent of slavery. Eventually most turned to sharecropping, a system under which blacks became even more dependent upon the planter as "planters and merchants consolidated and used their control over the rural credit system to keep black croppers in a virtual state of peonage" (Worthman & Green, 1971: 50). In the words of another historian,

> On "settling day" the dismayed and angered cropper not only found himself with no income but owing money. He had no other choice than to pledge his labor to the landlord for another year. If he were no longer a chattel bound to a master, he was not unlike a serf or peon bound to the soil. (Quarles, 1969: 150)

As the condition of blacks in agriculture continued to deteriorate, black workers in the towns and cities, especially those engaged in skilled labor, also found themselves losing ground. While at the close of the Civil War 5 out of every 6 artisans in the South (83%) were black, their numbers had been reduced to approximately 5% by 1900 (Quarles, 1969: 151; see also Worthman & Green, 1971: 54). Opposition to blacks in the skilled trades, always at a high level in the North but kept in check in the South by planters and other slaveowners before 1865, now intensified. White artisans, partially through the rise of craft unionism and the apprentice system during the years 1865–85 and partly through violence and intimidation, gradually pushed blacks out of the skilled trades (Ross, 1967: 10). In the few cities such as Pensacola, Florida, and Baton Rouge and New Orleans, Louisiana, where black artisans held on to their jobs or made some gains, they did so only by accepting lower wages than white workers. For example, where white carpenters received $2.07 to $4 per day, blacks were paid $1.82 to $2.50. Evidently, it was during this period that the concepts of "Negro jobs" and "clean" or "white men's work" were established, although it was always possible to redefine a job as "clean" through technological upgrading and to push black workers out of more occupations.

In the areas of unskilled labor and traditionally "Negro jobs," blacks fared somewhat better than in agriculture and the crafts. As the South slowly began to industrialize, blacks were hired to do the heavy, dangerous, and dirty work on the docks and in the manufacturing, mining, and transportation industries. Thus, as was true earlier in agriculture, black workers once more became the backbone of economic development in the South. By 1910, for instance, blacks constituted 55% of the coal miners and 80% of the iron ore miners in Alabama. In this same year, 71% of the black population was employed over ten years, compared to only 48% of the native whites (Worthman & Green, 1971: 53).

By the end of the 19th century, the greater occupational diversity that had occurred among blacks was primarily the effect of the opening of new unskilled industrial jobs that were unattractive to whites because they were heavy, dirty, or dangerous. In agriculture, where the bulk of the black population remained, most lived on a subsistence level. The position of blacks in the skilled crafts had been seriously eroded, in spite of the fact that they had held an edge in the South at the time of Emancipation. Although the condition of white workers in the South, particularly in agriculture, was also serious, whenever blacks had to compete with whites—native or immigrant—they generally emerged the losers. The pattern of confining black workers to the most menial, unskilled, and low-paying jobs became entrenched in the North and the South, and it was to continue in the 20th century.

The 20th Century: 1900–1930

METHODS OF ANALYSIS.   Before beginning our discussion of the economic position of blacks in the 20th century, it might be useful to explain the manner in which our analysis will proceed. A more sophisticated analysis is possible as the amount of census data and research becomes more extensive. Wherever possible, the economic position of blacks will be approached in two ways, from the perspectives of the black community alone and of the black community in relation to the white.

First, changes in the occupational distribution, unemployment rates, and income of black workers will be discussed to provide a general picture of shifts in the economic position of blacks, or of their mobility in an aggregate sense. This mode of analysis provides valuable insights into the changing economic status of blacks, but inasmuch as black workers are only a small fraction of the total labor force, this type of information is incomplete. The real concern is with the position of blacks *relative* to whites in the economy. For instance, was the economic position of blacks approximately equal to that of whites in any given year? Has the long-term trend in the 20th century been toward economic equality? The answers to these questions are complicated by the problem of measurement and by the fact that the economic position of any group is determined by its relative position in a minimum of three areas: occupational distribution, income, and employment status. A comprehensive index of black economic status relative to whites should therefore include all three components. While attempts have been made to construct indices for one or two of the areas combined (see Becker, 1957; Hiestand, 1964), no one, to our knowledge, has as yet developed an index using all three factors.

In the following analysis, two types of relative measures will be used. The first is a simple ratio. This is useful when considering the relative position of blacks in a single area such as income, or in a single occupation. Thus we will be making statements such as "In 1920 there were about eight times as many white (relative to their number in the total work force) as black male clerical and sales workers," or, "In 1965 the median income·of black families was only 55% that of white families." Since the issue of black economic equality is largely a question of their participation in a given occupation or income category in proportion to their numbers in the total work force, ratios are very helpful in determining the extent to which there is deviation from equality.

For questions of overall relative equality in a given area (e.g., occupational distribution) indices are more accurate than ratios, since indices are somewhat more sensitive to variations in different categories. Two indices are frequently used for this type of data, the index of dissimilarity (ID) or delta (see Duncan & Duncan, 1955) and the Gini index (see Miller 1966: 220–221). While the ID and Gini indices can be characterized as "generalized" or standard indices which are widely used for a variety of data (the ID, for instance, has been frequently used as a measure of segregation; Taeuber & Taeuber, 1965; Duncan & Duncan, 1955), there have been several attempts to develop special indices to measure the occupational position of blacks. The earlier (and less useful) attempts were by Becker (1957) and Rayack (1961). These two, as well as a later index developed by Hiestand (1964), are income-weighted indices. Becker, however, applied his index to 1910, 1940, and 1950 only, while Rayack's application of his own index was limited to the decade of the 1940s. Hiestand, on the other hand, applied his index to measuring the relative occupational position of blacks for the years 1910–60, at ten-year intervals. It is the Hiestand index that is utilized in our analysis. It should be noted that an index number has little meaning except in comparison with other index numbers preceding or following it. Thus an ID of 30 followed by one of 28 indicates a movement toward greater equality.

OCCUPATIONAL DISTRIBUTION.   The first really significant shift in the overall occupational distribution of blacks occurred after the turn of the century. This shift was very gradual but steady and resulted in a substantially different black occupational structure by 1930 (Table 2.1). The principal direction of this shift was a movement out of agriculture, where blacks

TABLE 2.1
Percent Distribution of Whites and Negroes Employed, by Occupational Fields, 1910–1970

	1910		1920		1930		1940		1950		1960		1970	
	White	Negro	White	Negro	White	Negro	White	Negro	White	Negro	White	Negro	White	Negro
All sectors	100%	100%	100%	100%	100%	100%	100%*	100%*	100%*	100%*	100%*	100%*	100%	100%
Nonfarm, total	72.0	49.6%	76.0	53.4%	80.6%	63.9%	82.3%	66.6%	81.6%	79.5%	89.6%	83.6%	96.1%	96.2%
White-collar sector, total	23.8	3.0	27.8	3.6	33.0	4.6	35.7	6.0	39.9	10.2	44.1	13.4	50.8	27.9
Professional and technical	4.8	1.4	5.3	1.5	6.5	2.1	8.0	2.7	8.6	3.4	11.9	4.7	14.8	9.1
Proprietors, managers, and officials	7.4	0.8	7.4	0.8	8.3	1.0	9.0	1.3	9.8	2.0	9.1	1.4	11.4	3.5
Clerical and sales	11.6	0.8	15.1	1.3	18.2	1.5	18.7	2.0	21.5	4.8	23.1	7.3	24.6	15.3
Manual and service sector, total	48.2	46.6	48.2	49.8	47.6	59.3	46.6	60.6	47.7	69.3	45.5	70.3	45.3	68.3
Skilled workers and foremen	13.0	2.5	14.5	3.0	14.2	3.2	12.2	3.0	14.4	5.5	14.3	6.1	13.5	8.2
Semiskilled workers and operatives	16.1	5.4	16.8	7.3	17.2	9.4	19.0	10.3	20.3	18.3	18.3	19.6	16.9	23.7
Laborers	14.3	17.4	13.4	20.8	11.7	21.6	6.1	14.3	5.0	15.7	4.0	12.6	4.1	10.3
Service workers	4.8	21.3	3.5	18.7	4.5	25.1	9.3	33.0	8.0	29.8	8.9	31.9	10.8	26.1
Farm, total	28.0	50.4%	24.1	46.6%	19.4%	36.1%	16.7%	32.8%	11.1%	19.0%	5.9%	8.1%	4.0%	3.9%

*Sum of items is not 100.0% because for some no occupation was reported.

Source: Dale L. Hiestand, *Economic Growth and Employment Opportunities for Minorities* (New York: Columbia University Press, 1964), p. 42; Eli Ginzberg and Dale L. Hiestand, "Employment Patterns of Negro Men and Women," in John P. Davis (ed.), *The American Negro Reference Book* (Englewood Cliffs, N.J.: Prentice-Hall, 1966), p. 220; U.S. Bureau of the Census, "Social and Economic Status of the Black Population in the United States, 1971," *Current Population Reports*, Series P-23, No. 42 (Washington, D.C.: U.S. Government Printing Office, 1972), Table 50, p. 66.

had been concentrated since their arrival in America, into the manual and service sector. Each decade witnessed a steady attrition of black farm laborers, from over half of all black workers in 1900 to slightly more than one third (36.1%) in 1930. This decline in agriculture was matched by an equally distinct rise in the manual and service sector where, until 1930, virtually all black occupational gains were registered. While the first two decades showed a modest shift in these sectors, it was in the 1920s that a really dramatic change occurred, with blacks in agriculture declining over ten percentage points (from 46.6% to 36.1%) and their representation in the manual and service sector increasing by about the same amount (from 49.8% to 59.3%). Most of this gain was in service and unskilled manual jobs in the North where, because of expansion or because whites were vacating unskilled jobs for better opportunities, industries had room for black migrants. These new job opportunities included employment in manufacturing, mechanical, mining, trade, and transportation occupations, as well as opportunities in "steel mills, auto plants, foundries, packing houses, highway construction, railroad maintenance, laundries, food industries, and some branches of the needle trades" (Ross, 1967: 13). By 1928 black workers had gained a foothold in many occupations as laborers or unskilled or semiskilled operatives. Thus in 1928, 21% of the unskilled jobs in the building industry were held by blacks; 24%, in the chemical industry; 14%, in iron and steel mills; 39%, in saw mills and planing mills, and 60% in the tobacco industry. Blacks even gained a sizable share of semiskilled jobs in a few occupations, such as glass workers (29% black), fish-packers (42%) and longshoremen (32%). As black women found employment in white households in the North, the number working as domestics rose from 715,000 in 1920 to 1,036,000 by 1930. It was these developments that led one writer to characterize the 1920s as "a high point of prosperity for the Negro in the Northern cities" (Ross, 1967: 13–14).

As is apparent from Table 2.2, these changes in occupational distribution differed somewhat for black males and females. The primary differences lay in areas of concentration. Both showed a similar decrease in the agricultural sector and an increase in the manual and service sector. However, from the beginning of this century there were always relatively more black men in agriculture than black women, and while black men overwhelmingly predominated in the unskilled and skilled occupations, black women always formed the majority of service workers because of their employment as domestics. In the semiskilled and operatives area there were relatively more black women than black men in 1910, but this disparity had almost disappeared two decades later. It is difficult to make a meaningful comparison of the relative occupational gains of black males and females because of the tremendous differences in occupational distribution.

Given the above changes in occupational structure, did black workers gain or lose relative to whites in the 1900–1930 period? To answer this

TABLE 2.2
Percentage Distribution of Black Labor Force in Occupational Fields, by Sex, 1910–1970

	1910		1920		1930		1940		1950		1960		1970	
Male Female	Male	Female	Male	Female	Male	Female	Male	Female	Male	Female	Male	Female	Male	Female
All sectors	100%	100%	100%	100%	100%	100%	100%*	100%*	100%*	100%*	100%	100%	100%	100%
Nonfarm, total	44.4%	59.7%	50.9%	58.9%	59.3%	73.1%	58.2%	83.0%	74.5%	89.0%	85.3%	93.8%	94.0%	98.0%
White-collar sector, total	3.2	2.6	3.6	3.7	4.4	5.0	5.7	6.6	8.8	12.8	13.7	18.0	22.0	36.0
Professional and technical	1.1	1.8	1.2	2.3	1.5	3.3	1.8	4.3	2.2	5.6	4.0	5.8	8.0	11.0
Proprietors, managers, and officials	1.1	0.4	1.0	0.5	1.2	0.6	1.6	0.7	2.3	1.4	2.7	1.8	5.0	2.0
Clerical and sales	1.0	0.4	1.4	0.9	1.7	1.1	2.3	1.6	4.3	5.8	7.0	10.4	9.0	23.0
Manual and service sector, total	41.2	57.1	47.3	55.2	54.9	68.1	52.5	76.4	65.7	76.2	71.6	75.8	73.0	62.0
Skilled workers and foremen	3.6	0.1	4.4	0.1	4.8	0.1	4.4	0.2	8.1	0.6	9.1	0.7	14.0	1.0
Semiskilled workers and operatives	4.7	6.8	6.7	8.6	9.0	10.1	12.2	6.5	20.1	14.8	24.4	15.1	28.0	17.0
Laborers	25.9	1.0	29.5	2.6	31.7	1.7	21.1	0.9	23.1	1.5	23.3	0.3	18.0	1.0
Service workers	7.0	49.2	6.7	43.9	9.4	56.2	14.8	68.8	14.4	59.3	14.8	59.7	13.0	43.0
Farm, total	55.6%	40.3%	49.1%	41.1%	40.7%	26.9%	41.3%	16.1%	24.1%	9.3%	14.7%	6.2%	6.0%	2.0%

*Sum of items is not 100.0% because for some no occupation was reported.

Source: Hiestand, Economic Growth and Employment Opportunities for Minorities, p. 44; U.S. Bureau of the Census, "Social and Economic Status of the Black Population in the United States, 1974," Current Population Reports, Series P–23, No. 54 (Washington, D.C.: U.S. Government Printing Office, 1975), pp. 73–74.

question it is useful to begin by briefly examining the occupational distribution of white workers. In any question of relative gain or loss, the starting points of the groups involved are extremely important. If the starting point of one group is very low relative to the other, even a more rapid rate of increase may be inadequate to enable it to catch up. Such is the case when we try to compare the economic progress of blacks and whites. A glance at Table 2.1 above shows immediately that the occupational distribution of white workers in 1910 was radically different from that of blacks. Looking at the three major sectors, it is apparent that while blacks were hardly represented among white-collar workers (3.0%), almost one quarter (23.8%) of the white labor force was in that sector. In the manual and service sector, what first appears to be a case of near equality turns out to be otherwise upon examination of the detailed occupations. White workers were highly represented in the more favorable end (skilled and semiskilled) of the distribution, while black workers were concentrated at the lower end (unskilled laborers and service workers). Thus although both groups come under the heading of blue-collar work, there is a significant difference in the meaning of this term for blacks and whites. Finally, by 1910 the proportion of whites in the farm sector was reduced to a level that blacks had not yet reached 30 years later.

Clearly, at the beginning of the period under consideration, the white labor force enjoyed a much more favorable distribution than the black labor force. This pattern continued throughout this period, in spite of the faster rate of change for blacks in both the manual and service and the farm sectors, and the favorable shifts of the twenties. It was a case of the turtle attempting to catch up with the rabbit which, unlike the fairy-tale hare, did not fall asleep. Throughout this period, white workers maintained their more favorable distribution over the several occupations in the manual and service sector and strengthened their monopoly of white-collar jobs, even though there was an actual decrease of white blue-collar workers, with most of the decline occurring in the unskilled category (from 14.3% to 11.7%). This decline was actually a gain for whites as they moved into the higher paying and "cleaner" semiskilled and skilled jobs. In the white-collar sector, most of their gains were registered in the clerical and sales category.

Another and more accurate way of comparing changes in the relative distribution of black and white workers is to examine ratios in each occupation (Table 2.3). The ratios should be interpreted as the relative overrepresentation or underrepresentation of blacks or whites in a specific area or occupation. A ratio of 1.0 indicates that both blacks and whites are represented in a given occupation in proportions relative to their numbers in the total labor force. If the ratio is larger than 1.0, blacks are underrepresented; if smaller than 1.0, they are overrepresented. The state of occupational equality would exist if all ratios were equal to 1.0. The advantage of ratios over simple distributions, as in Table 1.1, is their ability to measure the

TABLE 2.3
Ratio of White to Black Workers, by Occupational Field and Sex, 1910–1974

	Male								Female							
	1910	1920	1930	1940	1950	1960	1970	1974	1910	1920	1930	1940	1950	1960	1970	1974
All sectors	1.0	1.0	1.0	1.0	1.0	1.0	1.0	1.0	1.0	1.0	1.0	1.0	1.0	1.0	1.0	1.0
Nonfarm, total	1.5	1.4	1.3	1.3	1.1	1.1	1.0	1.0	1.5	1.6	1.3	1.2	1.1	1.0	1.0	1.0
White-collar sector, total	6.8	6.6	6.3	5.4	3.8	2.9	1.9	1.8	12.7	12.7	10.5	7.8	4.5	3.4	1.8	1.5
Professional and technical	2.9	2.9	2.8	3.2	3.1	2.8	1.9	1.7	6.6	5.9	4.8	3.4	2.3	2.4	1.3	1.3
Proprietors, managers, and officials	8.1	8.7	7.8	6.4	5.1	5.5	3.0	3.0	4.9	4.6	4.7	5.7	3.4	2.9	2.5	2.5
Clerical and sales	10.1	8.1	8.3	6.4	3.4	2.0	1.2	1.0	43.2	34.2	30.5	21.3	6.9	4.0	1.8	1.5
Manual and service sector, total	1.1	1.0	0.9	0.9	0.8	0.7	0.7	0.7	1.0	0.8	0.6	0.6	0.5	0.5	0.5	0.6
Skilled workers and foremen.........	4.3	4.0	3.7	3.6	2.4	2.2	1.5	1.3	30.5	13.9	12.1	7.1	2.5	1.6	1.0	2.0
Semiskilled workers and operatives	2.5	2.0	1.7	1.5	1.0	0.8	0.7	0.6	5.2	3.5	2.6	2.1	1.3	1.0	0.8	0.7
Laborers.................	0.7	0.5	0.5	0.4	0.3	0.3	0.3	0.5	1.5	0.9	0.8	1.1	0.5	1.4	*	1.0
Service workers	0.2	0.2	0.2	0.4	0.4	0.4	0.4	0.5	0.4	0.3	0.3	0.3	0.3	0.3	0.4	0.5
Farm, total	0.6	0.6	0.6	0.5	0.6	0.6	0.8	1.3	0.2	0.2	0.2	0.1	0.3	0.5	1.0	2.0

Note: The ratio of white to black workers is relative to their numbers in total work force.
*Less than 1% of white women worked as laborers in 1970, while black women accounted for 1%.

Source: Hiestand, Economic Growth and Employment Opportunities for Minorities, p. 48; U.S. Bureau of the Census, "Social and Economic Status of the Black Population, 1974," pp. 73–74.

"distance" blacks are from equality in a given occupation. Nevertheless, since gains or losses in the different occupations do not have the same meaning or value for the total group, ratios do not enable us to make very accurate statements about the overall trend in the occupational structure toward or away from equality.

Looking at the several sectors, it can be seen that in spite of the more rapid decrease of blacks in agriculture, their overrepresentation remained the same throughout this period, 40% for black males and 80% for black females. In the manual and service sector the underrepresentation of black males by 10% in 1910 changed to overrepresentation by 10% by 1930. The imbalance became even more pronounced among black females. The overrepresentation of both white males and females relative to blacks decreased only slightly in the white-collar sector. By 1930 white males were still over six times more numerous among white-collar workers than black males, relative to their numbers in the labor force, and white females were over ten times more numerous than black females.

The imbalance is seen to be even more pronounced when individual occupations are examined. Here it becomes much more important to take note of differences among males and females. Among clerical and sales workers, where women tend to predominate, the ratios for male workers do not tell the true story. With few males in this category, black or white, the overrepresentation of white males (about ten times as many white males in 1910) is not as significant as the overrepresentation of white females (43 times as many in 1910). Even though black females made some progress toward equality in these occupations, the initial advantage of white females was so great that in 1930 they were still 30 times more numerous than black females relative to their respective labor force totals. Another striking imbalance among women is in the skilled workers and foremen category, but here the importance is diminished because of the predominance of male workers in these occupations. Ratios reflect the simultaneous shifts of black and white workers, but it is difficult to draw an overall conclusion because of the separate ratios for males and females. In general, the overrepresentation of black males among laborers and service workers changed little or not at all between 1910 and 1930. There was a slight movement toward greater equality in the categories of skilled and unskilled workers, but in 1930 there were still almost four times as many white skilled workers as blacks, and almost twice as many operatives. Apart from the clerical and sales category, very little progress toward equality occurred in the white-collar sectors during this period among black males. Among black females the pattern of overrepresentation in the lower-skilled jobs and underrepresentation in the higher-skilled categories continued, although there was some movement toward equality in two occupations of high female concentration, operative and semiskilled workers and clerical and sales workers.

To accurately assess the meaning of the above shifts in ratios, it is necessary to turn to an overall index of occupational position of black workers compared to whites, such as the one worked out by Hiestand (1964). Such an index, employing seven occupational groupings[1] according to the average income level of each, goes a long way toward the goal of a comprehensive index of relative economic status. It should be noted, however, that because black workers tend to be concentrated in the lower-paying jobs in each occupational group, especially in the higher-skilled and professional occupations (for example, more black teachers and ministers than doctors and lawyers), this index probably understates the degree of inequality among the races. Even without applying this caution, Hiestand's index reveals that for black males the net effect of all combined changes in occupational groups during the years 1900–1930 was zero. *Relative to white males,* black males did not change their overall occupational position between 1910 and 1930, remaining at 78% that of whites. Black females fared even worse, suffering a loss of 3% during the same period, from 78% to 75% (Hiestand, 1964: 53). This finding is instructive. It reveals that the gains made by blacks in the manual and service sector were checkmated by white advances in white-collar and skilled occupations. It also serves as a caution against drawing conclusions about overall black economic gains from occupational data alone.

UNEMPLOYMENT AND INCOME.   As noted above, the economic position of blacks is reflective not only of their occupational structure but of their income and employment status as well. Unfortunately, there are no systematic data on either unemployment or personal income for the 1900–1930 period. The Census Bureau did not begin collecting personal income data until 1950, and detailed annual unemployment statistics by race were not available until 1948. Our discussion of these factors during this period will therefore be sketchy.

The unemployment rate of blacks does not appear to have been high relative to whites during this period. In the 1920s, especially, black unemployment was no higher than white unemployment (Ross, 1967: 14), probably because of the high concentration of blacks in agriculture (where unemployment is normally very low) and the growing demand for black workers in Northern industries during this entire period, but especially in the twenties. The high agricultural concentration of blacks was on the one hand an asset, and on the other a liability. Although unemployment is low in agriculture, underemployment is high.

The combination of high underemployment in agriculture, low-skilled blue-collar jobs, and underrepresentation in the high-paying white-collar sector probably kept black income low relative to that of whites in this period. Hiestand's occupational index, using as it does income weights, would lead to the conclusion that there was probably little or no gain in black income relative to whites, and perhaps even a loss among black females. The regional distribution of the black population would appear to be an important factor when considering relative income. In spite of the northern migration of blacks during this period, their overwhelming numbers remained in the South (90% in 1910), which was economically depressed compared to the North. This constituted a situation of double jeopardy in economic terms and pointed to a relatively low income for the entire black labor force. The only conclusion to be drawn about black economic gain during this period is that while there were favorable changes in the distribution of black workers—when compared with changes going on simultaneously among white workers—it appears that the overall relative economic position of blacks remained about the same throughout this time.

The 20th Century: 1930–1940

The argument might be advanced that the decade of the thirties, the time of the Great Depression, was a very special case in American economic history, and therefore its effect on blacks should not be unduly stressed in a study of long-term change. This line of reasoning might be acceptable were it not for the fact that economic downturns always have a more negative impact on the economic status of blacks than of whites. The depression hit black workers especially hard "because they were located at the bottom of the occupational pyramid, because they were concentrated in industries sensitive to the business cycle, and because they were subject to sharper discrimination in a period of job scarcity" (Ross, 1967: 14–15).

OCCUPATIONAL DISTRIBUTION. The impact of the depression is not completely evident from an examination of the changes in black occupational structure—pointing again to the need to consider employment and income data in any consideration of overall economic status. The trend toward a decrease in agricultural concentration continued in the thirties but was less pronounced (a decrease of only about 3% compared with more than 10% in the twenties) and was not matched by a corresponding increase in the manual and service sector, where blacks gained a meager 1% increase (Table 2.1 above). Within the blue-collar sector the major shifts occurred among laborers and service workers, with black males losing substantially and black females gaining. The overall effect of these changes must have been a loss for blacks, because of the lower income rate of female service jobs. The only other decrease was in the skilled area, and gains in the semiskilled and operative category and in the white-collar sector were too slight and the numbers involved too small to be significant. The primary effect of the depression on the black occupational structure was to bring to a standstill the favorable trends of the past decades and to even reverse this trend in some categories (unskilled and skilled work).

Of course, white workers were also affected by the depression, but not as severely as blacks. Although the trends of the previous decades favorable to the white occupational structure were slowed, the only areas of major concentration where these trends were reversed were in the skilled area—and perhaps the unskilled, where black employment declined at a faster rate than during the previous decade. Losses of skilled and unskilled jobs, however, were at least partially offset by gains in the semiskilled and operatives category.

Ratios of white to black workers (Table 2.3 above) for 1940 reveal a mixed bag that is difficult to interpret. In the sectors of major black concentration (farming and blue-collar workers), where 94% of black workers were found, they suffered an overall loss in the form of increased overrepresentation in agriculture. Among blue-collar occupations, which accounted for 60.6% of black employment in 1940 compared with 46.6% of white employment, black males moved away from proportionality in the unskilled category and slightly closer to it in the skilled, semiskilled, and service areas. The same was true for all white-collar occupations except professional and technical. It should be emphasized, however, that most gains toward proportionality were made in occupations where few blacks were employed. Much the same state of affairs held for black females relative to white females. Gains by black females in service employment were matched by an increase of white females, leaving black females overrepresented in this area by 70%. No other shifts except their loss in agriculture were of great importance, because of the small numbers involved.

Turning again to Hiestand's index of occupational position, we can note that the changes of the thirties did result in a deterioration of the economic status of black males (from an index of 78.1 to 77.5). Surprisingly, black females somewhat strengthened their position in the economy relative to white females (74.8 to 76.8). In spite of this gain by black females, it can be concluded that, because of the greater importance of males in the economy, blacks overall lost ground relative to whites in the thirties. Data analyzed by Sorkin (1971) for nonwhite[2] and white females 14 years old and over revealed a sharp regional difference in occupational status in 1940: a ratio of 0.41 for the South and 0.56 for the North and West. The same was undoubtedly true for black males relative to white males, perhaps even more so, when we consider the higher concentration of black males in agriculture.

UNEMPLOYMENT AND INCOME.   Black occupational losses during the depression of the thirties were paralleled by employment and income losses. As cotton agriculture collapsed in the South, blacks moving into southern cities or to the North found that nonagricultural jobs were not only declining but that "there was widespread invasion of Negro jobs by unemployed whites" (Ross, 1967: 15). Thus black workers not only lost much of the occupational progress of the previous decades in manufacturing, mechanical, and mining occupations, where their share of the jobs fell from 1,100,000 in 1930 to 738,000 in 1940, and in wholesale and retail trade, where their employment shrank from 398,000 to 288,000 in the same period; they found traditional "Negro jobs," such as waiter, porter, housemaid, elevator operator, and railroad laborer, also being taken away by whites. Under these conditions, a large unemployment differential appeared for the first time (Ross, 1967: 15; Sorkin, 1971: 396).[3]

As income is a factor of unemployment rates and occupational distribution, it can be concluded that since blacks lost significantly in both areas, their income must have also declined, both in absolute terms and relative to whites. Blacks who remained in the South during the thirties no doubt suffered more there than in other regions. Irrespective of region, however, the economic status of blacks deteriorated during this decade in all categories.

The 20th Century: 1940–50

Within the context of the 20th century and the history of black economic status, the 1940s provided a high point for blacks. The importance of the decade is further increased by its position, that is, following the disastrous decade of the thirties.

OCCUPATIONAL DISTRIBUTION.   The sharp shift of black workers from the farm to the manual and service sector that had been interrupted by the depression resumed in the 1940s. As Ross (1967: 16) points out, the recovery was slower for black than for white workers, but eventually it came; and with recovery came some relative progress, as by 1950 the number of black operatives had surpassed that of unskilled workers for the first time (Table 2.1). This development, along with a decline among domestic workers and a modest gain in the skilled worker and clerical and sales areas, were the principal occupational gains made by blacks in the forties.

Whites, of course, were also recovering from the depression and, as already noted, began their recovery earlier than blacks. By 1950 they had reduced their percentage in the agricultural sector to 11.1% (compared with 19.0% for blacks), and had 39.9% of their workers in the white-collar sector, compared with 10.2% for blacks. While total numbers of whites held steady in the manual and service sector, the position of blacks continued to improve as they moved out of service and unskilled occupations into semiskilled and skilled blue-collar jobs.

Relative to blacks, white workers were about four times as numerous in

the white-collar sector in 1950, and blacks continued their overrepresentation in lower-level blue-collar jobs. However, in one important area of unskilled jobs, black males achieved parity with whites, while in clerical and
sales positions, black females were rapidly closing the gap (Table 2.2). In
overall terms, both black males and females seemed to have improved their
economic position relative to whites, as measured by Hiestand's index of
occupational positions. The improvement appears striking—ranging from
an index of 77.5 in 1940 to 81.4 in 1950 for black males, and from 76.8 to 81.6
for black females (Hiestand, 1964: 53). Our caution that the unfavorable
position of blacks within occupational categories probably results in an
overstatement by such an index of the gains made by blacks still holds. Even
with this caveat, however, there seems to be little doubt that in the forties
blacks improved their overall occupational position *relative to whites* for the
first time in U.S. history. This conclusion is supported by another study
employing intracohort analysis (Hare, 1965). Using four age groups, 25–34,
35–44, 45–54, and 55–64, and the index of dissimilarity, Hare concluded that
there had been convergence (or movement toward similarity of occupational
distribution) for all age groups in the forties (p. 167).

Intraregional variations are evident from Table 2.4, which shows the
index of occupational positions of blacks relative to white males by states. All
but three southern states (Georgia, Kentucky, and Tennessee) showed gains
for blacks, some of which were quite substantial (in Louisiana, South
Carolina, and Maryland). All states in the Northeast except Pennsylvania
also showed some improvement. Only in the North-Central region was there
an overall decline in black occupational status.

UNEMPLOYMENT AND INCOME.   Although unemployment rates
fluctuated in the forties, black unemployment climbed from about 20%
higher than white unemployment in 1940 to about 80% higher in 1950
(Killingsworth, 1968: 23–24; Kahn, 1964: 18–19). Income data for the end of
the decade reveal that even after a period that was, according to all analysts, a
good one for blacks economically, the median income of black families was
only a little more than half (54%) the median income of white families (Table
2.5). In spite of the fact that this was a considerable improvement over the
1939 median ratio for black families and individuals (37%), it was still
indicative of a standard of living for blacks far inferior to that of whites.

An important point to note is the difference in the income ratios for
black male and female workers in 1950, 61.3 and 36.9%, respectively (Table
2.6). Income trends between the two sexes and between families also varied.
All groups experienced some rather sharp ups and downs between 1947 and
1950, but none so startling as black males, who suffered a loss of about nine
percentage points in 1949, only to regain those and more in 1950 (back up to
61.3% of white males). No doubt the higher income ratio of males reflects the

TABLE 2.4
Index of Occupational Position of Black Relative to White Males, by States, 1940–1960

	1940	1950	1960
United States, total	70	77	81
Northeast			
Massachusetts	81	84	88
Connecticut	82	84	83
New York	85	86	87
New Jersey	78	80	83
Pennsylvania	85	85	86
North-Central			
Ohio	87	86	86
Indiana	92	90	89
Illinois	89	88	88
Michigan	91	90	88
Missouri	87	88	86
South			
Maryland	71	75	78
District of Columbia	75	77	79
Virginia	73	76	76
North Carolina	71	72	73
South Carolina	62	65	69
Georgia	71	73	73
Florida	68	67	69
Kentucky	93	89	83
Tennessee	84	83	79
Alabama	75	77	74
Mississippi	63	66	64
Arkansas	73	74	77
Louisiana	66	70	74
Oklahoma	77	78	82
Texas	73	77	79

Note: Actually, the index is of nonwhite to white males; it includes all states with 100,000 or more Negroes in 1960 except California, where such a ratio may not be representative of Negroes.

Source: Eli Ginzberg and Dale L. Hiestand, "Employment Patterns of Negro Men and Women," in John P. Davis (ed.), The American Negro Reference Book (Englewood Cliffs, N.J.: Prentice-Hall, 1966), p. 226.

TABLE 2.5

Median Income of Families of Blacks and Other Races as a Percent of White Median Income, 1947–1974

Year	Income of Other Races as Percent of Whites'	Year	Income of Other Races as Percent of Whites'
1947	51%	1961	53%
1948	53	1962	53
1949	51	1963	53
1950	54	1964	56
1951	53	1965	55
1952	57	1966	60
1953	56	1967	62
1954	56	1968	63
1955	55	1969	63
1956	53	1970	64
1957	54	1971	63
1958	51	1972	62
1959	52	1973	60
1960	55	1974	62

Note: Excluding "other races" from these calculations indicates that the ratio of black to white median family income went from 0.54 to 0.58 between 1964 and 1974.

Source: Andrew F. Brimmer, "The Negro in the National Economy," in John P. Davis (ed.), *The American Negro Reference Book* (Englewood Cliffs, N.J.: Prentice-Hall, 1966), pp. 259; U.S. Bureau of the Census, "Social and Economic Status of the Black Population, 1971," p. 29, and "Social and Economic Status of the Black Population, 1974," p. 25.

presence of many unrelated individuals whose income, among black groups, was the highest of all (73% of the corresponding white group). Black females actually suffered a decline in relative income in the forties, from a high of 43.4% in 1948 down to 36.9% in 1950, which was nearly the same as their 1939 position.

The 1940s emerges as a mixed decade. Unemployment began to rise sharply for the first time, but so did income—presumably as a result of occupational gains. The result was a meaningful rise in overall economic status. Nevertheless, at the end of the decade, blacks were still relatively disadvantaged. They still occupied the bottom of the occupational scale, with an 80% higher unemployment rate and an income of only about 50% of that of whites. Further, when viewed in the context of the entire period thus far covered, the forties diminish in significance somewhat; for in the end it represents little more than a recouping of the losses suffered by blacks in the previous decade.

TABLE 2.6
Median Income of Male and Female Blacks and Other Races
as a Percent of White Median Income, 1939–1974

Year	Male	Female
1939	41.4%	36.4%
1947	54.3	34.0
1948	59.6	43.4
1949	50.0	40.5
1950	61.3	36.9
1951	61.6	42.1
1952	58.1	41.2
1953	59.4	48.5
1954	56.8	44.7
1955	58.8	43.3
1956	56.2	44.5
1957	55.4	45.5
1958	58.0	44.6
1959	58.0	53.2
1960	59.8	50.2
1961	57.0	51.3
. . . .	. . . .	. . . .
*1970	68	82
1971	68	88
1972	68	86
1973	67	85
1974	70	91

*Note: Data are for year-round full-time workers.

Source: Ginzberg and Hiestand, "Employment Patterns of Negro Men and Women," p. 232; U.S. Bureau of the Census, "Social and Economic Status of the Black Population, 1974," p. 28.

The 20th Century: 1950–60

During the fifties the economic seesaw continued, with both gains and losses sandwiched into the decade. As we will see later when discussing the factors related to black economic progress, for the first time in this century some long-term developments in the economy began to work to the disadvantage of black workers.

OCCUPATIONAL DISTRIBUTION.   During the first three years of the fifties, the prosperity brought on by the Korean War enabled blacks to continue improving their economic status. These three years, as Ross (1967: 18) argues, represent "the apex of Negro prosperity" relative to whites, to that date. The remainder of the decade, however, saw a slowing of the relative rate of progress of blacks and, to some extent, it seems, some retrogression. Accordingly, statistics for 1960 reflect the results of both trends.

The now-familiar trends in occupational change of past decades continued, except that the movement out of agriculture was not matched by a corresponding increase in the manual and service sector. The overall change of black workers in the latter sector was from 69.3% to 70.3% compared with 60.6% to 69.3% in the previous decade. These figures largely represent the higher unemployment rates for blacks in the fifties, but also to some extent an increase in white-collar employment, especially clerical and sales positions. Within the blue-collar sector, blacks improved their overall distribution as their numbers in unskilled occupations declined and their numbers in semiskilled and skilled employment increased. Trends in occupational shifts of the white labor force continued to be favorable to that group. Particularly significant was the fact that white workers were now almost equally represented among white-collar and blue-collar occupations, not only because of the continued decline in agricultural jobs held by whites, but also because of a new decline in blue-collar occupations, while the number of white-collar jobs held by whites continued to rise.

Relative to white males, black males did not reduce their overrepresentation in agriculture or among lower-level blue-collar occupations. In the operatives and semiskilled category, black males moved from a position of equality to overrepresentation, and they only slightly increased their representation in skilled jobs. Among white-collar occupations, the only improvement was in the clerical and sales area. In jobs important to females, black females had achieved equality with white females only in the semiskilled area, but they also continued to narrow the gap among clerical and sales workers (Table 2.2). At the same time, black females continued to furnish a disproportionate number of all domestic workers (45%) in 1960 (Russell, 1968: 100). Following the large jump in the index of occupational positions in 1950, there was an obvious leveling off for both black males and females, though black females improved their position more than black males.

UNEMPLOYMENT. Since the 1920s blacks have always had higher unemployment rates than whites, but it was not until 1954 that this rate increased to about twice the white rate and remained there for the rest of the decade (Table 2.7). This higher unemployment ratio was a very serious development which, even in the best periods, was to plague blacks in their struggle for economic equality for some time to come. In 1956, for instance, when the overall white unemployment rate dropped to 3.3%, the black rate

TABLE 2.7
Unemployment Rates, 1948–1974 (annual averages)

Year	Black and Other Races	White	Ratio: Black and Other Races to White
1948	5.9	3.5	1.7
1949	8.9	5.6	1.6
1950	9.0	4.9	1.8
1951	5.3	3.1	1.7
1952	5.4	2.8	1.9
1953	4.5	2.7	1.7
1954	9.9	5.0	2.0
1955	8.7	3.9	2.2
1956	8.3	3.6	2.3
1957	7.9	3.8	2.1
1958	12.6	6.1	2.1
1959	10.7	4.8	2.2
1960	10.2	4.9	2.1
1961	12.4	6.0	2.1
1962	10.9	4.9	2.2
1963	10.8	5.0	2.2
1964	9.6	4.6	2.1
1965	8.1	4.1	2.0
1966	7.3	3.3	2.2
1967	7.4	3.4	2.2
1968	6.7	3.2	2.1
1969	6.4	3.1	2.1
1970	8.2	4.5	1.8
1971	9.9	5.4	1.8
1972	10.0	5.0	2.0
1973	8.9	4.3	2.1
1974	9.9	5.0	2.0

Note: The unemployment rate is the percent unemployed in the civilian labor force.

Source: U.S. Bureau of the Census, "Social and Economic Status of the Black Population in the United States, 1971," p. 52, and "Social and Economic Status of the Black Population, 1974," p. 64.

was 7.5%, more than twice as high. When broken down by sex and age groups, the high unemployment rate for blacks remained consistently high, although the black/white female ratio tended to be lower than the black/white male ratio. Black teen-agers (male and female, 14–19 years) had the highest rates of all groups: as high as 26.2% for black females and 24.3% for black males in 1958. The corresponding white teen-age rates were 11.6% and 14.0% (Ross, 1967: 31).

Another revealing unemployment rate is that based on occupations. In 1960 some of the highest unemployment rates prevailed in occupations with the heaviest black concentration—laborers (12.5%) and operatives (8.2%) in the case of black males, and operatives (12.3%) and private household workers (6%) in the case of black females.

Still another indication of the growing seriousness of the unemployment problem for blacks is long-term unemployment (15 or more consecutive weeks), which since 1953 has constituted an increasing proportion of the total unemployed (Kahn, 1968: 20). Furthermore, blacks account for an even larger portion of this "under class," as one economist terms them (Kahn, 1968: 20): 22.5% in 1974, when they comprised only 11% of the total labor force.

While the above unemployment figures for blacks are already extremely high, it is believed that they are still an understatement of actual rates because they do not reflect the higher level of involuntary part-time employment and "hidden unemployed" or discouraged black workers.[4] Involuntary part-time employment for nonagricultural workers increased steadily during the fifties, with nonwhite percentages always about 50% higher than those of corresponding white groups (Batchelder, 1968: 85–86). Ross calculated that in 1963, 25.6% of all involuntary part-time workers were black, the equivalent of 130,000 full-time unemployed (pp. 28–29).

Hidden unemployment is difficult to calculate. One method of estimating this portion of black unemployment is to compare the labor force participation rates of blacks and whites. While participation rates for males of both races have been decreasing since the early 1940s, they have declined much more sharply for blacks than for whites. Participation rates for women, on the other hand, have been increasing, but more rapidly for white than for black women (Ross, 1967: 22–23). Between 1940 and 1960, black males showed an increase in participation in only two age groups: the 14–15 age category between 1940 and 1950 and the 30–34 age category between 1950 and 1960. In all other categories there were decreases in participation. White males suffered losses of more than 1% in only three categories among workers below 60 years (Ginzberg & Hiestand, 1966: 236).

It must be remembered that unemployment rates for blacks were increasing during this same period. These two facts, declining relative labor force participation and increased relative unemployment among black workers, have led to the conclusion "that many [Black workers] are not in the labor force because there is no work for them" (Ginzberg & Hiestand, 1966: 237). One estimate of the effect of different participation rates on the nonwhite civilian labor force was calculated by Ross. He found that if white participation rates had applied to the black labor force, in 1950 there would have been 42,000 more black males and 766,000 less black females, while in 1960 there would have been 66,000 more black males and 727,000 less black females (p. 26). If we were to make the conservative estimate that half of these black males were not in the labor force because of discouragement, this would still represent 33,000 among the hidden unemployed in 1960. The combination of higher relative unemployment rates together with a larger share of the long-term unemployed, the part-time employed, and the hidden unemployed points to a deteriorating economic position for blacks in the 1950s.

INCOME.   As expected, income trends reflect developments in the areas of occupational distribution and employment. Most of the gains in relative income made by blacks occurred in the 1940–55 period. During the second half of the fifties, the relative growth rate of black income was about the same or lower than that of whites.[5] While the average income of black families rose 58% compared with 46% for white families between 1947 and 1955, the rates were 31 and 35%, respectively, for the 1955–62 period (Henderson, 1967: 87).

The differences between the first and second half of the decade are clearest when we consider the income of families. The median income of black families rose from 54% of the white median in 1950 (with some fluctuations) to 56% in 1953 and 1954; thereafter it dropped rapidly to a low of 51% of white income in 1958, the same as the 1947 and 1949 levels. It recovered somewhat in 1959 and 1960 (to 55%) but never again reached the high points of the fifties (56% and 57%; see Table 2.5 above). Ratios for the median income of black males relative to white males demonstrated great instability during the 1950s and finally ended up lower than at the beginning of the decade. Only black females showed a marked gain in income relative to white females. Their ratio rose from 36.9% in 1950 to 53.2% in 1959, and ultimately surpassed black males (Table 2.6).

While blacks gained little or nothing in income relative to whites in the fifties, the absolute or dollar difference widened. This was true even in the early years of the decade, when the black rate of increase was higher than that of whites. For black families the absolute dollar difference in 1950 was $1,576, in 1954 it was $1,929, in 1960 $2,603. Clearly, black families were losing ground. Some researchers, when comparing incomes of blacks and whites, emphasize relative gains of blacks while ignoring the dollar difference. This is a misleading practice which led Henderson (1967) to comment,

This continual widening of the dollar difference is a significant dimension of the economic trap in which Negroes are caught. Relative improvements in the

Negro's economic status do not adequately alter the situation. People do not spend and save percentages; they spend and save dollars. Assessments of the economic position of Negroes that are confined to acceleration concepts and percentage gains obscure the real predicament: Negroes are losing rather than gaining ground in reaching dollar parity with whites. (p. 88)

The disadvantaged position of blacks in terms of income appears even starker when we examine the relative poverty status of blacks and whites. Statistics show that not only does a much higher relative proportion of black families live in poverty,[6] but also relatively fewer black families are escaping from below the poverty line. Between 1947 and 1962 the number of black families living in poverty declined by only 3%, compared with 27% for white families. Thus, in 1962 *almost half* (44%) of all black families were still living in poverty, compared with only 17% of white families (Henderson, 1967: 86).

As noted above, the low relative income of blacks directly relates to their occupational and employment status. Even though blacks were making some occupational gains in the 1950s, particularly during the first half, there was stagnation in their relative position. This condition was a result of both their relatively high unemployment rates and their low positions within occupational categories. When blacks advanced to higher occupational categories, it appears that they moved into the lowest income end of each occupation (Batchelder, 1968: 88).

REGION.   The regional differences in black economic status have become more and more evident as the 20th century advances. These differences are not surprising, given the economic disparity between the South and other regions of the country, and, until recently, the overwhelming concentration of blacks in the South. As late as 1940, nearly four fifths (77%) of the black population lived in the South, compared with only 27% of the white population (U.S. Bureau of the Census, 1971b: 9). By 1960 the Southern portion of the black population had been reduced from 77% to 60%, but the percentage of whites in the South had not changed. Another salient point is the fact that most blacks employed in the agricultural sector reside in the South.

Whether the regions are being compared by occupational distribution, unemployment rates, or income, statistics show very clearly that blacks in the South are far more disadvantaged than blacks in other regions. In 1960, only in one Southern state, Kentucky, did black workers show an index of occupational position equal to the lowest (83 in New Jersey and Connecticut) in the Northeast and North-Central regions (Table 2.4 above). During the fifties, not only were blacks in the South far behind blacks in other regions in terms of occupational position, but Southern blacks were losing ground while other blacks were either gaining ground or holding steady. For instance, outside the South 17.2% of black males held white-collar jobs, compared to only 6.9% in the South. For black women the corresponding figures were 24.5% outside the South and 11.5% in the South. The difference in employment ratio between white and black males (white collar) within the South expanded between 1940 and 1960 from 22% to 29%, but it changed very little in other regions. Among females, the ratio expanded in the South from 44% to 47% during the same period, while narrowing from 44% to 25% outside the South (Henderson, 1967: 97). The disparity held for other sectors as well. Batchelder (1968: 89) compared employment ratios for black and white males for four different occupational groups: clerical and kindred workers; craftsmen, foremen, and kindred workers; service workers; and laborers, except farm and mine. He found that, in both 1950 and 1960, with the exception of service workers, southern blacks tended to be far more overrepresented in the low-skilled occupations and underrepresented in the high-skilled ones than blacks in any of the other three regions.

Surprisingly, male and female blacks in the South in 1960 had lower unemployment rates than those in all other regions, except for black females in the Northeast (Killingsworth, 1967: 60). These rates are probably the result of a number of factors: the different type of economy of the South as opposed to that of other regions, with the South requiring more laborers and service workers; the "southern division of labor," with its tradition of "Negro jobs" and "white man's work"; and the larger numbers of southern blacks in agriculture, which has low rates of unemployment. As noted above, however, underemployment is a serious problem in the South.

On the other hand, between 1950 and 1960 only black males in the South experienced an *increase* in unemployment. Relative unemployment rates declined for black males in all other regions and for black females in all regions. At the same time, the South was the only region where neither black females nor black males increased their proportion of the total labor force (Batchelder, 1968: 82).

These disparities between the South and other regions were cumulative and showed up clearly during the fifties in income differences. Outside the South, black median income was about 75% of the white, but in the South it was less than 50% of the white. This difference in income by region was true for black males and black females in 1949 and 1959, although black females enjoyed higher *relative* incomes than black males in all regions (except the South) in 1949 (Batchelder, 1968: 71, 73). The proportion of black families below the poverty line was also much higher in the South than in any other regions. In 1959, 91.8% of nonwhite farm families were living below the poverty level, compared to 45.3% of white nonfarm families (U.S. Bureau of the Census, 1969, Table D). This estimate of the South—non-South disparity is only a rough one, but it is of some use, since about 85% of all black rural farm families resided in the South.

The 20th Century: 1960–1970

OCCUPATIONAL DISTRIBUTION. After a decade which for blacks was not much more than a standoff, the 1960s brought some significant change—most of which came after 1964. As before, the proportion of black workers in farming continued to decline, and now it reached a point of actual parity (Table 2.1). However, though blacks and whites were now represented in farming occupations in about the same proportions, relative to their number in the total labor force, blacks were far more likely to be farm laborers and whites farmers and farm managers. With the proportion of black workers in farming already very low, even in 1960 (8.1%), the most important developments were now taking place in the blue-collar and white-collar sectors. Since 1910, the proportion of black workers in the blue-collar sector had increased steadily—especially during the twenties and forties—to the point that blacks were highly overrepresented in the entire manual and service sector (45.5% for whites and 70.3% for blacks in 1960). In the 1960s this trend began to reverse itself, as the proportion of blacks holding blue-collar jobs declined to 68.3% in 1970. At the same time, blacks doubled their overall proportion in the white-collar sector, from 13.4% to 27.9% (see Table 2.1 above). These two trends, a decrease in overrepresentation in the blue-collar sector and a large increase in white-collar occupations, were the most important developments during the sixties.

We are now in a position to examine the trends of the past 60 years. What has been happening is clear. It began with black workers greatly overrepresented in the lower-level occupations and greatly underrepresented in the higher-level ones. Since then there has been a very slow process of upward mobility in an aggregate sense. But this "aggregate mobility" can be visualized as two groups of people climbing two ladders that are side by side. Both groups are moving up at the same time, but part of group A is always above the highest person in group B, and part of group B is always below the lowest person in group A. Since the beginning of this century blacks have been gradually reducing their overrepresentation in farming and in service and unskilled occupations, while at the same time attempting to increase their representation in *all other* occupational categories. By 1970 blacks had been able to eliminate their overrepresentation in only one of the three categories, farming. A decade earlier, equality had been achieved in the operatives area, only to be followed by overrepresentation in yet another low-skilled area. Although in the 1960s black workers seemed at last to be breaking into the white-collar sector, especially clerical, sales, and professional jobs, by 1970 they had not yet reached a position of equality in any occupation above the semiskilled level. Equality has proved very elusive for blacks in this 60-year period during which the United States has moved from a developing nation to a postindustrial economy.

It is difficult to compare the relative progress of black males and females because of their different occupational patterns or concentrations. It would appear, however, that in relative terms black women have made greater progress than black men. Although the index of dissimilarity for nonwhite females in 1950 was 53 compared with 37 for nonwhite males, by 1970 the two groups had almost identical indexes, 31 for males and 30 for females (Farley & Hermalin, 1972: 363). Another conclusion to be drawn is that in 1970 black males and females were about equally distant from occupational equality.

•   UNEMPLOYMENT.   The improvement in the economic position of blacks that began in 1964 is reflected in the unemployment rates. In that year unemployment rates for blacks dropped below 10% for the first time in seven years, and thereafter it continued to decline, to a low of 6.4% by 1969 (Table 2.7 above). However, this was still higher than the lowest rate of the fifties; black unemployment fell to 4.5% in 1953. Further, the unemployment rate began to climb again in 1970, reaching 8.2% for blacks in that year; and even during the best years, the black unemployment rate was never less than twice the white rate between 1954 and 1969. Black females suffered higher unemployment rates than black males, and by the end of the sixties, at least, their rates were increasing faster than those of black males. Another disturbing fact is that within the 13 largest black ghettos, the official unemployment rate was far higher than the national figure. Of the 13 largest black ghettos in 1966, 8 had official unemployment rates of from 10.1% to 15.6%, compared with 7.3% for blacks in the entire nation (National Committee against Discrimination in Housing, 1968).[7]

These official rates were only the tip of the iceberg, as an examination of the black share of long-term unemployment, involuntary part-time employment, and hidden unemployment will reveal. Between 1964 and 1974, blacks consistently accounted for approximately 20% of the long-term unemployed. In 1974 22.5% of the persons unemployed for 15 or more weeks were black (U.S. Department of Labor, 1975, p. 242), and they continue to have higher involuntary part-time employment.[8] Judged by labor force participation rates, black hidden unemployment also increased between 1960 and 1970. Black participation rates declined from 56.3% in 1960 to 54.2% in 1970. For whites, the corresponding figures were 55.2% and 55.7%, an increase in participation rates. Since black women increased their participation rates during the sixties, most of the burden of black hidden unemployment fell upon black males (especially the 14–24 age group), whose rates fell from 72.1% to 65.4% (U.S. Bureau of the Census, 1972a: Table 78, p. 372).

To get beyond the limitations of official unemployment figures, the Department of Labor developed two new measures of unemployment: the "subemployment index" for urban slums (U.S. Bureau of the Census, 1968b), and one for the entire nation (U.S. Department of Labor, 1968: 34–36). The subemployment index for urban slums combines measures of (1) the unemployed, (2) the involuntary part-time employed, (3) heads of households earning less than $60 per week and individuals under 65 earning less than $56 a week in a full-time job, (4) half the number of nonparticipants in the male age group 20–64 who are not in the labor force (the hidden unemployed), and (5) a conservative estimate of the male "under-count" group. This index yielded subemployment rates (for ten urban slums) of a "low" of 24% in Boston to highs of 45% and 47% in New Orleans and San Antonio, respectively, for November 1966 (National Committee against Discrimination in Housing, 1968).

The subemployment index for the nation includes measures of the long-term unemployed and of those workers who made less than $3,000 in 1966 for year-round full-time work. For 1966 the nonwhite subemployment rate was 21.6%, compared with 7.6% for whites (U.S. Bureau of the Census, 1968a: 17).

INCOME.   The pattern of unemployment for the 1960s also emerges in the area of income. Just as black unemployment declined beginning in 1964, so too did the median income of black families (in part reacting to unemployment trends) begin rising gradually in 1964 and 1965, take a sharp jump in 1966, and then resume its slow ascent, to reach an all-time high of 64% of the median white income in 1970 (Table 2.5 above). Since much has been made of the income gains of black families during the sixties, we will examine the data more minutely. The conclusion one draws depends in part upon the particular statistics used. A recent article by Farley and Hermalin (1972), for instance, reports ratios of nonwhite to white median family incomes for the years 1947, 1959, 1961, 1963, 1965, 1967, and 1969. The corresponding ratios are 51, 52, 53, 53, 55, 62, and 63, giving the impression that there was a *continuous* rise in median black income. This is not the case, however, as will be seen from an examination of yearly income data from 1947 to 1970. To begin with, there is no doubt that black median income rose considerably during the sixties, that is "considerably" when compared with the fifties, which was a decade of decline for blacks.[9] We do not know how the sixties compare with the forties, which was also a decade of large gains for blacks.

Further, the ratio of nonwhite to white family median income has demonstrated great instability. This point is extremely important in a discussion of black economic gains. Though the economic position of blacks has improved in this century, even in relative terms, it has not been 'a *steady*, rapid rise, but rather a very slow rise, with periods of stagnation (as during the years 1961–63) and many instances of reversals or losses. In the 1950s, a mediocre to bad decade for blacks in economic terms, the income ratio climbed to a high of 57% in 1952, only to fall almost steadily to a low of 52% by 1959 (Table 2.5). In the sixties most of the relative gain in income by black families occurred in 1965 and 1966, when the ratio jumped five percentage points, from 55% to 60% of white income. A similar jump of four percentage points occurred between 1951 and 1952—four percentage points which were eventually lost. The other gains of the sixties were made between 1963 and 1964 and 1966 and 1967. Before 1964 there was a period of stagnation, and after 1967 the rate of increase again declined sharply, remaining at 63% of white median income in both 1968 and 1969. In the context of the present discussion it is interesting to note that, during the years 1960–63, black families found themselves in the identical situation that existed between 1955 and 1956—with incomes declining from 55% to 53% of white median income (Table 2.5).

The important question is whether or not the factors influencing the income growth of blacks are beginning to be supportive of a steady and rapid rate of increase, or whether the 1960s was just another relatively good decade to be followed by a decade similar to the 1950s. A useful comparison might be made of the number of reversals suffered by blacks in different decades. During the fifties there were five reversals in the black/white income ratio, for a total loss of eight percentage points. There were only three reversals during the sixties, with a total loss of four percentage points. Only time will tell if there will be more or fewer reversals in the remainder of the seventies.

Two important points which should be made here involve the use of statistics for nonwhites and the absolute dollar gap. Since 1954 income data for blacks alone have been available. These statistics reveal that the black/white median income ratio for families has been two to three percentage points lower than the corresponding nonwhite-white income ratio, an indication that at least some of the other nonwhite groups are faring better than blacks. The second point is that even while the relative income gap has been slowly narrowing, the absolute dollar gap (using median family incomes), for the most part, has been widening. Between 1950 and 1960, the dollar difference in median income increased from $1,576 to $2,602. By 1965 it was $3,758. After decreasing to $3,445 in 1967, the gap increased to $3,603 in 1969 and $3,957 in 1970 and reached $5,548 in 1974.

A report on the social and economic status of the black population in 1971 (U.S. Bureau of the Census, 1972b) found two hopeful signs of development in the sixties: an increase of black families with incomes of $10,000 or more from 11% in 1960 to 28% in 1970 (p. 31), and a decrease in black families below the poverty line, from 48% in 1959 to 28% in 1969 (p. 39). Both trends were dramatic at first but showed signs of slowing down near the end of the decade, and they actually ended up in 1970 with a slight reversal among low-income families, as their proportion below the low-income level climbed to 29%. Though both of the above developments seem impressive, they pale in comparison with the trends among white families which raised their percentages in the $10,000-plus category from 31% in 1960 to 53% in 1969 (p. 31) and lowered their proportions below the low-income level from 15% in 1959 to 8% in 1970 (p. 39). White families suffered a slight reversal in the $10,000-plus category in 1970, with a reduction to 52%. Still they ended the decade with over 50% of white families having incomes of $10,000 or more, compared with only 28% of black families. On the other hand, while black families had the same proportion below the low-income level as in the $10,000-plus category, white families had reduced their proportion below the low-income level to less than 10%. Furthermore, for black families to achieve incomes of $10,000-plus required both the husband and the wife to work far more frequently than in the case of whites (U.S. Bureau of the Census, 1971a, pp. 6–8). On the national level, the only age categories (by age of the head of the household) of black families which reached a median income of $10,000 or more in 1970 were the 35–44 and 45–54 age groups. In the North and West the 25–34 and 55–64 cohorts also had median incomes of $10,000 or more. In *all* cases these were families in which both husband and wife worked. On the other hand, white families achieved this median income with only the husband working in both the 35–44 and 45–54 age groups on both the national level and in the North and West.

REGION.   Regional differences continued in the sixties. Two indicators of the continuing disparity between blacks and whites were to be found in statistics for median income of families, and the proportion of families with incomes of $10,000 or more. Though the median income of black families did increase during the 1960s from 46% of the southern white median in 1959 to 57% in 1970, this was far below the three other regions, in which black families had median incomes ranging from 71% of the corresponding white median in the Northeast to 77% in the West (U.S. Bureau of the Census, 1972b, p. 32). While 38% of black families in the North and West had median incomes of $10,000 or more, this was only true for 18% of black families in the South. Finally, in no age group did black families in the South attain a median income of $10,000 or more, even when both husband and wife worked (U.S. Bureau of the Census, 1971a, pp. 6–8).

It is quite clear now that blacks experienced some degree of economic progress during the 1960s relative to other decades in the 20th century. The sixties can be compared to the twenties and forties as high points in black economic progress. During each of these three decades significant changes took place. In occupational terms, the twenties and forties were noteworthy for the movement of black labor from rural farms to manual labor in the cities, especially in the North and West. The sixties are especially significant as the decade during which blacks began to crack the white-collar barrier for the first time; black median income relative to that of whites rose significantly; more black families' incomes reached $10,000 or more; and the percentage of black families below the low-income level sharply declined.

On the negative side, the rate of relative income gain began to slow near the end of the decade, and the absolute dollar gap continued to widen as whites also registered gains during the sixties. Although unemployment rates declined after 1963, they began to rise again in 1970. Furthermore, except for 1970, when the black/white ratio was 1.8, black unemployment rates were never lower than twice the white rate. In general it can be said that most of the gains experienced by blacks occurred betweeen 1965 and 1968, and although there were gains after 1968, rates for all economic indicators were slowing down considerably.

In the area of occupational distribution (see Table 2.1), by 1970 blacks finally had the same proportion of their workers in the white-collar sector as whites had in 1920. Among professional and technical workers, blacks now had a proportion slightly above that reached by whites between 1940 and 1950; among clerical and sales workers they were at the point reached by whites in 1920 but had not yet reached the 1910 relative proportion of white proprietors, managers and officials, or skilled workers. On the other hand, black workers in 1970 were overrepresented among operatives and unskilled and service workers. Only in the farming sector was there parity; and as noted above, it should be remembered that in all occupational categories blacks tend to hold the lower-paid positions. Having reviewed changes in the economic position of blacks up to 1970, the only question remaining to be considered in this section is the future of black economic status in the seventies.

The 1970s

Recent reports indicate that there has not been much relative change in occupational structure between blacks and whites thus far in the 1970s (*The New York Times*, July 23, 1973; p. 17). The report entitled "Social and Economic Status of the Black Population in the United States, 1974" (U.S. Bureau of the Census, 1975), provides further data on this (pp. 56–57). There were 9.3 million blacks in the civilian labor force compared to 76.6 million whites in 1974. Since 1970, black and white employment have each increased by 8%. In 1974, blacks were more likely than whites to be working at part-time jobs for economic reasons. In 1974, 5% of black men and 7% of black women reported they could not find full-time work and were forced to settle for part-time work (compared to 3% and 4% for white men and women). The proportion of black men in white-collar occupations increased from 22% to 24% between 1970 and 1974, while the proportion of white men in these occupations declined from 43% and 42%. During this time black women and women of other races increased their numbers in white-collar occupations from 36% to 42%, while white women maintained their positions at 64% (pp. 73–74).

Although there has been a trend toward upward occupational mobility among blacks, they are still overrepresented at the lower end of the occupational ladder in the low-skill and poor-paying jobs. In 1974 black workers composed approximately 9% of the employed population, but they accounted for 17% of nonfarm laborers and 19% of service workers (p. 75). Although blacks have been increasing their numbers in federal jobs in the 1970s, they are more concentrated in the lower pay grades than all other federal employees (p. 77).

By 1972 black unemployment had risen to the 10% level for the first time since 1963 and was twice the rate for whites. In 1975 the black unemployment rate was approximately 14%, and blacks were more likely than whites to remain jobless longer and to experience multiple unemployment.

After a decade of rising incomes, black families experienced a decline in income compared to whites in 1971, 1972, and 1973. Their income remained at only slightly more than half that of whites in 1974 (see Table 2.5).[10] The median dollar gap between blacks and whites rose to an all-time high of $5,548 in 1974, and the percentage of black families below the low-income level[11] ceased its steady decline of the previous decade. The percent of blacks living below the low-income level in 1973 and 1974 held steady at 31.4% (U.S. Bureau of the Census, 1975, p. 42). Meanwhile, the white rate rose from 8.4% to 8.9% during this time. The proportion of black families earning $10,000 or more remained at 38% from 1970 to 1974, while white families in that income bracket increased from 66% to 67% (p. 26). There were 5.5 million black families in March 1975, 19% of whom had incomes of $15,000 or more in 1974 and 23% of whom had incomes under $4,000. These proportions, as well as the median income level, have remained unchanged, in constant dollars, since 1970 (p. 24). The regional disparity described in earlier decades also continued. The momentum of the sixties has not only passed but seems to have played itself out. Whether the remainder of the seventies will be a repeat of the mediocre performance of the fifties or just a temporary setback remains to be seen.

Thus far we have attempted to develop as comprehensive a picture as possible of changes in black economic status, especially during the 20th century. This task has been accomplished chiefly through a description of what we consider to be the principal components or resources which determine the economic well-being of a group: its occupational distribution, employment and unemployment rates, and income. There are many handicaps to such an analysis, especially the unavailability of data and inadequacy of statistical measures. Before 1940, much of the data needed was either nonexistent or very inadequate, and consequently, our analysis had to be brief. From about 1940 on an increasing amount of data has been collected by the U.S. Census Bureau in its decennial censuses and current population surveys, and this enabled us to be much more comprehensive in our analysis in the latter part of this survey. Whenever possible, we attempted first to describe the absolute level of achievement of blacks on each component of economic status and the changes that took place over various periods of time. We then compared black achievements with white achievements to ascertain the relative position of blacks or the distance that remained to be traveled before equality would be achieved. The handicap of inadequate measures was partially overcome by using Hiestand's index of occupational positions, which is an income-weighted index and thus comes close to an overall measure of economic position.

FACTORS RELATED TO BLACK ECONOMIC STATUS

We turn now to the second part of our analysis, the factors related to black economic status. It would have been possible to include a discussion of factors in the first part, but in the interest of greater emphasis and clarity we delayed such an analysis. In the study of black economic status, there are a number of factors that have come to be recognized as causally related to one or more of the components of economic position. Some lend themselves more easily to accurate measurement and quantification and consequently are more frequently used, while others resist measurement and are not dealt with rigorously. Among the former are education, region, migration, and sex; among the latter are the economy, discrimination, personal values, and attitudes. Ideally one would like to be able to analyze the complex interrelationship of these and other factors as they causally relate to black economic status. An ideal tool for such a study would be path analysis (Land, 1969), since this method makes it possible to measure both the direct and indirect effects of factors. For instance, region may affect income through the influences of both education and higher wage rates. In the absence of a comprehensive causal model of the process by which the above factors determine black economic position, we must confine ourselves to discussing these factors sequentially. No doubt some factors are more closely related to one economic component than to another, and some factors have probably been more crucial at certain historical periods than others.

Education, a personal resource which is measurable (at least quantitatively), is one of the factors most frequently used in analyzing black economic change. It is a personal resource in the sense that it affects the value of human capital, making the individual more or less marketable. Sex is a personal variable which, while not strictly a resource, becomes an asset or liability in a world which is dominated by males and which frequently defines occupational roles in sexual terms. Most secretaries are females; most laborers are males. Region serves as a contextual variable; that is, if other variables, such as education and sex, are held constant, there will still be economic differences related to properties of the different regions, some of which interact with education and sex. Migration is a means used by individuals to alter their context and make their personal resources more valuable. Discrimination is in a sense the flip side of migration, in that it prevents the full utilization of personal resources in the market. Values and attitudes are personal characteristics which may or may not affect an individual's economic position. The hidden unemployed, for instance, are those who have become so discouraged that they have ceased looking for a job. Finally, the economy sets the overall conditions within which the other factors operate. Since we have already discussed the effects of sex and region to some extent, we will say no more about these two variables. The other factors—the economy, migration, education, discrimination, and attitudes—will be analyzed consecutively.

The Economy

Of all the factors heretofore mentioned, it appears that the state of the economy has been the most important single determinant of the economic status of blacks. The reason seems to be that discrimination lessens during periods of severe labor shortages and low unemployment. Both Ferman et al. (1968) and Ross (1967) concluded that occupational gains have only been made by blacks during periods of high labor demand and low unemployment. The way to understand the importance of the economy to black economic status is to think of the economy as establishing the broad conditions within which other factors operate and influence black occupational distribution, employment, and income. The level of manpower demand (tight or loose market), the general employment structure and trends, and the technological mix are all factors which operate in such a way as either to enhance or to limit the more "proximate" factors, such as education, sex, region, and discrimination. An important point that bears repeating is that all of these factors (including the economy itself) operate together in such a way that their influence on black workers is different from their influence on white workers. Not only are black workers affected differently from white workers by the economic forces, but, because of their more precarious position in the economy, black workers respond more quickly to negative economic forces (Ferman et al., 1968: 14). Thus there have been periods during which the workings of economic forces contributed to black economic progress, but there have also been periods during which these forces arrested or even reversed black gains.

We can perhaps distinguish two different types of economic forces which are important for the present discussion. The first is the short-term or temporary economic development, such as a boom, a recession, or even a depression. Though their effects are felt throughout the economy and by the black labor force, the fact that they do not continue for a long time (relative to the time perspective we are working with) makes them less important than the second type of economic force. The latter is a more "permanent" aspect of the structure of the economy; "permanent" in the sense that it may operate for decades rather than merely a few years and thus have a more far-reaching influence.

The 20th century can be divided into roughly two broad periods, each dominated by a separate deep-seated force which reverberated throughout the economy, determining much of what was happening. A convenient dividing point is 1956, the year in which white-collar workers outnumbered blue-collar workers for the first time in our history. The first period can be called the early industrialization stage, during which the blue collar sector predominated as the most dynamic and dominant area of the economy. That period was characterized by a steady attrition of agricultural occupations and a similar growth in manual jobs. During this first broad period there were several briefer periods marked by very intensive industrial growth, from which black workers especially profited. These briefer periods occurred shortly after the turn of the century, during World War I, the 1920s, World War II, and the postwar period and the Korean War to 1953.

Shortly after the turn of the century, industrialization was in full swing. From the last decade of the 19th century to about 1910, the gross national product grew from $13 billion to $22 billion, and by 1918 it had reached $40 billion. As industrial jobs became plentiful, the first wave of black migration out of agriculture and the South and into the North and blue-collar jobs occurred (Ross, 1967: 11). Though these were often the most dangerous, difficult, and lowest-paying industrial jobs, they still carried higher incomes than the agricultural jobs blacks had held in the South. World War I further stimulated industrial development and cut off the supply of European immigrants, thereby continuing the momentum of the black occupational shift which began a decade earlier. The prosperity of the twenties merely reinforced an already strong force, and it benefited black workers enormously. The depression of the thirties was a severe economic setback to blacks, but World War II created jobs through a special demand for industrial goods necessary for the war. This economic upswing was followed by a postwar boom and then the Korean War. Each period was characterized by high demand for industrial goods of one type or another, and each facilitated the transition of black workers out of agriculture and service jobs into manual occupations.

Although each of these subperiods built on the gains of the previous ones, it can be argued that the years of World War II and the two periods following (1940–53) represent the apex of the early industrialization phase, during which the demand for blue-collar employment was at its highest. But there were other forces at work during this period besides high labor demand which were especially beneficial to black workers. During World War II, as Killingsworth (1968) explains, there was:

> . . . a massive reduction in the civilian labor force; a massive restructuring of demand, resulting in the massive creation of low-skilled, repetitive jobs; massive government subsidies, both direct and indirect, for recruitment and training of inexperienced workers; and a massive increase in tolerance of low productivity. (p. 36)

The importance of this first broad period for the economic progress of blacks lay in its impact upon all three factors of economic status. The occupational distribution of black workers was greatly improved, relative to that of the beginning of the century, by their movement into blue-collar jobs; unemployment was at an all-time low during much of this time, both in absolute terms and relative to whites; and, finally, since blue-collar wages were rising faster than white-collar wages, blacks improved their incomes relative to whites. A weakness of this period lay in the fact that the economic gains of blacks depended in part upon what Michael Harrington has called "economic geography" (Kahn, 1968: 18), or the movement of black workers to areas of the country with better employment opportunities and higher wage rates. But since white workers were also taking advantage of economic conditions, within each region blacks remained at the bottom.

The most important factor during the second broad period (1953–76) has been the development of technology (automation), which has resulted in a decline in blue-collar jobs and an increase in white-collar ones. This development was in part a factor of the types of occupations created by the space industry in the 1950s and 1960s, and in part the result of the broad application of the new technology to industry as a whole. As a result, not only is the white-collar sector now growing faster than the blue-collar sector, but, even within blue-collar industries the demand for white-collar jobs is now outpacing the demand for blue-collar jobs. Manufacturing, one of the most important of the blue-collar industries, can serve as a barometer. Between 1953 and 1965, total employment in manufacturing changed very little, but in 1965 there were 1 million fewer blue-collar and 1 million more white-collar jobs in the industry (Killingsworth, 1967: 66). In other words, in this advanced stage of industrialization the service-producing industries are growing faster than the goods-producing industries.

Just how is this affecting the black labor force? Unfortunately, it must be said that the technological revolution is working to the disadvantage of black workers. While white workers were moving out of the blue-collar and into the white-collar sector (44.1% by 1960; see Table 2.1), black workers were moving from agricultural to blue-collar jobs (70.3% in 1960). We see now that this major trend of the first broad period, while beneficial to blacks up to 1953, has left them concentrated in the most vulnerable sector of the economy. Not only are blue-collar occupations declining in importance (within the total economy) and subject to slower growth and consequently to higher unemployment, but the income of white-collar jobs is now growing faster than that of blue-collar occupations. As a result, the relative income position of blacks is now slowly deteriorating, and the absolute dollar gap is widening. It should be noted that black income increased sharply between 1964 and 1968, and black unemployment declined somewhat during the same period, because of the economic growth spurred by the 1964 income tax cut and rising military spending for the Vietnam War, which accelerated factory production (and blue-collar jobs) in 1965 for the first time since 1953 (Ferman et al., 1968: 14). However, this period was of extremely short duration. On the whole, blacks remain overwhelmingly concentrated in the less dynamic (blue-collar) sector of the economy, and until the late sixties they had little success in penetrating white-collar occupations.

We believe there are reasons to argue that, in spite of the gains of the past, this second period into which the economy has entered (advanced industrialization) is a more difficult one for blacks. During most of the first period, jobs were plentiful in the blue-collar sector for black and white workers, and the white-collar sector was expanding just rapidly enough for whites who wanted to move to have some place to go. As a result, competition between the races was low. Black and white workers, in fact, were not competing for the same jobs, since blacks were moving into the low-skilled and low-prestige jobs as whites were moving out of these and into higher-skilled and higher-prestige jobs. Thus, general labor force conditions facilitated a limited upward mobility of black workers, for blacks provided what the economy then needed—cheap, low-skilled labor.

During the second period, black workers faced an entirely different set of market conditions. Jobs, especially blue-collar jobs, became scarcer, and since blacks were concentrated in these areas of declining importance, the unemployment they faced was more serious and intractable than during the first period because structural constraints were operating. Furthermore, after 1947, and especially during the fifties, the white departure rate from agriculture exceeded the black rate for the first time. The cause was improved technology, which pushed up the productivity curve in farming at a time when total demand for farm products grew more slowly than productivity. The result was increased competition for the least skilled nonfarm jobs in the urban areas to which both blacks and white workers were drifting, especially in the North-Central region (Killingsworth, 1968: 10).

For blacks to continue progressing under the new economic conditions, they must now win a substantial share of jobs within the most dynamic area of the economy, the white-collar sector. But it is precisely here that the difficulty lies. For millions of black workers with obsolete skills and low education, the loss of their blue-collar job leaves them no place to go but welfare. The forces of past discrimination have worked together in such a way as to prevent black workers from becoming truly competitive in a changing economy, with the result that the negative effects of the new technology fall most heavily upon them. But there is a second aspect which we believe is also very important. It is quite possible that blacks face greater (and more subtle) discrimination in their attempt to enter white-collar occupations than had existed in their entry into the blue-collar sector. These are not only the jobs that carry the highest prestige, but they are the only jobs which have the promise (or threat) of truly equalizing the two races. Heretofore, as blacks moved upward they found themselves "occupying land" that had been abandoned by whites who were moving still higher. Now there is no place for whites to go, and as a result competition and discrimination (which have always gone hand in hand throughout our history) are increasing in the white-collar sector. It is significant that as blacks began to move into the white-collar sector in large numbers for the first time in the late sixties, they occupied jobs with lower income and lower levels of authority. Relatively few blacks have been able to land jobs as salaried proprietors, managers, and officials (Table 2.1).

Migration

One of the principal ways in which blacks have sought to improve their economic lot in the 20th century is through migration. The overwhelming concentration of blacks in the South, which not only had a depressed economy relative to other regions but which discriminated more consistently and severely against blacks, made it necessary for them to migrate away from declining agriculture and toward growing industrial employment. The extent of this migration can be gauged from the following figures for net movement of blacks from the South, as estimated in U.S. Bureau of the Census (1971b: 11, Table 5):

1910–20	450,000
1920–30	750,000
1930–40	350,000
1940–50	1,600,000
1950–60	1,500,000
1960–70	1,500,000

Source: Killingsworth (1968), p. 7.

Except for the thirties there has been a steady increase in the number of blacks who chose to seek their fortune in regions other than the South. The result has been a steady decrease in the black population of the South, from 90% in 1900 to 53% in 1970. There are indications that this trend may be changing in the midseventies, but it is too early to state this emphatically. What has been the impact of this massive migration upon the economic status of blacks?

It is obvious from what has already been said that migration from the South has been an important avenue to greater occupational diversification for blacks. The movement out of agriculture into manual employment was accomplished by means of migration to the North and West. Without massive migration, blacks would have remained a predominantly rural people.

The impact of migration upon unemployment is somewhat more complicated. As we have already indicated, the employment problem of the South has been one of underemployment rather than unemployment. In fact, the South has consistently had lower black unemployment rates than any other region. Since the agricultural economy of the South has experienced both depressions and a sharp decline in manpower needs because of the introduction of modern technology, the low black unemployment rate must be a direct result of black emigration. This argument appears especially convincing when we realize that, until recently, there was a very low net emigration of whites from the South: 0.1% in the 1940s and 14% in the 1950s (Henderson, 1967: 83).

Although black migration from the South helped to keep their unemployment rate down in that region, this massive migration did not substantially increase the black unemployment rates of the other regions until the mid-1950s. Before that time black migrants had little difficulty securing jobs. After 1953, however, the situation changed drastically. Not only did white migrants to the Northeast and North-Central regions begin to outnumber black migrants for the first time (Fein, 1965: 111) and to compete for low-skilled jobs, but black migrants found that blue-collar jobs were no longer as plentiful as before. Black migrants were now contributing to the growing unemployment of the North and West. Extensive evidence for this assertion is lacking, but at least some research is supportive of such a conclusion. For instance, Sorkin (1969: 272–273) calculated the contribution of migrants to the nonwhite/white unemployment ratio in 10 standard metropolitan statistical areas (SMSAs) in 1960 and found that in 8 out of the 10 cases the inclusion of migrants increased the ratio.[12]

Migration appears to be related to the mounting black unemployment in the North and West in still another way. Killingsworth (1968) argues that past black migration, particularly during the forties, included an unusually high proportion of young adults. As a result, black "migration transferred not only population as such; it also transferred a substantial part of the reproductive capacity of the rural southern Negro population" (p. 18). The result was a higher black birth rate in the North and West than would otherwise have been the case, and consequently a higher growth rate in the black labor force in the North and West.

That migration has contributed to rising black incomes is obvious from what has already been said about regional differences in black median income. The greater occupational diversity and higher wage rates of the North and West relative to the South enabled blacks to improve their economic position far above the level that would have been possible had they not left the South in large numbers. The extent of this migration effect is far greater than might be imagined. Using data for urban males (25 years and older) in the South and in the North and West (1939–59) and for males and females in nonfarm occupations in both regions for the years 1949–67, Gwartney (1970a) estimated the proportion of relative income gain that was the result of education and migration. His findings reveal that during some periods, a substantial part of the gain was the result of migration alone. The greatest relative income gains for black urban males was during the 1940s, 12% or more within certain regions. For the 1939–59 period, the relative income gain for black urban males was 22.8% for the nation as a whole, or about 19% after controlling for the migration effect.

During the 1950s, however, the median income ratio for black males increased only slightly for the nation as a whole and actually declined within some regions. Most of the relative income gain of the fifties appears to be the result of migration. Gwartney made the same calculations for the 1959–67 period and concluded that, for that eight-year period, "almost all of the relative median income gains of nonwhites during the period are estimated to have resulted from regional migration" (p. 876). The increase resulting from migration was between 9.2% and 10.9%, while the increase before removing the migration effect was 11.2%.

For black women the impact of migration on relative income gains was less pronounced. For the nation as a whole, migration contributed between 5.9% and 6.8% to the relative median income gains of black females in the 1950s, and from 4.4% to 4.6% between 1959–67. Even after controlling for the migration effect, Gwartney found that black females gained in relative income between 25% and 30% for the years 1949–67 (p. 876). However, according to Gwartney, the failure of white females to increase their income as rapidly as black males, white males, and black females is "largely responsible for the substantial relative income gains of nonwhite females" (p. 877).

Migration emerges as one of the most important avenues of black economic progress in the 20th century. It was migration that enabled blacks to take advantage of the jobs created during the phase of early industrialization. By migrating from the South in large numbers to areas with more favorable employment opportunities and higher income rates, blacks were able to greatly improve their overall economic status. The effect in the South was to help keep their relative unemployment rates low and to raise their economic status relative to what it would have been had they remained. Migration led to greater occupational diversification in the North and West and to higher educational attainments (relative to the South) for the children of migrants. During some periods, as in the fifties and part of the sixties, relative income gains of black males were caused almost solely by the migration effect. And even though migration seems to have contributed to high rates of unemployment in the North and West after 1953, it is doubtful that blacks would have been better off had most remained in the South.

Education

It is a well-known fact that an investment in education does not bring the same economic return to blacks as to whites. A short time ago Brimmer (1966) could write that in 1960 "the financial advantage for Negroes of an additional year of educational attainment is just over half that of whites," and "a nonwhite man must have between one and three years of college before he can expect to earn as much as a white man with less than eight years of schooling over the course of their respective working lives" (p. 260). Ten years later the situation had not changed appreciably for black males, as can be seen from the following conclusions drawn by Farley and Hermalin (1972):

> In 1960, Black men with a college education had a median income lower than that of white males with one to three years of high school. Even after the progress of the 1960s, a college educated Black man had a lower median income than a white secondary school graduate in 1969. (pp. 361–62)

While the above observations are clear and incontestable, explanations differ for the unequal return to black males for the same quantity of education as white males receive.[13] Most researchers, leaning on the findings of the Coleman Report (Coleman and others, 1966) that there is great disparity in the educational attainments of black and white students, have been inclined to attribute the above discrepancy to difference in the quality of education received by blacks in segregated southern and inner-city northern schools. This explanation appeared to be given further support by findings that black students in racially integrated schools show higher scholastic achievement than those in all-black schools, and that "Negro adults who attended desegregated schools are more likely to be holding white-collar jobs and to be earning more than otherwise similarly situated Negroes who attended racially isolated schools" (U.S. Commission on Civil Rights, 1967: 102–104). The serious flaw in the above assumption occasioned by the Coleman Report is that until recently it has been an untested assumption. In the following pages we will first examine the findings on the observed relationship between education and the three economic status indicators: occupational attainment, unemployment, and income. We will then address ourself to two related questions: (1) Is education related to economic status? (2) is the difference in the black/white return for an equal quantity of education due to discrepancy in the quality of education received?

Since most data on the relationship of education to economic status began to be collected in the 1940s, our discussion will be limited to the past three decades. The observed relationships are sometimes surprising and not easily explained. Hare (1965) calculated indexes of dissimilarity between white and nonwhite occupational distributions by age and education for males during the years 1940, 1950, and 1960. He found that for all years, the dissimilarity was smallest at the two extreme educational levels (0–8 years of elementary school and four years or more of college) and smallest of all for those with four years of college or more (Table 2.8). The greatest dis-

TABLE 2.8
Indexes of Dissimilarity between White and Nonwhite Occupational Distributions, by Age and Education, for Employed Males, 1940, 1950, and 1960.

Years of School Completed and Census Year	Age Group			
	25–34	35–44	45–54	55–64
Total				
1940	46.02	43.11	41.79	36.04
1950	36.40	38.85	39.15	36.22
1960	35.39	37.46	38.27	38.82
Elementary 0–8 years				
1940	34.72	35.07	35.00	29.36
1950	27.26	29.84	30.52	32.04
1960	27.89	29.05	32.03	33.80
High school 1–3 years				
1940	40.71	41.11	37.44	38.21
1950	29.17	35.97	39.37	38.25
1960	29.79	31.13	34.16	38.71
High school 4 years				
1940	43.09	45.91	43.37	39.11
1950	32.14	37.05	40.35	36.92
1960	31.72	31.85	34.09	39.55
College 1–3 years				
1940	36.53	38.44	37.01	40.58
1950	30.19	33.54	37.10	29.23
1960	28.06	31.55	31.17	32.02
College 4 years or more				
1940	21.32	23.05	23.78	20.12
1950	11.90	13.01	20.23	17.10
1960	15.29	13.67	14.06	16.33

Source: Nathan Hare, "Recent Trends in the Occupational Mobility of Negroes, 1930–1960: An Intracohort Analysis," *Social Forces* 44 (December 1965): 172.

similarities were found among those with either partial high school education or the full four years. Whether we use cohort analysis or follow the same
age group over time, it is clear that convergence was strongest during the
forties,[14] especially among the two youngest age groups (25–34 and 35–44)
with four or more years of college. During the fifties convergence was less
pronounced and there were many instances of divergence, especially among
the two youngest age groups of college-educated black males. While young
college-educated black males seemed to profit more from good times than
other age-education groups, they suffered equally with others during bad
times. Still, the dissimilarities in 1960 were least for the college educated. The
above findings seem to indicate that the relative "payoff" to black males for
education is different for different educational levels.[15]

There is other evidence to support the contention that black males
profit less in occupational terms than white males from an equal amount of
education. Ginzberg and Hiestand (1966) found that at all educational levels
(elementary, high school, and college), black males were more likely to end
up in lower occupations than white males in 1960. For instance, they found
that in 1960 among male college graduates, 20% of the blacks were blue-
collar workers compared with only 9% of the whites (p. 241); and among
high school graduates, 40% of the white males landed white-collar jobs,
compared to only 21% of the black males (p. 243).

Although black males made educational gains in the 1960s, we do not yet
have extensive empirical evidence of the occupational return relative to
educational advances. However, using data for males in the central-city
poverty areas of 12 SMSAs[16] in March 1966, Harrison (1972) found that at all
grade levels (except four years of college) whites gained more in occupational terms than blacks. The greatest discrepancies were among those who
had completed high school or some college. For those who had completed
college, blacks had a slight edge.

Data on the relationship between education and unemployment in 1960
and 1964 indicate a remarkably similar relationship between education and
unemployment and between education and occupation (Killingsworth,
1968). While white males experienced steadily declining rates of unemployment with increasing years of education, black males experienced the
highest rates among the middle education ranges, especially high school
dropouts (11.3%). Except for those black males with college training, the
least educated (0–4 years) had the lowest unemployment rates (7.7%). Those
with the least education and those with *some* college actually had almost
identical unemployment rates (7.7% and 7.3%, respectively). The different
patterns for white and black males are reflected in the black/white unemployment ratios by years of schooling. At each educational level (elementary,
high school, and college), the greatest discrepancy exists among black males
with the most education, with the smallest discrepancies of all among those

with only elementary training. Killingsworth found that "adjustment for hidden unemployment raises the unemployment rates for the lower educational attainment groups by 40 to 50 percent, but by only a negligible amount for the college-trained group" (p. 25). On the other hand, while Harrison (1972) found the same relationship between education and unemployment for white males in his sample, he observed a "virtual absence for nonwhites of any relationship between education and unemployment, after the effects of age, sex, industry, city, training experience and full-time/part-time status had been removed" (p. 807).

In regard to the relationship between education and income, we have already cited the findings of Brimmer (1966) and Farley and Hermalin (1972) on the lower income gains of black males for equal education. We will cite two other sources. Gwartney (1970a) found that the largest black-white differences in income (both absolute and relative) during the 1950s and 1960s appeared at the higher educational levels. In fact, it appears from his analysis that, "even though the educational gap between white and non-whites has narrowed slightly in terms of quantity of education, the education effect for [black] males has either been negative or only slightly positive" during the 1940s, 1950s, and 1960s (p. 879). On the other hand, Weiss and Williamson (1972), using 1967 data from a Current Population Survey and a special sample drawn from low-income areas, concluded that education has had a strong and consistent impact on black incomes. It is difficult to reconcile these two conclusions, but perhaps the more positive findings of Weiss and Williamson result from the fact that they used only 1967 data, which was a time of relative prosperity (see Jencks and others, 1972: 242–243, footnote 51).

We turn now to the two questions raised above: whether education is related to economic status, and whether the difference in the black-white return for an equal quantity of education is due to a discrepancy in the quality of education received. It seems clear, thus far, that education is indeed related to economic status, but the relationship is different for whites and blacks. While the relationship between education and economic status is a direct one for white males (that is, as education increases, occupational status and income increase and chances of unemployment decrease), such is not the case for black males, except for income in the 1960s. We find explanations for the smaller differences in occupational status and unemployment rates between blacks and whites at the lowest educational levels to be unsatisfactory. Both Hare (1965) and Gwartney (1970a) suggest that differences are lowest at the lowest educational levels because poorly educated blacks and whites are at an equal disadvantage and therefore compete on more equal terms. We believe rather that blacks still serve the same economic role they always have, namely as a source of cheap labor to do the dirty work. Since the numbers of poorly educated white males are relatively small (and their occupational returns for low education are higher than for blacks), they probably tend to compete less for the lowest-status and lowest-paying jobs and more for the higher ones.

If blacks do not reap the same economic returns from an equal amount of education, what accounts for this inequity? Until recently it was customary to attribute much of this disparity to differences in quality of education. The American creed supports the belief that education is the avenue to equality for all, blacks included. If blacks do not receive the same rewards, surely it must be because they do not have the same quality product to offer. As noted above, those who advance this explanation are following an untested assumption occasioned by the Coleman Report. Recent research, however, contradicts this assumption and points to the conclusion that while quantity of education has some bearing on economic status, quality does not. This finding raised a storm of protest when it was recently advanced by Jencks and his associates (Jencks and others, 1972).[17] However, this finding was not new. Berg (1971) had earlier supported, with extensive research, the conclusion that it is credentials (quantity rather than quality) that have a high economic payoff. He found that, when employers were asked to justify their use of education as a screening device, they were unable to do so in any convincing way. Nor did they collect data that would help them to judge whether their assumption was correct.

Two other researchers recently arrived at the same conclusion about the irrelevance of quality of education. Harrison (1972), using data from the U.S. Department of Labor Urban Employment Survey of ten ghettos in 1966, concluded that even though white workers in the central cities could be assumed to have received education of similar quality to blacks of the same area, whites earned on the average *more than twice as much* in weekly wages per extra year of school completed than did blacks. Similar findings were made with respect to the relationship between educational quality and unemployment. Weiss and Williamson (1972) tested the effect of quality by stratifying their sample of blacks according to five regions which could be expected to yield different qualities of educational attainment.[18] Their conclusion was similar to that of Harrison, namely, "that interregional differences in the quality of black *education* have relatively weak effects on earning ability" (p. 379).

We have devoted considerable space to the relationship between education and black economic status because so much attention has been given to the belief that education is the avenue to economic success. The evidence examined seems to point to the conclusion that education is not as highly related to economic success as formerly believed, and that what effects it does have (especially in regards to occupational status and unemployment) are far less pronounced for black males than for whites. Finally, there is mounting evidence that the unequal return (to blacks) for an equal amount of education does not appear to be due to differences in quality.

Discrimination

The prevalance of economic discrimination in various forms during the 19th (Scruggs, 1971) and early 20th centuries (Worthman & Green, 1971; Marshall, 1965) is well supported, even though largely by qualitative data. The important question at present concerns the persistence of economic discrimination during the past few decades. While all researchers writing on the differences in economic status between blacks and whites will use discrimination as one of the explanatory variables, it is usually as a residual category, that is, as the probable explanation for differences that remain after other factors such as age, education, and region have been used. Discrimination in employment, in income, or in occupation is difficult to prove and difficult to measure with any high degree of accuracy. However, since the appearance of Becker's study, *The Economics of Discrimination*, in 1957, there have been increasing attempts to measure the impact of discrimination on economic inequality. Since most of this research examines data collected since 1940, and since we are primarily concerned with the question of the persistence of discrimination, we will undertake only an analysis of discrimination during the past three decades.

Discrimination can affect black economic status either directly or indirectly. Direct economic discrimination occurs, for instance, when an employer refuses to hire a black individual for no other reason than the color of his skin. However, if the same individual fails to get a job which requires a high school diploma because southern segregation policies prevented him from going beyond the 6th grade, or the conditions of the inner city led to his dropping out of school in the 10th grade, it can be said that his economic plight is being indirectly affected by discrimination. To put it more technically, many of the differences in "productivity factors" between black and white workers are the results of discrimination in *other areas*, such as education or housing (Gwartney, 1970b). Past discrimination (direct and indirect) is also a kind of present indirect economic discrimination. Although these indirect influences of discrimination are difficult to measure, they are very real in their consequences for the economic position of blacks. Because of the effects of past discrimination *alone*, Lieberson and Fuguitt (1967) have estimated that if economic discrimination were to end completely today, it would still take 60 to 80 years before occupational differences became negligible. The effects of past discrimination on income are probably even more serious. Soltow (1972) estimated that in 1962 the nonwhite level of wealth (not income) was still behind that of whites in 1870, and further, that it would be near the year 2000 before nonwhites had accumulated the level of wealth possessed by whites at the end of the Civil War.

Studies of the effects of direct economic discrimination indicate that they are both great and persistent in the North and the South. Becker (1957) concluded from his research that neither striking increases nor *striking decreases* in economic discrimination against blacks had occurred between 1910 and 1950. His finding is confirmed by others. Rosenberg and Howton (1967) concluded that "it is more the rule than the exception that hiring and promotion in the North follows a pattern in which the better jobs are reserved for whites—just as in the South, except that there it is open and official" (p. 337). Bloch (1965) has provided extensive documentation of a pattern of employment discrimination in New York City up to the early sixties, where his research ended. He divided the incidents of discrimination into three categories: (1) full restriction in employment (refusal to hire blacks in any capacity), (2) partial restriction in employment (hiring blacks for only menial jobs, tokenism, and so on), and (3) discriminatory employment retrenchment (firing blacks instead of whites in spite of the seniority of blacks, hiring blacks for only temporary jobs, and so on). Bloch found that discrimination was especially extensive and persistent in the hotel and transportation (ground and air) industries throughout the period studied.

Other researchers have attempted to measure the effect of discrimination on unemployment and income. After controlling for differences in unemployment rates due to different levels of skills between black and white males in 1950 and 1957–62, Gilman (1965) found that half the disparity in unemployment rates remained and was presumably due to discrimination. He recognized, at the same time, that differences in skill levels were probably also related to discrimination.

Gwartney (1970b), following the same approach as Gilman (1965), estimated that after controlling for differences in education, scholastic achievement, age, region, and city size, there remained unexplained differentials in income (for males 25 years and over) of between 14% and 25% for nonfarm occupations and between 13% and 19% for urban males in 1959. Again, this "unexplained" differential was presumed to be the result of discrimination. Rasmussen (1971) estimated that in 1960 discrimination was responsible for 17% of the income differential outside the South and 45% of it in the South. These are probably very conservative estimates, since all of the above researchers assumed that differences in *quality* of education accounted for some of the economic disparity.

One of the strongest reasons for arguing that economic discrimination continued at a high level even into the sixties is the finding cited above that quality of education has little or no effect on observed differences in economic status. The fact that an equal amount of education does not bring an equal economic reward to black males can no longer be attributed to differences in quality of training. Discrimination remains as almost the only explanation left for the disparity.

Our discussion of the influence of discrimination on economic inequality has been all too short, given the importance of this factor. This brevity was dictated in part by the fact that much of the present discussion was already implicit in the findings related to other factors, especially education.

Attitudes and Values

Thus far most of our analysis has proceeded at the aggregate level or in terms of groups (age, region, education, sex, and so on). The issue of the influence of attitudes and values on economic status can be dealt with in much the same way. Essentially the question here is whether blacks as a group, or certain subgroups within the black community, hold attitudes and values that are detrimental to their economic progress. The fact is that a country which believes in rugged individualism, which was "brought up" on the Protestant ethic (which teaches not only that success is the reward of hard work, but also that failure is somehow the fault of the individual who fails) still contains millions of poor people, and certain groups have a higher proportion of the poor than others. Many myths have been put forth to explain this discrepancy. In 1974 there were over 24 million persons living below the low-income or poverty level. Of these poor, nearly 7.5 million, or 31.4%, were black, almost three times their proportion (11%) in the entire population (U.S. Bureau of the Census, 1975: 42).[19] There must be some reason for the disproportionate share of poverty among blacks. Earlier myths held that blacks were lazy, shiftless, and less intelligent than whites, and therefore they were unsuited for any but menial jobs. However, as Worthman and Green (1971) observe, even as southern industrialists and planters were saying these things they contradicted themselves in practice during the late 19th and early 20th centuries:

> Most of the industrialists testifying before a congressional investigating committee that toured the South in 1883 agreed with one iron manufacturer who asserted: "We find the colored men . . . are fully as good as white men; they are as steady as workmen; they are as realiable in every way, and the product of their labor is fully as good as anything we have got from white labor . . . I believe that the future labor of the South in all industrial departments must be colored." (p. 52)

But myths die hard, and even as late as the forties the use of blacks as operatives in industry was initially an "experiment." After it became evident that the Great Society program was failing in its attempt to eradicate poverty, newer, less crass myths arose to account for black poverty.[20] One of these, the "culture of poverty" view, is hardly more than a sophisticated rationalization for older views of blacks as lazy and unambitious. The culture-of-poverty view merely places the burden of values allegedly detrimental to economic well-being on the environment rather than the individual. According to this view, blacks do not escape from poverty because, as a result of living in poverty for long years or growing up in an impoverished environment, they have developed values which now make it difficult for them to escape poverty (see H. Lewis, 1967; O. Lewis, 1968). The fact that a large proportion of poor blacks do work—a larger proportion than poor whites—is, of course, not dealt with by this theory.[21] Percentages for those not in the civilian labor force increased from 23% to 36% for black male heads of households, and from 33% to 47% for their white male counterparts. Only black females experienced a slight increase in unemployment, from 4% to 60% (U.S. Bureau of the Census, 1971b: Table 32, p. 41).

The culture-of-poverty theory as an explanation for what sometimes appears to be behavioral traits that are detrimental to economic progress or success has been challenged (in our opinion, successfully) by a number of researchers.[22] These writers have generally advanced a theory of "adaptation" as an alternative explanation. The poor, they argue, have the same economic aspirations and work values as other Americans who are not poor. However, since these aspirations cannot usually be realized by the poor, they adapt to the inevitable in various ways: by dropping out of the race, going on welfare rather than accepting work which does not provide them with sufficient income for the bare necessities, or resorting to various illegal occupations, such as numbers running (Perrucci, 1969). Given the opportunity of earning adequate incomes from respectable jobs, these same individuals would choose the jobs instead of an alternative form of behavior.

Another recent myth which purports to explain the economic disparity between blacks and whites is the allegation that blacks have genetically inferior IQs and therefore cannot be expected to reach the same levels of achievement as whites. Again this view, advanced by Jensen (1969) and Eysenck (1971), has been strongly challenged by other researchers.[23]

The question of the role of values and attitudes on the economic position of blacks has been a strangely persistent one. While many opinions have been expressed and many myths held about the supposed attitudes and aspirations of blacks and the effects of these attitudes and aspirations, in 1971 Tausky and Wilson could write that there was "a surprising lack of data" on the subject (p. 23). The situation has not changed much since then. Essentially, two distinct issues are involved. One is the question of the attitudes and aspirations of blacks in general, and the other is the question of the attitudes and aspirations of poor blacks.

Studies relating to the attitudes of blacks in general have usually focused on occupational aspirations of blacks and have generally utilized, as samples, high school or college students. These studies have generally found that black youths do not differ from white youths in their educational or occupational aspirations. This conclusion was reached by Gist and Bennett (1963), who studied the aspirations of 873 black and white 9th- and 12th-grade students in four large Kansas City high schools. It was also the conclusion of Stephensen (1957), who studied 1,000 ninth-graders, and Rosen (1959), who had at first hypothesized that the aspirations of black students would be different from those of whites. Rosen examined the achievement motivation of 954 mothers and sons in 62 communities in four Northeastern states. The sample consisted of members of six different ethnic groups: Greeks, Jews, white Protestants, Italians, French-Canadians, and blacks. While Rosen expected the values and aspirations of blacks to be among the lowest, he found that blacks possessed values and aspirations comparable to those of Jews, Greeks, and white Protestants, and higher than those of the Italians and French-Canadians. Finally, Tausky and Wilson (1971) found, in a national representative sample of 209 white and 57 black adult males, that there was a great similarity between the two groups in their desire for work that carried social prestige. The above review is obviously sketchy and inadequate; however, it does tend to contradict past and present negative stereotypes.

Research on the aspirations and work orientation of poor blacks is hardly more adequate than similar research for blacks in general. Investigations of work orientations of the poor are frequently of small groups of people. Basically, this research is concerned with the meaning of work for the poor and their orientation to work. Do the poor want to work, or do they prefer being on welfare? Liebow, in *Tally's Corner* (1967), describes the response of unemployed black men to an offer of a day's work by a white man in a pickup truck. Most of the men, he found, refused the offer, and Liebow attributes their refusal to their hesitation to commit themselves to a job because of general discouragement and uncertainty over the future. It would probably be more accurate to attribute their refusal to discouragement over obtaining a steady job with a decent salary. P. B. Doeringer and his colleagues found in their 1968 study of Boston labor markets that ghetto job seekers were usually placed in jobs similar in wage and working conditions to those they had just left. As a result, Harrison (1972) reports, Doeringer concluded that

> . . . the availability of alternative low wage job opportunities and the unattractiveness of such low wage work interact to discourage the formation of strong ties to particular employers . . . for wage rates higher than the "prevailing" ghetto wage, disadvantaged workers are more likely to be stable employees than other workers. (p. 808)

It appears that whether on the job or unemployed, black workers have ample reasons for discouragement. Since many blacks have experienced discrimination in employment, long periods of unemployment, and involuntary part-time employment, many become discouraged, despair of bettering their condition, and eventually withdraw from the labor force into the ranks of the hidden unemployed. Those who manage to find and keep jobs frequently experience blocked mobility, whether their occupation is blue collar or white collar. Garbin and Ballweg (1965) found, in a study of black blue-collar workers in a Midwestern meat-packing plant, that they tended to remain in, or experience mobility to, production-oriented departments, while white more frequently moved to service and mechanics departments. More recently a survey by Fields, Freeman Associates Inc. of 500 highly educated blacks holding white-collar positions in corporations such as IBM, Zerox, Procter and Gamble, and General Motors found that "Three out of five of those interviewed claimed that their chances of promotion were smaller than those of their white co-workers, and felt that they usually could not expect advancement into important managerial posts" (Jet, August 16, 1973, p. 24). Clearly, discouragement is a rational response of black workers to realistic situations.

In spite of the unequal economic returns for equal amounts of effort and resources documented above, a number of studies reveal that poor blacks possess work orientations that are the same as or superior to those of whites. Thus Kaplan and Tausky (1972) concluded from their study of 275 hard-core unemployed that these men and women exhibited:

> . . . a commitment to work as frequently as that found among employed white- and blue-collar workers. Our subjects did not want to remain idle and accept public assistance; many indicated moral indignation toward persons who did not want to work. The fascinating aspect we encountered was the seeming internalization of the dominant work ethic, with its negative stereotype toward people who accept welfare, by a group of extremely disadvantaged people. (p. 481)

In a much larger study of 4,000 blacks and whites, Goodwin (1972) drew the same conclusion as Kaplan and Tausky. He found that the poor fathers, poor mothers, and the sons of poor mothers (whether the mothers worked or not) identified with work and tended to reject quasi-illegal activities. He did find, however, that the poor tended more often to lack confidence in their ability to succeed and were more ready to accept welfare as an alternative than the nonpoor were. Acceptability of welfare, however, was correlated with lack of confidence. One of the most striking findings was the positive orientation to work of teen-agers (sons of both working and nonworking mothers) who had spent all of their life in poverty. This finding led Goodwin to conclude: "That these poor youths start with the same positive orientations as do more affluent youths indicates that a later loss of self-identification with work would be the result of environmental experiences, not of childhood rejection of the importance of work" (p. 81).

Again, research on the work orientations of the poor is not extensive, yet the best of it contradicts the stereotype of lazy freeloaders who prefer to be idle on welfare than to work.

CONCLUSION

In this review of research on the economic position of blacks, we have attempted to give a comprehensive picture of the changes that have occurred in their occupational distribution, unemployment rates, and income, and to analyze some of the factors related to these components of economic status. While considerable economic progress has been made by blacks during the 20th century, whites have also made progress, and consequently the disparity in economic position was still great in 1970. The rate of change varied greatly from decade to decade, with the twenties, forties, and sixties as high points. The principal change in black occupational distribution was the gradual movement of black workers out of agriculture and domestic work and into manual jobs. Not until the 1960s did black workers gain a real foothold in the white-collar sector. While the occupational distribution of blacks was gradually improving, they experienced a steady rise in their unemployment rates, especially since 1954, when the rate reached twice that of whites and remained there. Black median income has risen in both absolute and relative terms, but this rise has been accompanied by many reversals and an actual widening of the absolute gap. At the present time the future of black economic status remains uncertain, as the rapid gains of the sixties have first slowed down and then reversed.

A number of factors believed to be related to black economic status were analyzed: region, sex, the economy, migration, education, discrimination, and values. From this analysis it appears that black economic progress has been strongly dependent upon a healthy economy and is very sensitive to economic downturns. There is evidence that throughout most of the 20th century, migration has been responsible for most of the improvement in the black economic position. Though education is positively related to economic gain, it is quantity rather than quality that seems important. Furthermore, the fact that there is great disparity in the economic return to blacks for the same quantity of education as whites points to the continuation of high levels of economic discrimination. Finally, contrary to popular myths, recent empirical research supports the idea that blacks, poor and nonpoor, have the same occupational aspirations and work orientations as whites.

NOTES

1. These seven groupings are: professional and related workers; nonfarm proprietors, managers, and officials; clerical and sales workers; skilled workers, or craftsmen and foremen; semiskilled workers, or operatives; service workers and nonfarm laborers; and farmers and farm workers (Hiestand, 1964, p. 52).

2. Since about 90% of nonwhites are black, we use *black* throughout this analysis, even when the statistics refer to nonwhites.

3. For females 14 years and over the ratio of female nonwhite to white unemployment rates in 1939 was 202. It had been 102 in 1930 for females 16 years and over (Sorkin, 1971: Table 3, p. 396).

4. Part-time employment is defined as less than 35 hours a week. The hidden unemployed or discouraged workers are those individuals who would like to work but have given up looking because they despair of finding a job (see Ross, 1967: 21).

5. Rates vary depending on the group being compared: families, males, or females.

6. The low-income threshold varies from year to year, depending upon the state of the economy. For a nonfarm family of four it was $3,968 in 1970, $3,743 in 1969, and $2,973 in 1959 (U.S. Bureau of the Census, 1971b: 35).

7. These 13 ghettos were in the following cities: Boston, Cleveland, Detroit, Los Angeles, New York, Philadelphia, Phoenix, St. Louis, San Antonio, and San Francisco–Oakland.

8. E.g., 25% of the total in 1968.

9. If we add up the gains and losses of the fifties and sixties, we find that there was a net loss of two percentage points in the fifties and a gain of eight in the sixties.

10. These rates are for black families alone. Earlier income figures were for blacks and other minorities.

11. This was $5,038 in 1974 for a family of four.

12. The ten SMSAs were New York, Philadelphia, Chicago, Los Angeles, Detroit, Indianapolis, Boston, San Francisco–Oakland, Kansas City, and Cleveland. Unemployment rates were for those nonmigrants who lived in the same houses in 1960 as in 1955, and for those migrants who arrived in one of the ten SMSAs between 1955–60.

13. Much of this discussion will be about black males, both because many researchers looking into the relationship between education and economic status have confined themselves to data on males, and also because recently it has been found that the same discrepancy no longer exists for black females, or at least not to the same degree as in the case of black males.

14. There were only two cases of divergence in the forties, one in the 45–54 age group and the other in the 55–64 group.

15. That is, the relationship between education and occupational status is not linear for black males.

16. Baltimore, Chicago, Cleveland, Detroit, Houston, Los Angeles, New York, Philadelphia, Pittsburgh, St. Louis, San Francisco, and Washington, D.C.

17. In our opinion, Jencks has been much maligned and even more misunderstood. A careful reading of his work makes it clear that he was not advocating that education was not at all important, nor that educational reform should be abandoned. He was merely saying that education is not a realistic avenue to equality of income for the poor, and that if poverty is to be overcome more direct methods will have to be used.

18. The five regions were rural South, small-town South, small southern SMSAs, large southern SMSAs, and North or West.

19. The actual numbers of poor blacks is undoubtedly higher, since the above figures do not include the undercount (especially) of young black males, most of whom are probably among the hidden unemployed.

20. It should be emphasized that, for whatever reasons, these myths—even the newer ones—are usually applied only to blacks or other nonwhite minorities, not to the white poor.

21. In 1959, 67% of black male heads of poor families worked, compared with 60% of white male heads of poor families. Black and white female heads were employed in identical proportions, 31%. In 1969 the employment rates for male heads of poor families were 58% for blacks and 50% for whites, and for female heads of poor families the rates were 29% for blacks and 28% for whites. The decrease in employment rates was probably the result of high rates of unemployment continuing for a long time (Table 2.7), followed by discouragement and withdrawal from the labor force, since in the case of both white and black males, percentages not in the civilian labor force increased drastically and unemployment rates (for heads of poor families) declined.

22. See, for instance, Valentine (1968), Gans (1968), Spilerman and Elesh (1971), and Rainwater (1968).

23. See, for instance, the review of Eysenck's book by Leggett (1973) and a discussion of IQ by Cohen (1972).

REFERENCES

Batchelder, Alan B. "Decline in the Relative Income of Negro Men." In Louis A. Ferman, Joyce L. Kornbluh, and J. A. Miller (eds.), *Negroes and Jobs: A Book of Readings.* Ann Arbor: University of Michigan Press, 1968.

Becker, Gary S. *The Economics of Discrimination.* Chicago: University of Chicago Press, 1957.

Berg, Ivar. *Education and Jobs: The Great Training Robbery.* Boston: Beacon Press, 1971.

Blauner, Robert. *Racial Oppression in America.* New York: Harper & Row, 1972.

Bloch, Herman D. "Discrimination against the Negro in Employment in New York, 1920–1963." *American Journal of Economics and Sociology* 24 (October 1965): 361–382.

Brimmer, Andrew F. "The Negro in the National Economy." In John P. Davis (ed.), *The American Negro Reference Book.* Englewood Cliffs, N.J.: Prentice-Hall, 1966.

Cohen, David K. "Does IQ Matter?" *Intellectual Digest* 2 (July 1972): 35–38.

Coleman, James S., and others. *Equality of Educational Opportunity.* Washington, D.C.: U.S. Government Printing Office, 1966.

Duncan, Otis Dudley, & Beverly Duncan. "A Methodological Analysis of Segregation Indexes." *American Sociological Review* 20 (1955): 210–217.

Eysenck, Hans J. *The IQ Argument: Race, Intelligence and Education.* New York: Library Press, 1971.

Farley, Reynolds, & Albert Hermalin. "The 1960s: A Decade of Progress for Blacks?" *Demography* 9 (August 1972): 353–370.

Fein, Rashi. "Educational Patterns in Southern Migration." *Southern Economic Journal* 32 (July 1965): 106–124.

Ferman, Louis A., Joyce L. Kornbluh, & J. A. Miller. *Negroes and Jobs: A Book of Readings.* Ann Arbor: University of Michigan Press, 1968.

Franklin, John Hope. *From Slavery to Freedom.* 3rd. ed. New York: Alfred A. Knopf, 1967.

Gans, Herbert J. "Culture and Class in the Study of Poverty: An Approach to Anti-Poverty Research." In Daniel P. Moynihan (ed.), *On Understanding Poverty: Perspectives from the Social Sciences.* New York: Basic Books, 1968.

Garbin, A. P., & John A. Ballweg. "Intra-Plant Mobility of Negro and White Workers." *American Journal of Sociology* 71 (November 1965): 315–319.

Gilman, Harry J. "Economic Discrimination and Unemployment." *American Economic Review* 25 (December 1965): 1077–1097.

Ginzberg, Eli, & Dale L. Hiestand. "Employment Patterns of Negro Men and Women." In John P. Davis (ed.), *The American Negro Reference Book.* Englewood Cliffs, N.J.: Prentice-Hall, 1966.

Gist, Noel P., & William S. Bennett, Jr. "Aspirations of Negro and White Students." *Social Forces* 42 (October 1963): 40–48.

Goodwin, Leonard. *Do the Poor Want to Work? A Social-Psychological Study of Work Orientations.* Washington, D.C.: Brookings Institution, 1972.

Gwartney, James. "Changes in the Nonwhite/White Income Ratio—1939–67." *American Economic Review* 60 (December 1970): 872–883. (a)

Gwartney, James. "Discrimination and Income Differentials." *American Economic Review* 60 (June 1970): 396–408. (b)

Hare, Nathan. "Recent Trends in the Occupational Mobility of Negroes, 1930–1960: An Intracohort Analysis." *Social Forces* 44 (December 1965): 166–173.

Harrison, Bennett. "Education and Underemployment in the Urban Ghetto." *American Economic Review* 62 (December 1972): 796–812.

Henderson, Vivian. "Regions, Race, and Jobs." In Arthur M. Ross & Herbert Hill (eds.), *Employment, Race, and Poverty.* New York: Harcourt, Brace & World, 1967.

Hiestand, Dale L. *Economic Growth and Employment Opportunities for Minorities.* New York: Columbia University Press, 1964.

Jencks, Christopher, and others. *Inequality: A Reassessment of the Effect of Family and Schooling in America.* New York: Basic Books, 1972.

Jensen, Arthur R. "How Much Can We Boost IQ and Scholastic Achievement?" *Harvard Educational Review* 39 (Winter 1969): 1–123.

Kahn, Tom. "The Economics of Inequality." In Louis A. Ferman, Joyce L. Kornbluh, & J. A. Miller (eds.), *Negroes and Jobs: A Book of Readings.* Ann Arbor: University of Michigan Press, 1968.

Kaplan, H. Roy, & Curt Tausky. "Work and the Welfare Cadillac: The Function of and Commitment to Work among the Hard-Core Unemployed." *Social Problems* 19 (Spring 1972): 469–483.

Killingsworth, Charles C. "Negroes in a Changing Labor Market." In Arthur M. Ross & Herbert Hill (eds.), *Employment, Race, and Poverty.* New York: Harcourt, Brace & World, 1967.

Killingsworth, Charles C. *Jobs and Income for Negroes.* Joint publication, Institute of Labor and Industrial Relations of the University of Michigan and Wayne State University and the National Manpower Policy Task Force. Ann Arbor, Mich., 1968.

Land, Kenneth. "Principles of Path Analysis." In Edgar Borgotta (ed.), *Sociological Methodology 1969.* San Francisco: Jossey-Bass, 1969.

Leggett, John C. "Review of *The IQ Argument: Race, Intelligence and Education,* by Hans J. Eysenck," *Society* 10 (July–August, 1973): 79–84.

Lewis, Hylan. *Culture, Class and Poverty.* Washington: Cross-Tell, 1967.

Lewis, Oscar. *A Study of Slum Culture: Backgrounds for La Vida.* New York: Random House, 1968.

Lieberson, Stanley, & Glenn V. Fuguitt. "Negro-White Occupational Differences in the Absence of Discrimination." *American Journal of Sociology* 73 (September 1967): 188–200.

Liebow, Elliott. *Tally's Corner: A Study of Negro Street Corner Men.* Boston: Little, Brown & Co., 1967.

Marshall, Harvey, Jr. Black-White Economic Participation in Large U.S. Cities. *American Journal of Economics and Sociology* 31 (October 1972): 361–372.

Marshall, Ray. *The Negro and Organized Labor.* New York: John Wiley & Sons, 1965.

Meier, August, & Elliott Rudwick. *From Plantation to Ghetto,* Rev. ed. New York: Hill & Wang, 1970.

Miller, Herman P. *Income Distribution in the United States.* Washington, D.C.: U.S. Government Printing Office, 1966.

National Committee against Discrimination in Housing. *The Impact of Housing Patterns on Job Opportunities.* New York, 1968.

Perrucci, Robert. "The Neighborhood Bookmaker: Entrepreneur and Mobility Model." In Paul Meadows & Ephraim H. Mizruchi (eds.), *Urbanism, Urbanization and Change: Comparative Perspectives.* Reading, Mass.: Addison-Wesley Publishing Co., 1969.

Quarles, Benjamin. *The Negro in the Making of America.* New York: Macmillan, 1969.

Rainwater, Lee. "The Problem of Lower-Class Culture and Poverty-War Strategy," In Daniel P. Moynihan (ed.), *On Understanding Poverty: Perspectives from the Social Sciences.* New York: Basic Books, 1968.

Rasmussen, David W. "Discrimination and the Income of Non-White Males." *American Journal of Economics and Sociology* 30 (October 1971): 377–382.

Rayack, Elton. "Discrimination and the Occupational Progress of Negroes." *Review of Economics and Statistics* 43 (May 1961): 209–214.

Rosen, Bernard C. "Race, Ethnicity, and the Achievement Syndrome." *American Sociological Review* 24 (February 1959): 47–60.

Rosenberg, Bernard, & F. William Howton. "Ethnic Liberalism and Employment Discrimination in the North." *American Journal of Economics and Sociology* 26 (October 1967): 387–398.

Ross, Arthur M. "The Negro in the American Economy." In Arthur M. Ross & Herbert Hill (eds.), *Employment, Race, and Poverty.* New York: Harcourt, Brace & World, 1967.

Russell, Joe L. "Changing Patterns in Employment of Nonwhite Workers." In Louis A. Ferman, Joyce L. Kornbluh, & J. A. Miller (eds.), *Negroes and Jobs: A Book of Readings.* Ann Arbor: University of Michigan Press, 1968.

Scruggs, Otey M. "The Economic and Racial Components of Jim Crow." In Nathan I. Huggins, Martin Kilson, & Daniel M. Fox (eds.), *Key Issues In the Afro-American Experience,* Vol. II, *Since 1865.* New York: Harcourt, Brace, Jovanovich, 1971.

Soltow, Lee. "Age and Color in a Century of Personal Wealth Accumulation." In Harold G. Vatter & Thomas Palm (eds.), *The Economics of Black America.* New York: Harcourt, Brace, Jovanovich, 1972.

Sorkin, Alan L. "Education, Migration and Negro Unemployment." *Social Forces* 47 (March 1969): 265–274.

Sorkin, Alan L. "Occupational Status and Unemployment of Nonwhite Women." *Social Forces* 49 (March 1971): 393–398.

Spilerman, Seymour, & David Elesh. "Alternative Conceptions of Poverty and Their Implications for Income Maintenance." In Larry L. Orr, Robinson G. Hollister, & Myron J. Lefcowitz (eds.), *Income Maintenance: Interdisciplinary Approaches to Research.* Chicago: Markham Publishing Co., 1971.

Stephensen, Richard M. "Mobility Orientation and Stratification of 1,000 Ninth Graders." *American Sociological Review* 22 (April 1957): 204–212.

Tabb, William K. *The Political Economy of the Black Ghetto.* New York: W. W. Norton & Co., 1970.

Taeuber, Karl E., & Alma F. Taeuber. *Negroes in Cities: Residential Segregation and Neighborhood Change.* Chicago: Aldine Publishing Co., 1965.

Tausky, Curt, & William J. Wilson. "Work Attachment among Black Men." *Phylon* 32 (Spring 1971): 23–30.

U.S. Bureau of the Census. "Recent Trends in Social and Economic Conditions of Negroes in the United States." *Current Population Reports,* Series P–23, No. 26. Washington, D.C.: U.S. Government Printing Office, 1968. (a)

U.S. Bureau of the Census. "Social and Economic Conditions of Negroes in the United States, 1967." *Current Population Reports,* Series P–23, No. 24. Washington, D.C.: U.S. Government Printing Office, 1968. (b)

U.S. Bureau of the Census. "Revision in Poverty Statistics, 1959–1968." *Current Population Reports,* Series P–28, No. 28. Washington, D.C.: U.S. Government Printing Office, 1969.

U.S. Bureau of the Census. *Differences between Incomes of White and Negro Families by Work Experience of Wife and Region: 1970, 1969, and 1959. Current Population Reports,* Series P–23, No. 39. Washington, D.C.: U.S. Government Printing Office, 1971. (a)

U.S. Bureau of the Census. "Social and Economic Status of Negroes in the United States, 1970." *Current Population Reports,* Series P–23, No. 38. Washington, D.C.: U.S. Government Printing Office, 1971. (b)

U.S. Bureau of the Census. "General Social and Economic Characteristics." *Census of Population: 1970, U.S. Summary.* Final Report PC(1)–C1. Washington, D.C.: U.S. Government Printing Office, 1972. (a)

U.S.Bureau of the Census. "Social and Economic Status of the Black Population in the United States, 1971." *Current Population Reports,* Series P–23, No. 42. Washington, D.C.: U.S. Government Printing Office, 1972. (b)

U.S. Bureau of the Census. "Social and Economic Status of the Black Population in the United States, 1974." *Current Population Reports,* Series P–23, No. 54. Washington, D.C.: U.S. Government Printing Office, 1975.

U.S. Commission on Civil Rights. *Racial Isolation in the Public School: Summary of a Report.* Publication No. 7. Washington, D.C.: U.S. Government Printing Office, 1967. Reprinted in Harold G. Vetter & Thomas Palm (eds.), *The Economics of Black America.* New York: Harcourt, Brace, Jovanovich, 1972.

U.S. Department of Labor. *Manpower Report of the President.* Washington, D.C.: U.S. Government Printing Office, 1968.

U.S. Department of Labor. *Manpower Report of the President.* Washington, D.C.: U.S. Government Printing Office, 1975.

Valentine, Charles A. *Culture and Poverty: Critique and Counter-Proposals.* Chicago: University of Chicago Press, 1968.

Weiss, Leonard, & Jeffrey G. Williamson. "Black Education, Earnings, and Inter-Regional Migration: Some New Evidence." *American Economic Review* 62 (June 1972): 372–383.

Worthman, Paul B., & James R. Green. "Black Workers in the New South, 1865–1915." In Nathan I. Huggins, Martin Kilson, & Daniel M. Fox (eds)., *Key Issues in the Afro-American Experience;* Vol. II, *Since 1865.* New York: Harcourt, Brace, Jovanovich, 1971.

CHAPTER 3

Dimensions for the study of work-related values in Mexican-American culture: An exploratory essay

Joseph Spielberg Benitez

INTRODUCTION

This chapter cannot provide a comprehensive description of the work-related values of Mexican-Americans in the United States because such a task is impossible given the current conceptual development of the social sciences with respect to the notion of values or national character (Hsu, 1975: 378–393) and the enormity of the research effort required. Rather, we will limit our effort to an outline and description of the dimensions which shape, color, or otherwise determine what the nature of these values might be or how they might be manifested theoretically.

The dimensions which appear to have the greatest potential in determining what might be called the *meaning of work* in Mexican-American culture are: (1) the core of the Mexican-American cultural heritage, (2) stratification, and (3) self-identity. These dimensions will be defined and described later. It is important, however, to point out that these dimensions

Note: The author wishes to acknowledge the generous, helpful assistance of William A. Faunce, Department of Sociology, Michigan State University, for his reading and critique of the manuscript and his gracious permission to use ideas from his forthcoming book which enhanced this chapter. The author, of course, bears full responsibility for its errors and faults.

are only analytically separable; this is especially true of the last two, which can only be explored as interrelated levels within one social structural complex, as manifested in the context of an actual, physical community.[1] They are separated only for the purpose of a more orderly presentation, as well as to allow the possibility of discerning their implications for issues concerning alienation, adaptation, and centrality of possible work-related values.

Before proceeding with a description of these dimensions, some prefatory remarks concerning the central concepts involved in this topic will be given, to provide a better idea of the limitations of this chapter. The first concept which requires definition is that of *work*. Following Udy (1970: 2–4), we prefer to treat work as a system of physical or mental effort (or activity), the purpose of which is the modification of the individual's physical environment. Such a system of activity involves a *work organization pursuing production objectives by means of a technology*. This definition of work is restricted and differs from broader social science conceptualizations. Our definition, we feel, will help us avoid the redundancies common to the more sociologically or psychologically oriented definitions. In short, we need to define work in a way that will clearly distinguish it from the social or psychological phenomenon we are attempting to explain.

As in the case of defining work, the exercise of picking a definition or conceptualization of *values* is to a certain extent arbitrary, depending on the nature of the problem and the data involved. For present purposes, the definition provided by Goldschmidt (1959) is appropriate. According to him, "Values . . . may be defined primarily as those individual personal qualities which are considered to be desirable by people in a given culture" (pp. 72–73). Of particular significance here is the emphasis Goldschmidt places on "the needs of the social system in the context of its environment and technology" (p. 74), as reflected in (if not determining) the general character of its value system. Values, then, are notions and manifestations of the attitudes and behaviors which constitute a proper person within a given work system (or set of systems). As we will show, an added feature of this view of values is that it liberates us, to some extent, from having to derive the set of values of one "minority" group from those of a "dominant" group in a simultaneously pluralistic and class-oriented society, such as is manifested in the notions of a compensating shadow system of values (Liebow, 1967: 208–231) or value stretch (Rodman, 1963: 205–215).

Finally, we need to define the population under discussion. Who are the Mexican-Americans, and what is the nature of Mexican-American culture? In the broadest sense of the term, the label "Mexican-Americans" refers to either citizens or residents of the United States whose ancestry can be traced back to colonial or republican Mexico. Both the population and ancestry components of this definition of Mexican-Americans offer the analyst a number of obstacles with respect to generalizations or sharp delineation of the group.

As a population, this group, commonly referred to as the second largest minority in the United States, has come to have significant variation in its distribution—from the mountains of New Mexico to the mountains of the Pacific Northwest; from the great plains and the coastal deserts of central and south Texas to the flood plains of the upper Mississippi and the Ohio. Furthermore, their distribution is far from being stabilized. With continuing streams of migration from Texas to California and the Midwest, as well as from Mexico to various regions within the United States, the distribution of this population will continue to be in a state of flux for some time to come. The same is true for their distribution with respect to urban-rural regions, although the rate of urbanization is considerable (Grebler, Moore, & Guzman, 1970: 61–81 & 82–100). With respect to size, it is one of the fastest growing "ethnic groups" in America, especially in the Southwest, the area generally regarded as the home base of Mexican-Americans (Barrett 1966: 159–163).

While generally considered to be one of the most underprivileged of the ethnic groups, with respect to income, occupation, and education, such a cumulative profile or portrait tends to mask a considerable amount of socioeconomic stratification and, more importantly, mobility (Grebler et al., 1970: 13–34 & 317–349). As Lyle (1973) has pointed out, "Popular mythology views Chicanos as largely migratory rural labor, although in fact less than 1/10 of employed Mexican American men are 'farm workers' and migratory farmworkers are an even smaller proportion" (p. 11). In another study of the economic situation of Spanish-Americans (Ryscavage & Mellor, 1973), it has been shown that in 1970 as many, if not slightly more, Mexican-Americans of both sexes were to be found in the professional, technical and kindred category as in the farm worker category, with nearly 1 out of 5 employed men in skilled craft occupations. With respect to income, Mexican-Americans again show considerable variation, although by occupational categories they tend to earn less than whites. The range, likewise, is not as great as that among other whites (pp. 6–7).

In terms of educational attainment, Mexican-Americans also exhibit a rather normal distribution, although they lag far behind other Americans in this regard. Recent figures, for example, show that nearly the same proportion of Mexican-Americans 25 years of age or older had completed four years of high school or more (i.e., 25.8%) as had completed less than five years of school (i.e., 26.7%) (Ryscavage & Mellor, 1973: 6–7). The citation of these statistics is not intended to minimize the economic, occupational, and educational problems of Mexican-Americans. It merely aims to show that, internally, this population is diverse when considered in terms of the differential distribution of socioeconomic characteristics along a scale or continuum (a necessary condition for stratification).

More subjective approaches to the problem of defining Mexican-Americans are not necessarily less fraught with problems. Some indication of the subjective variation in definition can be derived from an examination of the terms used for self-designation; *Mexicano,* Mexican-American, *Hispano,* Spanish-American, Latin-American, *Raza,* and *Chicano* (Grebler et al., 1970: 385–387). While some of these terms may be simply indicative of individual or regional preferences, others (such as *Chicano*) are not so simply dismissed. Rather, they connote social characteristics and consciously adopted patterns of behavior, sentiments, and values which are sharply distinctive and perhaps discontinuous with the larger cultural tradition. Indeed, I recall, as a young man growing up in the *barrio* of a small south Texas town, that the term *Chicano* was merely a stylish *pachuco*-derived synonym or contraction for the term *Mexicano,* used exclusively in ingroup situations. Today the term *Chicano* is a consciously adopted and publicly touted badge of identity signifying a militant commitment to the organized struggle for civil rights. As such, it tends to identify the relatively well-educated young adult, usually a person involved in organized and concerted efforts to promote democracy within an ethnically particularistic framework of power (Gutierrez 1970; Alvarado et al., 1970).

The historical (or ancestral) aspects of our definition of Mexican-Americans, as mentioned earlier, also pose problems. Generalizations or definitions of Mexican-Americans based on ancestry are complicated by factors of time of origin, generation, social or ethnic class background of first generations, and conditions or motivations in migration or resettlement (Gamio, 1970; McWilliams, 1949; Samora, 1971; Lummis, 1969; Galarza, 1964).

. One such variable which, while posing problems with respect to generalization, is nevertheless useful as a point of departure for an operational definition of "traditional" Mexican-American culture is that of region. To the layman, the country and culture of Mexico may appear as one large, undifferentiated mass. Nothing, however, could be further from the truth. Although certain aspects of national culture, especially since the 1950s, pervade the society, Mexico nevertheless is and has been a culturally pluralistic society. While a number of frameworks might be useful for understanding its historical and contemporary pluralism, in our opinion this pluralism is best understood, in overall terms, within a regional framework. In other words, Mexican diversity, with respect to historical development, ecological adaptation, and cultural institutions, is made more intelligible when looked at in terms of areas or regions.

Thus, while the different regions of Mexico, in varying degrees, have undoubtedly contributed to the formation of Mexican-American society and culture, one region is central to the development of what might be called the core features and serves as a useful baseline in defining the traditional cultural orientations of Mexican-American society. The region we refer to is the one denominated (not coincidently) as the Mexican-American West by the anthropologist-historian Miguel Leon-Portilla (1972). Geographically, this region comprises what is today the Mexican Northwest and the Southwestern part of the United States. Culturally, Leon-Portilla calls it the *Norteño* variety of Mexican culture, a variety which ignores national boundaries and is manifested, in various ways, on both sides of the border among the Spanish-speaking people. Our observations here will be limited to those populations of Mexican-Americans that share this milieu. In this case, then, we will be referring primarily to the Spanish-speaking populations of the Southwest. The extent to which our remarks may be considered applicable to Mexican-Americans elsewhere is limited by their degree of socialization within this particular regional variety of Mexican culture.

THE CULTURAL HERITAGE DIMENSION

The cultural heritage of the Mexican-American, it can be argued, has its principal roots in the type of society and economy which developed in the northern frontier of colonial and early republican Mexico. This is not to imply that no significant variations existed within this vast region, nor that the contemporary culture of Mexican-Americans (and even that of northern Mexico) has not experienced significant changes. But in our search for the continuities and general aspects in the cultural life of the Spanish-speaking people, it is important to assume a particular definition of culture (and its dynamics) which lends itself to questions of persistence in ethnohistorical reconstruction. Definitions of culture too closely tied to the material or the sociological are inadequate, given the ecological and social variations (in both time and space) presented by any given situation. What is required is a definition of culture linked to the more subjective or ideological aspects of a way of life or culture—its general orientations. Leon-Portilla thus prefers to attack the problem of persistence and change in *Norteño* culture from the point of view of what has been called the *ethos.* That is, the cultural heritage of a given group is composed of the motivations, values, attitudes, and types of relationships typical of various populations (Leon-Portilla, 1972: 10). His definition of ethos, then, is similar to those extant in social science literature, particularly Edward Sapir's (1924) notion of Genuine Culture.

In addition, Leon-Portilla (1972), assumes that the

culture of the Mexican north, a consequence of its own historical process, has been able to assimilate the various external pressures and to preserve to date many of its ancient characteristics. It should be added *that some elements in this Norteño culture have also persisted among the Spanish-speaking people established in what today is the U.S. Southwest.* (p. 109; emphasis added)

Without going into too much detail, we will look at some of the more salient features of this historical process (as summarized by Leon-Portilla) and the resultant characteristic orientations or ethos components of this, the *Norteño* culture.[2]

The process of Spanish settlement of this vast and generally hostile frontier environment was a gradual one, extending over a period of at least two centuries. Nevertheless, two features are important. First, the macro-environment penetrated northward, however gradually, and presented essentially the generally familiar features—arid plateaus and *llanos* interspersed by mountain outcroppings, and hostile populations, first Indians and later white American settlers and "filibusters." Thus, the basic adaptations, insofar as the possibility of settlement was concerned, did not require drastic alterations as Spanish-Mexican civilization crept northward.

Second, and this was especially true of those who came with principally agrarian (as opposed to mining) intentions, the movement northward did not occur in leapfrog fashion; rather, each advance tended to stem from the preestablished fringes. Indeed, settlers bent on an economy based on animal husbandry who were already established on the frontier tended to be pushed ahead as large-scale mining and cities developed (Leon-Portilla, 1972: 93–94). This fact also argues for the persistence of adaptations. Such a pattern of colonization, Leon-Portilla argues, may have had the effect of a peculiar pattern of natural selection in the evolution of this culture. As he puts it:

> Without a doubt there was great diversity in the purposes and behavior of people . . . so different among themselves. But despite the differences, all had to confront in their own manner the realities that characterized the northern lands. Those vast expanses were a frontier country. To create any form of settlement there was álways difficult in the extreme. . . . In that context, throughout the colonial period, many of the cultural characteristics developed. Traits common to the great majority of new arrivals were determination, courage in the face of danger, *and a will to work. All this implied physical strength.* (p. 92)

Thus, according to Leon-Portilla,

> A first characteristic almost constant in the attitudes of those who, since the colonial era, established themselves in the Northwest, seems to be a determination to confront all kinds of dangers and difficulties in order to obtain the riches and advantages which supposedly or really exist there. . . . It then led to the creation, from their very roots, of the original colonial settlements *in which one had to work strenuously in order to subsist.* Such was the case in the mining camps, the haciendas, the ranches, and new towns.

and, again,

The ethos of the Norteno has been shared, thus, in his . . . attitude of confronting danger, *dedicated to any work that would permit him, if not to secure coveted riches, at least to achieve a better way of life.* Stock raising, particularly, was for the Norteno not only a significant source of income but an institution that coloured his way of life. (pp. 110–111; emphasis ours)

The message in these quotes, with respect to what may have resulted as "proper qualities" of persons with the *Norteño* ethos, is clear. Physical stamina—the ability and willingness to withstand physical deprivation and punishment, if necessary—and the ability and willingness to adapt to whatever production-oriented activities were necessary for survival were not only requirements for existence but probably became central features of what constituted a proper person or *hombre Norteño.*

Environmental factors or exigencies which seemed to determine or shape these values also played a significant role in shaping other corollary values or sentiments, via their effects on the work system. The inconsistencies between an economy based on stock raising, within the context of a very isolated, harsh, and dangerous environment, on the one hand, and an inherited and rigidly hierarchical social system based on origins and wealth, on the other, appears to have been resolved in favor of the environmental parameters via the establishment of a "production-determined work organization." Udy (1970) defines this type of organization as one which

. . . is expected to adopt production objectives as given by the social setting. It is then expected to devise, on physical grounds, a technology suited to the achievement of those objectives, and, similarly on physical grounds, to structure itself so as to be able to carry on the technology effectively. Because it is not expected to adapt either the technology or its own structure directly to the social setting, it is free to make the prescribed physical adaptations with the work system without regard to possibly conflicting social constraints. (p. 9)

Indeed, the only example Udy can offer of this type of work organization is Plains Indian buffalo hunting, an activity not only similar to stock raising on open ranges but also an activity carried on by Spanish settlers (*Ciboleros*) on the northern fringes of the frontier (the Llano Estacado), and also one which was carried on by their principal adversaries or competitors.

The technology devised, on physical grounds, was neither new nor necessarily a very complicated one; neither did it require significant amounts of education or sophistication. More than anything, it required physical prowess and stamina, and not a little courage. Similarly, on physical grounds, this technology structured itself in such a way as to blur distinctions, not only of education or cultural refinement but of wealth and ownership as well, in order to get the work done and to provide itself with protection while doing it. Nearly everyone engaged in or related to this type of enterprise, from the large stockman and land grantee and his family, on down to his meanest peon or *agregado* (temporary assistant or helper), was expected to be able to do everything—ride, shoot, rope, shear, brand, and cook. Fabiola Cabeza de Baca's memoirs (1954) of life on the Llano Estacado (in eastern New Mexico and West Texas) is replete with such examples.

Of particular significance was the *patron–partidario* system—the practice whereby peons, cowboys, and herdsmen could acquire a herd of stock from large stockmen on a share basis (Cabeza de Baca, 1954: 58–59). This practice or system was present throughout this area—from the province of Nueva Viscaya (present day Chihuahua and New Mexico) to Nuevo Santander by the Gulf. It was practiced until the turn of the century, disappearing along with the open range, although it still operates, to some extent, in the more remote communities of northern Mexico (Olson, 1972).

This system of tenant herding was by no means a leveler of men with respect to wealth and power, nor did it lead to a more egalitarian society (Gonzalez, 1969: 57–58; Rubel, 1971: 25–29). It did, however, impose certain expectations or attitudes toward the method by which such wealth was acquired and maintained, and, more importantly, as concerned its use. A wealthy stockman-*hacendado* who inherited his wealth in stock but did not possess the physical ability and skill to work his holdings alongside his employees and, more importantly, who never shared his good fortune was less a man than those who could and did do so. This work organization also imposed limits on the unilateral use of wealth, power, and prestige by large herd proprietors and landowners in still another way, equally linked to the environmental setting. The combination of multiple economic alternatives (mining, tenant herding, and, later, seasonal employment in the United States), sparse population, and the need for protection from raids by predatory Indians and whites not only prevented the development of debt peonage in this northern area but also created, simultaneously, a sense of interdependence and self-reliance which cut across the owner and laboring classes (Katz, 1974).

In this particular pattern of production-determined work organization, then, we can see the beginnings of what we call the second component of the *Norteño* ethos. Specifically, we can hypothesize that the system resulted in a generalized attitude toward labor and its reward which stresses the degree of individual self-reliance involved and its benefit for the producer and those dependent on him (generosity).

The isolation of this region as a whole, as well as the exploitation suffered at the hands of hostile Indians, bandits, and, later, white "nesters" and "filibusters," seems to have added still another (the third) component to the ethos of the *Norteño*: that of *familism*. Familism was manifested in two ways. First, as Leon-Portilla (1972) points out, it accentuated the need for protection which "produced a greater family cohesion and a more persistent preservation of ties of Kinship." He adds,

> To date, in several northwestern states, the family, as an institution, displays greater stability than in central and southern Mexico. . . . In fact, both in colonial times and more recently when other migrations began to take place, those who arrived in the North frequently came accompanied by their wives and children. (p. 111)

The persistence of this pattern among Mexican-Americans today is particularly evident in the patterns of seasonal migration and work among agricultural laborers.

On another level, this isolation and need for protection placed an aura of familism on entire communities. Towns were few and far between and usually were principally administrative, market, and educational centers. As a general rule, people resided in scattered settlements and *rancherias*, made up of the families of the *patron* and his *empleados* (employees). Cabeza de Baca (1954) and Schunior Ramirez (1971) provide vivid pictures of large, extended family relations on these *rancherias*, which were established only of necessity and with all the strains inherent in such an institution.

The prolonged isolation of the North from the cultural and political centers of the Colony and, especially, the Republic, created the fourth component of the *Norteño* ethos. This component is a curious paradox. That is, while the area and its people were isolated from the actual and symbolic centers of Mexico, to them fell much of the responsibility of violently defending the domain and integrity of the nation-state. This was a responsibility they did not shirk and which, according to Leon-Portilla (1972) gave rise in the *Norteño* to "an even stronger consciousness of his Mexicanism." He states:

> Proof of this is found in several facts already mentioned. There is the belligerence of the North during the war with the United States, in dealing with invasions by filibusters, and also at the time of the French intervention. These forms of participation in the life of the country, in turn, determined a desire for stronger ties with the integral reality of Mexico. Perhaps this explains, too, the decisive role of the North in the Mexican Revolution, when, in several border states, leaders emerged who effectively opposed the dictatorship. They also fought to put an end to the alienation represented by the great landholding, the mines, and other concessions in the hands of foreigners. *From another point of view, this ethos helps to explain the preservation of determined cultural values and elements among the Spanish-Mexican groups that continue to live in the U.S. Southwest* (pp. 112–13; emphasis ours).

Thus, the cultural heritage has as its core four components: (1) an emphasis on physical ability and stamina, (2) an emphasis on self-reliance with generosity, (3) familism, and (4) a heightened sense of nationality or ethnicity, or "Mexicanness." This is not to say that this list is all-inclusive of the ethos or the value components of Mexican-American (and *Norteño*) culture. Nor is it to be taken as synonymous with that culture, in the broad sense of the term. We only hypothesize that these are to be counted among the basic components of the ideological aspects of that culture, which, in various ways, alongside and in interaction with our other dimensions, must be taken into account as essential elements in the determination of work-related values of Mexican-Americans.

STRATIFICATION AS A DIMENSION

Let us assume that the ethos components of Mexican-American culture hypothesized above reflect the attitudes with which these people confront the realities of life, and especially their adaptations to the socioeconomic changes which overtook their existence after 1850. It would be impossible here to describe the totality of this subjective mind–objective world confrontation in all its aspects. We will restrict our speculation to those aspects of social structure experienced within a context of invidious, qualitative, status comparisons with significant others. More directly, we will attempt to sketch the interrelations between stratification and the subjective tendencies inherent in the ethos components hypothesized.

Before doing this, however, it will be useful to construct a model of stratification which is suited to the social structure which emerged from the Anglo domination in the Southwest. In the social science literature, the nature and function of stratification in Mexican-American society and culture comprise one of its least known or emphasized aspects. Studies of Mexican-Americans tend to assume its presence (based on rather lifeless categories or scales of income, occupation, and education) and then proceed to look for significant correlations with other sociocultural aspects (e.g., indices of acculturation). Or they tend to ignore such variables in order to provide a monolithic view of the culture, usually with an eye to its role in delaying or preventing acculturation or assimilation into the larger society. In either case, stratification is usually linked to acculturation, and, not infrequently, the two are confused. Such a simple-minded view tends to obscure the nature of Mexican-American culture, making it appear undifferentiated, passive, and without a history.

Another deficiency is evident in these approaches; that is, these studies tend to have a rather one-dimensional view of stratification, in that stratification is objectively presented as a scale or continuum along which is measured a single criterion (e.g., income) or multiple but highly correlated criteria (e.g., income, occupation, and education). Such a view is more a function of statistical operations than relevant to the nature and functioning of the society in question. The unequal distribution of certain characteristics among individuals, inclusive of the value attributed to these characteristics by members of a society, is meaningful only when examined on the basis of a discontinuous set of groupings (i.e., stratum or social class), each with a particular combination or set of socially relevant characteristics, and in interaction with each other. In short, stratification is not merely a scale or continuum but a system made up of different strata or social classes—a system held together by its involvement in one economic structure and the subjective glue of invidious status comparisons and concomitant social attitudes and practices.

The Anglo-American conquest of the Southwest and that region's subsequent development as an agri-industrial complex created a unique system of stratification which, we hypothesize, along with the ethos components, deeply affects the nature and manifestations of work-related values among Mexican-Americans. This is not to say that stratification was unknown in this area and appeared only with the coming of the Anglos. The pre-Anglo situation was a highly stratified system, but one wherein this aspect of the social setting was, to some extent, checked by the physical exigencies of the work system. By the same token, the new economic organization which developed in the wake of Anglo social and economic expansion into the Southwest brought drastic alterations to the preexisting system of stratification and, we hypothesize, to the contexts wherein related values could be and were manifested. In other words, there developed within the Spanish-speaking Southwest a dual but interrelated system of stratification similar to the situation described by Stavenhagen (1965) in the Chiapas highlands of Mexico.

Following Stavenhagen, we can describe this as a stratification system composed simultaneously of colonial relations[3] and social-class relations. Social class is a stratified system wherein the quantitative status characteristics are not associated with any qualitative factors, such as race or ethnicity. In a colonial system, however, such qualitative factors are associated with the quantitative status characteristics of income, education, or occupation. Furthermore, according to Stavenhagen, "The primary characteristics of the colonial situation are ethnic discrimination, political dependence, social inferiority, residential segregation, economic subjugation and juridicial incapacity" (p. 70).

Colonial relationships, then, are those wherein Mexican-American society, as a whole, is confronted by Anglo-American society as a subordinate or less privileged group. In this situation, the key link between these two strata (which together make up the totality of the colonial society) were the Anglo commercial farmer and the Mexican-American agricultural wage laborer, a nexus which colored the general system of mutual or interethnic group images and invidious comparisons. In the eyes of the less numerous but politically and economically more powerful Anglo-Americans, there existed no real differences within the population of Mexican-Americans, nor between Mexican-Americans and Mexican *Nationale*. All were essentially peons whose physical abilities (but not their particular talents) were necessary, indeed indispensable, for the modernization of agriculture and the continued economic development of the region. According to Rubel (1971), for example,

> Anglos continue to lump together as "Mexicans" . . . all those with a Spanish or Mexican ancestor, regardless of the side of town on which they reside. The entire *chicanazgo*—laborer and professional alike—is lumped together by Anglos into a subordinate group based on ascribed characteristics. (p. 19)

Two important factors contributed to the maintenance of this system of colonial relations, despite the presence and incrementation of socio-economic differentiations among Mexican-Americans. The first was the continued flow of "new" Mexican immigrants (i.e., wetbacks and *braceros*) replacing "established" Mexican-Americans within the ranks of agricultural wage labor: those who migrated to other areas of the United States or those who had climbed out of the agricultural wage labor. The second factor is the fact that, among Mexican-Americans, socioeconomic mobility does not lead to a change in ethnic identity. As Penalosa and McDonagh (1966) have pointed out, "Upwardly mobile Mexican-Americans do not shed their ethnic identification significantly. . . . It is the shedding of lower class culture rather than ethnicity which is most related with upward mobility" (p. 498).

Simultaneously, and intermixed with this system of colonial relations, there exists (especially since World War II) a system of class relationships, both within the Mexican-American population and between the Anglo-American and Mexican-American segments of the population. In a general sense, class relationships were possible for the following reason: While the principal and original link between these two major status groups (and the one which "colored" the entire nature of their relationship) was Mexican agricultural wage labor and Anglo-owned farms and packing sheds, labor relations as such were not, strictly speaking, between these two societies but between two (or more) specific sectors within each one. Furthermore, the specific sectors within Anglo and Mexican-American society were not static but rather were sectors which were constantly adapting to socioeconomic changes in the society as a whole. Of particular importance were the changes experienced and still being felt in the ever-increasing industrialization and capitalization of American farming.

More specifically, the initial agribusiness complex, established in many parts of the Southwest during the first two decades of this century, had at its center local commercial farmer-capitalists, most of whom apparently came directly from the Midwest. Unlike their experience in the Midwest, these farmers lived in towns, most of which were founded in the twenties. Almost immediately, these "farmers" pooled their capital for the purpose of establishing (1) cooperative gins and professionally managed citrus and vegetable plants and packing sheds; and (2) the necessary credit institutions, especially local banks. Since in its initial phases this commercial agriculture development was heavily dependent on cheap mobile labor, the social and political machinery which developed in these communities was oriented, de facto, toward discouraging the social and political development of the Mexican-American citizenry and encouraging the perpetuation of a system of colonial relations advantageous to these local farmer-capitalists.

However, such a system was doomed to failure, apparently for two important reasons. The first was a demographic one. Any inspection of census records will reveal that the local Anglo population within these communities has literally failed to reproduce itself. Both in relative proportions to Mexican-Americans and in absolute numbers, the number of young Anglos capable of managing the economic reins of this society (which they presumably would have inherited) has declined drastically, especially since World War II. Consequently, if the middle-management and white-collar positions and occupations are to be filled at all, the system has been increasingly forced to seek its recruits from among the qualified Mexican-American population.[4]

Second, and perhaps more importantly, it appeared that if post–World War II agriculture was to survive, it had to modernize (essentially, to mechanize) and capitalize beyond the capability of the local farmer-capitalists. As elsewhere in the United States, there began a gradual displacement of local capitalists (and other entrepeneurs) by larger, externally controlled corporations. Such a displacement made the future of *Juan Cuervo* (Jim Crow) in the Southwest highly uncertain.[5] In short, the "new" capitalist owners and management had no particular regional interests in maintaining a system of ethnic discrimination and social inferiority. On the contrary, they required a smaller but more dependable and more disciplined industrial work force. If a Mexican-American filled the bill, generally speaking, these managers had no strong, traditionalist objections to his or her employment. At the same time, however, this system created even more unemployment and underemployment among those Mexican-Americans whose capabilities were limited to agricultural wage labor or those who had the capability for the new system but for whom there was no place, since employment does not grow rapidly in this particular type of industrialization. The latter phenomenon, incidently, has created a two-pronged exodus from Texas which significantly altered the regional distribution of

Mexican-Americans in the United States: the more mobile went west, to California, while the less fortunate went to the Midwest.

More importantly, what remained was a situation wherein ethnic barriers to mobility were lessened (somewhat), but class distinctions within the Mexican-American population were intensified, side by side with the remnants of the preexisting system of colonial relationships. Some evidence of this effect can be found in Lyle (1973) who found that

> . . . once Spanish surnamed men penetrate the large firms, their level of education is not critical in their ability to "make the breaks" for themselves. Chicanos . . . do better in breaking into high status occupations in high wage center firms where employment is not growing rapidly. The assimilated worker is conspicuously absent in the service sector, where the demand for labor is expanding but where wages remain relatively low. (p. 14)

This brief history of the development of a dual stratification in the Southwest, and the principal factors which have brought it into existence, can perhaps be best summarized by Stavenhagen, (1965):

> Colonial and class relationships appear intermixed . . . while the former primarily answered to mercantilist interests, the latter met the capitalist ones. Both kinds of relationships were also opposed to each other: the development of class relationships came into conflict with the maintenance of colonial relationships. (p. 70)

To return to our principal point, any attempt to understand the role and meaning of work (and related values) among Mexican-Americans must deal with the types of invidious comparisons made within the framework of stratification which exists within this society. More specifically, it is necessary to see how work is involved in invidious comparisons in the system of colonial relations and system of class relations with Mexican-American society.

Invidious Comparisons in Colonial Relations

As noted above, the Anglo conquest of the Southwest and its subsequent development as an agri-industrial complex has led to a system of colonial relations between Mexican-Americans and Anglos. Along with the ethos components of Mexican-Americans, this system deeply affects the nature and manifestations of work-related values. In short, what quickly evolved (no doubt furthered by the Anglo-Mexican animosities established during the Texas War of Independence and the War with Mexico) was an economic system oriented to the maintenance of the "Mexican" in the inferior position of cheap wage labor. According to Paul Taylor, as reported in Shockley (1974b), "The Americans here [Texas] have always held the idea that the Mexicans are here just to work" (p. 16).

Even the physical structure and functioning of the new Anglo-founded communities reflected this point of view. Commenting on Crystal City, Texas, one Anglo (Shockley, 1974b) stated "All this town was ever intended to be was a labor camp" (p. 14). Indeed, Shockley summarizes the nature of this work organization and its social imperatives very neatly when he states:

> With the influx of these Mexicans, race lines became class lines. Mexicans did the manual labor, Anglos owned the land and made the money. . . . In being forced to migrate (in the U.S.) because of their dependence upon stoop labor, the Mexicans reinforced the Anglo's attitude towards them as being "here just to work." (p. 16)

Madsen (1964) presents some opinions expressed by South Texas Anglo farmers:

> An Anglo regarded Latins as the best of all farm laborers, "Man for man a Mexican can out-plant, out-weed, and out-pick anyone on the face of the earth."

> Perhaps the most common Anglo sentiment was voiced by a rancher, "If it were not for those hard-working *Meskins,* this place wouldn't be on the map. It is very true about the Anglo know how, but without those *Meskin* hands no one could have built up the prosperity we have in this part of the nation." (p. 12)

Not surprisingly, the Mexican-American shares this view concerning his own capacity or ability to do hard work, when necessary. In other words, Mexican-Americans generally would agree that, physically, they are stronger and possess greater endurance than Anglos or other Americans, although there is some indication that this self-view or stereotype is not held to the same degree by all social classes within Mexican-American society. Madsen (1964b), for example, attributes this attitude primarily to the lower-lower class. As he puts it, "Working the land seems to him to be a natural and noble labor. He is usually dependent on seasonal work in the fields. He takes jobs as they come and rarely complains to anyone outside his family about his pay or working conditions" (p. 31).

In a survey of favorable self-stereotypes conducted among Mexican-Americans in Los Angeles and San Antonio (Grebler et al., 1970), there was found to be a general consensus on this attitude. Mexican-Americans tended to agree with the statement "Other Americans don't work as hard as Mexican-Americans," although this opinion was held to a greater degree in the lower income brackets and for all classes was more commonly held by Mexican-Americans of San Antonio than those of Los Angeles. As Grebler et al. put it,

> The greatest consensus is on personal qualities. In some statements where responses vary with income of household head, there may well be a real

difference in the phenomena perceived. Thus, low-income people *are* likely to work harder. If a Mexican American observes his friends working like *camellos* (or camels, which is a distinct virtue), he may well interpret it ethnocentrically as applying to all Mexican Americans. (p. 388)

Another set of cross-ethnic views related to the value and meaning of work has to do with other personal qualities. According to Madsen (1964b), "Although the Anglos fully recognize the economic importance of the un- skilled Latin labor, they tend to regard the Mexican American as childlike, emotional, ignorant and in need of paternalistic guidance" (p. 12). Similar statements on the part of Anglos can be found in almost all works dealing with Anglo-Mexican relations. The stereotypes of "childlike" and "emo- tional" are especially important, as they tend to be operationalized and used against Mexican-Americans in their work and efforts at self-improvement. Thus, in the view of the Anglo, the emotional and childlike quality of Mexican-Americans makes them (1) "suspicious" and "quarrelsome" and therefore unable to get together to help themselves, (2) "unable to defer gratification," and (3) "superstitious," relying more on the saints than on science or unable to think scientifically.

Mexican-Americans tend to respond with complementary and equally unflattering views of the Anglo.[6] To quote Madsen (1964):

> Many Latins believe that Anglos lack true religion and ethics and are concerned only with self-advancement. . . . "The Anglo will do anything to get ahead, no matter who gets hurt. . . ." A similar view came from the teacher. . . . "Personal gain and achievement are the main Anglo goals in life and the ethics used to attain these goals will be worked out along the way." A Latin crop picker phrased the same sentiment in more transcendental terms, "The Anglo does what his greed tells him. The Chicano does what God tells him."

> The Latin feels that blind dependence on science and the ceaseless push for advancement have fettered the Anglo's integrity and intellectual ability. The Latin male sees himself meeting life's problems with intelligence and logic, which he finds lacking in the Anglo. An educated Latin pointed up the contrast in these words, "The Mexican American has no disdain for thinking, no mistrust of it. He wants to arrive at his own convictions, do his own thinking. The Anglo American will fit into almost any organization in most any way if he can only get ahead. . . . He accepts many facts although he does not understand them." (pp. 12–13)

In more direct terms, the above stereotypes of Anglos as expressed by Mexican-Americans reflect the opinion that, in contrast to themselves, Anglos are materialistic (or greedy) and conformist or dependent. The survey by Grebler et al. on favorable self-stereotypes held by Mexican- Americans demonstrated that the majority, at all levels of income, tended to agree with the view of Anglos as strongly materialistic. In another (in our opinion, less reliable) survey, Dworkin (1965) noted that native-born Mexican-Americans overwhelmingly agreed with the characterization of Anglos as "materialistic" and "conformist."

To summarize, we can say that at the level of colonial relations, the qualitative, invidious status comparisons made by Mexican-Americans are consistent with at least two of the "traditional" ethos components of their culture: physical strength and prowess, and self-reliance with generosity. This does not mean that these are the only Mexican versus Anglo images held. "Stronger family ties," as a reflection of the "familism" component, is another that is frequently mentioned. It is significant, however, that the elements highlighted here are directly related to how Mexican-Americans view themselves as workers, and these elements reflect continuities in traditional culture of possible work-related values and not compensatory modifications of their values.

We can tentatively conclude, then, that at the level of colonial relations, Mexican-Americans view themselves as "good workers," capable of adapting to any work requirements (i.e., self-reliant) and more humane in their search for a better life through their labor.

Invidious Comparisons in Social-Class Relations

This section will be limited to a discussion of invidious distinctions and comparisons, across social class lines, within the Mexican-American group. While a comparison of similar phenemona within the Anglo group would in itself be interesting and instructive, it is beyond the scope of this chapter.

How are internal class differentiation and social mobility interpreted within Mexican-American society, and what sort of invidious status comparisons (reflective of work-related values) do they give rise to? In order to answer these questions, we need to look at interclass relations and comparisons from the "upward" and "downward" views on the social class ladder.

In the pre-Anglo situation, stratification was part of the *Norteño* Mexican culture. While essentially composed of two classes (i.e., *los ricos*, or *hacendados*, and *los pobres*, or *peones*), this society was nevertheless homogeneous racially and culturally. Furthermore, both strata were linked through a paternalistic system of reciprocity or multiplex relations which went beyond purely economic ties (Rubel, 1971: 29). The appearance of full-fledged commercial capitalism (on both sides of the border) tended to remove these paternalistic links between the classes. The result seems to have been the development of an internal pattern of class consciousness with invidious cultural overtones.

In northern Mexico, for example, Olson (1972: 86–91) reports that the poorer elements of the community, in general, expressed resentment toward the "new" rich families, or *patrones*, often referring to them as *capitalistas*, while simultaneously expressing nostalgia for the old *hacendada-patrones* who supposedly shared their wealth (through prestation) and cared for the poor. According to his informants, the relationships which develop *within* the upper classes of the community are based on *puro negocio* ("all business") and lack the more personal qualities of *voluntad* (friendship and mutual trust). More importantly, the poor in Mina (Nuevo Leon) attribute this situation to a loss, on the part of the upper classes, of the traditional cultural values. Indeed, according to Olson, this rationale and the antipathy toward these *capitalistas* are among the principal elements which have given rise to a cultural revitalization movement centered around a folk-saint healer, *El Nino Fidencio*. This particular movement, among others, is to be found on both sides of the border (see Macklin & Crumrine, n.d.; Romano, 1965).

An anecdote provided by Bustamante (1971) poignantly describes this attitude. While masquerading as a wetback, Bustamante and Juan (a "real" wetback) slipped across the river near Reynosa and were hitchhiking north. A Mexican-American gave them a ride and tried to make some helpful suggestions for avoiding the U.S. Border Patrol. Bustamante suggested that the Mexican-American seemed like a nice, sympathetic person. Juan disagreed:

> That guy was very suspicious. I think he wanted to turn us in to the Border Patrol himself . . . .
>
> You [Bustamante] will learn very soon that you cannot trust a person who wears a tie; rich people hate us in this country even if they are of our race. (p. 117)

In the anthropological literature on Mexican-Americans, much has been made of the concept of *envidia* (envy) as a leveling mechanism and, by implication, as an inhibitor of social mobility. Most of these reports, however, tend to be cases wherein the envy is imputed to other Mexican-Americans (and directed to oneself), especially when one has experienced success or good fortune. This concept is rather troublesome in that it does not distinguish between class status placement as a factor promoting envy and the process of mobility. In our opinion, it is probably more a reflection of evaluations of the latter, particularly within the context of a small community and between persons familiar with one another, than actual evaluations of the meaning of established social-class status differences in general. It is our contention that invidious social-class distinctions on the part of the poor or lower classes are not manifestations of *envidia* but rather manifestations of class consciousness, summarized in terms of loss of ethnicity and legitimate cultural values. In short, the lower socioeconomic strata of Mexican-American society attribute to "known" aggregates or individuals in the higher strata the same work-related attributes or values they attribute to Anglos: materialistic, greedy, conformists, and dependent. In the case of the

Mexican-Americans, however, these characteristics are not seen as stemming from some inherent or genetic racial make-up, but rather as a result of assimilation or simulation of Anglo values and culture. In local jargon, such Mexican-Americans are referred to as *agringados* or *agabachados* (Madsen, 1964b). In the view of the lower classes, such a state implies moral, physical, and mental decay.[7]

From the standpoint of the downward view, the invidious status comparisons are not exactly reciprocal or opposite counterparts of those of the upward view. In other words, the higher socioeconomic strata in Mexican-American society do not necessarily accept themselves (or their way of life) as Americanized or Anglicized, and that of the lower classes as Mexican or Mexican-American. As mentioned before, Penalosa and McDonagh (1966) demonstrated that upwardly mobile Mexican-Americans tend to remain loyal to their ethnic identity; it is their conclusion that "It is the shedding of lower class culture rather than ethnicity which is most related with upward mobility." Others also have noted this tendency (see Simmons, 1952: 508; Madsen, 1964b: 36–43). In other words, the upper strata (including the middle classes) would not consider it un-Mexican to have high aspirations for oneself and children, smaller families, more education, greater fluency in English, and better or more prudent consumption patterns.

At most, the upper strata of Mexican-American society might attribute the lack of mobility or the low economic well-being of the lower classes to personal deficiencies stemming from a corruption or exaggeration of traditional Mexican values, such as confusing physical prowess and strength with sexual or violence-prone *machismo*; self-reliance with xenophobia or backwardness; or familism with large, financially crippling families. Such attitudes, to some extent, are manifested in the self-directed humor of Mexican-Americans (Paredes, 1973; Spielberg, 1975), which is especially common among middle- and upper-class types. Such attitudes, however, must not be confused with attitudes of ethnicity as the principal obstacle to mobility among members of these strata. The importance of class and class awareness among these types is one which cuts across the ethnic boundary or division. Rubel, in *Across the Tracks*, for example, points out that "some of the aspiring Mexican-Americans give as their reasons for not moving across the tracks the undesirability of living next door to 'white hilly billies' or to 'white trash'" (p. 19). Madsen (1964b) also reports an anecdote indicative of class awareness among upper-strata Mexican-Americans.

The [Mexican-American] elite are friendly to upper-class Anglos but regard them as boorish, ignorant and lacking in manners. During a conversation with a wealthy Anglo, a Latin aristocrat made a subtle jest using the symbolism of Cervantes. When the Anglo looked confused rather than amused, the Latin said, "Of course you have read Don Quixote." The Anglo brightened and

replied, "No, but I saw the movie." The Latin later shrugged and commented to
a friend, "What can you talk about to such people outside of cotton and the
comics?" (p. 42)

We can tentatively conclude, then, that in the minds of the upwardly
mobile or upper strata of Mexican-American society, mobility and success
are seen primarily from the standpoint of class variables, as opposed to
acculturation or assimilation to Anglo ways. The latter is more typical of the
interpretations by lower-class Mexican-Americans of wealth and social-
standing differences within their own ethnic community.

To summarize, as a dimension in the determination of work-related
values, stratification can be said to operate on two distinct levels of invidious
status comparisons. First, on the general interethnic level, there exists a
stratification system based on colonial relations between two hierarchically
arranged societies, the Anglo and the Mexican-American. It is at this level
that personal qualities stemming directly from selected aspects of the general value system of the Mexican-American ethos are applied in the derivation of favorable self-other evaluations. These aspects are (1) physical
strength and prowess and (2) self-reliance with generosity. Thus Mexican-
Americans tend to view themselves, in comparison with Anglos, as good
workers (i.e., physically more capable) who are better able to do all types of
work and are also more humane in their search for a better life through their
labor.

The second level of invidious status comparisons involves the various
social classes which exist within Mexican-American society itself. In this case,
however, a different set of variables is used for the derivation of favorable
self-other evaluations. While, as we have shown, class consciousness exists at
all levels or classes of Mexican-American society, manifestations of this
consciousness are not the same for all strata or classes. In the case of the
lower classes, a more particularistic aspect of the general value system or
ethos (i.e., "Mexicanism") is utilized in explaining class variation and in the
derivation of favorable self-other evaluations.

For the upwardly mobile or upper classes, on the other hand, more
universalistic social criteria, such as education, occupation, and skill, may be
involved in such explanations and evaluations. These criteria are hard to
account for, since they do not seem to stem from the ethos components of
Norteño culture outlined above. Neither do they necessarily represent uni-
versally held values of the dominant Anglo culture adopted by Mexican-
Americans. A possible explanation for this may be that they represent values
derived from middle- and upper-class segments of *both* Hispanic and Anglo
culture.

In either the upward or downward views, however, it is difficult to
derive any specific set of work-related values. In both cases, it would seem,

these views reflect estimations of the opportunity structure, the cultural costs in seeking to manipulate it, or the differential, class-determined abilities to manipulate more than they reflect any values related to work per se.

THE FRAMEWORK OF SOCIAL ROLES AND SELF-IDENTITY

The final dimension we are postulating as critical in the determination of work-related values (or the meaning of work) among Mexican-Americans is that of social roles and the different configurations of self-identity that are constructed from them. It is by no means, however, the least important dimension. On the contrary, as we shall show in our conclusions, it is probably the most important of these dimensions, in that it provides the mechanisms by which the other dimensions interact with one another in shaping the meaning of work.

The concept of social roles, as used here, refers to a named social position or term, including the institutionalized expectations (i.e., patterns of rights and duties) generic to that label or term, in any given society.[8] At the level of the society, all such labels or social roles are further seen here as being organized into a framework or system. The framework or systemic nature of social roles derives from the fact that all such roles, or social labels, are meaningful only in the context of complementary binary combinations with other relevant labels or terms.[9] True, some terms may have more than one relevant binary combination or counterpart, but all must have at least one, if they are to exist meaningfully. A second systemic quality derives from the degree to which such binary combinations are inclusive or exclusive with respect to their appropriateness of application or use, as determined by the reference group in question for any particular event or situation. In other words, specific binary combinations are to be found appropriate only to certain terminological domains. These domains, in turn, may be appropriate for either a very restricted or a relatively broad range of social situations. The notion of exclusive and inclusive domains implied here is conceptually similar to Service's fourfold table of terminological domains (1971: 95–113).

Self-identity, as we have implied, is a set or collection of individualized anchor points derived from the various social roles (and domains) known and participated in by the individual. Individuals, then, may be conceived operationally, as a selectively organized system of social-role labels. Such a system, in combination with evaluative dimensions (i.e., good/bad, ugly/beautiful, and so on), is what we are here referring to as self-conception or personality organization.

It would be impossible to give here a succinct description of the framework or system of social roles or domains in which Mexican-Americans participate. It probably includes all those social roles acknowledged in the everyday life of the larger society of which they are a part. For those social roles lexically distinct or peculiar to Mexican-Americans, we can assume that these would have, at least, recognizable counterparts or translations within specific role domains of the larger society. By looking in some detail at the self-designated identities, however, we can get not only an idea of major patterns in self-conception but also a glimpse of the more important societal-level role domains in their everyday lives.

Unfortunately, most studies of self-concepts of Mexican-Americans have focused on the evaluative aspects, such as degree of self-esteem or other subjective traits (see Dworkin, 1965; Carter, 1968). Few systematic studies have focused on the categorical (substantive) role identity aspect, and even these have tended to look at very specialized or particular segments of Mexican-American people, such as teen-agers, psychiatric outpatients, migrant laborers, or the very poor. Despite these limitations, it is still possible to retrieve patterns which at least are indicative of tendencies.

Gecas's (1973) study of self-concepts of poor migrant and settled Mexican-Americans in the Yakima Valley of Washington State revealed some significant tendencies worth citing here. Utilizing a slightly modified version of the Kuhn and McPartland Twenty Statements Test (TST), Gecas found the following:

> An overall inspection of identity patterns indicates poor Mexican Americans tend to locate themselves most frequently in the structural identities provided by the society (i.e., those based on ascribed characteristics or social organizational units). Family, gender and work constitute the most frequently mentioned identities for adults, *with family being consistently the highest.* (p. 586; emphasis ours)

He further states,

> We also asked our respondents to indicate which of the statements they had made about themselves was most important to the way in which they think of themselves. . . . For both migrant and settled parents, the parental identity emerges as the most important, and family in general (comprising family statements not specifically referring to family position) is rated high in importance. (p. 592)

With respect to the more subjective, or qualitative, aspects of self-concepts (which, in general, were less frequently mentioned than the substantive or categorical ones), only one was mentioned with the same high frequency as the categorical aspects, and that was what Gecas (1973) labeled "a sense of altruism." According to him, "the conception of self as a helpful, generous person was very frequent for all four categories of respondents (i.e., Fathers, Mothers, Sons and Daughters), with 70 percent mentioning it. It is clear that poor Mexican Americans think of themselves as helpful and unselfish people" (p. 588). The findings of this study (at least those reported above) tend to confirm the existence of at least two of the core values mentioned by Leon-Portilla and discussed above: familism and generosity.

Another of the few self-concept studies to stress substantive or categorical self-identities is Farris and Brymer (1970). Their findings are more difficult to interpret because of deficiencies in the method by which they present their findings and the conceptual constructs which underlie their categorization of responses. They administered twenty statements tests (TST) forms to school classes composed of "Latins" and Anglos at three levels (elementary, junior high, and high school) within the San Antonio, Texas, school system. Even though our interest here is not, strictly speaking, a comparative one vis-à-vis Anglos, the presentation of the data by the authors renders an analysis of the Latin children's responses alone meaningless here. Some parallels with the Gecas study findings can be drawn or inferred, however.

Farris and Brymer found that in contrast to Anglo youths, in general, Mexican-American school children assigned themselves to fewer social categories, as designated by the average number of social roles and social categories referred to on their TSTs. They interpret this finding by emphasizing the negative. Namely, they see a presumed low frequency of social encounters and participation in a fewer number of groups as resulting in "the Latin 'subjective social world' [being] smaller than that of Anglo by the time high school age is reached" (p. 415).

From a more positive standpoint, the results could be interpreted as indicating the overwhelming importance of certain social groups (i.e., the family), and certain associated social roles (i.e., sons and daughters), as opposed to other types of social groups and roles. Our alternative interpretation, we submit, is substantiated by another of their findings; namely, that while Anglos fluctuated drastically in the percentage of students making identity statements concerning family (i.e., 20%, 69%, and 29% in the three school levels), Latins demonstrated considerably greater consistency in this regard (41%, 47%, and 36%, respectively).

With respect to self-identities based on gender or sex roles, we also find some significant results in the Farris and Brymer study. That is, while sex role (as a qualifier to other statements of identity) decreases as the Anglo moves from elementary to high school levels, Mexican-Americans remained consistent along this dimension; slightly less than 50% mentioned this factor at all three levels.

Mexican-American students also tended to demonstrate a more developmental view of age as part of their self-concept or identity than did Anglos. That is, the frequency of statements implying age status made by Mexican-American students is low at elementary and junior high levels (20–25%) and then increases significantly among high school students (56%); while Anglos maintain a relatively high and consistent concern with age status throughout the three levels. We could interpret this finding as indicating that the maturation process is a significant variable in the self-concept of Mexican-Americans, especially as age brings with it new and perhaps more conscious responsibilities and privileges within relevant social groupings such as the family. Unfortunately, Farris and Brymer do not report what, if any, statements involving work as an element of self-identity were made.

What then, are we to make of these admittedly selective findings and interpretations in formulating a composite portrait of the categorical and substantive Mexican-American self-concept, or internalized matrix of social roles? Secondly, what would its significance be for the place and meaning of work in their lives?

It is one of the more lamentable characteristics of highly formal and ·systematic studies of self-conception, such as those based on TSTs, that analysis of the integral unity or the structural arrangement of responses is rarely undertaken. It would not be too unreasonable, however, to assume that each of these dimensions of the self-identity (i.e., kin status, age, sex) stands in some organic or systemic relationship to every other one and to the totality or configuration which they create. The latter is what this writer has always thought of as "personality organizations." The vagueness of this concept, however, is understandable, since "personality," as such, is not amenable to any type of holistc observation or measurement; only in one dimensional part can we catch a glimpse of it. Despite this methodological handicap, we must now consider, assuming such integration exists, what this organic configuration or constellation of self-identities would look like for Mexican-Americans.

We propose that "the family" could stand as an observable model for the presumed configuration or constellation of predominant dimensions of self-identity among Mexican-Americans. We suggest that the family, as a social group, is what basically defines and coordinates the relevance of age, sex, and kinship roles for determining "Who am I?" We further postulate that among Mexican-Americans, the family stands for the coordination of self-identity dimensions through a particularly well-delineated pattern of differential privileges and obligations made evident (or observable) in the behavioral manifestations of authority, respect, and division of labor within the family.

Looking at the qualitative aspects of the self-conception of Mexican Americans, it may well be that what Gecas identified as a sense of altruism is the self-concept element which provides or reflects the motivational force behind the performance and priority of familistic social roles and observance of its pattern of reciprocal rights and obligations. As a reflection of basic core values, we might designate this self-concept system as *altruistic familism*. Too often this pattern of familistic behavior and its value underpinnings has been couched in negative terms as dysfunctional, amoral familism, paternal authoritarianism, *machismo,* or, in the case of women, a martyr complex.[10]

Our postulated interconnections between kin position, age, and sex receive support from more in-depth studies. Romano (1960), for example, in his analysis of patterns of *Donship* (i.e., the application of the respectful term *Don* or *Dona* to a person) links intimately the dimensions of age and the sexually differentiated performance of parental position obligations, especially in provisioning, protection, and socialization functions within the family.

What then is the place of work (as distinct from occupation) in this family-coordinated system of self-identities, and its central value of altruistic familism? In our view, work, defined as physical or mental effort for the purpose of modifying the individual's environment, is the manifestation of the principal social roles (kin position, age, and sex) and the altruistic quality or trait attached to these roles. The principal or focal physical environment this activity seeks to modify or maintain is the family household.

This view of work vis-à-vis the principal subjective social world of Mexican-Americans is to some extent substantiated by Goodman and Berman's study (1974) of children in an urban *barrio.* After noting the unqualified precedence of kinsmen, particularly their parents, in their value hierarchy, the "others orientation," and the clear recognition of a parental sexual division of labor among *barrio* children, they state, "The Mexican children perhaps value work less for itself than as participation and contribution" (p. 153). The emphasis is on the contribution that work makes to the ongoing activity of the group most important to ego, i.e., the family. As they put it,

> Both boys and girls accept work as they accept play; it is expected, a taken for granted part of life. It is good to work, bad if father does not have a job. One should not avoid work. We asked "at your house, who works and what do they do?" Unlike Anglo and Negro children, the Mexican children answered including those who help at home, as well as wage earners. (p. 153)

For Mexican-Americans, then, work is first important and meaningful in the particular context of the family, where one's composite role is predetermined, and then is judged in terms of itself (personalistic criteria) and not in terms of competition judged from some external or universal standard. Work performance, in this context, is judged in competition against one's self, as defined by other core qualities or values, such as generosity and self-reliance, and, more importantly, from the standpoint of how it tests one's own capacity for physical endurance and stamina. These qualities are in line with Genovese's observation that the African and European peasant tradition or "work ethic" stressed hard work as a moral duty (1974: 311–312). If we may paraphrase him, the Mexican-American man might well agree with the French peasant: a brave man (a *macho,* if you will) is by definition a hard-working family man (p. 732).

WORK, SELF-IDENTITY, AND SELF-ESTEEM

It is now a commonplace in social science literature to analyze both the social and psychological place or meaning of work along a continuum of instrumental vs. expressive value; that is, work as a means to an end or work as an end in itself. While such a dichotomy may be useful for broad comparisons between distinct sociocultural types or populations, it is of limited value in understanding the role and meaning of work within a given population, because the distinction is really one of degree and not of kind.

On a more theoretical level, such a continuum is especially deficient as an aid to the understanding of the dynamics of the interrelationship between social structure and self-identity, as these shape or define the value and meaning of work. Its deficiency here is due, perhaps, to the fact that this continuum combines (or fails to distinguish between) two distinct levels of reality: work as an activity, on the one hand, and work activity as a status label or as "job," on the other. In other words, work, as an activity, is always a means to an end, from the standpoint of important social goals. Whether or not it is expressive of the social values of a society depends on whether the activity is conceived of as a labeled status, in and of itself, and, further, how it is worked into a hierarchically arranged system of such labels. What we propose, then, as an alternative to the instrumental vs. expressive continuum is a twofold construct which recognizes the dual but distinct nature of work as an activity and as a label, and simultaneously recognizes the place of each element in the individual's estimate of himself.

. In this construct, we begin by accepting the fact that all work is activity. As an activity, however, it has two aspects: particularistic and universalistic. The particularistic aspect of work activity refers to what such an activity accomplishes (food, housing, money, vacations) and for whom (what on-going social relationships it facilitates). The universalistic aspect of work activity refers to the fact that activity is labeled within the occupational domains of the larger society and evaluated relative to other occupational labels, and therefore it is expressive of a universal social value.

This rather schematic construct is not entirely new. Marshall (1963: 186 ff.), for example, distinguishes between *personal social status* and *positional social status.* According to Marshall, "The former refers to the actual social position accorded [to the individual and his activities] by the attitudes or behavior of those among whom the individual moves." On the other hand, "Positional social status is the social position accorded by the conventional values current in the society to the group or category of which the individual is representative" (p. 186 ff.). A crucial difference between these two types of social status (again according to Marshall) is that the standing or evaluation acquired in the case of personal social status is in comparison with a restricted and role-specific reference group, such as the role of the father and his standing within the family. The positional social status is the standing of that person, by virtue of his activities or personal characteristics, in comparison with all other members of that society; that is, sweepers of floors vs. teachers of schools, or Mexican descent vs. Anglo.

Viewed from the standpoint of this dichotomy, all working Mexican-Americans, by virtue of what they do, have simultaneously a personal social status and a positional social status. The most important psychological implication (or self-esteem implication) of this particularistic-universalistic duality in their work activity involves the relative amounts of self-investment, by ego, in the personal social status and the positional social status. According to Faunce (n. d.), "self investment refers to the extent to which an evaluated self identity is implicated in any activity; some activities may have immediate relevance to aspects of self concept while other activities have little or no relationship to what we think about ourselves" (p. 3). Thus, we can now posit our second intersecting dichotomy or dimension, namely, each social status may have either a high or low level of self-investment.

For purposes of clarity, we can go one step further and assume that a high level of self-investment, by definition, implies a relatively high estimate by the actor of his abilities or performance within the particular status involved. Low self-investment, on the other hand, carries neither a high nor a low estimate of one's own particular abilities or performance; those qualities are simply taken for granted. In this case, one is neither better nor worse than others in the same or a comparable category or status; it is a matter of indifference.

Before proceeding to an illustration of the status vis-à-vis self-investment alternatives possible under our twofold dichotomy, we need to clarify our view of self-esteem. For our purposes, self-esteem means a generalized sense of satisfaction with one's self as a total person. Thus, the notion of loss of self-esteem implies a situation akin to an inferiority complex. Inadequacy, on the other hand, refers to negative feelings about one's abilities in the performance of *specific* statuses or roles. The use of this distinction here is not purely arbitrary nor self-serving. For example, it constitutes the crux of a very important debate among Mexican psychologists concerning the basic nature of the Mexican personality (see Ramos, 1962, and Uranga, 1951). In addition, it is a useful distinction to keep in mind here because it is based on some very crucial assumptions about the system or hierarchy of values. As conceived of by Mexican psychologists, the sense of inferiority (i.e., loss of self-esteem) presumes the undermining of a person's sense or hierarchy of values: for example, the notions of what qualities constitute a proper person, in the traditional sense, and one's failure to measure up to those qualities. Consequently, a new or more compatible hierarchy of values may develop to mask one's failure as a person. Inadequacy, on the other hand, does not presume such an undermining or abandonment of the traditional or acceptable structure of values, and more importantly, because the value system is left essentially intact, feelings of inadequacy do not lead to the masking or pretense of being a different sort of person—*el disimulo,* as it is more commonly referred to in Spanish.

The important implication of this distinction between loss of self-esteem and feelings of inadequacy is as follows: If failure is experienced in the performance of a fundamentally important status (as defined by the hierarchy of values), then a loss of self-esteem is a likely consequence. If, on the other hand, failure is experienced in a status of less value, then a sense of inadequacy may result, but no loss of self-esteem would necessarily follow.

We can now posit the following: Among Mexican-Americans, work activity may occupy any one or more of four possible positions on a fourfold table of personal or positional social status vs. high or low level of self-investment. Graphically, the four possible alternatives can be illustrated as in Figure 3.1.

FIGURE 3.1

The Interaction of Self-Esteem, Social Status, and Work Activity among Mexican-Americans: A Theoretical Portrayal

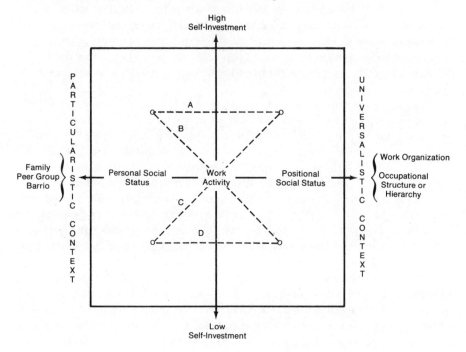

Assuming that the most important particularistic aspect of work activity among Mexican-Americans is the self-fulfillment or realization of a person's own social status within primary groups such as the family, such a personal social status and its concomitant activity may be a matter of either high or low self-investment for that person. His particular work activity, however, also earns the hypothetical Mexican-American a positional social status by virtue of where it fits within an occupational status or job domain. Likewise, this positional social status may be an object of either high or low self-investment.

In Figure 3.1 we have designated the various combinations of self-investment and social status as follows: A, high self-investment in both personal social status and positional social status; B, high self-investment in personal social status and low self-investment in positional social status; C, high self-investment in positional social status and low self-investment in personal social status; and D, low self-investment in both positional social status and personal social status.

Which of these four alternatives, generally speaking, will prevail will depend on what Faunce (n.d.) has called the process of selective self-investment. He describes this process as the one that articulates status assignment and self-esteem maintenance. The process is defined as one through which activities (or attributes) come to have more or less effect upon self-esteem. Furthermore, according to Faunce, the specific results of this process (e.g., A, B, and so on) are highly influenced by the degree to which the status hierarchies or structures which subsume the important categorical or substantive statuses are bounded and consensually validated. In his formulation, "clearly bounded and consensually validated status hierarchies are likely to have a wider range of effects than ones which do not have these characteristics" (pp. 20–21).

Applying Faunce's ideas to work activity among Mexican-Americans, which of the four alternatives illustrated in Figure 3.1 would be most likely to prevail? It is our contention that among adult Mexican-Americans of all classes, the more probable alternatives will be either A or B. Our reasoning is based, first, on the proposition that the assumed core value of familism and its concomitant sense of altruism among Mexican-Americans would in any case (or any type of work activity) lead to a high level of self-investment, as this activity contributes to the maintenance and modification of the household environment and constitutes the fulfillment of their role within it. Second, the family household can be said to constitute one of the most clearly bounded and (ideally) consensually validated status hierarchies or structures and, consequently (following Faunce), it is more important as a basis for self-evaluation.

It remains to be determined, however, which of these alternatives, A or B, will prevail in the case of any given Mexican-American and his work activity. In this kind of analysis, the element of intraethnic stratification (class) would seem to play a significant role. We hypothesize that in the case of middle- and upper-class Mexican-Americans, alternative *A* would be the most likely result; while alternative *B* would be most likely in the case of lower-class or blue-collar Mexican-Americans.

We postulate, further, that in the case of a middle-class or white-collar Mexican-American worker (one presumably with profile *A*), the degree to which he may experience or suffer from a sense of inadequacy vis-à-vis his "job" (i.e., positional social status) will depend on whether the work organization itself represents a clearly bounded status hierarchy (say, a bank teller in a banking institution), and whether his own positive estimate of his position or value within this institution is consensually validated in terms of that institution's most important symbols (e.g., salary, private office). Following Faunce's ideas, if both of these conditions obtain, then we would *not* expect to find a sense of inadequacy in this Mexican-American. If, however, his own estimate of his value or worth in this positional social status is not consensually validated, it would be reasonable to expect that he would experience a sense of inadequacy, *but not necessarily* a loss of self-esteem or a sense of alienation from his work activity. His self-esteem would be maintained because of the support such activity receives from his personal social status within the particularistic context of the family, and the values it supports. To some extent, this proposition is validated by the findings of Zurcher, Meadow, and Zurcher (1965), although they indicate that high self-investment on the job (positional social status) may be rare or not present.

In the case of the blue-collar, lower-class Mexican-American (or profile *B*), self-investment in the job qua job is, in our hypothesis, low to begin with. Consequently, whether the job is to be found in a clearly bounded organization (e.g., "janitor" at the bank) or not (e.g., a migrant farm worker), and, furthermore, whether or not a high estimate of one's abilities or performance is consensually validated, are matters of indifference to the maintenance of one's sense of adequacy or self-esteem.[11]

It is important to emphasize that in the case of either white-collar "inadequacy" or blue-collar "indifference," we need not expect to find a loss of self-esteem and alienation from work, nor, as a consequence, compensatory behavior in other nonwork activities. Given the assumed high level of self-investment in the personal social-status dimension of work activity, seeking other, nonwork, achievement-oriented activities through which to regain or maintain a positive self-image would not be necessary. On the contrary, if we may paraphrase Faunce the nonwork activities of Mexican-Americans may be characterized as involving *privatization,* that is, activities which tend to be centered primarily in the immediate family. To the extent that extrafamilial social relationships exist, they appear to occur in contexts in which all kinds of status differences and status seeking are minimized. The *palomilla* or male peer group (Spielberg, 1975; Rubel, 1965) is an example of a social group with minimal differences in status and status seeking.

So far we have looked only at work as activity and occupation in terms of the fourfold table of Figure 3.1. The dichotomy involved in this table also has relevance for other aspects of the self-identity of Mexican-Americans (vis-à-vis core values) in other, less clearly bounded status hierarchies, such as interethnic comparisons and invidious class comparisons or distinctions within the Mexican-American community. What we are asking here, first, is what the self-esteem consequences of such loosely bounded distinctions as Anglo vs. Mexican or upper-class Mexican vs. lower-class Mexican are. For the sake of brevity, we hypothesize the following: In invidious interethnic distinctions between Anglo and Mexican, being "Mexican" (as a component of social role or identity) occupies a relatively low level of self-investment as a personal social status, for example within the contexts of the family, the *palomilla*, or the *barrio*. On the other hand, a high level of self-investment (ethnic pride, if you will) is hypothesized with respect to the positional social status, in the context of colonial (or castelike) relations and structures of the larger society, that is, vis-à-vis dominant Anglos. Graphically, this hypothesis can be portrayed as in Figure 3.2. This hypothesized low level of self-

FIGURE 3.2
The Relationship between Personal and Positional Social Status and Self-Esteem among Mexican-Americans

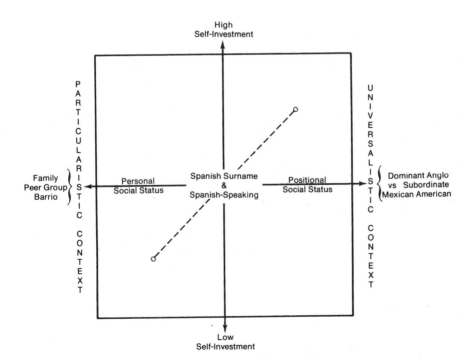

investment in ethnicity, within the contexts common to Mexican-American ethnic community life, is to some extent verified by the findings of Gecas (1973) and Farris and Brymer (1970). In both studies, ethnicity (Mexican) was very infrequently invoked as a dimension or element in self-identity.

As we have tried to show, however, when asked to contrast themselves to Anglos, Mexican-Americans achieve favorable ethnic self-evaluations by citing their qualities or capacity for hard work, self-reliance, and generosity—all work-related values. In short, Mexican-Americans have a high degree of self-investment in their ethnicity when the latter is defined by these core values or (presumed) work-related qualities, vis-à-vis Anglos. This is a radically different view from the one expressed by many writers, too numerous to cite, that growing up Mexican in an Anglo society almost inevitably leads to a low level of self-esteem or negative self-concept.

In the case of invidious comparisons of one's class position vis-à-vis higher or upper classes, we hypothesize a self-investment–social-status pattern which would look like Figure 3.3. In this case, the personal social status of being poorer, less important, and so on would demonstrate a high level of

FIGURE 3.3
Relationship between Social Class and Self-Esteem among Mexican-Americans

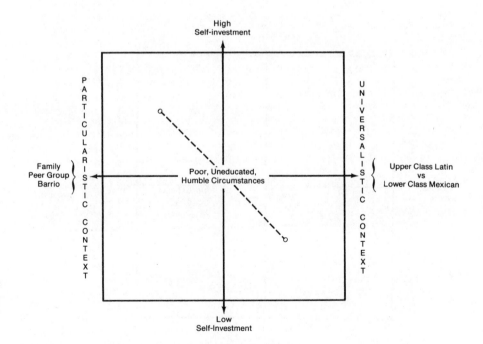

self-investment, while the positional social-status implication of this same condition (lower-class, Mexican) would receive a low level of self-investment. In this case, an invidious comparison of a lower-class Mexican-American with a middle- or upper-class Mexican-American would not necessarily lead to a sense of inadequacy. Given a low level of self-investment, it would be a matter of indifference. On the other hand, being poor but humble in the particularistic or personal social-status context (family, neighborhood, *palomilla*) could be seen as a validation of one's fidelity to one's culture and Mexican community. While the latter type of self-evaluation does not directly invoke work-related values, we submit that notions of "hard-working" and "self-reliant" are subsumed within this self-conception of being a "true" Mexican.

To conclude the discussion on self-esteem, it is not our intention to give the impression that Mexican-Americans do not suffer from loss of self-esteem or alienation from work activities. What we have tried to show is that—because of interrelationships among core values, social structure, and self-identity—the work-related situations or attributes which might cause loss of self-esteem, alienation, or compensatory status seeking in other populations might not have the same results among Mexican-Americans. To put it another way, the loss of self-esteem among Mexican-Americans results more from the dysfunctions which failure in work might occasion within the particular contexts of the ethnic community than from occupational or on-the-job implications of such failure or inadequacy.

SUMMARY

In this chapter we have attempted to delineate and describe what we consider the most important dimensions which, taken together, determine the value and meaning of work in Mexican-American culture. We have considered three dimensions. First, we have attempted to describe the ethos of Mexican-American culture and its development in the context of the northern colonial and republican frontier of Mexico. The principal components of this ethos are an emphasis on physical strength and stamina, self-reliance with generosity, Mexicanness, and familism. It is our contention that these elements have shaped the general value system of Mexican-American culture, and consequently they contribute to the place and meaning of work in the lives of these people.

The second dimension we have dealt with is that of stratification. Here we have tried to demonstrate that Mexican-Americans are to be found enmeshed in two distinct but interrelated systems of stratification; a system of colonial relations which, generally, places Mexican-Americans in a subordinate position to Anglos, and a social-class system which differentiates Mexican-Americans into distinct and hierarchically organized strata. In addition, we have tried to show that the distinct patterns of invidious comparisons which occur in these two systems reflect significant aspects of their value systems. Thus, in contrasting themselves to Anglos in general, Mexican-Americans view themselves as harder workers and better able to endure the demands of physical labor; they would attribute the "success" of the Anglo to his greed and lack of scruples. However, from the lower-class point of view, Mexican-Americans attribute the success and wealth of upper-class Mexican-Americans not to work-related qualities but to the abandonment of basic Mexican values and, perhaps, to their Anglicization. From the upper-class point of view, we postulate, the absence of economic and social well-being among poor Mexican-Americans is attributed not to cultural factors but rather to lower-class behavior.

The third dimension in our schema is that of social roles and self-identity. Here we have tried to show that the principal social roles which determine the self-identity of Mexican-Americans are those of kin status, age, and sex. Further, we postulate that these central elements of the Mexican-American's self-identity are most meaningfully organized in the system of family and familial relations, thereby being reflective of one of the central components of their value system. Work in this context is seen as being inextricably linked with the individual's concern for the maintenance and well-being of the family.

In the final section of this chapter we dealt with the interconnections among work, self-identity, and self-esteem of the prevailing system of values of the Mexican-American. More specifically, we tried to show, by means of schematic drawings, that the work activities of the Mexican-American simultaneously result in two distinct types of social status: a personal social status reflective of the significance and contribution of work activities in the primary-group (or particularistic) context, such as family, neighbors, or peers; and a positional social status reflective of the social worth of activities within the universalistic context of an occupational hierarchy. Each of these statuses, in addition, could be said to be the object of either high or low self-evaluation. It is our contention that Mexican-Americans place high self-evaluation emphasis on work activities with respect to the personal social status it earns them, and either high or low self-evaluation emphasis on the positional social status, depending on the individual's class standing.

Given this framework, we hypothesize that "failure" to achieve or perform in work-related situations or attributes (as defined by the larger, job-oriented society) would not necessarily lead to a sense of inferiority or loss of self-esteem, given the support work activity receives as a measure of the individual's personal social status, especially in the family. In short, the extent to which success or failure in work shapes the individual's estimate of himself depends on Mexican-American values more than the judgment of the impersonal world.

NOTES

1. Such a context, in our opinion, provides more meaningful *in vivo* manifestations of values or value orientations via the use of invidious comparisons with significant, known others.

2. Leon-Portilla's work deals primarily with the Mexican Northwest, and his article includes many good historical references. For the Northeast of the Mexican-American West, consult Alessio Robles (1946), Saldivar (1945), Hill (1926), Roel (1938), or Solis Garza (1971).

3. To avoid confusion, we will refrain from using the term "caste" (with all its other implications) and refer to this as a colonial system.

4. Another important but neglected source of occupational differentiation and subsequent intraethnic stratification resulted from the apparent lack of interest on the part of Anglos in the commercial exploitation of Mexican-Americans. There was and is little of the "company store" phenomenon. Also, each segment of these communities (Mexican and Anglo sections of town) usually had its own complement of stores, service establishments, and merchant organizations to serve its own particular segment. Both types of commercial districts (but especially the Mexican-American) declined severely with the coming of large, externally controlled discount and chain stores. See Rubel (1971: 3–4) and Galarza, Gallegos, & Samora (1969: 34–35).

5. The importance of this factor, especially in the political mobilization of Mexican-American communities and the development of leadership, is very aptly described in Shockley (1974).

6. A myth often heard by the author among Mexican-Americans in South Texas is that the Anglo will ignore or even encourage sexual advances on his wife or daughter by his boss or business partner in order to advance himself. This observation was usually contrasted to the Mexican norm of keeping their wives and daughters at home and completely out of their work or occupational affairs; a norm observed more in the ideal than in practice, by necessity.

7. To some extent, a similar connection appears to have been made among the more radical elements in the Chicano movement. Much of the rhetoric in these groups associates poverty with *chicanismo* and the manifestation of middle- or upper-class attributes with being a *vendido*, or sell-out. In this case, however, it is difficult to determine whether such an association stems from the Chicano experience or world view or from the culture of Third World or civil rights movements. Perhaps all are involved and are mutually reinforcing.

8. Our usage of the concept of social role is essentially identical to Edmundson's (1958: 6) idea of "status term." However, we refrain from using the adjective *status* to avoid confusion with its use as prestige or relative standing. The latter is conceived of here as a quality of all social roles, relative to other roles or labels.

9. For an example of the analytical virtues of this type of construction, see Adams's (1960) analysis of family dyads.

10. For a good discussion of the deficiencies and analytical problems presented by the a priori acceptance of such concepts as *machismo* and authoritarianism see Miguel Montiel's "The Social Science Myth of the Mexican-American Family" (1973)

and Michael V. Miller, "Variations in Mexican-American Family Life" (1975). For a rigorous historical study which casts doubt on the "stressful" or dysfunctional thesis of Mexican-American familism, see R. Griswold del Castillo, "La Familia Chicana" (1975).

11. If we are correct in this assumption, then Mexican-American blue-collar workers are apparently not too different from other blue-collar workers in American society. Wilensky (1966) found the same kind of "indifference" to on-the-job status seeking or evaluation among Detroit auto workers.

REFERENCES

Adams, Richard N.   "An Inquiry into the Nature of Family." In Gertrude E. Dole & Robert L. Carneiro (eds.), *Essays on the Science of Culture: In Honor of Leslie A. White.* New York: Crowell Co., 1960.

Alessio Robles, Vito.   *Coahuila y Texas Desde La Consumacion de la Independcia hasta El Tratado de Paz de Guadalupe Hidalgo.* 2 vols. Mexico City: Talleres Graficos de La Nacion, 1946.

Alvardo, Roger, et al.   *La Raza.* New York: Pathfinder Press, 1970.

Barrett, Donald N.   "Demographic Characteristics." In Julian Samora (ed.), *La Raza: Forgotten American.* Nortre Dame, Ind.; University of Notre Dame Press, 1966.

Bustamente F., Jorge A.   "Through the Eyes of a Wetback—A Personal Experience." In Julian Samora (ed.), *Los Mojados: The Wetback Story.* Notre Dame, Ind.: University of Notre Dame Press, 1971.

Cabeza de Baca, Fabiola.   *We Fed Them Cactus.* Albuquerque: University of New Mexico Press, 1954.

Carter, Thomas P.   "Negative Self-Concepts of Mexican American Students." *School and Society* 96 (March 1968): 217–219.

Dworkin, Anthony G.   "Stereotypes and Self Images Held by Native-Born and Foreign-Born Mexican-Americans." *Sociology and Social Research* 49 (January 1965): 214–224.

Edmundson, Monroe S.   *Status Terminology and the Social Structure of North American Indians.* Seattle: University of Washington Press, 1958.

Farris, Buford, & Richard A. Brymer.   "Differential Socialization of Latin and Anglo-American Youth: An Exploratory Study of the Self Concept." In John H. Burma (ed.), *Mexican Americans in the United States: A Reader.* Cambridge, Mass.: Schenkman Publishing Co., 1970.

Faunce, William A.   *Work, Status and Self Esteem.* East Lansing: Michigan State University, Department of Sociology, n.d.

Galarza, Ernesto.   *Merchants of Labor: The Mexican Bracero Story.* San Jose, Calif.: Rosicrucian Press, 1964.

Galarza, Ernesto, Herman Gallegos, & Julian Samora.   *Mexican-Americans in the Southwest.* Santa Barbara, Calif.: McNally and Loftin, Publishers, 1969.

Gamio, Manuel.   *Mexican Immigration to the United States.* Chicago: University of Chicago Press, 1970.

Gecas, Viktor. "Self Conceptions of Migrant and Settled Mexican-Americans." *Social Science Quarterly* 54 (December 1973): 577–595.

Genovese, Eugene D. *Roll, Jordan, Roll: The World the Slaves Made.* New York: Pantheon Books (Random House), 1974.

Goldschmidt, Walter. *Man's Way.* New York: Holt, Rinehart, & Winston, 1959.

Gonzalez, Nancie S. L. *The Spanish-Americans of New Mexico: A Heritage of Pride.* Albuquerque: University of New Mexico Press, 1969.

Goodman, Mary Ellen, & Alma Berman. "Child's Eye Views of Life in an Urban Barrio." In Joseph Jorgensen & Marcelo Truzzi (eds.), *Anthropology and American Life.* Englewood Cliffs, N.J.: Prentice-Hall, 1974.

Grebler, Leo, Joan W. Moore, & Ralph C. Guzman. *The Mexican-American People.* New York: Free Press, 1970.

Griswold del Castillo, Richard. "La Familia Chicana: Social Changes in the Chicano Family of Los Angeles, 1850–1880." *Journal of Ethnic Studies* 3 (Spring 1975): 41–58.

Gutierrez, Jose Angel. "Mexicanos Need to Control Their Own Destinies." In Manuel P. Servin (ed.), *An Awakened Minority: The Mexican-Americans,* 2nd ed. Beverly Hills, Calif.: Glencoe Press, 1970.

Hill, Laurence F. *Jose de Escandon and the Founding of Nuevo Santander.* Columbus: Ohio University Press, 1926.

Hsu, Francis L. K. "American Core Value and National Character." In James Spradley & Michael Rynkiewich (eds.), *The Nacirema: Readings on American Cultures.* Boston: Little, Brown & Co., 1975.

Katz, Friedrich. "Labor Conditions on Haciendas in Porfirian Mexico: Some Trends and Tendencies." *Hispanic American Historical Review* 54 (February 1974): 1–47.

Leon-Portilla, Miguel. "The Norteño Variety of Mexican Culture: An Ethnohistorical Approach." In Edward H. Spicer & Raymond H. Thompson (eds.), *Plural Society in the Southwest.* New York: Interbook, 1972.

Liebow, Elliot. *Tally's Corner.* Boston: Little, Brown & Co., 1967.

Lummis, Charles. *Land of Poco Tiempo.* Albuquerque: University of New Mexico Press, 1969.

Lyle, Jerolyn R. "Factors Affecting the Job Status of Workers with Spanish Surnames." *Monthly Labor Review* 96 (April, 1973): 10–16.

Macklin, Barbara June, & N. Ross Crumrine. "Three Northern Mexican Folk Saint Movements." New London: Connecticut College, Department of Anthropology, n.d.

Madsen, William. "The Alcoholic Agringado." *American Anthropologist,* 66 (February 1964): 355–360. (a)

Madsen, William. *The Mexican-Americans of South Texas.* New York: Holt, Rinehart & Winston, 1964. (b)

Marshall, T. H. *Sociology at the Crossroads.* London: Heinemann, 1963.

McWilliams, Carey. *North from Mexico: The Spanish Speaking People of the United States*. New York: J. B. Lippincott Co., 1949.

Miller, Michael V. "Variations in Mexican-American Family Life: A Review Synthesis." Paper presented at the annual meeting of the Rural Sociological Society, San Francisco, August 1975.

Montiel, Miguel. "The Social Science Myth of the Mexican-American Family." In Octavio I. Romano (ed.), *Voices: Readings from El Grito 1967–1973*. Berkeley, Calif.: Quinto Sol Publications, 1973.

Olson, Jon. "Economic and Social Alternatives in a Northern Mexican Community." Unpublished Ph.D. dissertation, Michigan State University, East Lansing, 1972.

Paredes, Américo. "Folk Medicine and the Intercultural Jest." In L. I. Duran and H. R. Bernard (eds.), *Introduction to Chicano Studies*. New York: Macmillan Co., 1973.

Penalosa, Fernando, & Edward C. McDonagh. "Social Mobility in a Mexican-American Community." *Social Forces* 44 (June 1966): 498–505.

Ramos, Samuel. *Profile of Man and Culture in Mexico*. Austin: University of Texas Press, 1962.

Rodman, Hyman. "The Lower-Class Value Stretch." *Social Forces,* 44 (December 1963): 205–215.

Roel, Santiago. *Nuevo Leon: Apuntes Historicos*. 2 vols. Monterrey, Mexico: Talleres Linotipograficos Del Estado, 1938.

Romano, Octavio I. "Donship in a Mexican-American Community in Texas." *American Anthropologist* 62 (August 1960): 966–976.

Romano, Octavio I. "Charismatic Medicine, Folk-healing and Folk-Sainthood." *American Anthropologist* 67 (October 1965): 1151–1173.

Rubel, Arthur J. "The Mexican American Palomilla." *Anthropological Linguistics* 7, part II (April 1965): 92–97.

Rubel, Arthur J. *Across the Tracks*. Austin: University of Texas Press, 1971.

Ryscavage, Paul M., & Earl F. Mellor. "The Economic Situation of Spanish Americans." *Monthly Labor Review* 96 (April 1973): 3–9.

Saldivar, Gabriel. *Historia Compendiada de Tamaulipas*. Mexico City: Editorial Beatriz de Silva, 1945.

Samora, Julian. *Los Mojados: The Wetback Story*. Notre Dame, Ind.: University of Notre Dame Press, 1971.

Sapir, Edward. "Culture, Genuine and Spurious." *American Journal of Sociology* 29 (January 1924): 401–429.

Schunior Ramirez, Emilia. *Ranch Life in Hidalgo County after 1850*. Edinburg, Texas: New Santander Press, 1971.

Service, Elman. *Cultural Evolutionism: Theory in Practice*. New York: Holt, Rinehart and Winston, 1971.

Shockley, John S. *Chicano Revolt in a Texas Town*. Notre Dame, Ind.: University of Notre Dame Press, 1974.

Simmons, Ozzie. "Anglo-Americans and Mexican Americans in South Texas: A Study in Dominant Subordinate Group Relations." Unpublished Ph.D. dissertation, Harvard University, 1952.

Solis Garza, Hernan. *Los Mexicanos del Norte.* Mexico City: Editorial Nuestro Tiempo, 1971.

Spielberg, Joseph. "Humor in Mexican-American Palomilla." *Revista Chicano-Requena* (Indiana University, Bloomington), 2 (1975): 41–50.

Stavenhagen, Rodolfo. "Classes, Colonialism, and Acculturation." *Studies in Comparative International Development.* (Social Science Institute, Washington University, St. Louis, Mo.), 1 (1965): 53–77.

Udy, Stanley H., Jr. *Work in Traditional and Modern Society.* Englewood Cliffs, N.J.: Prentice-Hall, 1970.

Uranga, Emilio. "Notas Para un Estudio del Mexicano." *Cuadernos Americanos,* 57 (May–June 1951): 114–128.

Wilensky, Harold L. "Work as a Social Problem." In Howard S. Becker (ed.), *Social Problems.* New York: John S. Wiley & Sons, 1966.

Zurcher, Louis A., Arnold Meadow, & Susan Lee Zurcher. "Value Orientation, Role Conflict, and Alienation from Work: A Cross-Cultural Study." *American Sociological Review* 30 (August 1965): 539–548.

CHAPTER 4

Concepts of work and situational demands on New York City Puerto Ricans

Elena Padilla

INTRODUCTION

Although work activities must be carried out in all human societies, concepts of work, work preferences, and occupational choices are relative rather than universal. Situational settings determine the status assigned to work and to those who perform it. Innovations and the implementation of new technological applications may affect not only the economic base of a society but also its concepts of work, the value and behaviors attached to it. New ways of doing work are developed, while others are either modified or may become extinct. Thus, work comprises more than utilization and economic aspects. Society provides rationales for making desirable work either available or unavailable to various sectors of its membership. Selected members of a society may be "excused" from work because of their wealth, illness, or disability, or because of their primary status (e.g., housewife, student, or retired). Members of certain segments of society, for whom work is considered normal and who possess the required skills, may find no jobs available, even though they search for them.

Examples of the relationships between work as an economic activity and the social-status system, family, religious beliefs, and moral norms can be identified, from simple, preindustrial to industrial and postindustrial societies. Work, thus, is not simply an economic activity, since it has to do with all aspects of behavior expected of members of society. Not all work, however, is "good" or socially desirable. In Western capitalist society, work has been associated with diverse values (the social good, exploitation, and oppression) and, psychologically, has been considered as a measure of social worth and individual accomplishment. Where capital resources are concentrated in the hands of a relatively small portion of the population and, most often, organized on a corporate rather than an individual basis, work is generally equated with employment and payment or sale of products and services. The life span of corporations is independent from that of their individual owners, managers, officials, and employees. Corporations are large-scale operations, designed to operate at minimum costs and to earn maximum profits, rather than to create meaningful work experiences.

Today, as in preindustrial times, many workers are underemployed, paid relatively low wages, subjected to seasonal layoffs, and required to perform tasks which machines could do more efficiently (National Commission on Technology, Automation and Economic Progress, 1966). When local workers are no longer willing to work for such enterprises, migrant workers are either encouraged to come into the area or are brought in through contracts or other assurances. In addition, there is always some unemployment, under even the best conditions of the market, and a pool exists of individuals who are neither employed nor looking for work—the nonparticipants in the labor force. Workers can be drawn from these two groups if the demand should develop.

The needs and requirements for workers are also affected by modifications of the marketplace induced by international agreements and governmental rules. Some of these external forces are regulation of prices and profits, tax incentives, contracts and subsidies, gifts, and direct governmental investments. Government also has played a major role in modifying manpower utilization through public policies that expedite, restrict, or delay the entry of individuals into and out of the labor force, as well as those that affect their occupational mobility. Such measures as financing of scholarships, stipends and loans, manpower development programs, supplementary assistance payments for underemployed workers, restricted minimum wages, social security payments for older citizens, Neighborhood Youth Corps, and day-care centers for children of working-age mothers are examples of governmental actions which directly or indirectly affect the size and characteristics of the labor force. Although there are no consistent or comprehensive middle- or long-range manpower policies in the United States, the federal government plays a key role in matters affecting education, technology, capital investment, production and productivity rates, wages and profits—all of which affect the conditions of workers and their chances for employment in the public and private sectors.

There are two diametrically opposite beliefs or ideologies regarding work in the United States. These are that (1) there is a job for anyone who wants to work, and (2) social barriers to employment prevent people who want to work from finding work. The first view places the responsibility for not working on the unemployed individual; the second places the responsibility for lack of work opportunities on social inequities. Both views are predicated on assigning an intrinsic value to work and on recognizing its function in social control. Psychological needs for self-development, and the values which mediate between individuals and the social contexts of their lives, are residual elements in both assumptions. The overriding issue is why there are large numbers of people not working and, among them, many who cannot work. Generalizing that those not working are "chiselers" ignores basic facts about the social system and the economy.

How can the plight of workers who react against the alienation and dehumanization of their jobs by retaliating against quality standards in the production of goods and services be explained, or the behavior of working women who cannot make arrangements for care of their children during work hours, and so leave them alone as "latch-key" children? How can the fact that skilled college-trained blacks or Puerto Ricans are turned away from jobs for being "overqualified" or the job struggles of physically disabled individuals whose training, education, and skills have overriden their disabilities be explained? Or the difficulties of any worker whose skills have become obsolete as a result of automated processes? These and related questions concerning the contradictions between society's expectations of its members and the often subtle but effective barriers which deny many of them entrance and mobility in work are crucial but as yet unanswered issues concerning values and policy. While it is true that legislation and court decisions of recent decades have attempted to redress a long history of discrimination by race, nationality, sex, and religion, as well as other forms of group-based discrimination such as against the mentally or physically handicapped, many members of these groups are still excluded from the work force or relegated to menial jobs. One consequence of this practice is that even those who are employed may require supplementary public assistance to maintain minimum living standards. It can be argued that the public welfare system is subsidizing low wages. An economic system that promotes social inequities in work and income distribution denies meaningful and creative human experiences to those discriminated against. This situation can only be reversed by a sociopolitical structure that rewards merit with opportunity. Concepts of work fall within historical and social contexts, and their meaning and place in the scale of values of a society change with the context of the life experience of individual members. In this chapter we examine the main sociocultural factors affecting the concepts of work among Puerto Ricans in the New York City experience, in historical perspective and in the continuum of New York–Puerto Rico relationships.

CULTURAL AND HISTORICAL ANTECEDENTS OF
CONCEPTS OF WORK AMONG PUERTO RICANS

For more than 400 years Puerto Rico was an agricultural society organized into a rigid class system of landholders, peasants, and slaves. At first, the Spanish conquerors reduced the native Indians to slavery, and later in the early 16th century slaves from Africa were introduced as property, like the land itself. Slavery, although on a smaller scale than on other Caribbean Islands, was an important social institution for three centuries. It left its mark on social institutions, social values, patterns of social and race relations, and the concepts of work in Puerto Rican society (Steward et al., 1956). The condition of slavery in Puerto Rico, however, was neither permanent nor hereditary. Slaves could achieve the status of free men and women through purchase or payment, escape, Catholic baptism, or being freed by their masters. Slavery was finally abolished by law in 1873.

The overriding inequities of the social system of the island were a product of Spanish colonial exploitation. Access to wealth was possible through the profitable exploitation of land grants from the Spanish royal government. Slaves, sailors, and soldiers often ran away and established themselves on small plots of land, engaged in contraband trade, or worked as artisans and merchants in the rising towns and cities of the island (Steward et al., 1956). In these ways a frontier developed where direct control by the colonial government could be avoided and where values of individualism and reliance on kinship and ritual kinship (such as *compadre* relations, which extended family obligations and reciprocal assistance) developed and continue to this day. In this context racial concepts became associated with social position, prestige, and rank.

After American forces invaded the island in 1898, the conditions of life of the population did not change very much. One of the principal trends which developed after the American occupation was unionization and politicalization of the labor movement. Sugar cane production was intensified, becoming the only crop grown in large landholdings, which employed seasonal, unskilled workers. Raw sugar cane was processed and exported to the United States for refinement. The control of the most productive and profitable sugar cane land and manufacturing was in the hands of American corporations. Agricultural production, such as of tobacco, coffee, and food crops, was usually undertaken by farmers who hired seasonal laborers or worked the land with their families. Most agrarian workers were squatters or sharecroppers. Major seaports, which were centers of commerce and transportation and had developed on the island since early Spanish colonialization, became centers for the distribution and merchandising of American imports and for increasingly large numbers of rural migrants, many of whom eventually moved into the San Juan slums. As the saying goes "the island emptied itself in San Juan." Urbanization is thus not a recent phenomenon in Puerto Rican society. Economic reforms started during World War II and gained momentum in the postwar period, during which large-scale emigration to the United States took place.

Situational Contexts of Work

CULTURAL NORMS RELATING TO WORK. Traditionally, in rurally oriented Puerto Rican society, work has been considered characteristic of a good person. Work is related to family life and to the status of individuals in the household and in the community. Beginning in childhood, individuals are taught about work roles. The concept of work cuts across two dimensions: sex, and kind of skills and activity. Men's work is different from women's. Men work outside or "downstairs" (*abajo*); women work inside the house or "upstairs" (*arriba*) (Buitrago-Ortiz, 1974). Ideally, men are expected to support their families and to own a house and some land. Women are expected to work in the household, keeping it clean, cooking, and coordinating and supervising the work of their children. The differences in the responsibilities between men and women are taught from childhood by example, performance, and didactic explanations which direct children to behaviors which will be characteristic of adult roles and which separate their roles by sex. Boys are expected to help with heavy tasks, to mind animals, and to help their fathers. Girls are expected to be upstairs helping their mothers in household chores. When necessity forces women to seek employment, the preference is for "cottage" industries in which the work is done at home. If they must they will work outside in the fields or in town. Still their work is expected to be womanly.

Laziness is disapproved for both men and women. A lazy person is considered dirty and prone to vice. Those who are single and earn money are expected to contribute to the support of their families, even if they no longer live in their parental homes. Older brothers and sisters are also expected to help younger siblings to pursue their education or find employment. A person who works and contributes financially to the family receives extra privileges such as special food, attention to clothing, and, perhaps, a single room or a bed that does not have to be shared. A person who does not work can maintain a status of respect and acceptance for only a short time. Only illness or disability can protect a nonworking person from being assigned the status of lazy (*vago*).

Work is also the main avenue for establishing credit for purchasing food, clothing, furniture, and other necessities. Installment buying is preferred, since available cash may be needed for emergencies. Work is considered a necessity and an attribute of being a good, honest, and decent person, contrary to Gillin's (1955) observation of it as a "necessary evil."

From the standpoint of skills and activity, work falls in two categories:

work of the mind (*trabajo de la mente*) and brute work (*trabajo bruto*) (Buitrago-Ortiz, 1974). Work of the mind, such as the professions or other white-collar occupations, can be done by men or women, provided they are educated. Brute work, which includes heavy physical labor, factory or farm work, kitchen and maintenance jobs requires little or no education and also can be done by men or women. It is more characteristic of men than women, however. Although work of the mind is not only cleaner and better paying than brute work, it is believed that too much of it can "tire the brains and make people mentally ill." Brute work, on the other hand, can also affect health and may result in crippling accidents which may make a person *inútil*, literally useless. Individuals who are accustomed to doing work of the mind may also become *inútil* if they become unemployed and cannot find work for which they have acquired skills. Thus, illness may become a face-saving outlet for the frustrations of unemployment and the difficulties in finding work. This illness is neither malingering nor avoidance of work but a result of inability to obtain it.

Good work can be work of the mind or brute work and involves more than tasks and pay. It is something one enjoys doing in a situation one likes and in which one is liked.

WORK AND LIFE SITUATIONS IN NEW YORK.   The norms about work which were derived from the rural, agrarian background of Puerto Ricans have been modified or abandoned in the urban context. For instance, in New York family obligations may be recognized and used as a yardstick for judging behavior, but alternative norms have emerged to contravene the disadvantages entailed by too many family obligations. Such new norms excuse individuals responsible for supporting their households from the additional responsibility of contributing to the support of their parents, siblings, and other relatives. Traditional norms are often inconsistent with the social and economic requirements of modern urban life, in which individual work, earnings, and personal expenditures substitute for cooperative work, contributory joint earnings, and family-centered expenditures and services. Family obligations continue to be emotionally strong, particularly within the nuclear family, even after children reach adulthood and establish their households (Padilla, 1958; Raneri, 1958).

Intrafamilial obligations are also important components of emigration and job hunting in the United States. Networks of emigration assistance and support have been established through the years among Puerto Ricans, and they are reinforced by frequent visiting between New York and Puerto Rico. Looking for work continues to be linked to family and friends.

The traditional division of labor between men and women has changed among Puerto Ricans in New York; necessity has forced many women in New York to work outside the home. This trend began during the pre–World War

II migration to New York, when women rather than men had the skills required for work in the garment industry, which was one of the main sources of work for Puerto Ricans. Many women have thus had to become breadwinners and heads of households, with sole responsibility for the support, guidance, and education of their children. These women, who are considered *struggling women,* may assume the role of both father and mother in their families. In effect, these are complete families, even if the father is not in residence and assumes no responsibility for the family. The presence and support of the family by the husband-father, however, continues to be the preferred mode for family life. Other household-familial arrangements have developed in response to conditions of life, such as the visiting husband, whose role includes being a surrogate father for children of the household and a mate and companion to their mother. These latter kinds of arrangements, which have long existed in urban societies, are becoming more widely accepted because of the "sexual revolution." The changing image of women entering into these relationships is enabling them to develop their capacities more fully.

Although earning a living through illegal activities is not a desirable condition, it may become acceptable if there is no other way of supporting one's family. Gambling on the numbers is regarded as a method of raising cash for the down payment on furniture or a house, for an airplane fare, or for sending a child to high school or college. In the same vein, welfare assistance may be a necessity, but it is often embarrassing and kept secret from friends and family. Frequently welfare payments are described as government pensions or as support for only the children.

Education and learning are seen as avenues for social mobility and achieving more desirable work, namely that "of the mind." Blocked opportunities frustrate these avenues. Hard work does not always reward an individual, and luck and destiny may be used to explain past events and their relation to the future.

PUERTO RICAN MIGRATION TO NEW YORK CITY

The migration of Puerto Ricans to the United States has been mainly to New York City. This migration is closely related to the conditions of the labor force in Puerto Rico, the demands for workers in the United States, and the concepts of work and work aspirations held by Puerto Ricans. Although this migration has been a continuing phenomenon, the flow may be subdivided into four stages, to facilitate analysis: (1) pre–World War I to the Great Depression, (2) World War II and the early postwar years; (3) the 1960s: the Civil Rights movement and the War on Poverty, and (4) the 1970s. The continuity of migration, the residential accommodations in the United

States, and the dependency of Puerto Rico itself on migration all have contributed to the unique character of Puerto Rican life in the United States.

The migration has been essentially one of youthful unemployed persons looking for work. In explaining the role played by Puerto Rico itself in relation to migration, Barton (n.d.) wrote: "In the labor market, it has been the function of Puerto Rico to contain people at very low or zero wages until an effective demand for workers arises either at home or abroad." The United States, in turn, has offered to Puerto Ricans a variety of occupations that are undesirable to white workers in terms of tasks, wages, or uncertainty of employment. The job market for Puerto Ricans has been generally in labor-intensive occupations requiring limited skills.

Pre–World War I to Great Depression

Migration to the United States started before the turn of the century, when a number of Puerto Ricans in political exile were living in New York. Several relatively small contract-labor migrations, primarily to Arizona, Florida, and Hawaii, occurred àfter the American military occupation of Puerto Rico.

The migration from Puerto Rico to New York between World War I and World War II was mainly of women who searched for work in the garment industry. (In Puerto Rico, the needle trades were done on a piecework basis at home rather than in factories, and they had been a major source of employment for women and children.) Immigrant men tended to work in the factories or in the merchant marine. A few businessmen and professionals settled in Midwestern cities such as Chicago, as well as in New York.

World War II and Postwar Migrations

After World War II, following demobilization and the reduction of civilian workers in the military, male migration predominated over female. The demand for workers resulting from postwar economic developments and readjustments encouraged migration of contract and independent labor. The movement of Puerto Ricans throughout the United States was primarily to urban areas where, because of their poverty, they settled in older sections of the cities where dilapidated housing at affordable rents was available.

In 1950, nearly two thirds of all employed Puerto Ricans in New York City were in blue-collar occupations, one fifth were service workers, and one sixth were white-collar workers. At that time, the proportion of nonwhites in white-collar work was 3% higher than that of Puerto Ricans, and there were proportionately three times as many whites as Puerto Ricans in such occupations. Puerto Ricans were overrepresented in the blue-collar category and nonwhites in the service categories (Bienstock, n.d.). Differences between Puerto Ricans born in Puerto Rico and those born in New York suggested some occupational mobility for the second generation, particularly toward the clerical and sales jobs. However, these new job categories and differences in income are not sufficient indicators of mobility, since the size of the adult, second-generation working population was very small (Bienstock, n.d.; U.S. Department of Labor, n.d.).

As the economy of the United States in the postwar years shifted toward automated production of goods and services, postindustrial activities, and the exodus of city residents to the suburbs, Puerto Ricans, like blacks, found themselves increasingly isolated from the expanded sources of work and from housing accessible to places of work. Housing restrictions in the suburbs and the lack of cheap public mass transportation contributed further to their isolation. The demands for skills that they did not have and could not obtain further limited their opportunities.

Unanticipated circumstances on the island itself also contributed to the movement of large numbers of Puerto Ricans to the United States. Among these were local industrial and economic development programs which influenced the labor pool and the aspirations for mobility on the island. It has been observed that the industrialization program had no effect on the unemployment rate of Puerto Rico, although it expanded the labor force. According to an analysis published in 1972 by the Puerto Rican Resources Center for the Federal Office of Civil Rights:

> . . . There is evidence that migration of Puerto Ricans to the United States has been due to a structural crisis in the Island's economy. . . . The lack of integrated planning consequently led to a reliance on the export of Puerto Ricans as the only way of achieving economic growth. . . . We repeat that the inability of Puerto Rico's development program to reduce unemployment is at the very basis of the demographic movement of Puerto Ricans to the United States. . . . The rate of unemployment has remained constant (in the neighborhood of 12%) since 1947 . . . in spite of the fact that the population increase has been neutralized by the mass exodus of workers to labor markets in the United States. (pp. 15–16)

Employment of migrants in the United States spread through the major cities of the East and Midwest, as well as into farm areas. Seasonal farm work for individuals who remained in the States between April and October and returned to Puerto Rico at the beginning of the frost became a new pattern of employment. After the end of World War II, private labor agents and contractors searched for workers on the island for employment in factories, mines, steel mills, farms, and household service. These activities led to abuses of workers under contract, and the government of Puerto Rico adopted legislation designed to protect Puerto Ricans in the United States.

Migration of Puerto Ricans to farms in the States has continued since the end of World War II. Still working and living under deplorable conditions, these workers have been victims of physical abuse, peonage, and other violations of their individual liberties and rights. Since the protection offered to them is guaranteed only under the laws of Puerto Rico, and U. S. state and federal officials have generally been indifferent to their plight, their situation has not appreciably improved. "Escape," as breaking away from their condition is described, is perhaps the only viable alternative for these farm workers. Many do not return to Puerto Rico but move into nearby cities where other Puerto Ricans live. In cities where few or no Puerto Ricans reside or no institutional resources have been developed by the Puerto Rican community, farm workers encounter severe difficulties, since their chances for finding work and adapting to the community are often contingent upon the existence of supportive social and emotional support of the kind provided by local Puerto Rican groups and organizations. The process of settling down by migrants is thus facilitated where Puerto Rican communities are present.

The 1960s: The Civil Rights Movement and the War on Poverty

By 1960, migrants were no longer coming only from urban centers in the island, and increasingly larger numbers were rural and small-town people. In a rural community in the interior of Puerto Rico studied by Buitrago-Ortiz in 1962–63, at least two persons per household were reported to have migrated to the United States either permanently or temporarily for the agricultural harvest. In that rural area, emigration had clearly become an absolute economic necessity and was virtually the only way young men could earn enough to get married and to establish a family (Buitrago-Ortiz, 1974). Migration during this period had already extended throughout all sectors of Puerto Rican society.

Migration of Puerto Ricans to New York City in 1960 had increased by 367,000, or 149.2%, over 1950. The median age of Puerto Ricans in New York was 21.9 years; they were the youngest population living in the city. Almost one third of the reported Puerto Ricans in the city were born in the United States (Bienstock, n.d.). The majority of Puerto Rican migrants (53%) who came to the United States between 1957 and 1961 were young and had had no previous work experience; 65% were between 15 and 34 years old, and an additional 20% were children under 15 (Gray & Gonzalez, 1970). The majority of Puerto Ricans held blue-collar jobs, but the job market had increased demands for white-collar workers. At that time, 65% of employed Puerto Ricans were in blue-collar occupations, 16% in services, and 19% in white-collar positions. Among employed whites, the situation was reversed: 58% were in white-collar occupations, 32% in blue-collar jobs, and 10% in service work. Additionally, Puerto Ricans had the highest unemployment rate in the city, 9.9%, compared to 6.9% among blacks and 4.3% among whites. Over one third of Puerto Rican families had annual incomes of less than $3,000.

The median education of Puerto Rican adults was 7.6 years; 13% had high school diplomas, and less than 1% had completed college (U.S. Department of Labor, 1968), in contrast, 8.2% of whites and 4.1% of blacks had completed college. The avenues for both education and employment in white-collar occupations were virtually closed to Puerto Ricans, and even those who were well educated had difficulty entering into white-collar employment (U.S. Commission on Civil Rights, 1972a). The Civil Rights movement, the antipoverty effort, and other domestic programs stimulated the Puerto Rican community into neighborhood and communitywide political action. Part of the struggle became translated into affirming the integrity of the Puerto Rican community, leading to an enriched sense of national identity. This movement encompassed all Puerto Ricans and led to the development of creative solutions to the problems of cultural inconsistencies and pressures for conformity from the dominant American society. These developments were reinforced by the interaction between Puerto Ricans in the United States and those in Puerto Rico, by the influence of the Puerto Rican media, and by direct appeals to Puerto Ricans to participate in the political process.

By the end of the 1960s, programs in economic development, formal education, employment, housing, health, and access to government were still unavailable to most Puerto Ricans. The 1964 civil rights legislation and subsequent affirmative action programs, manpower traning, education and community development, Model Cities efforts, and other Great Society programs did not have a visible effect on the lives of Puerto Ricans. By this time official statistics subsumed Puerto Ricans under other populations, such as white, nonwhite, Hispanic, Latin, persons of Spanish surname, or Spanish-speaking persons, while the category Puerto Rican was ignored.

Submerging the Puerto Rican community within larger categories tends to make their needs and aspirations invisible, and their priorities become unidentifiable in the political arena. Statistics which merge Puerto Ricans with other categories of the population conceal the accomplishments and rights of the Puerto Rican community, particularly when Puerto Ricans comprise the majority among groups of so-called Hispanics, persons of Spanish surname, or Latins. Since statistical categories and groupings are technically selected on the basis of their usefulness in dealing with large numbers of units or events, they are merely convenient ways of organizing and analyzing numerical data. Rarely do statistical categories reflect sociopolitical groups, communities, or organized constituencies. Using such categories to denote communities or sociocultural groups is misleading, illogical, and serves the purpose of discrimination by concealment. The use of any other term than Puerto Rican for Puerto Ricans blurs the political identity of that community and its ability to make legitimate claims within the political system.

The Seventies

According to recent estimates, 1 million Puerto Ricans live in New York City, nearly 200,000 more than the 1970 census, which reported 811,843. Between 1960 and 1970, the number of Puerto Ricans increased in each borough of the city except in Manhattan, where there was a decline in the overall population. The largest Puerto Rican neighborhoods were in the Bronx, Brooklyn, and Manhattan, in rank order of size (Bienstock, n.d.). In 1970, when 40% of all New York City residents lived in the 26 poverty areas of the city, 82% of all the Puerto Ricans in New York City lived in those areas. Puerto Ricans congregated in the poverty areas in all the boroughs in the city (U.S. Commission on Civil Rights, 1972a). The median age of the Puerto Rican population was 19.

Urban renewal of decayed neighborhoods and high rentals continue to push Puerto Ricans into ghettoized slum neighborhoods, where relatively cheap and dilapidated housing is still available. Public housing in New York imposes requirements of income and number of persons per room that Puerto Ricans with large families can seldom meet (Burstein, 1973).

In 1969 Puerto Ricans living in New York City had a median family income of $5,575, 43% lower than the $9,682 median family income for the entire city. Nearly 30% of Puerto Rican families had annual incomes of less than $3,000. An estimated 30% of all Puerto Rican families received some type of public assistance in 1969 for aid to the blind, the aged, dependent children, home relief, and supplementary allotments to low-paid wage earners. Nearly one third of the heads of Puerto Rican households were unemployed. Only 4.5% of all Puerto Rican families in New York earned $15,000 or more that year; only 15% of adults had a high school diploma, and 1.5% had completed college.

Although the school system of New York City is philosophically oriented toward the assimilation of newcomers, it has not acted forcefully to correct the problems of low student achievement, high attrition rates, and limited opportunities for high school education which confront Puerto Ricans to a greater extent than other city residents (U.S. Commission on Civil Rights, 1972b). These problems have been exacerbated by failure to recruit teachers who are bilingual and familiar with the cultural characteristics of the Puerto Rican children, and by attempts to discourage children from developing a sense of their cultural heritage and language. Furthermore, the adversary position of the teachers' union and community school boards over matters of decentralization, educational content, and personnel selection has created sharp conflicts between the Puerto Rican communities and the schools.

Puerto Rican parents and educators throughout the city have supported bilingual and bicultural education in the schools. However, these programs have been slow to develop and difficult to implement because of the rigidity of the educational bureaucracy and its failure to eliminate outmoded educational philosophies.

In 1969, when over 260,000 Puerto Rican children were attending New York City public schools, less than 1% of over 59,000 teachers in the public school system were Puerto Rican. English as a second language was taught by less than 200 teachers. Bilingual school and community relations programs were manned by a staff of only 300. The largest number of non–English-speaking children in the state of New York were Puerto Ricans (New York State Board of Regents, 1972). Of these children, 25,000 were receiving instruction in English as a second language, and less than 6,000 were receiving bilingual-bicultural instruction. Under this system, Puerto Rican children experience major difficulties in learning and have little reason to appreciate the educational experience.

The public educational system, furthermore, has failed to keep children from dropping out of school before their education is completed. Only about 30% of Puerto Rican children in the ninth grade will complete high school, and few pursue a college education. Universities and colleges in the city, as well as state university facilities, while beneficiaries of public funds, have been generally indifferent to the educational needs of the Puerto Rican community. The colleges of the City University have exhibited a limited but somewhat more responsive approach. Puerto Rican students primarily attend community colleges in the City University system. Cuadrado and Hernandez (1972) have called attention to the disparity between the claims by the City University concerning its responsiveness to the Puerto Rican community and the reality of the situation. Of more than 200,000 students registered in the 19 colleges operated by the City University in 1971, slightly more than 10,000 students of "Spanish surnames" were registered, and most were attending community colleges. Since the City University does not report Puerto Ricans, the figure is an inflated estimate of the number of Puerto Rican students. According to Cuadrado and Hernandez, most Puerto Rican students are beset by economic, health, and social problems. Lack of adequate housing, increased financial obligations to their families, and lack of adequate counseling often forces them to obtain full-time employment which eventually compels them to leave school. The City University has discouraged orientation programs which might enable these students to cope with their difficulties. Assigning students to colleges by a lottery system, rather than providing a regional match between colleges and students by residence, creates inequities, particularly for Puerto Rican students who must travel long distances to attend college in areas of the city where part-time jobs are inaccessible and housing facilities are not available.

Programs of Puerto Rican studies, following the model of black studies programs, have provided a niche for Puerto Rican students, faculty, and administrators in the colleges, while the liberal arts, sciences, and professional schools continue to have relatively few Puerto Rican students. Few Puerto Ricans have been recruited to faculty and administrative positions by the City University. In 1971, there were 281 Puerto Ricans in the noninstructional staff of CUNY, most of them being employed as maintenance workers. Only 4 of the 936 full professors on the instructional staff were Puerto Ricans. The state university system and private institutions, however, have even fewer Puerto Ricans among their faculties, administrations, and student bodies. The precarious financial situation of New York City has also affected the educational opportunities of Puerto Ricans and other minority groups. Decisions to end the open-admissions policy and charge tuition at the City University will inevitably deter aspiring students from pursuing higher education (Peterson, 1975: 5).

PUERTO RICANS AND THE ECOLOGY OF WORK IN NEW YORK CITY

Between 1960 and 1970, the population of New York City increased slightly, by 113,000 or 1.5%, reversing the trend toward an overall drop in population which had started after World War II. This increase originated mainly from the black and Puerto Rican communities. In that decade, the number of adults between 25 and 64 years old declined by 318,000; the increases in population were noted in the 14 years old and under (14,000), in the 15 to 24 years old (283,000), and in the 65 years old and older (134,000) categories. Puerto Ricans comprised 8% of the population of the city in 1960 and 13% in 1970; between 1960 and 1970, the Puerto Rican population increased by 74%. As noted before, increasing numbers of Puerto Ricans continue to come to the United States from rural areas, with no previous employment experience or only agricultural work experience. Employment options in New York for people with this type of background are limited, and wages are low. Among the major employers of Puerto Ricans are hotels and restaurants, laundries, construction companies, bakeries, confectioneries, warehouses, retail stores, canning plants, and maritime services, and manufacturers of electronic components, television sets, luggage, paperboard boxes, paints and varnishes, photographic supplies, jewelry, and toys (U.S. Department of Labor, 1971a: 15–21). According to Gray & Gonzalez (1970), "Even with growing union interest in job training and upgrading, Puerto Ricans are mainly employed at the bottom of the occupational ladder," and are "grossly under-represented relative to other ethnic groups in the policy making levels of unions." From a Puerto Rican perspective, moving into New York City in search of employment is, nonetheless, a rather uncomplicated process. With family and friends on both sides, the ease of transportation and the frequent interaction between New York and Puerto Rico minimize the unfamiliar and the unexpected. The Puerto Rican economy, furthermore, depends on emigration to reduce unemployment and alleviate social problems on the island.

A recent analysis of the occupational distribution of Puerto Ricans in New York City in 1970 (Gray, 1975) revealed that more than half of the employed Puerto Ricans worked in semiskilled and unskilled operative and service jobs (see Table 4.1). Puerto Ricans occupied the lowest niche in the earnings scale of every major occupational group, and less than 1% of employed persons in the prestigious and financially rewarding occupations of medicine, law, education, and engineering. One fourth of employed Puerto Rican men worked as operatives, and they were also overrepresented in low-skilled, food-associated work; for example, they accounted for one fifth of the city's male dishwashers and dining room attendants (Gray, 1975: 12–13).

Although their educational level is below that of the general population,

TABLE 4.1
Occupational Distribution of Puerto Ricans in New York City, 1970

	Both Sexes	Men	Women
White-collar workers,			
total	57.9	27.2	46.5
Professional and technical	4.8	4.0	6.5
Managers, officials, and proprietors	3.6	4.5	1.7
Clerical workers	20.2	13.7	34.0
Sales workers	4.8	5.0	4.3
Blue-collar workers,			
total	48.1	51.6	40.6
Craftsworkers and supervisors	11.3	15.5	2.4
All others[1]	36.8	36.1	38.2
Service workers, total	18.5	21.2	12.9
Private household workers	.3	.1	.8
Other service workers	18.2	21.1	12.1

Note: Data are for New York area including New York City, Nassau-Suffolk, Westchester and Rockland Counties; however, 96% of the Puerto Ricans in these areas lived in the city.

1. Includes operatives, laborers, and farm workers. Farm managers and laborers constituted less than 1% of the total.

Source: Adapted from Lois Gray, "The Jobs Puerto Ricans Hold in New York City," *Monthly Labor Review* 98 (October 1975): 13.

discrimination no doubt plays a role in their lower earnings and higher unemployment. Gray (1975: 16) reported that regardless of skills level, Puerto Ricans have higher rates of unemployment than the general population in the same occupation. She also found evidence indicating that Puerto Ricans suffered from higher rates of underemployment than the rest of the labor force.

The disparity between the number of Puerto Ricans in white-collar occupations and the rest of the labor force has narrowed over the past two decades. Puerto Ricans more than doubled their numbers in white-collar jobs between 1950 and 1970, and during this time they made significant increases in white-collar positions within the city government (Gray, 1975: 15). However, large numbers of Puerto Ricans are employed in manufacturing.

New York has become more white-collar oriented, and industry has moved out. From a high of nearly 900,000 manufacturing jobs in 1964, the city went to a low of 573,000 in 1975. More than 37,000 manufacturing jobs were lost in 1975 alone (U.S. Department of Labor, 1975). The decline of manufacturing industries, particularly in the apparel and needle trades, together with dwindling port, trade, and wholesale operations have contributed greatly to the reduction of jobs at a time when the population of the city has become increasingly black and Puerto Rican; these had been the major sources of employment for unskilled and semiskilled workers. The closing and relocation of factories, mergers, increases in taxes and in foreign competition, the concentration of Puerto Ricans in manufacturing, and the city's deteriorating labor market have all contributed to changes in the occupational structure of the city. From 1969 to 1975 the city lost over 510,000 jobs. These factors promise to increase the employment problems of Puerto Ricans in the future.

The movement of middle- and upper-income families from the city to the suburbs has further affected the city's job market. Suburbanites continue to depend on jobs in the city and to use city services, but they tend to spend the money earned in the city in the suburbs; they pay relatively no taxes in relation to the services, amenities, and protection they obtain from the city; and they do not participate in the city's political and civic life. Commuting to jobs in Long Island, New Jersey, and the northern suburbs of New York, where there has been an expansion of jobs, has been one of the solutions for the employment of New York City Puerto Ricans.

Until recently, job losses in New York City had been partly offset by the growth of jobs in local government and in medical and other health-related services which receive public funds. During the period of national economic recovery, from November 1970 to February 1973, however, the rate of employment in New York City continued at the same level as it had been during the national recession of November 1969 to November 1970 (Golden,

1974: 5). In spite of the fact that New York City continues to be the financial center of the country and still provides more than one half of all jobs generated in the New York–New Jersey area, unemployment rates for city residents have been among the nation's highest. Furthermore, the city's large-scale layoffs of government personnel in the fall of 1975 to avoid default further intensified the employment crisis. In 1975 there was a 10.3% decline in government employment, representing a loss of 59,000 jobs (U.S. Department of Labor, 1976). Unemployment rates for New York City residents were among the highest for large cities in the country in the fall of 1975.

In 1968–1971, Puerto Ricans had the highest unemployment rates and the highest rate of nonparticipation in the labor force. The latter rate is of particular importance, since it includes persons out of work who are no longer counted as unemployed. Young Puerto Rican men, however, had the highest proportion in numbers of those actively seeking employment. In 1969 and 1970, the unemployment rate among Puerto Rican males and females aged 16–20 was 40% and 30%, respectively. In 1968 through 1969, the unemployment rate among Puerto Ricans living in poverty areas was nearly three times higher than that of the city as a whole. Among Puerto Ricans in the labor force who lived in poverty areas, over one fourth (26.9%) had problems either holding their jobs or finding better ones. More than two fifths (43%) of all unemployed Puerto Ricans living in these areas had problems finding work.

Even though nearly one half of all the working Puerto Ricans in New York City held blue-collar jobs, the largest recent increases in the seventies in white-collar employment in the city have been among blacks and Puerto Ricans. Overall, the proportion of Puerto Rican men in the labor force is higher than that of white and black men, but Puerto Rican men are more likely to be in blue-collar jobs than any other workers. The proportion of Puerto Rican women in the labor force is lower than that of black and white women. Puerto Ricans also had substantially lower incomes than blacks or whites.

In 1970–71, roughly one half of the men in the age group 16–21 who lived in low-income areas of the city and were not participants in the labor force were Puerto Ricans, in comparison to 35% among blacks and 33% among whites (U.S. Department of Labor, 1971a: 15–21; 1971c). Older Puerto Rican men were more likely not to be in the labor force than older blacks and whites. Puerto Rican women were less likely to be in the labor force (46.1%) than black or white women.

In 1970 the Puerto Rican population continued to be the youngest in the city, with 75% of all Puerto Ricans being between 16 and 45 years old. Puerto Rican families tended to be larger than other families, and 1 out of 3 was headed by a woman. These factors, together with the low level of educational attainment, the lack of work experience, the confusions regarding the Puerto Rican presence, and discrimination against Puerto Ricans in a city which has been losing jobs for over 20 years, combine to make the conditions of life of Puerto Ricans in New York precarious in a self-perpetuating system of inequities.

Blau and Duncan (1967) have argued that social origins have a considerable influence on an individual's chances for occupational and career success, but education, training, and early work experiences are even more influential in determining success. These factors are interrelated, but in the case of minorities like blacks and Puerto Ricans, they become cumulative. The social origins of individuals reared in poverty tend to reinforce perspectives of inadequacy and negative views on opportunities for education and training, and thus they serve to limit jobs and career opportunities. The social and emotional resources provided by the family and the community of origin may counteract such forces by changing the conditions of life and the opportunity structure through the formulation of goals and the organization of political efforts to combat societal indifference. Traditionally, Puerto Rican family obligations of mutual assistance have been explicitly recognized. In large families, the first born are expected to go to work at an earlier age than later siblings to aid in supporting the family. Thus the tendency is for younger children to be more educated than their older siblings. Younger siblings are also expected (and are more likely) to have more prestigious occupations and careers than older ones.

The New York median is 12.1 years of schooling, compared to 8.3 years for Puerto Ricans (U.S. Department of Labor, 1971b: 8–10). Limited formal education has been associated with the unfavorable occupational distribution and high unemployment of Puerto Ricans. In New York City, where the minimal qualification for skilled work is the arbitrary requirement of a high school diploma, large numbers of Puerto Ricans face the prospects of lifetime unemployability or low wages and limited increments or promotions. Since 4 out of every 5 Puerto Rican males 18 years old and over, and 3 out of every 4 Puerto Rican women living in low-income areas have not completed high school, they face special problems in obtaining employment. In a sense, Puerto Rican workers must compete for jobs in a market dominated by men and women who are more than three times as likely to have completed high school and gone to college (U.S. Department of Labor, 1972). When Puerto Ricans are matched by educational level to other workers, they still have a higher unemployment rate; thus, limited education alone is not a sufficient explanation for high unemployment rates among Puerto Ricans. The role of discrimination cannot be underestimated as an element of unemployment and as a major difficulty for Puerto Ricans in finding employment outside their community.

The method of looking for work varies for Puerto Ricans by

socioeconomic and educational status, and by their knowledge of access to work and their cultural expectations in this country. Looking for work is mainly done through a network of personal contacts: friends or family who know about job vacancies believe employment can be secured for someone they introduce to a supervisor or employer. Such employers are likely to be considered friends who would hire as a favor. Other, more impersonal and bureaucratized methods of finding jobs, including employment agencies, are less acceptable. A major obstacle in searching for work in an impersonal manner is the expectation of being stereotyped and discriminated against or being denied individuality and uniqueness. Often the interaction in job interviews revolves around stereotypes interviewers have about Puerto Rican applicants. Common remarks are that the applicant "does not look or talk like a Puerto Rican." There may also be an attempt to anticipate responses on the basis of "knowing Puerto Ricans." Stereotyping ethnic groups is an entrenched American tradition which has been reinforced by fiction, the press, movies, radio, and television, as well as by "scientific" sociology and anthropology. This is often done without an intent to offend, and perhaps even in an effort toward mutual understanding. Stereotyping, which is a form of racism, is entrenched in the socialization of Americans beginning in early childhood, and it is extremely difficult for individuals to overcome.

The common stereotype of the Puerto Rican in the United States is a composite of a short individual, with dark skin color, who not only cannot speak English but who speaks poor Spanish and is uneducated. Amateur linguists perpetuate this stereotype when they note that Puerto Ricans do not speak Castillian and imply that this is a mark of inferiority. Actually, Castillian is a dialect spoken only by peasants in central Spain. Puerto Ricans are also considered to be easily excitable, to gesture frequently with their hands, and to display a "Latin temperament." Individuals who do not conform to the stereotype are not considered to be "really" Puerto Ricans, but something else, like Spaniards or Latin Americans. The negative expectations embodied in stereotypes of Puerto Ricans profoundly affect the self-images of Puerto Ricans, and thus their relationships with each other and with non–Puerto Ricans. Unemployment and the search for work are difficult problems for Puerto Rican families, since lack of job security is common, and the search for work may involve painful and difficult steps which often violate the self-esteem of job seekers. In looking for work, Puerto Ricans have the added burden of having to combat negative stereotypes about them which surface in job-seeking situations and the performance of their work.

SUMMARY AND CONCLUSIONS

Puerto Rican concepts of work are historically derived from the rural, agrarian, colonial backgrounds of the island. Work ethics or moral norms about work are found in all societies. Among Puerto Rican migrants, the norms of work or work ethics are related to family background and one's sense of obligations and concept of a good person. The problems faced by the masses of Puerto Ricans in New York, particularly by those with non-transferable or inadequate skills, is a part of the larger problem of the increased displacement of persons in American cities. In human terms, for Puerto Ricans living in the city, the problems are worsened by discrimination. Under such conditions and with such experiences, Puerto Rican institutions have been recreated and the sense of Puerto Rican identity strengthened. Cultural nationalism has become a protective ideology.

Forced to migrate because of the conditions of life in Puerto Rico, over a million Puerto Ricans have sought a brighter future in the United States since World War II. The Puerto Rican population, nonetheless, is the poorest, the youngest, and the least educated in New York City, and the victim of political neglect. Most Puerto Ricans who are in the labor force are in blue-collar work. The unemployment and nonparticipation work force rates of Puerto Ricans are the highest in the city. The key factors considered crucial to employment—advanced schooling, experience, and skills—are virtually denied Puerto Ricans. Overcoming the problems of the Puerto Rican community requires an organized political effort by Puerto Ricans based on culturally meaningful values, the development of Puerto Rican institutions, and the enhancement of Puerto Rican self-identity. Only the Puerto Ricans can initiate the actions necessary to create a vital political force to change the climate of life in their community.

REFERENCES

Barton, H. C., Jr. "The Employment Situation in Puerto Rico and Migration Movements between Puerto Rico and the United States." In *Summary of Proceedings: Workshop on Employment Problems of Puerto Ricans.* Manpower Training Series, Center for the Study of Unemployment. New York: New York University, Graduate School of Social Work, n.d.

Bienstock, Herbert. "Labor Force Experience of the Puerto Rican Worker." In *Summary of Proceedings: Workshop on Employment Problems of Puerto Ricans.* Manpower Training Series, Center for the Study of Unemployment. New York: New York University, Graduate School of Social Work, n.d.

Blau, Peter, & Otis D. Duncan. *The American Occupational Structure.* New York: John Wiley & Sons, 1967.

Buitrago-Ortiz, Carlos. *Esperanza: An Ethnographic Study of a Puerto Rican Community.* Viking Fund Publications in Anthropology No. 56. Tucson: University of Arizona Press, 1974.

Burstein, Abraham C. "A Demographic Profile of New York City." Mimeographed. Human Resources Administration, New York City, September 1973.

Cuadrado, Maria, & Carmen Hernandez. "The Status of Puerto Ricans in the City University." Mimeographed. New York, 1972.

Gillin, John. "Ethos Components in Modern Latin America Culture." *American Anthropologist* 57 (June 1955): 488–500.

Golden, Sonia. "Recession Is Not a Threat, It's a Fact in New York City." *The New York Times,* September 1, 1974, p. 5.

Gray, Lois. "The Jobs Puerto Ricans Hold in New York City." *Monthly Labor Review* 98 (October 1975): 12–16.

Gray, Lois, & Edward Gonzalez. "Puerto Ricans as Union Members." Mimeographed. Brooklyn College, Center for Migration Studes, March 13–14, 1970.

National Commission on Technology, Automation and Economic Progress. *Employment Impact of Technological Change,* Appendix. Washington, D.C.: U.S. Government Printing Office, 1966.

New York State Board of Regents. *Bilingual Education.* Albany, 1972.

Padilla, Elena. *Up from Puerto Rico.* New York: Columbia University Press, 1958.

Peterson, Iver. "As CUNY Cuts Back, Those Who Suffer Most are the Minorities." *The New York Times,* December 21, 1975, Sect. E:5.

Puerto Rican Research and Resources Center. *Puerto Rican Migration.* March 1, 1972.

Raneri, G. N. "An Analysis of Unemployed Puerto Rican Migrants in New York City." M. A. research report, Montclair State Teachers College, 1958.

Steward, Julian, et al. *The People of Puerto Rico.* Urbana, Ill.: University of Illinois Press, 1956.

U.S. Commission on Civil Rights. *Demographic, Social and Economic Characteristics of New York City and the New York Metropolitan Area.* Staff Report. February 1972. (a)

U.S. Commission on Civil Rights. *Public Education for Puerto Rican Children in New York City.* Staff Report, February 1972. (b)

U.S. Department of Labor. *Some Facts Relating to the Puerto Rican and the Labor Market.* Bureau of Labor Statistics, 1968.

U.S. Department of Labor. *The New York Puerto Rican: Patterns of Work Experience.* Bureau of Labor Statistics. Washington, D.C.: U.S. Government Printing Office, 1971. (a)

U.S. Department of Labor. *Poverty Area Profiles: The Job Search of Ghetto Workers.* Bureau of Labor Statistics, Middle Atlantic Regional Office, Regional Report, June 1971. (b)

U.S. Department of Labor. *Working Age Non-Participants.* Bureau of Labor Statistics, Middle Atlantic Regional Office, Regional Report No. 22, June 1971. (c)

U.S. Department of Labor. *Social, Economic and Labor Force Characteristics of Residents in New York City's Low Income Areas.* Bureau of Labor Statistics, Middle Atlantic Regional Office, Regional Report No. 30, 1972.

U.S. Department of Labor. "Spanish-Speaking Americans: Their Manpower

Problems and Opportunities." Reprint from the 1973 *Manpower Report of the President*. Washington, D.C.: U.S. Government Printing Office, 1973.

U.S. Department of Labor. "New York City Job Loss Since 1969 Hits Half-Million Mark in September." Press release from Bureau of Labor Statistics, Middle Atlantic Regional Office, December 3, 1975.

U.S. Department of Labor. "November Job Rise in New York–Northeastern New Jersey Area Below Seasonal Expectation. . . ." Press Release from Bureau of Labor Statistics, Middle Atlantic Regional Office, January 26, 1976.

U.S. Department of Labor. *Some Perspectives on New York in Transition*. Bureau of Labor Statistics, n.d.

CHAPTER 5

Poverty and work among American Indians

Joseph G. Jorgensen

INTRODUCTION

How modern American Indians are integrated into the American political economy has received some anthropological analysis during the past 30 years. Anthropologists who have concerned themselves with contemporary Indian life have usually disregarded the politicoeconomic causes of Indian conditions and instead have employed an "acculturation" schema to explain why living Indian societies differ from their precontact forebears and from the dominant, contemporary, white society.

Stages, contexts, or levels of acculturation achieved by Indians are usually loosely defined and measured in relation to the hypothesized norms for white society. Though actual measurements of white societies are seldom made, and variation in white society is almost never accounted for, in general the more similar an Indian society is to white society, the more "acculturated"

Note: Part of this essay appeared as Chapter 2, "Indians and the Metropolis," in Jack O. Waddell and O. Michael Watson (eds.), *The American Indian in Urban Society* (Boston: Little, Brown & Co., 1971). This essay has been abridged and revised for this volume. The revisions, especially pp. 171–72 and 188–97 are copyright © 1977 Joseph G. Jorgensen.

the Indian society is said to be. In this view the dominated society accommodates itself to the dominant society in stages.

The underlying assumption in these studies is that the direction change takes is from a primitive, underdeveloped society (i.e., a society with low economic output and low standard of living) to a civilized, developed society which becomes fully integrated into the dominant white society. Integration is achieved when "acculturation" is complete. The actual steps involved vary from context to context. There is no single path.

The acculturation framework provides a rather euphoric way to think and talk about what has happened to American Indians since contact with whites. It assumes that before this contact Indians were "underdeveloped," and it avoids analysis of why Indians are as they are today. Because this framework assumes that Indians will eventually become fully integrated into the U.S. polity, economy, and society, just like whites, it is also meaningless. No matter what the condition of Indian society is when analyzed by the anthropologist, it is always somewhere along the acculturation path, headed toward full acculturation. Because acculturation explains everything, it explains nothing.

Recently the clichés and erroneous concepts of acculturation research have been challenged by Vine Deloria, Jr. (1969), an Indian author. Deloria's criticisms are sound, although he probably attributes to anthropologists, especially applied anthropologists, more power than they possess. One theme in Deloria's analysis—and in the analysis of Stan Steiner (1968), a white author—is that Indian culture is different from Anglo capitalist culture, and that Indian culture has preserved its differences from the dominant culture for generations, in spite of "acculturation," "assimilation," "integration," and annihilation schemes perpetrated by the dominant culture. In an important way the cultural-differences theme developed by Deloria and several Indian authors is different from the acculturation or culture-in-conflict scheme developed in various fashions by anthropological experts. Indians, for instance, focus on traditional Indian ethics, concepts of spirit, and lifestyle to explain why Indians have resisted the Protestant ethic, the technological and rapacious approach to expropriation of natural and human resources, and the acquisitive, competitive, nuclear-family lifestyle of the dominant culture.

Because the first devotion of anthropologists has been to the structures of cultures, it is somewhat surprising that the cultural features emphasized by Indians about Indian culture have not been recognized earlier and more fully by anthropologists. Indeed, it is most interesting that acculturational anthropologists have not focused on the cultural features specified by Indians as those that cause them to reject "acculturation." Toward the end of this chapter the question of Indian culture vis-à-vis work expectations will be taken up because it is critical to its theme. Suffice it to say here that whereas cultural differences are important, they do not adequately explain why

Indians are as they are. On the other hand, it is clear that the political, economic, and social conditions of American Indians are not improving, and it is necessary to deal with this issue before turning to the role of Indian culture in interpreting and responding to these conditions.

Underdevelopment, in our view, has been caused by the development of the white-controlled national economy, and the main reason the political, economic, and social conditions of Indians are not improving is because the American Indian is, and has been for over 100 years, fully controlled by the national political economy. Underdevelopment, paradoxically, has been caused by the development of the capitalist political economy of the United States. This postulate is in direct opposition to the postulate that seems to underlie acculturation, and it also suggests a basic contradiction in the American political economy. Before exploring this postulate, we will survey Indian conditions in the past several decades, since they have *become* underdeveloped, and in a very cursory way, develop some idea of what the basic features of modern Indian life have been for these "acculturating" or "developing" people.

THE PROBLEM: THE PERSISTENCE OF INDIAN POVERTY

The History of Indian Deprivation

In 1926 Lewis Meriam was commissioned by Secretary of Interior Hubert Work to survey Indian administration and Indian life. His report demonstrated that federal legislation and the niggardly funds allocated for Indian programs had injured rather than helped American Indians (Meriam, 1928). It also showed that the Bureau of Indian Affairs (BIA), the government agency responsible for implementing federal policies and managing Indian affairs, had a long tradition of dry rot—that is, unimaginative and undereducated mismanagers caught up in red-tape procedures—that had made it incapable of helping Indians with their economic, health, education, housing, and legal problems.

Following the passage of the General Allotment Act (Dawes Act) of 1887, which was intended to civilize Indians and "free" them from communal land ownership, Indian reservation land was drastically reduced by allotting acreage to each Indian family head and, in some instances, to other living Indians. The unallotted land became part of the public domain. By 1926, much Indian land was tied up in complicated heirship status, much had been sold or leased by Indians to whites, and Indian economic conditions, in general, were deplorable. Employment was almost nonexistent; family farming and ranching were not meeting subsistence needs. Thus, between 1887 and 1926 the underdeveloped Indians became more underdeveloped.

Meriam and his associates further showed that Indian health tended to be poor, with a high incidence of disease, especially those related to poverty, such as tuberculosis and trachoma. Also, the infant mortality rate was high. Indian housing was so substandard (dirt floors, no doors, wretched sanitation, no running water) and Indian diet so poor that the two coalesced greatly to exacerbate Indian health problems.

Federal education policy since the 1880s took preadolescent children away from their homes, and the so-called restrictive, backward influences of tribal life, and educated them in all-Indian boarding schools. The intention of the policy was to force rapid acceptance of white ways, and the optimistic notion behind it was that if a man has been given an education, he will, ipso facto, make his own way successfully as a wage earner or petty capitalist-farmer or shopkeeper in white society. The Meriam report was critical of this education policy as well as of the General Allotment Act of 1887, which was intended to bring the education-economic program to fruition and to achieve, in a short time, the desired goals set by the white policy makers.

The Meriam report criticized the current state of Indian affairs, especially land and education policies, and made suggestions for solving the problems: Indian health and housing were to be improved; preadolescents were to be educated on home reservations; loss of Indian land through sale or lease was to be stopped; and greater federal appropriations were to be made to increase salaries and entice better qualified people to join the BIA. Characteristically, the report did not cover such questions as the need for massive funds to develop industries—agricultural or otherwise—under the ownership and control of Indians. Rather, it directed itself to the symptoms of the Indians' problems and to cleaning up the bumbling, underfunded BIA, hoping that good advice administered through this special appendage of the federal welfare program would improve the individual Indian's lot until he became self-sufficient.

During the Hoover administration federal appropriations doubled, but they slackened by nearly 20% in 1933 during the depths of the Great Depression. Most of the money went for education expenses, salaries of better trained personnel, and health and medical expenses, including the salaries of doctors, nurses, nutrition experts, and others involved in Indian health programs. Thus funds were provided for the education dream, for a larger and better trained welfare bureaucracy to administer Indian affairs, and for maintaining and hopefully improving Indian health. This welfare program served to expand the BIA, improve health slightly, and keep the Indian education system going.

In 1934, during Franklin Roosevelt's first administration, the Wheeler-Howard Act, known best as the Indian Reorganization Act (IRA), was passed. The IRA provided for sweeping changes in Indian policies. Following the recommendations of the Meriam report, it allowed for consolidation of Indian land and purchase of more land; development of tribal governments with constitutions and charters; financial loans to the tribal governments for the development of tribal resources; and development of day schools for Indian children on home reservations. John Collier was appointed Commissioner of Indian Affairs to implement these policies, which were considered "radical" at the time (see Haas, 1957).

The IRA did not decrease the powers of the BIA over Indian lives, even though tribal governments with constitutions were created. In fact, the IRA actually increased the powers of the Secretary of Interior over Indians. Many Congressmen and lobbyists became irritated at Collier's implementation of the IRA, but their fears were premature. Because the program allowed land to be purchased for Indians, thus removing it from state tax rolls, and because it was thought that it would be more difficult for private corporations to exploit resources on those lands if they fell into Indian ownership, state governments as well as agribusiness and mineral lobbies were opposed to the IRA and to Collier. Actually, mineral, farm, and range-land exploitation became cheaper on Indian-owned land than on company-owned or leased federal land, because a special tax exemption was implemented for lessees of Indian lands.

Shortly after World War II, Commissioner Collier was replaced and the Indian Claims Commission Act was passed, allowing Indian tribes to sue the United States for redress of grievances, particularly for the loss of lands and broken treaties. Many thought that legal redress for these things and for inhumanities perpetrated against the American Indians was only just.

The Indian claims legislation also paved the way for a new federal policy, the goal of which was the dissolution of the BIA and the termination of all treaty obligations of the United States to American Indians. It was argued that once the old scores over land thefts and other inhumanities had been settled and Indians were taught how to spend money wisely, they could make their own way as responsible citizens (see Lurie, 1957).

Aiming toward this goal of termination, following the passage of the Indian Claims Commission Act, the House Committee on Interior and Insular Affairs (U.S. House, 1953, 1954) conducted an investigation of the BIA and research on all U.S. Indian groups. The results clearly indicated that the Indians were in dire straits and overwhelmingly opposed termination of federal government control and involvement. Nevertheless, between 1950 and 1960 some groups were terminated with (it is alleged) their consent, and others without it. Most American Indian groups were not terminated, but they felt the pressure of such proceedings and were frightened by them (U.S. House, 1954).

In response to the termination policy, the Commission on the Rights, Liberties and Responsibilities of the American Indian was financed in 1957 by The Fund for the Republic to begin a private investigation of federal

Indian policies and the general living conditions of Indians. The investigation was a sequel to the Meriam investigation three decades earlier. An extensive summary of all investigations made by this commission was not published until nine years later (Brophy & Aberle, 1966).

If the Meriam report's analysis of the "Indian problem" had been correct, and if the solution to that problem attempted through the implementation of the IRA had worked, in 1957 there would have been no need for another investigation. The solution suggested by Meriam, in our view, missed the crux of the problem, but the IRA did work satisfactorily, given the analysis and solution suggested by Meriam and accepted by Collier. Neither man, nor his advisors, seemed to realize that the "Indian problem" was caused by the growth of the political economy of the metropolis.[1]

The results of the commission's investigation showed the economic position of the Indian about 1960 to be less favorable than that of any other American minority group. Indian income was scandalously low; employment was meager, unstable, and temporary; and the Indian land base was smaller than in the previous decade. Indian health was poor when contrasted with whites, as was Indian housing, education, and local government (see Brophy & Aberle, 1966). Very little had changed for the American Indian since 1934, except that some land had been reacquired, schools had been developed near reservations (about half of all funds went to education), the BIA staff had grown, and Indian governments exercised a modicum of control over reservation societies which were poverty ridden and often pervaded with factionalism.

DEPRIVATION AMONG CONTEMPORARY INDIANS IN CALIFORNIA

The conditions of American Indians in California (California State Advisory Commission, 1966; California Fair Employment Practice Commission, 1966; U.S. Congress, Senate, 1974; U.S. Bureau of the Census, 1973) illustrate the lot of Indians throughout the country. California is particularly good to assess because of its relatively large Indian population (88,000 in 1970), of which about 25% have migrated to California since 1955, primarily in quest of on-the-job training and employment. Moreover, only 19% of all California Indians live on, or adjacent to, reservations, and more than three fourths live in urban areas. The national rural-urban migration, Indian and non-Indian, since 1955 has been marked, and California's urban areas have received huge numbers of migrants from other states and from its own rural areas. Nevertheless, the proportion of California Indians living in rural areas is still greater than that of any other ethnic group there—even though the many out-of-state Indian migrants to the Los Angeles and San Francisco–Oakland areas are included in the California Indian total.

In all measures of economy, education, health, and housing, the Indians of California rank below the white population and significantly below all other ethnic groups. Because family household size is related to household economics, it is not surprising to learn that Indians exceed all other ethnic groups in size of family households, with more than 15% having six persons or more. In California, the Indian population is the most youthful ethnic group, whereas senior citizens are predominantly white. Non-Indians live longer because of better nutrition, medical care, housing, and the preconditions of better education, occupation, and income. Moreover, the comparatively affluent whites can afford to move there to retire.

A survey of these preconditions to longevity reveals that in California only 3% of the Indian population 25 years and over, including immigrants, had college degrees in 1970, and 23% had not attended school beyond the eighth grade (U.S. Bureau of the Census, 1973: 21). On the other hand, 13.8% of the white population 25 and over had completed college, and only 8.9% had not gone beyond the eighth grade (U.S. Bureau of the Census, 1972: 383). These percentages do not reveal the quality of education received, of course, and there is good reason to suspect that the Indian generally gets a poorer education. It can also be inferred that if approximately half of all federal funds for Indians are being used for education, either too few funds are being allocated, or, more likely, other factors are causing Indians to drop out of school.

In 1970 the median annual income of California Indian families ($7,952) was about two thirds that of whites—$10,969. In 1969, 8.4% of all the families in California were living below the poverty level, compared to 17.6% of all Indian families. In 1970, the unemployment rate for male Indians, using a narrow definition of employability,[2] was 11.4%, nearly twice the state unemployment rate. Using the state's broader definition of employability, the same definition used for the rest of the U.S. population, the figures are more startling. In 1969 only 61% of California Indian men and only 38% of Indian women[3] were employed.

In what kinds of jobs are Indians employed? Table 5.1 compares the percentage of employed Indians and whites in California by occupation and sex. Significant differences in the distribution of occupations are revealed. When education and access to capital are requisites, as for such occupations as professionals, proprietors, farm owners, and managers, Indians fare far worse than the general population.

California Indians generally are either out of work or have work that is often unskilled and temporary. They stand on the lowest rungs of the occupation ladder, filling jobs that require few skills and no capital. These figures are more interesting, however, in view of the fact that 25% of the California Indian population has migrated there since 1955 in search of work. This is evidence of their self-selection of skills or motivation to acquire

TABLE 5.1

Comparison of Employed Indians and Total Employed Population in California, 1970, by Occupation

	Percent of Total Employed Population		Percent of Employed Indian Population		Difference in Percent	
	Male	Female	Male	Female	Male	Female
Professional, technical, proprietors, managers, officials	29.1%	20.3%	15.0%	13.6%	−14.1%	−6.7%
Clerical, sales	15.3	44.2	9.1	39.1	−6.2	−5.1
Craftsmen, operatives	33.2	10.7	48.1	17.9	+14.9	+7.2
Laborers, farm laborers ...	7.8	1.3	16.9	2.6	+9.1	+1.3
Domestics, service workers	8.6	17.0	9.8	29.5	+1.2	+12.5
Occupation not reported	6.1	6.5	—	—		

Note: Columns do not add to 100 due to rounding errors.

Source: U.S. Bureau of the Census, "General Social and Economic Characteristics—California," *Census of Population: 1970, U.S. Summary* (Washington, D.C.: U.S. Government Printing Office, 1972), p. 383, and "American Indians," *Census of Population: 1970, Subject Reports,* Final Report PC (2)–1F (1973), p. 106.

skills; these Indians probably possess more skills and more "desire" to improve their circumstances through working than Indian populations in other western states.

Some indicators of economic well-being show Indians to be in the lower percentiles. Predictably, California Indian housing is below the standards of comfort, decency, and safety set by the U.S. Department of Health, Education, and Welfare. A 1964 survey by the California State Advisory Commission on Indian Affairs (1966) classified 90% of the houses as inadequate; 39% of these could be improved, and 51% needed complete replacement because of unsafe and unsanitary conditions. Sewage disposal facilities were unsatisfactory in about 65% of the homes; contaminated water was used in approximately 45%.

The health problems experienced by California Indians are great in comparison with the total California population; these problems are clearly related to lack of employment; poor housing, sanitation, and nourishment; inadequate medical care; and the apathy generated by these conditions. The leading causes of death among California Indians contrast markedly with those for non-Indians.

Causes of death among Indians are: heart disease, 20%; accidents, approximately 20%; influenza, pneumonia, and tuberculosis, about 10% (except newborn); and cirrhosis of the liver, 7%. In contrast, 37% of non-Indians die from heart disease, 6% from accidents, 4% from influenza, pneumonia, and tuberculosis, and 2% from cirrhosis of the liver. The majority of diseases attacking Indians are either respiratory or gastrointestinal—health problems closely related to inadequate shelter, sanitation, and diet—whereas only about 20% of non-Indians contract such diseases.

These statistics lay bare the discrepancy between the non-Indian and Indian norms. In the mid-1960s, despite all programs, the American Indians were relatively as underdeveloped as in the mid-1920s. Even in a statement of averages, Indian conditions are extremely low on all measures of education, skills, employment, income, and comforts; they suggest extreme deprivation. The acculturation has been to rural poverty and, more recently, urban poverty as well. Surprisingly, on all these measures of the quality of life, the Indians of California are much better off than their counterparts in other states and much closer to the standards of living considered adequate for the average U.S. citizen than their congeners (California State Advisory Commission, 1966; U.S. Department of Health, Education, and Welfare, 1974).

THE ENDEMIC POVERTY OF CONTEMPORARY INDIANS

To consider the endemic poverty of U.S. Indians generally, we will contrast California Indians with other groups and assess how Indian family household organizations have adjusted to economic deprivation.

The relative "prosperity" of California Indians is partly due to the self-selected migrants to major urban areas, many of whom have some employment, and to generally high welfare standards observed in that state. For the nation as a whole, the family income of Indians in 1970 was $6,857, $1,784 less than for California Indian families. Their median family income was $5,832. In 1970, also, 38% of all Indians were living below the poverty level, and 33% of all families had incomes below the poverty level. (U.S. Bureau of the Census, 1973: 120). The unemployment rate is between 40% and 50% on almost all reservations. But of the employed 50–60%, over half are either temporary or part-time employees; that is, underemployed.

According to the President's Task Force on American Indians (Brophy & Aberle, 1966), the present poverty on Indian reservations and among urban ghetto Indians is deplorable. Housing is grossly dilapidated; the incidence of disease, especially upper respiratory and gastrointestinal forms, is seven or eight times the national average; Indian life expectancy is only two thirds the national life expectancy; and one third of all adult Indians are illiterate. As youthful populations grow on the reservations, many young Indians spill off into the ghettos of urban areas, replacing rural poverty with urban poverty. Though adequate statistics on urban Indians are not available, particularly from the BIA—the agency responsible for sending many Indians to cities—it is estimated that 380,000 American Indians currently live in urban areas.

In contrast to California Indians, 38% of whom use contaminated water, the national average of such usage by Indians is 74%, and while 48% of California Indian families haul all domestic water, 81% of the national Indian population does so. Among California Indians, 73% have unsatisfactory facilities for disposal of excreta; 83% is the Indian national average.[4] All Indian households, including those of California Indians, average more than five (5.4) occupants in less than two rooms, whereas the non-Indian household averages only 2.9 occupants in more than four rooms (California State Advisory Commission, 1966; Wagner & Rabeau, 1964; U.S. Bureau of the Census, 1967).

The composition of Indian households differs significantly from the nuclear-family, conjugal-pair, and single-person types that predominate in white America. In California 30% of all Indian households are composite, including such combinations of kin and nonkin as grandchildren, nieces and nephews, brothers or sisters of the husband or wife, a married child with spouse or children or both, and even more distantly related kin and affines (in-laws). Of all California household heads, 61% are men and 39% are women—the latter being widowed, separated, or divorced. The composition of California Indian households is not an anomaly but a regular feature of Indian poverty and poverty in the Western Hemisphere generally.[5]

Though there are no national statistics on the subject, research confirms the California Indian household composition distribution. This includes the work of Munsell (1967), among the Salt River Pima-Papago of Arizona; Robbins (in press), among the Blackfeet of Montana; Jorgensen (1972), among Shoshones and Utes on five reservations in Idaho, Wyoming, Colorado, and Utah; Mochon (1968), among the Stockbridge-Munsee of Wisconsin; De la Isla (in press), among the Umatilla of Oregon; Maxwell (1973), among the Spokane-Colville of Washington; and Dowling (1973), among the Oneida of Wisconsin. These studies do demonstrate that there are relatively more composite Indian households outside of California than in that state, and those outside are larger. This situation is to be expected, given the greater average family income for California Indians.

The studies cited above clearly demonstrate that household size varies inversely with the amount and stability of income. The less stable and lower the amount of income among American Indian family households, the larger the households. The explanation for this phenomenon is that people with meager means join together to pool resources. It is better to crowd together under a single roof, or adjacent roofs, and share resources than it is to live apart in less crowded households where resources are less predictable. This grouping together characterizes poverty-stricken households among other ethnic and racial minorities within, as well as outside of, the United States (see footnote 5).

Through sharing funds from several diverse sources—welfare (e.g., Aid for Dependent Children, Old-Age Assistance, Federal Aid to the Blind), per capita payments from Indian Claims Commission judgments, lease income from land, wages from part-time labor, cash from piece work, goods received as welfare commodities or procured in hunting and fishing—these composite family households have adjusted to their lack of resources. Where nuclear-family households occur among American Indians, they usually have a *stable* source of income, males tend to be the household heads, and, to a lesser extent, someone in the household is employed.

American Indian family household compositions tend to change in a rather predictable cyclic manner, from composite to nuclear. If a son gains regular employment, he and his wife and children move out of his father's home and establish a separate household. In 15 years or so, this man's nuclear family is likely to become a composite household. His wife's parents may move in to share his resources, or as his children marry they may establish temporary residence in the household.

American Indian composite households and family household cycles are not retentions of aboriginal customs but are products of their meager and unstable incomes, lack of skills, and lack of control over resources. They do not have money or resources to allow them to cope with life as do the gainfully employed and nonpaternalistically guided lower (working), middle, and upper classes of U.S. society. Indian family households change from composite to nuclear to composite as their economic conditions change, making the Indian family similar to other families living in poverty in the Western world. Yet the peculiar niche occupied by Indians in American poverty—as super exploited and paternalistically guided wards of neocolonialism, the vast majority of whom reside on reservations—separates them from, for example the Mestizo in Mexico, the Callampa dwellers in Chile, the rural poor and the black urban ghetto dwellers in the United States, and the Black Caribs of Latin America and the West Indies.

Although the major problems of American Indians are rooted in economy and polity, as are the problems of the other groups mentioned, a difference is that Indians often have resources. But the access of American

Indians to their resources is severely restricted, and the major exploitation of these resources is carried out by non-Indian local, national, and multinational corporations.

THE POLITICOECONOMIC NICHE OCCUPIED BY AMERICAN INDIANS

A brief survey of the niche of reservations in the national economy reveals that they generally have land bases that are arid or semiarid, and because some segments of the land are tied up in questions of inheritance, they are not suitable for the development of profitable agribusiness. Moreover, most reservations do not have sufficient land, even if all of it were consolidated, to provide decent livelihoods from agriculture for all inhabitants on them (the rural economics surrounding most reservations are basically agricultural). Reservations are generally located long distances from major markets, big cities, and industrial plants, so there are no large job markets. Moreover, the greater the distance to market, the less profitable, generally, is the agribusiness on reservations. Reservations are also often located considerable distances from railroads and major highways, making transportation expensive and profitable development of heavy industry on reservations unlikely. Industrial development has been further inhibited because Indian populations are undereducated and underskilled (Brophy & Aberle, 1966: 62–116).

Rural economies adjacent to reservations in most of the western half of the United States have withered, as large farms in the Midwest with access to capital and improvements in technology—including hybrid crops, fertilizers, and pesticides—have become more productive and have grown at the expense of small agricultural operations everywhere. Federal farm policies have worked with the large farm corporations to protect them through price supports and soil-bank payments, encouraging large farm corporations to gobble up small farms (President's National Advisory Commission, 1967). In general, the greater the productivity, the greater the government assistance. Since 1920 the farm population of the United States has decreased by two thirds, and its percentage of the total population has plummeted from 30 to 6. Although the average size of all farms has increased, the number of farms has decreased by more than half since 1920. Since 1940 the average size of farms in the United States has increased by well over 200% (U.S. Bureau of the Census, 1968: 613–624, 1967: 608). As examples of federal benefits, in 1967 48% of U.S. farmers with incomes less than $2,500 per year received 4.5% of the federal farm subsidies. On the other hand, 65% of federal subsidies went to the *top* 10% in the farm production pyramid, most of them being large corporations or food-processing trusts. (See President's National Advisory Commission, 1967, for a complete analysis of the subsidy program, especially the programs designed to "encourage, promote, and strengthen the family farm.")

The livestock business has followed a similar course in the past decade, as quasi-cartels are beginning to control all aspects of beef production from feeder lots, to packing houses, to supermarket distribution. Grass-fed (range-fed) mature beef is less marketable because of the time needed for fattening the animals for slaughter and the difficulty in controlling the size of range-fed beef. Weight can be controlled on feeder lots, yielding animals of standardized size, which greatly eases slaughtering and packing. In addition, there is a lower demand for grass-fed beef by packing houses and distributors (both processes often carried out by the same corporation) because, they allege, the meat is not sufficiently marbled with fat, and the increased production costs, including transportation for range-fed beef, are pushing the producers of grass-fed beef off the market. This squeezes small operators out of the business, especially those in the western United States who are long distances from the main markets.

Though the rural economics around Indian reservations are dwindling and farm consolidation is occurring rapidly, there is some money to be made in agriculture on reservations. The U.S. Bureau of Indian Affairs (1968) reports that $170 million were grossed from agriculture on all reserves (50 million acres) in 1966. These figures are rather liberal as they include the *estimated* value of all fish and game taken by Indians on their reservations (perhaps $20 million) and consumed by the procurers, but this modest amount of overestimating is not the critical point. Of the $170 million, the Indians realized only $58.6 million, $16 million of which was derived from rents and permits to non-Indians. This means that $127.4 million, or 75% of the gross from agriculture, went to *non-Indians* who paid Indians $16 million, or roughly 12% of their gross, for exploitation of Indian lands.

The BIA statistics clearly reveal what can happen to Indian resources when Indians have neither access to capital nor the skills or adequate counsel to utilize their own resources. Of the estimated $170 million from agriculture in 1966, the Indian share approximates $58.6 million, of which $16 million (27%) is from leasing to non-Indians (as noted above), $23 million (39%) is from farming and ranching (this, too, is an estimate and includes all goods produced *and* consumed by Indians), and $19.6 million (34%) is from hunting and fishing for their own consumption. There is no way to know how inaccurate the latter two estimates are.

The BIA statistics on further exploitation of Indian resources are also revealing. In 1967 about 803 million board feet of lumber were cut. Only 100 million board feet, or about 12%, were processed in tribal sawmills. Indians were selling their natural resources yet maintaining practically no control over production. Timber sale brought $15 million to Indian tribes in 1967. There are no figures pertaining to the non-Indian gross, non-Indian profits, or the costs to Indian tribes to maintain their resources (see U.S. Bureau of Indian Affairs, 1968).

As for oil and all other minerals, including uranium, sand, gravel, phosphate, gilsonite, gypsum, coal, limestone, copper, lead, and zinc, the exploitation of these resources by national and multinational corporations brought $31 million to tribal coffers in 1967 through bids and lease royalties. Again, the tribes do not control production, and few jobs are generated for Indian employees. Though there are no figures on corporate profits or gross income, the corporations are generating capital for themselves and offering Indian tribes carrots in the form of lease and royalty incomes, and the Indians are losing their resources.

Finally, since the early 1950s the U.S. Bureau of Indian Affairs (1955) has encouraged the location of industries on or near reservations to provide employment for Indians. The emphasis has not been on development of Indian-owned and Indian-controlled industries. Tribes have been urged to use their modest amounts of capital from land claims judgments and mineral royalties to build plants and lease them to private corporations at low rates. The corporations, the Indians have been told, will then move onto the reservations, even though they are a great distance from markets, because they can operate at low costs and use cheap Indian labor.

Nothing much came of this program until 1962, when a few industries moved onto reserves to take advantage of provisions made for them. Between 1962 and 1968, 10,000 jobs were created through the development of industries on or near reserves. Characteristically, 6,000 (60%) of these jobs have gone to *non-Indians* (U.S. Bureau of Indian Affairs, 1968: 7). Private corporations are using Indian capital to expand, yet using Indian labor only when it is adequate to the task. Indians do not maintain ownership or control.

"Industrial development" has been mostly talk; development has benefited industry and not Indians or Indian-owned and Indian-controlled industry. In 1967 private non-Indian development of Indian lands on a lease basis, including all industrial, commercial, and recreational uses, brought $4 million to Indian tribes. Recreation brought $1.9 million of that total (U.S. Bureau of Indian Affairs, 1968). The irony of this is that whites are paying low-lease fees to exploit Indian lands for white leisure use.

Why are things as they are, even after so much has been done to improve the Indians' lot? From 1955 to 1968 the BIA grew from 9,500 employees to 16,000 (1955, 1968). From 1949 to 1969, federal government appropriations for American Indian affairs increased from $49 million to $241 million (1949, 1968). In fact, in the 1968–69 fiscal year, about $430 million were spent on federal programs intended to benefit Indians, yet the average annual income for all Indian families was about $1,500.

Part of the failure of Indian policies is attributable to mismanagement by the BIA. For example, the BIA has encouraged the development of livestock operations at a time when quasi cartels have been taking over the industry, and the Bureau has advised tribes to allow non-Indian corporations to exploit Indian resources. But the causes of persistent Indian problems cannot be solely attributed to the BIA. Indeed, the growth of the BIA and the federal budget for Indian affairs is indicative of the more important causes of Indian poverty. Federal welfare institutions and funds have increased as exploitation has continued. The growth of the BIA is an effect of the way in which the national political economy has grown. Poverty is perpetually created, and welfare measures are used to heal the most gaping wounds.

A HYPOTHESIS ABOUT INDIAN UNDERDEVELOPMENT:
THE METROPOLIS-SATELLITE POLITICAL ECONOMY

The Indians of the United States, in our opinion, have been controlled by the U.S. political economy since they were conquered. As shown above, Indians are currently deprived and have been deprived for the past several decades. This is not a coincidence or a fortuity; Indian poverty does not represent an evolutionary "stage of acculturation" somewhere between the underdeveloped *tabula rasa* and the developed non-Indian polity, economy, and society. In our hypothesis, Indian underdevelopment is the product of the full integration of U.S. Indians into the U.S. politicoeconomic society— albeit as superexploited victims of that society.

With this general proposition in mind, the term "metropolis-satellite"[6] is used here rather than "urban-rural" in a characterization of political economy, because the latter implies a city, a locational unit filled with people. "Metropolis" implies the concentration of economic and political power and political influence. "Urban" and "metropolis" are not, of course, completely independent, as the directors of the metropolis, their corporations, research houses, and liquid capital are located in the great urban areas. But, as the economic and political power and influence of the metropolis have grown, especially in the past decade, the great urban centers have withered. Although urban areas have generally grown in number of inhabitants, they have decreased in economic and political influence, social services, and the quality of life. Ghettos have grown as a result of natural increase and migration of the rural poor, especially from the South and Southwest (Shannon & Shannon, 1967: 19–75; Shannon, 1969: 36–56). Moreover, unemployment has risen, and rebellion with subsequent repression is more and more a characteristic of the largest cities (President's National Advisory Commission, 1968).

This withering of the locational cores of urban areas, too, can be accounted for through the nature of the metropolis-satellite politicoeconomic structure. As the satellites, *or the resources and labor of the rural areas or those areas that do not concentrate political and economic power,* are exploited and technological advances are made, fewer and fewer man-hours are required to produce more and more goods on greater amounts of land or from greater areas within mines. Because men who do not control the resources, or whose resources are meager, can no longer cope, selective migration of the poor and displaced, as well as of the upwardly mobile, takes place from the withering rural areas to the urban areas. As a partial effect, middle-income families move to the suburbs of these cities.

To develop the hypothesis, the conditions of the "backward" modern American Indians are not caused by rural isolation or a tenacious hold on aboriginal ways, but result from the way in which U.S. urban centers of finance, political influence, and power have grown at the expense of rural areas. The rapid development of urban areas after the mid-19th century brought the Indian social ruin, as measured in status and self-worth; poverty, as measured in access to strategic resources, the distribution of surpluses from one's own region, employment, housing, and general welfare; and political oppression and neocolonial subjugation, as measured by decimation of Indian populations through warfare, the dissolution of aboriginal politics, the loss of self-direction, the lack of access to the locus of political power, the general denial of citizenship (with a few exceptions) until 1924, and the increasing role of the BIA and the Secretary of Interior in directing the conduct of Indian affairs.

These results were brought about by expropriation of Indian land and resources by the railroads, mining corporations, farmers, and ranchers. Economic surpluses were taken from the rural areas and used for the growth of the metropolis. For instance, from an estimated 16 million bison on the American plains in 1860, the bison population was reduced to about 1,000 in 1885 through systematic killing by whites (Klose, 1964: 79–80), because there was a market for tongues and skins in the eastern United States, and, more importantly, because the plains could then be farmed and cattle raised without interference from the bison or the Indians who lived off them (Klose, 1964: 83–84). The railroads, which received vast amounts of right-of-way (i.e., Indian territory) free from the U.S. government, in turn sold his land to farmers and ranchers. The railroads profited from the sales and later began moving products from these farms and ranches to markets in the East.[7] Indians were the first rural inhabitants to suffer from this development and the first people to be forced into underdevelopment from their previous condition of self-support and self-governance. Mining industries expanded throughout the West, from the 1850s to the turn of the century, and they too expropriated Indian land and resources.

With the growth of technology influenced and controlled by the metropolis, particularly as it affected agribusiness and the mineral industries, non-Indian ranchers, farmers, and miners in rural areas were also adversely affected. For instance, the beef production industry, once based on range-fed cattle, has been revolutionized by development of hybrid crops, feeder lots, mechanized packing techniques, and the growth of large supermarket quasi cartels which are beginning to control all aspects of production. Since 1935 the man-hours (labor time) to produce beef (measured in live weight) has been cut nearly in half, and it has been cut by one fourth since 1959 (U.S. Bureau of the Census, 1968: 629). Only those producers that control the greatest amount of capital are able to survive. Technology has influenced the grain, vegetable, and cotton industries through mechanization and fertilizers. Again, only the largest producers are able to survive. The small producer is losing his land due to costs or taxes, or both. He cannot get loans because he is a bad risk, and the large producer, in turn, is consolidating the land made available through the former's liquidation. But this trend is not solely a product of technology and capital; political influence and power, too, are critical in maintaining it.

Underdevelopment of rural areas is a result of the development of urban centers of finance, and the latter wield considerable influence in enacting legislation to maintain their growth. The mineral industries have long lived under special tax-privilege umbrellas; they have profited from the special-use tax (allowance) applicable to the exploitation of Indian lands, as well as the tax-depletion allowances offered to oil, gas, and mineral producers generally. The influence of the mining lobbies prior to the General Allotment Act and of the multinational oil and mineral corporations in maintaining the privileged tax-depletion allowance and protective import laws that have sheltered them for decades is solid evidence of the relationship between polity and the growth of the metropolis.

Agribusiness, too, has had long-term special federal privileges in the form of price supports, soil banks, and government-sponsored research which benefits huge producers but displaces the small operator. A recent investigation (President's National Advisory Commission, 1967: 142) reports that not only is farm policy dominated by acreage and price supports, but about 70% of the federal cost of assistance to farmers is correlated with attempts to bring supplies into alignment with demands for farm commodities. Farmers receive benefits from this assistance in proportion to their production or contribution to total farm output. This is not a policy to alleviate rural poverty; it is a commercial farm policy.

This internal contradiction of capitalism in the development of the metropolis (or the urban financial center) at the expense of the satellites (or the rural areas) was as apparent in the 1960s as it was in the 1860s. But it is more poignant now, perhaps, because the progeny of non-Indian pioneers—farmers, cattlemen, miners, and shopkeepers—are feeling the sting of underdevelopment which the Indians felt because of their pioneering forefathers.

As the metropolis grows and the resources of the satellites nourish that growth, many people living in rural areas choose to better their conditions by moving to urban areas. Some are successful, especially if they are white, yet many trade rural poverty for urban poverty. For Indians, who stand in a special neocolonial relationship to the rest of society, the latter is usually the case (Price, 1968; Hodge, 1969; Graves, 1971; Weppner, 1971; Snyder, 1971; Bahr, Chadwick, & Stauss, 1972). This is not to say that all Indians are doomed to poverty. Just as some native Africans once living in colonial Kenya, for example, can be educated at Oxford and through help open businesses in London or Nairobi or even enter the British colonial service, so can some U.S. Indians move from reservations, gain university educations, and become popular authors or high-ranking officials in the Indian Service. But the odds and the context in which both colonial Africans and neocolonial Indians live weigh heavily against such happenings. In both colonialism and neocolonialism, however, some subjects have made their way out of their native predicaments, just as some non–Indian ghetto dwellers and rural whites have.

To distinguish between Indians and non–Indians in the rural milieu is critical. The immediate local economies, including banks, shops, farms, and ranches, are controlled by non–Indians—usually the progeny of those non-Indian pioneers who "settled" the west. In the rural areas, too, the non-Indian populations control the churches, the education system, and the local government. The representatives from these areas to state and federal governments are almost always non-Indian. The obvious generalization from these and earlier generalizations is that whereas the satellites are exploited so that the metropolis may grow, the rural areas are in the immediate economic, political, and social control of non-Indians.

The Indian lives on or near reservations, agencies, colonies, or rancherias in a special wardship status not inflicted on non-Indians. His tribal government has only limited control over tribal resources and tribal affairs. Ultimate authority is vested in the Secretary of Interior, with local BIA employees having lesser authority over scores of aspects of the personal lives of Indians, such as the disposition of funds in their Individual Indian Monies accounts. The average Indian, then, is subject to local, state, and federal governments like everyone else, plus special neocolonial institutions such as tribal governments, which exercise only a modicum of control over their affairs, and the BIA, which serves as a caretaker of these tribal governments. Also, the Secretary of Interior and the House Committee on Interior and Insular Affairs can and do intervene in the lives and affairs of Indians, having decision-making powers which they do not have over any other race or ethnic group.

To summarize the hypothesis presented here, the growth of the metropolis caused the Indians of the United States to be underdeveloped; Indians did not begin that way. Non-Indians who originally settled in rural areas, expropriated Indian land and the resources thereon, and manned the satellite sector of the economy did meet with some success. Yet the past four decades have brought economic reversals for their progeny. Only the largest producers have been able to cope, profitably, with the changes in their industries as the metropolis has grown. As a consequence, outmigration of rural non-Indians has been substantial since 1920, farm and ranch consolidation has been enormous, and rural labor needs have been greatly reduced.

As the satellite economies, especially in the western states, have withered and the threat of economic demise has become more pressing, the non-Indians who own the shops, manage the banks, and operate the ranches and farms in rural areas have hired non-Indians rather than Indians for the permanent and temporary jobs they control. They tend to provide jobs for kin, friends, and others of the same race as the owner or manager. The Indian is most generally a consumer, seldom a wage earner, almost never an owner or controller of the production of anything in the economic satellites. As in the initial westward expansion of the metropolis-satellite economy, the Indians have been the first to suffer in the subsequent growth of the economy.

As a corollary, the greater the contribution of a producer to the national farm, ranch, or mining economy, the greater the federal benefits to the producer. Those that have, get. Though the rural areas exert little political influence, any influence that is felt, especially in state government, is that of the non-Indian. Another corollary is that as satellites have withered and small producers have gone bankrupt, those people who contribute least to the economy also exert the least political influence and receive the fewest benefits—usually only welfare assistance. The Indian, who has almost never produced anything, has the least influence and the least control over his own resources and the federal welfare he receives.

Finally, because Indians have few skills, little education, no capital, poor housing, poor health, and no influence or power, they are discriminated against by local non-Indians. The people who took their resources have denied status to Indians and have rebuked their morality because they have not been productive members of the society and because they have been special "wards" of the federal government. The cycle is vicious.

ON INDIAN EMPLOYMENT AND INDIAN CULTURE

The final question we will consider in this chapter is Indian culture and the Protestant ethic. Indians and their articulations with the dominant culture have been depicted in several ways by social scientists and other commentators, as we suggested in the opening paragraphs. It will be of some value to typologize the various ways in which Indians have been characterized. John Greenway (1969), a folklorist from the University of

Colorado, alleges that Indians are, and always have been, lazy, rapacious, and cruel. In Greenway's view, prior to European contact, Indians used to do as little work as possible and engaged in warfare as much as possible. Since European contact they have turned to the welfare dole and heavy drinking as alternatives to those specific traits they can no longer practice. Greenway's simple analysis of contemporary Indian behavior suggests either that Indian culture, in some undefined manner, is disposed to cause Indians to behave as he has characterized their modern behavior, or that Indian racial features have caused them to be rapacious and lazy (in his view).[8]

Greenway's "racial" or "cultural" theory that it is unclear whether biology or culture causes Indians to behave as they do has as its opposite the explanation of Indian work and drinking behavior offered by Ted Graves (1971). Graves argues that, all things being equal, Indians will work as hard, as well, and as often as non-Indians: Inherently, Indians are neither rapacious nor lazy. Neither Indian racial features nor Indian cultural features dispose them to be underemployed or heavy drinkers. Indeed, in their study of Navahos who have in the past or are at present residing in Denver, Graves (1971) and Weppner (1971) point out that all migrated to that city in search of work; most were undertrained when they got there, were not hired for the jobs for which they were trained, and received less pay than their non-Indian counterparts. Graves further notes that, depending on the manner in which they were confronted by attempts to satisfy Indian and non-Indian expectations, some, but not all, Indians began drinking heavily. Graves suggests, then, that Indian values on the reservation are different from non-Indian values off the reservation, and that the conflicts between these value expectations must and can be resolved—regardless of job training, job procurement, and regular paychecks—in order for the Indian to live in the city. He does not think that Indian culture predisposes Indians either to drink heavily or to fail at jobs. Whereas Graves fully recognizes that Navahos are socialized to Navaho values, or ideology, he argues rather persuasively that Navaho ideology does not doom Indians to failure in coping with non-Indian ideologies. Indeed, the most successful Navahos in Denver are those who expect to operate well in Indian *and* non-Indian contexts.

Between the racist-tainted Social Darwinism of Greenway, which argues that Indians are predisposed to be deadbeats and would be eliminated in life's competition were it not for liberal federal intervention, and Graves's hypothesis that Indian and non-Indian ideologies are different, but differences can be resolved and will not deter an Indian from successful participation in the economy, there are two middle-ground positions about Indian—non-Indian cultures. The position generally held by anthropologists and sociologists[9] is that Indian and white cultures (ideologies, values, or norms) are different, yet the differences are not so great that Indian culture cannot adjust to white culture. It is suggested that Indians will jettison their culture as they become more assimilated (a covert tautology). Nevertheless, Indian cultures, depending on their traditions, change at different rates and in different fashions as they accommodate to the dominant white culture. This view says that acculturation is a linear, inevitable phenomenon, although the amount and direction of variation from the trend line for each Indian culture might differ from other Indian cultures.

The final position, offered by Vine Deloria, Stan Steiner, and others, alleges that Indian culture is not only different from white culture, it rejects much of that dominant culture. This position holds that Indians, because of persistent Indian cultures (1) want to work, but at their own pace, (2) want employment, but want to be their own bosses, and so forth. The focus is on the persistence of Indian notions of work in a capitalist society. Indians want to maintain their culture without being swallowed by the Protestant work ethic and without destroying reservation societies.

It is our hypothesis, as should be clear in part from the preceding, that the metropolis-satellite capitalist economy has harnessed the military and the BIA to conquer and control North American Indians, and it is this political economy that has maintained Indian deprivation. Now the question is, have structural features of traditional Indian culture also served to inhibit Indian economic success from the white view? Our answer is simple and equivocal: They could have, but we doubt the causal importance of these vague structures. That is to say, Indians have seen their resources expropriated and exploited by non-Indians, they have been dominated on reservations by non-Indians, and they have been the recipients of several forms of government assistance—sometimes in payment for land appropriated by the government and given to railroads, mining, and ranching interests; sometimes in the form of government jobs (during the Great Depression and the War on Poverty, for instance); and sometimes in the form of welfare payments and commodities. But throughout the transformations from traditional economies to the contemporary part-time-wage work and welfare economic niche occupied by most Indians, a certain number have maintained some cultural integrity that separates them from other Indians.

Needless to say, reservation life and special relations to the federal government have helped to maintain Indian culture in a way unanticipated by federal planners. Even though livelihoods could not be procured in traditional ways in traditional territories, and native political organizations lost their autonomy and authority, and native sodalities dissolved, and kinship organizations, (such as corporate patrilineal and corporate matrilineal descent groups) withered and lost their meanings, and religious movements (such as peyotism) swept throughout the Indian reserves—still Indian cultures did not lose all that was once theirs. Let us explain by providing some generalizations about Indian work attitudes.

INDIANS AND WORK

Utes and Shoshones seek work on and near reservations, but with little success (Jorgensen, 1972). The same is true for Blackfeet (Robbins, in press), Oneidas (Dowling, 1973), Umatillas (Wagner, in press), and Pimas (Munsell, 1967), to mention a few tribes on which we have good data. These tribes are distributed from Wisconsin to Oregon, and from Idaho to Arizona. Furthermore, Indians on these reserves take pride in their jobs (see the sources above) and despair when they are laid off. The simple fact is that in areas near reservations jobs are few and temporary, and all things being equal, the Indian is the last person hired.

In two careful studies, Weber (in press) and Wagner (in press) have demonstrated there is no relationship between education and occupation and employment for the Blackfeet and Cree of Montana and the Umatilla of Oregon. Whites get jobs and Indians do not, and it is not because Indians desire to work less or have significantly less education than their white counterparts.

In another work we have further provided an inductive and detailed explanation of Indian underemployment and the contradictions in Indian economic life (Jorgensen, 1972, esp. Part II). At best we can summarize these contradictions and their "resolution" here (see also Aberle, 1966, for a related account of the Navaho).

During their reservation tenure, Indians have been urged by government officials at all levels, Christian missionaries, local entrepreneurs, and white taxpayers to practice the Protestant ethic. That is, they have challenged Indians to work hard (in wage work or as entrepreneurs), to be thrifty (economizing resources so as to maximize benefits), to develop skills, to care for the nuclear family by providing for them while instilling the need to do well in the eyes of God; and to dissociate themselves from the behaviors and demands of collateral kinsmen and "pagan" tribal friends. Indeed, Indians have been asked to leave their reserves and tribal ways and civilize themselves. Indians have been challenged to pay land taxes, thus ensuring responsible citizenship.

Yet Indians, especially since 1934 and the Wheeler-Howard Act, have also been urged by the federal government to move in a contradictory direction. That is, Indians have been prompted to create tribal corporate bodies, to conduct agricultural businesses, craft businesses, and the like. Thus, while individual Indians have been told to sever themselves from their tribes and become farmers, ranchers, or craft store proprietors, their tribes have been encouraged (and aided through legislation) to compete with them. Furthermore, tribal corporate bodies have been thrown into competition over extremely meager federal funds to finance these corporate ventures. To add to these problems, tribal corporations have been pushed toward competition in the agribusiness sphere which, for the reasons specified above, has doomed the vast majority of such enterprises to failure. In other words, the very nature of the production relations of agriculture defeat tribal corporate ventures almost before they begin.

In contrast to the federal- and white-induced Protestant and corporate ethics (which contradict each other), Indians are oriented toward narrow, individualistic hedonism. That is, given the absolute deprivation in reservation life in such things as jobs, income, and political autonomy, they are disposed to avoid obligations to kin and friends and use their scarce resources for their own pleasures. More often than not this means that some people will disrupt family and reservation affairs by engaging in heavy drinking bouts, thus becoming a burden on, rather than a asset to, kin and friends. Fist fights can break out, and animosity can smolder in households as a consequence of such behavior. It is obvious that to succumb to hedonistic impulses conflicts with Protestant ethic individualism and corporate collectivism, and unrestrained pursuit of personal pleasure can even lead to death through consumption, malnutrition, and cirrhosis. Indeed, narrow hedonism is the antithesis of the Protestant ethic, and it is this hedonism, parodied as rapaciousness and lust, that so animates Greenway and causes him to argue that Indians, by nature, are inclined to forsake the work ethic. Our position is that hedonistic impulses might well reside in all humans, but the forces affecting Indian life for the past century have given Indians proportionately more cause than their white cousins to act on these impulses.

The final tug on Indian behavior is provided by a generalized, communitarian Indian ethic. Among Indians it is referred to as "The Indian Way," "The Way," "The Way of the 'Old People,' " and so forth. In general it beckons Indians to honor the needs of the aged, the infirm, the children, and the less fortunate. This ethic, so prominent in religious movements (Aberle, 1966; Wallace, 1970; and Jorgensen, 1972), calls on Indians to respect their obligations to share with kin and friends and avoid narrow ends—material and spiritual. In brief, Indians should share, rather than save; cooperate, rather than compete; and observe Indian beliefs, rather than those of the whites. Quite obviously this ethic is directly contradictory to the Protestant ethic, which calls for narrow family achievements and competition. It is also contradictory to the corporate ethic, which calls for competition among tribes (handled by business committees), and it is contradictory to narrow hedonism, which threatens the communitarian fabric and life itself.

Because reservation and urban Indian life is deprived, Indians are constantly tempted to sever their ties with kin and friends, and the obligations these relationships entail, and to seek crumbs of wealth in the city or to save crumbs from their paychecks on the reserves. When Indians so behave, they are nevertheless mindful of the needs of their larger family networks, and it is not easy to deny kinsmen in need when one's own "successes" are limited in amount and duration. To be sure, today's donor is often tomorrow's recipient.

The contradictions among hedonism, corporate collectivism, Protestant ethic individualism, and the communitarian Indian ethic are resolved for very few people caught in the neocolonial niche of the metropolis-satellite structure of the U.S. political economy. To satisfy the Protestant ethic is to sever ties with the tribe. Only the communitarian Indian ethic provides a reasonable, albeit temporary, solution to the conditions in which Indians live. Does this communitarian ethic eschew work? The empirical answer is a flat no. It lauds work, but it eschews narrow, competitive striving, or the gain of one Indian at the expense of others.

Finally, let us address the question of whether the communitarian Indian ethic rejects the Protestant and corporate ethics because they are not the ethics of past Indian cultures. Our answer is still equivocal. In part, the communitarian Indian ethic is reported, in one way or another, for most American Indian tribes at contact. Sometimes the bilateral extended family shared and cooperated, sometimes it was matrilineal or patrilineal descent groups, sometimes whole villages and bands emphasized cooperation and sharing in various degrees in various situations.[10] At present the corporate descent groups, villages, and bands are defunct, and redemptive religious movements rather than "traditional" (precontact) religions preach communitarian Indian ethics. On the whole these ethics are created on traditional bases, but they are responses to odious oppression and persistent poverty. In our view, precontact Indian culture, in general, helps account for the emphasis on communitarian values in the present, but the systematic oppression of Indians on reservations, the federal maintenance of the reserve communities, and the deprivation which has characterized Indian life on these reserves because of the Indian position within the metropolis-satellite political economy explain why the communal values persist and why they are different from their precontact forms.

The communitarian values, on the other hand, do not explain the metropolis-satellite economy nor the neocolonial niche occupied by Indians within it.

NOTES

1. *Metropolis* as used in this chapter is not synonymous with *urban area location,* or *city.* The hypothesis advanced later in this chapter reveals its special meaning in this context.

2. *Employability* here means all Indians of working age who are not physically or mentally disabled, not students, not retired, and not encumbered by family responsibilities.

3. Indian unemployment was so severe in the recession of 1974–1975 that they were designated a special manpower target group, and over $57 million was allocated for public service employment programs for them (U.S. Department of Labor, 1975: 84–85).

4. The proportion of Indian households in dwellings in urban areas without toilets is 14 times greater than for the total U.S. population. Almost half of all Indian dwellings in rural areas do not have toilets (U.S. Department of Health, Education, and Welfare, 1974: v).

5. See, for example, the following analyses of family household organization among people living in poverty who have little access to resources: Black Caribs of Guatemala and British Honduras (Gonzalez, 1969); Mestizos of Latin America (Adams, 1960); blacks of the West Indies (Smith, 1962; Otterbein, 1965); Mestizos in Mexico and Mexican-Americans (Borah & Cook, 1966); and blacks in the United States (Moynihan, 1965).

6. André Gundar Frank (1967) fully develops the concept of the metropolis-satellite economy, although Frank's conception varies from ours in that he treats the metropolis-satellite as nexus, whereas we treat it as *nexus* and *locus*. Furthermore, Frank stresses exchange relations, whereas we emphasize relations of production.

7. The transcontinental railroad, completed in 1869 with the extensive use of Chinese labor, was such an expensive project that the railroads could not pay off their loans from the federal government. The government, in turn, cleared the loans without payment and left ownership in the hands of the railroad "financiers."

8. Greenway's (1969) essay is bombastic and error-ridden, but it represents a Social Darwinist view that has been popular in Congress since the 1860s (see Jorgensen, 1976).

9. See Walker (1972) for a host of essays centered around the acculturation scheme, in *The Emergent Native Americans*.

10. See Jorgensen's forthcoming inductive analysis (in press). The economies, politics, social organizations, and religions of 172 tribes at European contact are analyzed.

REFERENCES

Aberle, David F. *The Peyote Religion among the Navaho.* Viking Fund Publications in Anthropology, No. 42. Chicago: Aldine Publishing Co., 1966.

Adams, R. N. *An Inquiry into the Nature of the Family.* In Gertrude E. Dole and Robert L. Carneiro (eds.), *Essays in the Science of Culture.* New York, Crowell, 1960.

Bahr, Howard M., Bruce A. Chadwick, & Joseph H. Stauss. "Discrimination against Urban Indians in Seattle." *The Indian Historian* 5 (Winter 1972): 4–11.

Borah, Woodrow, & Sherburn F. Cook. "Marriage and Legitimacy in Mexican Culture: Mexico and California." In Jacobus tenBroek (ed.), *The Law of the Poor.* San Francisco, Chandler Publishing Co., 1966.

Brophy, William, & Sophie D. Aberle. *The Indian: American's Unfinished Business.* Norman, University of Oklahoma Press, 1966.

California Fair Employment Practice Commission. "Minority Groups in California." *Monthly Labor Review* 89 (September 1966): 978–983.

California State Advisory Commission on Indian Affairs. "Indians in Rural and Reservation Areas." Report submitted to the Governor and Legislature of California, Sacramento, 1966.

De la Isla, Jose. "Household Composition and Economics within the Umatilla Indian Reservation Community." In Joseph G. Jorgensen (ed.), *Western Indians: A Comparative Analysis of the Indians of Western North America.* San Francisco: W. H. Freeman & Co., in press.

Deloria, Vine, Jr. *Custer Died for Your Sins: An Indian Manifesto.* New York, Macmillan, 1969.

Dowling, John. "Wisconsin Oneida: The Economics of the Culture Change." Unpublished Ph.D. dissertation, University of Michigan, Ann Arbor, 1973.

Frank, André Gundar. *Capitalism and Underdevelopment in Latin America.* New York: Monthly Review Press, 1967.

Gonzalez, Nancie L. Solien. *Black Carib Household Structure.* Seattle: University of Washington Press, 1969.

Graves, Theodore D. "Drinking and Drunkenness among Urban Indians." In Jack O. Waddell and O. Michael Watson (eds.), *The American Indian in Urban Society.* Boston: Little, Brown & Co., 1971.

Greenway, John. "Will the Indians Get Whitey?" *National Review* 21 (March 11, 1969): 223–28, 245.

Haas, Theodore H. "The Legal Aspects of Indian Affairs from 1887 to 1957." In George Simpson and Milton Yinger (eds.), *American Indians and Indian Life.* Annals of the American Academy of Political and Social Sciences. Vol. 311 (May 1957).

Hodge, William. "The Albuquerque Navahos." *University of Arizona Anthropological Papers,* No. 11, 1969.

Department of Interior. *Indian Record.* Special issue: Economic Development. Washington, D.C.: U.S. Government Printing Office, October 1968.

Jorgensen, Joseph G. "The Ethnohistory and Acculturation of the Northern Ute." Unpublished Ph.D. dissertation, Indiana University, Bloomington, 1964.

Jorgensen, Joseph G. *The Sun Dance Religion: Power for the Powerless.* Chicago: University of Chicago Press, 1972.

Jorgensen, Joseph G. (ed.). *Reservation Indian Society: Studies in Economics, Politics, Families and Households.* Stanford, Calif.: Occidental Publishing Co., 1976.

Jorgensen, Joseph G. *Western Indians: A Comparative Analysis of the Indians of Western North America.* San Francisco: W. H. Freeman & Co., in press.

Klose, Nelson. *A Concise Study Guide to the American Frontier.* Lincoln: University of Nebraska Press, 1964.

Lurie, Nancy Ostereich. "The Indian Claims Commission Act." In George Simpson and Milton Yinger (eds.), *American Indians and American Life.* Annals of the American Academy of Political and Social Sciences. Vol. 311 (May 1957).

Maxwell, Jean A. (Nordstrom). *The Contemporary Spokane and Colville Indians.* Ph.D. dissertation, University of Michigan, 1973.

Meriam, Lewis. *The Problems of Indian Administration*. Baltimore; Johns Hopkins University Press, 1928.

Mochon, Marian. "Stockbridge-Munsee Cultural Adaptations: 'Assimilated Indians.' " *Proceedings of the American Philosophical Society* 112 (June 1968): 182–219.

Moynihan, Daniel. *The Negro Family–The Case for National Action*. U.S. Department of Labor, Office of Policy Planning and Research, 1965.

Munsell, Marvin. "Land and Labor at Salt River." Unpublished Ph.D. dissertation, University of Oregon, Eugene, 1967.

Otterbein, Keith F. "Caribbean Family Organization: A Comparative Analysis." *American Anthropoligist* 67 (1965): 66–79.

President's National Advisory Commission on Civil Disorders. *Report of the National Advisory Commission on Civil Disorders*. New York: Bantam Books, 1968.

President's National Advisory Commission on Rural Poverty. *The People Left Behind*. Washington, D.C.: U.S. Government Printing Office, 1967.

Price, John A. "The Migration and Adaptation of American Indians in Los Angeles." *Human Organization* 27 (1968): 168–175.

Robbins, Lynn A. "Economy, Household and Family among the Blackfeet." In Joseph G. Jorgensen (ed.), *Western Indians: A Comparative Analysis of the Indians of Western North America*. San Francisco: W. H. Freeman & Co., in press.

Shannon, Lyle W. "The Economic Absorption and Cultural Integration of Immigrant Workers: Characteristics of the Individual vs. the Nature of the System." *American Behavioral Scientist* 13 (September–October 1969), pp. 36–56.

Shannon, Lyle W., and Magdaline Shannon. The Assimilation of Migrants to Cities: Anthropological and Sociological Contributions. In Shannon and Shannon (eds.), *Urban Affairs Annual Review*. New York: Sage, 1967.

Simpson, George, and Milton Yinger (eds.). *American Indians and American Life*. Annals of the American Academy of Political and Social Sciences. Vol. 311 (May 1957).

Smith, M. G. *West Indian Family Structure*. Seattle: University of Washington Press, 1962.

Snyder, Peter Z. "The Social Environment of the Urban Indian." In Jack O. Waddell and O. Michael Watson (eds.), *The American Indian in Urban Society*. Boston: Little, Brown & Co., 1971.

Steiner, Stan. *The New Indians*. New York: Harper & Row, 1968.

U.S. Bureau of the Census. *Statistical Abstract of the United States, 1966*. Washington, D.C.: U.S. Government Printing Office, 1967.

U.S. Bureau of the Census. *Statistical Abstract of the United States, 1967*. Washington, D.C.: U.S. Government Printing Office, 1968.

U.S. Bureau of the Census. "General Social and Economic Characteristics—California." *Census of Population: 1970, U.S. Summary,* Final Report PC (1)—C1 (Washington D.C.: U.S. Government Printing Office, 1972.

U.S. Bureau of the Census. "American Indians." *Census of Population: 1970, Subject Reports*. Final Report PC (2)–1F. Washington, D.C.: U.S. Government Printing Office, 1973.

U.S. Bureau of Indian Affairs. *Answers to Your Questions about American Indians.* Washington, D.C.: U.S. Government Printing Office, 1949, 1955, 1968.

U.S. Congress, House, Committee on Interior and Insular Affairs. *Investigation of the Bureau of Indian Affairs.* 83rd Cong. Washington, D.C.: U.S. Government Printing Office, 1953, 1954.

U.S. Congress, House, Committee on Interior and Insular Affairs. *Indian Unemployment Survey.* Committee Print No. 3, 88th Cong., First Sess. Washington, D.C.: U.S. Government Printing Office, 1963.

U.S. Congress, Senate, Committee on Interior and Insular Affairs. *California Indian Oversight Hearings, Part I: Issues and Problems Affecting Reservations and Rural Indians in California.* Washington, D.C.: U.S. Government Printing Office, 1974.

U.S. Department of Health, Education, and Welfare. *American Indians: A Study of Selected Socio-Economic Characteristics of Ethnic Minorities Based on the 1970 Census.* Office of Special Concerns. Washington, D.C.: U.S. Government Printing Office, 1974.

U.S. Department of Labor. *Manpower Report of the President, 1975.* Washington, D.C.: U.S. Government Printing Office, 1975.

Waddell, Jack O., and O. Michael Watson (eds.). *The American Indian in Urban Society.* Boston: Little, Brown & Co., 1971.

Wagner, Carruth J., and Erwin S. Rabeau. "Indian Poverty and Indian Health." *Health, Education, and Welfare Indicators,* March 1964.

Wagner, Nancy Owens. "Earning a Living at Umatilla." In Joseph G. Jorgensen (ed.), *Western Indians: A Comparative Analysis of the Indians of Western North America.* San Francisco: W. H. Freeman & Co., in press.

Walker, Deward E., Jr. (ed.). *The Emergent Native Americans.* Boston: Little, Brown & Co., 1972.

Wallace, A. F. C. *The Death and Rebirth of the Senecca.* New York: Alfred A. Knopf, 1970.

Weber, Kenneth R. "Economy, Occupation, Education and Family in a Tri-ethnic Community." In Joseph G. Jorgensen (ed.), *Western Indians: A Comparative Analysis of the Indians of Western North America.* San Francisco: W. H. Freeman & Co., in press.

Weppner, Robert S. "Urban Economic Opportunities." In Jack O. Waddell and O. Michael Watson (eds.), *The American Indian in Urban Society.* Boston: Little, Brown & Co., 1971.

CHAPTER 6

Women at work in America: History, status, and prospects

Adeline Levine

The need to work is a fact of life for most people, and American women are no exception to this rule. As women have increasingly participated in the nation's work force the locale of their work has changed, as have the tasks and the forms of remuneration. But women have been the victims of cultural lag. Technology permits and encourages forms of behavior which are as yet unsupported by coherent sets of cultural ideas. Women must work, but our society's values, beliefs, and norms prevent their achieving full status as workers with the attendant rights, privileges, rewards, and obligations of their positions.

For well over a century there has been serious questioning of attitudes, practices, and laws affecting women. It has reached a high pitch of intensity as more women than ever before are working and studying for longer times in locations away from their homes. Some of the attitudes, practices, and laws will be analyzed in this chapter, as well as the challenges to established ways. The chapter will also discuss the work role in women's lives in the context of

Note: I want to thank Lucy Calkins and Murray Levine for critical readings of the early drafts of this paper; Roy Kaplan who suggested, criticized, and waited for the paper; the State University of New York at Buffalo for a sabbatical leave which gave me time to write it; Norma Burk who typed and retyped with patience and an air of good cheer.

the changing situation of American women. Discrimination against women is assumed as a given condition, not needing to be proven once again. However, some of the forms and consequences of discrimination that particularly affect working women will be discussed.

A review of the current position of women in the labor force will be followed by a brief description of some historical and contemporary forces of discrimination, and some forms of resistance to discrimination within the larger context of underlying changes in our technology and economy. The discussion will stress married women for four reasons: (1) historically, their legal status and their obligations have differed more markedly from men's than those of single women have, (2) most American women do marry, (3) it is the increase of married women workers which has created the most extreme change in the labor force over the past few decades, and (4) it is that increase which has the potential for great changes in the family and socialization of the young.

WOMEN IN THE CONTEMPORARY LABOR FORCE: SOME FACTS AND FIGURES

Numbers

In 1974 there were nearly 36 million women in the labor force. Women comprised almost 40% of the labor force, and 4 out of 10 worked full time and year round (U.S. Department of Labor, 1975: 62). Approximately one half of all women between 18 and 54 were in the labor force, with the rates of participation highest among women 18 to 24 and 35 to 54. The sheer increase in the numbers of women in the labor force over the past few decades, and particularly the increase in the percentages who are married and mothers, has been of interest to many writers (Blood, 1965; Oppenheimer, 1974; Sweet, 1973; Waldman & McEaddy, 1974; Wolfbein, 1964). Nearly three fifths of the 36 million women workers are married "with husband present." Two fifths of the women are mothers; a total of 26.2 million children, 6 million of them under age six, had working mothers in 1973 (U.S. Bureau of the Census, 1973c, Table 1; U.S. Department of Labor, 1973b, 1974a, 1974b).

These figures provide a starting point for learning about working women. Let us turn first to their earnings.

Earnings

Women earn a good deal less money than men. In 1973 the median income for full-time working women was 58% that of men ($5,900/$10,200), a decline from 1956, when women's median earnings were 63% of men's (U.S. Department of Labor, 1969a: 133; 1974a). Within every occupational group, women's median salaries are lower than men's. Even in clerical jobs, where women dominate numerically, the median salaries are 65% those of men (Kreps, 1971: 2; Sommers, 1974).

The range of median salaries of couples working in 1959 and 1969 differed not only by occupational groups but by sex. For all husbands in a large-scale census sample the difference between high and low median salaries in 1969 was $8,164. For wives, working full time and year round, that difference was $1,884 (Oppenheimer, 1974: 18). The difference in earnings by sex is the result of complex factors. The most obvious one, indicated by the limited range of median earnings, is that women are concentrated in low-paying jobs. Even where sex desegregation is occurring, men are entering "women's occupations" and reaching high-level jobs within them, while the movement of women into men's occupations has been a slower process (Gross, 1968).

Women's Occupations

Over one third of all employed women are clerical workers (U.S. Department of Labor, 1974a). If we examine women's chief occupations, at the highest level we find the semiprofessionals: nurses, teachers, librarians, and dietitians. The rest of the jobs may be characterized as requiring readily available skilled and semiskilled laborers, but the workers are not organized into strong unions. They are easy-entry jobs—the requisite skills can be easily learned, and substitute personnel can be taught quickly. They are jobs not threatened by familial mobility, for they are found all over the country; they do not depend on a difficult-to-establish private clientele; long-range commitment is not essential; and lack of continuity in the labor market does not impede the performance of the jobs. In these jobs there is little, if any, authority over men; many are of a nurturant variety, concerning the care of clothes, and children, and, often, of male bosses (U.S. Department of Labor, 1969a; Sommers, 1974). They are jobs which can be carried on from time to time, when and where women are able to find employment, and obviously, when and where they can fit the jobs in with family responsibilities.

Higher Education and Work

What of the best educated women? Not only are they the most likely of all to be working at any time,[1] but they are the women most able to choose from a variety of jobs with the highest earning potential (Kreps, 1971: 27; Sweet, 1973: 14). But even these women are clustered in lower-paying areas. In 1971, the median annual salary for women with college degrees, working full time and year round, was lower than for men with high school diplomas (U.S. Department of Labor, 1973a).

The fields in which women earn their undergraduate, master's, and doctorate degrees indicate some of the occupations they enter. In 1966–67, women were educated chiefly in education and the humanities. Basic science, mathematics, the highest level professions, business administration, and economics accounted for the lowest concentrations of women degree earners (U.S. Department of Labor, 1969a: 187–199). In short, in the mid-1960s, women did not prepare themselves to hold jobs in the mid-1970s in well-paid occupations where some power is exercised in our society: in big business, government, and high-level professional, scientific, and technological fields.

The Need to Earn Money

Today, most working women occupy secondary places in the labor force. When they are in the same occupational groups as men, they are not found in the top-level positions in proportions reflecting their numbers. Even where they do hold the same positions as men, employers and even union spokesmen justify discriminatory pay scales by claiming that women are not the breadwinners for the family, and holding a job is a secondary aspect of their adult roles. This belief is so widespread that women themselves often concur, which may account in part for their acquiescence to inequitable practices.

In fact, however, a recent Women's Bureau bulletin summarized the important subsistence role which work plays in women's lives:

> Millions of women who were in the labor force in March 1973 worked to support themselves or others. This was true of most of the 7.7 million single women workers. Nearly all of the 6.3 million women workers who were widowed, divorced, or separated from their husbands—particularly the women who were also raising children—were working for compelling economic reasons. In addition, the 3.7 million married women workers whose husbands had incomes below $5,000 in 1972 almost certainly worked because of economic need. Finally, about 3 million women would be added if we take into account those women whose husbands had incomes between $5,000 and $7,000. (U.S. Department of Labor, 1974c: 1)

After accounting for over 20 million women workers, the Department of Labor points out that about 1 in 10 women workers were family heads, and over 2 million women seeking work had nonworking husbands. There seem to be excellent economic reasons why women work—to support themselves and to support their families (Parnes, Shea, Spitz, Zeller et al., 1970: 212). While not all of the women household heads were in the labor force, the realities of women's economic needs refute the rationalizations for paying women lower wages.

WOMEN'S ROLES AND SOCIAL ATTITUDES

To understand the contemporary status of working women and the forces of discrimination affecting them, we must explore some general attitudes about women and the relations between the sexes. The attitudes date from earliest times and have long been an integral part of our own cultural heritage.

Since records have been kept, women's place in society has been subservient to men and to their needs, interests, and desires. Women have been men's slaves, workers, concubines, housewives, mothers, assistants, and entertainers. Only in rare instances have women been independent, in charge of economic decision making on the familial level, or in positions of authority in formal structures (Bullough, 1974). It is true that when noble Romans were engaged in the Punic wars their wives managed their enterprises. Similarly, mistresses of great estates managed them in the medieval period of unceasing warfare and crusades, as did wives on Nantucket Island who took care of the family home and business or farm, when their men were off on long whaling voyages. These and other rare instances did not violate the general male-female relationship: a basic exchange of male support and protection for female obedience and assistance, one where the male is dominant both in law and in everyday behavior.

The Colonial Period

By the early days of our colonial period the patriarchal system was already centuries old. The colonists and their British relatives learned from the Bible, and inferred from women's anatomy, that women's behavior and capabilities were to be limited and guided by men. In the colonies, as in England, the status of wife and mother was considered the proper one for adult women. Girls were educated almost solely in the household arts; their minds were considered unsuitable for intellectual development (Spruill, 1972: 214 ff.). Berkin (1974) describes the women of the time as follows: "Trained as a daughter in the womanly skills, taught the passive womanly virtues, discouraged from intellectual activity, and encouraged to expect her ultimate fulfillment in marriage and motherhood, the average colonial woman led a life of narrow focus" (p. 6).

After marriage, following the English custom, a woman became a part of the family unit, her individual identity virtually lost, her legal status that of *femme covert*. The doctrine of *coverture* has been described as one where the husband and wife are one, and that one is the husband. As a *femme covert*, a woman could not control, manage, or transfer her own property; she could not make contracts; she could not be sued. She was treated, in short, as a person incapable of understanding the consequences of her behavior. Whatever practical rationalizations were offered, the status of *femme covert* helped to perpetuate "the feudal theory of 'natural male dominance' " (Kanowitz, 1971: 35–37).

However, in the American colonies, prevalent British customs and laws underwent continual modification. For one thing, there was a great shortage of women, and they were desperately needed, from the beginning, to work, to make homes, and to bear children. In the earliest period of settlement, in 1619, the chief profits connected with the colonies came to "sea-going entrepreneurs who shipped eligible young girls to Virginia and sold them in marriage at 80 pounds of tobacco a head" (Berkin, 1974: 4)

The shortage of women resulted in their being offered various protections from abuse by husbands. As the colonial period went on, the laws continued to deviate from those of Britain, and many of them focused on women's property and status. The long and complex challenge of common law by equity proceedings, for example, preceded, and underlay in part, the rapid changes in women's status which took place in the 19th century (Beard, 1962: ch. 4–8; Melder, 1965: ch. 1).

Most colonial women lived busy, purposeful lives, working on the family farm or in their husbands' business enterprises. It was a rare instance when a woman started a business of her own. There are some recorded cases, however, of colonial women who invested their endowments or inheritances and prospered. There were women working alone who were shopkeepers, newspaper owners, or innkeepers; however, those who worked alone were usually carrying on a deceased husband's business.

There were not many options open for women who did not marry. The status of *femme sole* was recognized in law and was of importance for unmarried or widowed women who possessed money or skills or both. The community benefited by recognizing these women legally, as individuals who could make contracts, sue, and buy and sell property. Such recognition meant that neither their skills nor their capital were lost to the community, while they remained responsible for their own support. Most spinsters, however, lived with married brothers or sisters, performing the same chores as married women (Berkin, 1974).

By the last decade of the 18th century important industrial changes were occurring in the new country with the growth of household manufacturing, primarily spinning, weaving, and knitting. The man was the master in the home industries, the woman his hard-working assistant. When the first textile mills were built in the late 18th century, Secretary of the Treasury Alexander Hamilton hailed them as industries to be developed without removing men from the fields, and he glowingly described the English system of factory employment for women and children. Public economists and moralists urged women to work in the new factories (Baker, 1964: 1–6). The idea of woman's proper role expanded to include work out of the home as well as in it, at least for some women.

On the other hand, the role also expanded to include little or no work for some women (Klein, 1971: ch. 2). This latter development accompanied the growing affluence in the colonies:

> . . . by the first quarter of the eighteenth century relatively stable and settled communities were appearing in the colonies, towns and cities had developed, wealthy planters and merchants, and middle class tradesmen, artisans, and professional men had appeared. Accompanying the new society came new values concerning women: women of the upper classes and the higher middle classes were not required to work; instead they patterned their lives after those of the British gentry, emphasizing the cultivation of leisure, engaging in fashionable pursuits, and concentrating their attention on manners. (Melder, 1965: 47)

In England, of course, frivolity had been raised to an art form after the Restoration of the 1660s, providing a pattern for America. The leisurely ideal was accentuated early in the 19th century by the Romantic movement, which affected literature and the theater and influenced attitudes about women's true nature and destiny.

Since few women could afford an idle existence, the ideal of the lady, with her finer nature and her delicate ways, was probably realized most fully among the wealthiest classes. But for most women the expectation of ladylike behavior created problems:

> While Americans were officially adopting the belief that women were made of finer fabric, not suited for the more mundane tasks of life, the vast majority of Americans were still living on farms where women worked, and in fact pulled a fair share of the load so the family farm would not collapse. The result was a continuing contradiction between myth and reality which often led foreign visitors to make fun of the Americans. When myth and reality clash the result is often a kind of hesitancy about what is proper, and when the myth is adopted as proper there is still no certitude of what is right conduct because it is so far from reality. Reality, except in the more backward parts of the country, was considered poor manners, and this meant that women were caught in a kind of trap in which they were damned if they did and damned if they did not. (Bullough, 1974: 312)

The 19th Century

In the early decades of the 19th century the "true nature of woman" and "woman's place" began to be topics of popular interest. Women were thought to be endowed with a finer nature than men, yet to be easily susceptible to seduction. Women were to be modest and decorous and yet sexually attractive to men. Morally strong, but physically frail, they were dependent and in need of men's protection, while able to buttress his efforts and dissuade him from evil ways.

Whether women worked, and no matter what the work, a good wife molded herself to her husband's desires, and women generally remained responsible for the care and moral guidance of young children. Ridley (1972: 377) suggests that at this time, when the mortality rates declined more quickly than fertility rates, women may well have experienced a great increase in child-rearing tasks, because more infants and children survived and fathers increasingly worked away from home. Married women of the middle classes certainly found much of their time absorbed within the home caring for their children. A cult of motherhood was reflected in journals and books written for this audience. "Compared with maternal influence," women of the 1830s were told, "the combined authority of law and arms, and public sentiment are little things" (Melder, 1965: 44).

There was, however, some lessening of household duties for many women, as well as some increase in leisure and education which accompanied industrialization (Flexner, 1959: 17). Despite contradictory expectations for their behavior, women at all social-class levels increased their activities outside the home during the 19th century. Poorer women worked in the factories and in domestic service. Middle-class women were basically homemakers and mothers, but many, particularly unmarried women, became involved in reform movements of all sorts, some of which led to the organized Women's Rights movement in the United States (Barnes, 1933; Melder, 1965).

Some women took advantage of the new opportunities to become educated. By the 1830s women were being hired as teachers, and by the 1840s they were being sought. Men were finding opportunities in business and the skilled trades more attractive than teaching, while "the phenomenal growth of public schools created an alarming shortage of teachers" (Baker, 1964: 56). In order to educate them, high schools began to admit girls, with the first public high school for girls opening in 1824. Prior to the Civil War, as free elementary and secondary schools appeared throughout our country, girls were admitted to them along with boys, in part because the population was so sparse that in some areas there were not enough boys to fill a grammer school and a high school.

After the Civil War there was a shortage of men in the northern and western states. By that time, more women than men were teaching in the public schools, "and after that time, as men went west, both elementary and secondary schools went largely into the hands of women" (Baker, 1964: 58). From the beginning, women teachers were paid less than men—a quarter of their salaries, in some cases. This disparity made them attractive employees to taxpayers. With no other professional opportunities open to them, educated women accepted these poorly paid positions (Flexner, 1959: ch. 8; Smuts, 1971: 91).

The shortage of men was of importance for another reason. In New York State after the Civil War, women of marriageable age outnumbered men by 39,000, and in Massachusetts by 27,000. Parents concerned with their daughter's welfare may well have viewed teaching as a guarantee of a secure, respectable future for their child. By 1870, about 5% of working women were teachers. Only servants, waitresses, agricultural laborers, dressmakers, and laundresses outnumbered them.

During the Civil War, and the ensuing period of economic and industrial expansion, women were employed in a number of semiskilled jobs. Labor shortages of various sorts opened some occupations to women who constituted a pool of cheap labor. By the 1870 census, nursing was a professional career for young women, and women were entrenched as saleswomen in retail stores. Inventions also resulted in new occupations for women. Clean, light work as telephone operators and typists attracted women described as "well-bred" and "young women of education" (Baker, 1964: 69).

Turn of the Century and Later

By 1900, the Census Bureau counted more than 5 million "gainfully employed" women, about 18% of all workers aged 16 and over. One out of every five females over age 10 were included in this number, triple the amount in 1870. The largest group (40%) were employed in domestic and personal services. Next in order were those employed in manufacturing, and then those on farms. The professions, chiefly teaching, were the fourth biggest employers of women, and the trade and transportation sector was the smallest. This sector, however, had grown remarkably in the final decades of the 19th century, so that in 30 years the number of women employed in white-collar occupations had increased from 19,000 to 503,000. These saleswomen, telegraphy and telephone operators, stenographers, typists, clerks, copyists, bookkeepers, and accountants were of middle-class origins, and they had more education than any other working women except professionals (Baker, 1964: ch. 5).

The phenomenon of women entering and staying in the paid work force was a subject of general discussion throughout the 19th century. A growing minority stressed that jobs were important for women; that, in reality, not all women could depend upon anyone else for their support. Mary Livermore, a suffragist and lecturer, stated the case that "no girl should be considered well educated, no matter what her accomplishments, until she has learned a trade, a business, a vocation, or a profession" (Baker, 1964: 85). The majority of writers predicted worrisome changes in sex roles; as women encroached on men's domain, men would find themselves aproned, holding the baby, and stirring the pudding. There was a good deal of lamenting about the good old days when women knew their place.

By the end of the 19th and the beginning of the 20th century, the phrases "the new woman" and "the modern woman" were used liberally by journalists and by women to describe themselves. As women assessed the changes in their activities, they could see they had achieved greater freedom in a number of directions. Not only were women working outside the home, but they were graduating from a variety of women's colleges. There was even a new emphasis on clothes that allowed women greater freedom of movement. Women were joining women's organizations by the thousands, becoming major forces for the reform of schools and juvenile courts. They worked for temperance, women's suffrage, and in settlement houses (Levine & Levine, 1970). This story has been told in fascinating detail by a number of authors (Flexner, 1959; Melder, 1965; O'Neill, 1969, 1971; Sinclair, 1965).

Once again, women's new activities were additions to their tasks as wives and mothers. Traditional activities and ideas were altered but not discarded, and they continued to influence women. Gilman (1966) argued that sexual equality was essential for the betterment of the human race, and she advocated changes in housekeeping arrangements so radical that they would free women to take part fully in all activities, especially in the economic sphere. However, women were urged by other spokesmen to create expanded role definitions based upon recognized ideas of women's proper duties.

By the end of the 19th century, women were doing important work as social reformers, organized as they had never been before and have scarcely been since. Leaders argued that when women used their energies to improve the world they benefited their families. Jane Addams, for example, called upon women to exercise womanly responsibility by engaging in political and social activities as "housekeepers for the world." Early in her days at Hull House, she passed the examination for garbage inspector and served in that capacity for some time (Davis, 1967: 120). This bold move was a means of entering the local political fray; Addams thereby deprived a ward boss of a patronage position while actively engaging in problems relevant to the neighborhood people she served. But her exhortations to women to do likewise were couched in terms designed to provide a justification for women hesitant about overstepping traditional boundaries.

> Many women today are failing properly to discharge their duties to their own families and households simply because they fail to see that as society grows more complicated it is necessary that woman shall extend her sense of responsibility to many things outside of her own home, if only in order to preserve the home in its entirety. (Addams, 1908: 41)

The suffragists "brilliantly exploited traditional assumptions about women's unique place." Stating that women as more noble, more spiritual creatures would improve governmental morality and functioning, they argued that since "the nation was simply a macrocosm of the home," their vote would transfer women's expertise in home matters to solving the human problems created by growing industrialization and urbanization (Chafe, 1972: 13; see Kraditor, 1965).

ENUMERATION.   "Gainfully employed" women were not married as a rule. A married working woman was an embarrassment, an indication that her husband could not support her, or perhaps could not control her, to the detriment of family prestige and masculine self-esteem. In fact, Smuts (1960) has pointed out that the prohibitions against married women working for pay may have contributed to their underenumeration by the Bureau of the Census. People responding to census enumerators may have been reluctant to admit that the women of their families were employed. The census enumerators themselves shared the negative attitude about women's employment, and, as a result, "most white married women were automatically counted as housewives." For example, while there were about 4 million white married women living on farms in 1890, only 23,000 were counted in agricultural occupations (Smuts, 1960: 74, 76).

Even today many of the occupations held by women are still not enumerated, and never have been: housework, volunteer work, part-time employment, seasonal employment, unpaid work on farms, and work in family businesses (U.S. Bureau of the Census, 1973c: App. 10–11). The question here can be a subtle one, for whether or not one is counted is an indication of membership in a group, as well as an indication of whether one's activities are of consequence in the economy.

LABOR UNIONS.   By the end of the 19th century women were in the work force but were treated differently from male workers. Labor unions provide an important case where sex-role factors have operated to the detriment of women workers. Even in industries where labor unions experienced their first growth, women had little involvement, despite the sporadic efforts of some women throughout the 19th century to form, join, or participate in these organizations (Brooks, 1964; Flexner, 1959: ch. 14). There were various reasons. First, the unions organized originally along craft lines, drawing leadership for many years from craftsmen. But women were generally a low-wage, low-skill group, for few had been admitted to apprenticeship training (Baker, 1964: 81). Second, as a readily available pool of cheap labor, women had served employers often and well as scabs and undercutters. They were thus exploited by employers while they earned their fellow workers' hostility. Third, working women lacked both authority and experience in self-assertion, and they had a lesser understanding of economic and industrial questions. As a younger group likely to work only until marriage, they were not concerned about potential union benefits affecting paid work at a possible future time (Cook, 1968). Older working women had little leisure time to devote to union matters, even less than working men, for they had to rush home at the end of a working day to cook, clean, and care for children (Dorr, 1971: 188).

Since there were few women in the unions, those who did join were criticized as thoroughly unfeminine creatures. Many young women workers were not permitted by their families to attend evening meetings, and few women were willing to risk their reputations by joining discussions of union activities that took place very often, in the early days, in working men's clubs and saloons. Finally, since there were few women organizers or officials, women workers felt constrained about voicing their concerns about unsanitary working conditions, sexual exploitation, and the "female problems" of menstruation and pregnancy (Boone, 1942: 58 ff).

Several commissions investigated the conditions of workers' lives in the early 1900s and reported that since women lacked the influence that came from "combination and association" with others, their wages were lower than men's (Baker, 1964: 81).[2] Women's lesser involvement in unions in all ways—membership, leadership, and pertinent concessions obtained through collective bargaining—has persisted and hampered working women to the present time. By 1959, Flexner observed, in states where equal-pay laws had been enacted they remained "largely ineffectual" because women were "so inactive and so little represented in the leadership of . . . the trade unions." (p. 329; see Falk, 1973: 57–65).

The increase in women trade unionists has not kept pace with the numbers of women in the labor force. In the late sixties, 12.5% of American women workers were trade union members, compared to over 30% of men workers. One fifth of the union members in the late sixties were women, but they were scarcely represented in leadership positions; in 1968 4.6% of the union officials listed in the *Labor Bureau Directory* were women. By 1971, when women made up 75% of the clothing-worker union memberships, in the Amalgamated union there was one female vice president out of 28, and in the ILGWU, only 1 of the 20 was a woman (Dewey, 1971; U.S. Department of Labor, 1969a: 82).

Union contracts have often included separate categories and pay scales for men's and women's jobs. Cook (1968) describes one contract, for example, where unskilled men received a minimum straight-time hourly rate of $3.22, while the women earned $2.74. The difference in median earnings for union and nonunion women in 1971 was $1,540, which means that union membership is beneficial, but in comparable organizations, union women received lower wages than did men (Dewey, 1971: 44).

In some of the craft unions there have been problems presented by job incumbents who still feel it inappropriate for women to become skilled workers. They refuse to teach women or to offer them opportunities that depend upon a comradely social network (Cook, 1968). While many women have indeed benefited from union strength and negotiations in their behalf, it is little wonder that some of the earliest cases of discrimination brought to the attention of the Women's Equity Action League in the 1960s concerned women complaining of their union's treatment of them (U.S. Congress,

House, 1970: Part 1, p. 32 ff). Obviously, as women become more active in the labor force, they are increasingly concerned about seeing that unions represent their interests as women as well as workers.

PROTECTIVE LAWS.   Tracing the background of some laws governing women's work provides a good way of understanding how cultural attitudes take on great force as they are formalized. The prevailing social attitudes about working women in the 19th and early 20th centuries were expressed in a series of important legal decisions. The case of *Bradwell* v. *Illinois* was a landmark, of import precisely because it was a legal decision, with language that provided a basis of resistance to subsequent legal challenges. Mrs. Myra Bradwell had been educated in the law. In 1870 her application to practice in the state of Illinois was rejected because of her sex. The Illinois Supreme Court decision to deny her this right states in part: "We are certainly warranted in saying that when the Legislature gave to this court the power of granting licences to practice law, it was not with the slightest expectation that this privilege would be extended equally to men and women." They also questioned whether "to engage in the hot strifes of the Bar, in the presence of the public, and with momentous verdicts the prizes of the struggle, would not tend to destroy the deference and delicacy with which it is the pride of our ruder sex to treat her." (Flexner, 1959: 120–121).

When the case was appealed to the U.S. Supreme Court, Justice Joseph P. Bradley stated in his concurring opinion:

> Man is, or should be, woman's protector and defender. The natural and proper timidity and delicacy which belongs to the female sex evidently unfits it for many of the occupations of civil life. The constitution of the family organization, which is founded in the divine ordinance, as well as in the nature of things, indicates the domestic sphere as that which properly belongs to the domain and function of womanhood. The harmony, not to say identity, of interests and views, which belong, or should belong, to the family institution is repugnant to the idea of a woman adopting a distinct and independent career from that of her husband.

> The paramount destiny and mission of woman are to fulfill the noble and benign offices of wife and mother. This is the law of the Creator. And the rules of civil society must be adapted to the general constitution of things, and cannot be based upon exceptional cases. (Kanowitz, 1971: 151–152)

These attitudes were paramount over 30 years later in justifying protective legislation, which in turn has had important consequences for working women. Protective legislation codified legally the principle that women, as a class of persons, must be accorded treatment different from men.

Basically there are two broad types of state protective legislation:

(1) *laws conferring supposed benefits,* such as minimum wages, a day of rest, a meal or rest period, maternity benefits, provision of chairs for rest periods, and (2) *laws prohibiting women from working* in certain jobs, such as in mining or bartending, or under certain conditions—i.e., weight limits and hour limits have been imposed on women's jobs, and nightwork and work before and after childbirth is either prohibited or restricted. (Ross, 1970: 394)

It is interesting that these laws focused on women, who were a minority in the labor force. Throughout the 19th century laws were sought to protect *all* workers from harsh working conditions. The first such legislation, in the 1840s, regulated the hours of work of children in Massachusetts under age 12. As workers gained organized strength and the vote, laws were passed in various states shortening the working day. Evidently, the passage of the laws appeased working male voters, while their frequent nonenforcement appeased powerful manufacturing interests (Baker, 1964: ch. 7).

By the 1870s, and continuing over the next few decades, organized labor was one of the many groups pressing for eight-hour days for women, first in the state of Massachusetts and then in other states as well (Brooks, 1964: ch. 8). Perhaps organized labor made the attempt for women and children first in the hope that legal protection would in practice apply equally to men (Baker, 1964: ch. 7). There may have been the desire to limit competition from low-wage groups as well (Freeman, 1971).

By 1900, despite legal controversy, 14 states had laws on their books limiting the hours of women's work (Baker, 1964: ch. 7). While the earlier efforts concerned all workers, evidently those laws covering women and children were more likely to be supported by the U.S. Supreme Court when the inevitable challenges occurred. There were two important decisions in this regard.

In 1905 in *Lochner* v. *New York,* the Supreme Court invalidated a New York statute limiting the working hours of both men and women employees. Then, in 1906, in *Muller* v. *Oregon,* the Supreme Court upheld a limitation on working hours for women. The result of this pair of decisions was "to convince the state legislatures that half a loaf was better than none, leading to widespread passage of protective legislation for women only" (Kanowitz, 1971: 278).

The language of the *Muller* v. *Oregon* decision was especially important, for it was used thereafter to uphold the principle that sex is a valid basis for classification. The court stated in part:

That woman's physical structure and the performance of maternal functions place her at a disadvantage in the struggle for subsistence is obvious. This is especially true when the burdens of motherhood are upon her.

Differentiated by these matters from the other sex, she is properly placed in a class by herself, and legislation designed for her protection may be sustained, even when like legislation is not necessary for men and could not be sustained.

The limitations which this statute places upon her contractual powers, upon her right to agree with her employer as to the times she shall labor, are not imposed solely for her benefit but also largely for the benefit of all.

The two sexes differ in structure of the body, in the functions to be performed by each, in the amount of physical strength, in the capacity for long-continued labor, particularly when done standing, in influence of vigorous health upon the future well-being of the race, the self-reliance which enables one to assert full rights, and in the capacity to maintain the struggle for subsistence. The difference justifies a difference in legislation and upholds that which is designed to compensate for some of the burdens which rest upon her. (Freeman, 1971: 223–224)

The *Muller* decision was hailed as a victory by feminists who had pressed for the improvement of women's conditions by emphasizing their distinct nature, contributions, and place. They did not anticipate two types of negative consequences, which soon became apparent.

First of all, treated as a class, rather than as individuals whose capabilities could be assessed competitively with other workers, some women found they had lost free choice about working in certain jobs, certain places, and at certain hours. Some of them were "protected" out of jobs they had held for years (Nelson, 1974).

Second, even though *Muller* concerned hours of work, the "difference principle" was evoked in a variety of subsequent decisions. By using the language of the *Muller* decision rather than taking into account the particular conditions that the decision was intended to remedy, judges made decisions which kept women from jury duty, treated their applications for professional licenses differently from men's, and kept women out of state-supported colleges (Kanowitz, 1971: 154)

Overall, while protective legislation of all sorts was helpful to women in industries dominated by women, in those dominated by men the laws sometimes kept women from higher pay, promotions, or even from the opportunity to take a job (Nelson, 1974). It is interesting to note that while the *Muller* decision was justified on the grounds of women's motherhood or potential motherhood, protective legislation has been criticized for not providing protection for women in specific areas related to motherhood.

In 1954, Caplow observed that requirements had fallen behind usage in many states and that the laws were falling into disuse (Caplow, 1954: 236). However, the laws became a center of contention in the mid-1960s when some protective regulations were used by employers and unions to circumvent antidiscriminatory legislation. They are currently the subject of discussion in regard to the Equal Rights Amendment (Ross, 1970).

There are arguments for retaining protective legislation, or at least not giving it up without guarantees against the exploitation of women (Jordan, 1970; U.S. Congress, Senate, 1970). It is clearly possible to find legal approaches which preserve the beneficial effects for workers of either sex, while bringing practices into compliance with the proposed Equal Rights Amendment (Kanowitz, 1971: xiii). Arguments aside, during the past few years many advances in women's rights have come about through Title VII of the Civil Rights Act of 1964, which voided protective laws that conflict with it (Freeman, 1975: 187).

In the end, the 19th-century pressure for protective legislation for all workers yielded results applicable chiefly to women. Important discriminations became imbedded in the law, influencing the course of later decisions about all women. The lesson that later feminists were to draw was that "sex-specific legislation will become sex-restrictive" (Freeman, 1971: 231).

WOMEN IN THE LABOR FORCE IN THE 1970s: FULL PARTICIPATION AND CONSTRAINTS

Women today have more years available to them for leisure, retirement, education, and work than ever before. Since 1900 the life expectancy for women has increased by about 26 years (Taeuber & Taeuber, 1971: 500).[3] While the average woman in 1900 spent one third of her lifetime bearing and caring for children, that percentage declined to one seventh in the late 1960s (Sullerot, 1971: 75).

In fact, more women are spending more time in the work force (Wolfbein, 1964; Taeuber & Taeuber, 1971: 206), from 20% of women 16 and over in 1900 to 45% of women 16 and over in 1973 (U.S. Department of Labor, 1974a). The increase in the proportions of women in the labor force, most marked since 1940,[4] can be described in several ways. First, the labor force composition is changing as the rate of increase of employed women exceeds that of men. Of the total increase in the labor force between 1940 and 1968, 65% was accounted for by women (U.S. Department of Labor, 1969a: 5).[5]

Second, as noted above, the characteristics of the female labor force have changed considerably. In 1900 the typical "gainfully employed" woman was young and single. The greatest rates of increase in the labor force have occurred among married women and mothers. By 1969, as indicated in Table 6.1, the demographic characteristics of the female labor force, while not identical with the general population of women, closely resembled them (Kreps, 1971: 81–82).

Third, the pattern of women's participation in the labor force is changing. Paid work activity for women 20 to 24 peaked in the early part of the 20th century, and it steadily declined for all other ages thereafter (Oppenheimer, 1970: 7). By 1950 women were entering or reentering the labor

TABLE 6.1

Characteristics of Women in the Population and in the Civilian Labor Force, 1969

	Women in Population	Women in Labor Force
Median age (years)	42.2	39.5
Median education (years completed)	12.2	12.4
Percent married	65.7%	63.9%
With Children 6–17	28.2	34.4
With Children under 6 . .	28.4	20.6
Percent nonwhite	11.0	12.7
Percent farm workers	4.8	4.2

Source: Janice Hedges, "Women Workers and Manpower Demands in the 1970s," *Monthly Labor Review* 93 (June 1970): 21.

force in their late thirties, as well as participating in the years prior to marriage and childbearing. Today, women in the early childbearing years are still less likely to be in the labor force than they are at other times, but that picture is also changing (Waldman & McEaddy, 1974). In short, while women's pattern of participation still differs from that of men, the differences are increasingly less marked (Kreps, 1971: 12).

All sorts of women work, yet working women are sometimes categorized as amusing oddities. For example, in the summer of 1974, U.S. Senator Barry Goldwater reportedly quipped to journalists who asked him his opinion of the possibility of a woman for vice president that he would certainly support the idea so long as the woman could get her work done in time to hurry home and make supper! Both the reporters and the senator must have assumed an audience that would chuckle at that comment (also see Hole & Levine, 1973: 228–242).

Working women's needs are often ignored. In recent years, for example, challenges to "men's only" bars such as Morey's in New Haven or McSorley's in New York have been amusingly photographed and described. While the challenges can be made to appear frivolous, it is unthinkable to imagine men excluded from locations where important business discussions take place in informal surroundings. More important however, according to Caplow (1954), working women are "everywhere confronted with a vast network of special statutes, rules and regulations—some are designed for their protection, some intended to reduce their effectiveness as competitors, and some adroitly contrived for both purposes at once" (p. 236).

Protective legislation has been discussed above. Antidiscriminatory legislation has been in existence since the passage of the Equal Pay Act and

Title VII of the Civil Rights Act in the early 1960s. It provides the legal authority for challenges to discriminatory legislation as well as to "civil service requirements, statements of company policy, union bylaws, and the entrance qualifications of professional schools all of which exclude women gratuitously from many types of employment . . . bans on employment of married women . . . rules relating to nepotism and seniority" (Caplow, 1954: 236–237).

Antidiscriminatory legislation will be described briefly in a later section. In addition there is a pot pourri of other laws shaping working women's opportunities and behavior.

Laws Affecting Women

Innumerable laws affect working women, because they are intended to affect *all* women. They are by no means relics of the past. As with protective legislation, many of these laws differentiate between men and women, regardless of individual capacity, merit, or performance. In some areas they accord women less favorable treatment than men, as in banking and credit (despite recent remedial legislation), and sometimes they accord women what seems to be more favorable treatment; for example, women are not liable for military conscription. Kanowitz (1971) argues, however, that legal rules which "emphasize irrelevant differences between men and women cannot help influencing the content and the tone of the social, as well as the legal, relations between the sexes" (p. 4). In fact, women have not only not been drafted but have had to meet higher age and educational standards to join the military (*The Spokeswoman*, February 15, 1975, p. 4). By restricting women from the armed forces and assigning them a limited number of duties, the military has prevented them from moving up an important career ladder used by many men and denied them important veteran's benefits, such as the G.I. Bill.

The unintended consequences of the complex of laws distinguishing between men and women may perpetuate the working woman's second-class status as much as blatantly discriminatory regulations do. Some examples follow.

SOCIAL SECURITY. Some laws affect working women adversely because they assume all women will be cared for. Social security regulations, for example, assume that *the* worker in the family where both husband and wife are present is always the man.

A wife is, therefore, entitled to identical social security benefits at age 62 or 65, whether or not she has ever worked. Thus, even though most working women pay social security premiums throughout their working lives, the benefits they draw at age 62 or later are based on their own *or* their husband's earnings, whichever is larger, but they cannot collect two full benefits. In fact, a working couple's benefits may be somewhat smaller than if total family earnings were the same but only the husband had worked (U.S. Department of Labor, 1973a).

The working woman who has contributed to the fund cannot even demand the return of her payments. The social security premiums are collected from individuals, but payments are made to families (Alberts, 1974). Furthermore, while the wife or widow of a worker receives full benefits, a dependent husband or widower has been eligible for benefits *only* if his wife provided at least half of his support when she was alive. Recently, important rulings in Federal District Court (Seigel, 1975) and in the Supreme Court (*The Spokeswoman,* April 15, 1975, p. 2) have struck at this gender-based discrimination. Decisions were made or upheld in favor of the widower-plaintiff, who, like most married men, provided over half of their own support during their wives' lifetimes.

Even though the intent of the Social Security Act was to provide income for dependents, while taking into account women's lower earnings, shorter work life, and longer life expectancy, in practice working women and their husbands have been affected inequitably as compared to couples with non-working wives. Certainly over the years, social security provisions have not provided incentives for married women to work.

INCOME TAX AND CHILD CARE.   Income tax laws reflect the same assumptions about family units. While they do not discriminate between single men and women, the tax for a working couple may be higher than if both parties were single. The provisions for joint income taxes favor the couple with a nonworking member. Perhaps of more importance, the cost of child care is to be met largely by the parents. Prior to 1971, costs of child care for working mothers were not deductible from gross income. Since that time, a working wife can deduct up to $400 a month for child-care expenses if the combined husband-wife income is below $18,000. The deduction goes down to zero as the combined income goes from $18,000 to $27,000 (U.S. Department of Labor, 1973a). Again, such a law does not provide incentives for women to earn higher incomes.

CONTRACTS.   Married working women are subject to other regulations, based upon the assumptions that the unit that counts is the family, that once married a woman is the husband's responsibility, and that once married a woman cannot appreciate the consequences of agreements she enters. In the early 1970s an observer pointed out, "Four states require a married woman to obtain a court order before establishing an independent business. Eleven states place special restrictions on the right of a married woman to contract. In three states, a married woman cannot become a guarantor or surety" (Freeman, 1971: 212). In four of the eight community property states a woman cannot control her own earnings!

DOMICILE.   The law governing legal domicile is a good example of one which unintentionally adversely affects working women. In all but five states, the legal domicile is the one selected by the man (Freeman, 1971: 212; Pilpel & Peyser, 1965). A wife who owns property in one state while her legal domicile is in another may find her property taxed at the latter rate, even if it is higher. She cannot vote or run for office other than in the state of her legal domicile, even if she in fact resides elsewhere, although there are exceptions. In all states, couples may establish separate domiciles for purposes of divorce, but in only 18 states is it possible for a couple to establish two domiciles by mutual consent (Kanowitz, 1971: 46–52).

A woman who quits her job to move with her husband cannot collect unemployment compensation. It is possible, however unlikely, for her to be divorced for desertion if she does not move with him (Freeman, 1971: 211; see Kanowitz, 1971: 52).

CREDIT.   Restrictions on the granting of credit to married women provide a good example of laws based on the assumption that all women are supported by men, and, as a corollary, that men are totally responsible for their wives' debts. It was not until 1974 that New York State passed a bill prohibiting "discrimination based on sex, marital status or childbearing capacity in any credit transaction" (Shack, 1974). By no means was New York the last state with regulations hampering women's freedom in credit transactions. The Federal Equal Credit Opportunity Act, which went into effect in late October 1975, makes it illegal to deny or terminate credit on the basis of sex or marital status. The enforcement of the law depends upon complaints of individuals adversely affected by inequitable credit regulations. It is too early at this writing to speculate about the effects, although the intent seems to be in the desired direction (see Porter, 1975).

UNEMPLOYMENT INSURANCE.   Inequitable unemployment insurance and private retirement programs may adversely affect working women. In some instances insurance benefits for maternity and related disabilities, as well as other fringe benefits, cover the spouse of a male employee but not a female employee herself (Freeman, 1971: 233; U.S. Congress, House, 1971: 56).

Two recently filed suits indicate some of the inequities in insurance coverage for working women. In one, the New York Civil Liberties Union filed suit against the New York State Superintendent of Insurance. He was charged with approving the sale of disability income-protection policies which discriminate against working women. Numerous unfair practices in disability income-protection policies were alleged, in addition to lower benefits for higher premiums:

> . . . coverage for women often begins after one or two weeks of disability while men are covered from the first day of illness. Low-income women are often unable to purchase disability policies on any terms while such policies are available to men of similar age and income. Some policies offer men full benefits to age sixty-five in the event of total disability while women may only purchase policies providing benefits for one year. (New York Civil Liberties Union, 1974: 8)

The Women's Equity Action League filed a complaint with the Equal Employment Opportunity Commission (EEOC) in an attempt to rectify unequal insurance coverage offered by the Teacher's Insurance and Annuity Association of America (TIAA) to the spouses of working women, as compared with the spouses of working men (*The Spokeswoman,* June 15, 1974: 4). In 1973, the National Organization for Women and the American Nurses Association joined forces to file complaints against TIAA focusing on the unequal retirement benefits paid to men and women. TIAA argues that since women live longer than men, their monthly payments in retirement must be lower, if contributions to the fund are equal (Teacher's Insurance and Annuity Association, 1973). However, the EEOC ruled favorably on the charge brought by the American Nurses Association (*The Spokeswoman,* September 15, 1974, p. 4).

The purpose of including these examples of recent rulings* is to illustrate some discriminatory laws and practices and to show some of the legal changes taking place. It would be naive to assume that the problems will now disappear, for there will be legal challenges and appeals in cases where compliance with new rulings creates inconveniences, particularly to vast corporations with great resources. Legal rulings must be put into practice, administered, and supervised, in some instances, before they truly command compliance. Finally the effects must be internalized and demonstrated in people's attitudes and behavior.

Women's Orientations to Family and Work: First Things First

For the most part women have adopted as their own guiding principle the idea that they will have and *should* have work roles which are secondary: secondary in the work force, in relation to men, and in relation to family roles. Sociologists call the desired result of socialization the internalization of

---

* See Chapter 8 below for a review of recent court decisions on maternity-related issues.

norms; Betty Friedan called the result "chains in the mind." Using notable achievement, educational attainment, and earnings as gross indicators, it is obvious that women have not yet achieved equality with men, in part as a consequence of the "chains."

Women's orientation toward work, the choice of jobs, the decision whether or not to work, and the degree of commitment are influenced by tradition, cultural assumptions about women, laws and associated practices common in employment and educational settings, and family background. Women's work is also affected by practical matters, where they live, and whether jobs and transportation are available nearby. Personal characteristics, education, skills, appearance, health, and experience make a woman more or less attractive to employers. Her economic circumstances also play an important part (Parnes et al., 1970).

In this section we will describe women's orientation to work and their achievements as a consequence of several interrelated factors: familial responsibilities, social support, job demands, and social class and ethnic considerations.[6]

CONTINGENCY PLANNING.   Young girls' attitudes toward work reflect the dominance of sex-related aspects of their views of themselves. For example, Sullerot (1971) was shocked when she asked young men and women to describe a day in their lives when they would be 50 years old. In contrast to young men, who were able to cooperate in this challenge to their imaginations, the young women indicated they preferred to imagine themselves dying well before 50, rather than "lose a single hour thinking about a future in which they would no longer be seductive" (p. 77).

Epstein (1970b) describes the social forces operating to keep women in their place. Work is a part of a picture of success for men, while for women it is part of a syndrome of failure: "A woman may start thinking about working because a man let her down" (p. 74). We may infer that when a girl is counseled to choose a career in some traditional, easy-to-enter occupation, *not* because she is interested in doing the tasks related to that job but in order to "have something to fall back on," she is being told that working, once a female reaches adult status, is correlated with personal disaster.

When young women do engage in future planning, they keep their desire to marry or "settle down" with someone someday uppermost among their priorities. For some women, the decision to marry will depend in part upon the man's feelings about the woman's career ambitions. But not quite knowing what that future partner, lifestyle, and family size will be means that contingency planning is a common theme in the thinking of single women (Angrist, 1972; Douvan, 1972: 48).

Rose (1951) once concluded that women college students were unrealistic in their future planning, for they had not taken preparatory steps essential for the career they wanted to pursue. They were preparing, in fact, to concentrate on marriage, with work as a secondary consideration. There is a decline in grades and plans to attend graduate school when college women become engaged (Wallace, 1966). It is common knowledge that for many years, college women not engaged by the end of their senior year felt all the anxiety of once again being faced with an uncertain future, while the lucky ones showed off their new rings to admiring friends, at special parties given in their honor.

Despite their greater commitment, graduate and professional-school students also operate with contingency plans. At Yale University the women in the one-year Master of Arts in Teaching program were taunted by their alleged motto "A ring before spring, or your money back!" This was a derogatory way of noting the decline in educational endeavors and forms of preparatory stages for work when women place marital and familial needs first.

In the same study, which I conducted, many of the student nurses and teachers emphasized that their choice of occupation had been strongly influenced by a desire for a "feminine career." Future female lawyers and physicians were interviewed as well, and all of them had considered the question of family plus career very seriously. Future physicians stated that their choice of speciality was the result of many variables, including their own interests and the level of discriminatory practices they perceived in an area of medical practice. Important among the variables, however, were considerations about specialities whose hours and demands would allow them to be wives and mothers (Levine, 1968, 1975; Feldman, 1973; Lopate, 1968: 119 ff).

Such planning is *not* unrealistic, but very much in tune with realities (Poloma & Garland, 1971). Many times, jobs which allow women to utilize their education or skills fully, jobs with better pay, or even promotions may be ruled out by family responsibilities which are more important to them (Waldman, 1970).

HUSBANDS' ATTITUDES.   A husband's feelings about his wife's working (or her perception of his attitude) has an important influence on her work life and on the future of the marriage. Lifetime labor force participation by a sample of over 5,000 women was related to their holding of permissive views about mothers working; a permissive attitude was also strongly associated with a woman's report of her husband's attitude toward her working (Parnes et al., 1970: 47, 76). A husband's type of work, income, and hours of work are variables which could be examined for their effect on women's work, as well as on the husband's feelings about that work.

An ambitious and productive scholar made the following personal statement to a House subcommittee hearing on discrimination: ". . . how grateful, how lucky, to have a supportive husband. It is not a "condition" [a professional woman] is fortunate to have as a base for being something more than homemaker, mother and husband relaxer. It is something she looks for and if she finds it, she marries him" (Rossi, 1971b: 1066).

While sympathetic, helpful wives undoubtedly make all phases of life happier and easier for their fortunate husbands, women say that supportive husbands are a *necessity* if both a high-level career and the continuation of the marriage are to be achieved.[7] Bailyn concludes that "a husband's mode of integrating family and work in his own life is crucial for the success—at least in terms of marital satisfaction—of any attempt of the wife to include a career in her life" (Bailyn, 1970: 114; see Holmstrom, 1972).

MOBILITY. Mobility presents a complex problem for women which frequently results in their settling for less than the optimal job or work situation (Long, 1974). Decisions about where to live are usually made by husbands who initiate most family moves to further their careers or to obtain jobs. There are some major effects of such mobility on women. Many working women must leave their jobs and hope for suitable opportunities in the new area. Some must take licensing examinations in a new state, start school once more, forego accrued seniority, build up a new clientele, or reestablish a reputation, whether or not they would have chosen to move at that time in their own work lives.

On the other hand, women tend to be less residentially mobile than men (Long, 1974). Where such mobility is essential for workers to be promoted or to be able to accept a variety of assignments, women are generally at a disadvantage, unless their husbands are willing and able to move.

Holmstrom (1971: 518) found that partners in the professional couples she studied had made decisions about where to live based upon career considerations for both. Most reports, however, stress the sort of finding that Kashket and others (1974) described in a study of 237 women and 578 men, all members of the American Society for Microbiology. When asked about moving, 93% of the women microbiologists with Ph.D.s said that they would move only if their husbands obtained good positions, while only 17% of the male Ph.D.s indicated a corresponding attitude toward their wives' careers. Since the women worked slightly fewer hours per week than the men, since the married women interrupted careers to have babies, and since the women held lower ranks and earned less than the men at every level of education (10% less at the BA level, 15% less at the MA level, and 32% less at the doctoral level), their jobs *were* less important than their husbands', along a number of dimensions (Kashket, Robbins, Leive, & Huang, 1974).

In cases like these, assigning second priority to the career needs of the individual in the poorer competitive position is understandable, but approaching both careers as being equally important might help both members of a professional pair to get satisfactory positions (Bergmann & Adelman, 1973).

CHILD CARE.   In 1960, Smuts argued that general disapproval of married women working was disappearing because working women clearly showed they "value their role in the family far above their role in the labor force" (Smuts, 1971: 147). Women do not, as a rule, have continuous work patterns over their life cycles, and every sort of measure of labor force participation shows that lower rates of women's participation are correlated with the presence of children, and the younger the children, the less likely women are to work at all (U.S. Department of Labor, 1973a).

Survey data from 1936 to 1960 demonstrate that men and women feel that the care of children is a prime reason why women should not take full-time jobs outside the home (Oppenheimer, 1970: 54). We certainly cannot dismiss these concerns, for the loving, continuous, and creative care of our children is of paramount importance to individuals, families, and society. But these concerns stem from the assumption that the family must be totally responsible for child care, except for unusual circumstances, and within the family the person responsible for child rearing is mother, whether or not she holds a job (see, e.g., Poloma & Garland, 1971).

DAY CARE.   At home, mother's work comes second to household tasks and child care. Outside the home, facilities for the care of children when mothers work are totally inadequate. There are about 1 million registered places for children in day-care centers in the United States, but few, if any, places for 7- to 12-year-old children to play in supervised settings after school, and few, if any, easily available arrangements for day care at home by trained people. Most children of working mothers (26 million under age 18; 6 million under age 6) are cared for through private arrangements, made by the parents, in their own or someone else's home (Waldman & Whitmore, 1974).

Despite the mobility of our population, we have not developed a network of publicly supported, excellent child-care services to help families that are cut off from relatives and close friends. Rossi (1972a: 127) attributes this deficiency to our cultural emphasis on individuality. But, as Steinfels (1973) points out, policy makers have had a negative perspective about day care, traditionally viewing it as a stop-gap or patchwork method of caring for children in desperate situations where simple custodial care suffices. This is not to say that there are no good day-care centers, but day care has not been perceived as a part of the educational system which should be publicly funded and treated as essential for families.

Former President Richard Nixon's veto of the Comprehensive Child Development Act is instructive. He stated that he did not want to bring the forces of government to bear in undermining the sacred responsibilities that parents have to rear their children: "For the Federal Government to plunge headlong financially into supporting child development would commit the vast moral authority of the National Government to the side of communal approaches to child-rearing over against the family-centered approach" (cited in Steinfels, 1973, p. 19).

There were other reasons for the veto, but Nixon knew he could expect a vast, sympathetic response to his statement. The measure was defeated with scarcely a ripple of interest by anyone but affected women. In New York State and New York City, where day-care appropriations are currently being reduced, the chief protesters are women who must work and who need care for their children, and their sympathizers (Garson, 1974).

TIME OFF FOR CHILD CARE. There are few formalized arrangements being utilized to accommodate working mothers. While many women work part time, many more would do so if they could find part-time jobs which are not boring and dead-end (e.g., Brozan, 1973). Employers rarely provide day care for children of employees (U.S. Department of Labor, 1971a). Women's behavior on the job reveals their attempt to strike a balance between family and work obligations. For example, women's absenteeism and job turnover rates are very close to those of men in similar jobs, at similar levels of skill and experience. But women with children take more time off than childless women, and women lose more time from work for acute illness than men do. The "acute illness" however, may well be time taken for children's needs, for provisions for "personal" and "family" leave are exceptional. There is no evidence that women workers are less healthy than men. In fact, their absenteeism for chronic illness is lower than men's (Wells, 1969).

Home responsibilities are not legitimate reasons for collecting benefits. Two state courts recently upheld decisions by state unemployment security agencies denying benefits to women unable to work at certain times for personal reasons. In one case, the reasons cited included babysitting problems. In the other case, a mother of four children wanted to resign from night work because she could not sleep during the day with her children at home ("Good Cause Refusal to Work," 1974).

CAREER INTERRUPTIONS. What is perceived as career interruptions or part-time status can differ markedly for women and for men. Arguing that, in fact, employers do make arrangements for individuals to work part time or to take leaves of absence with no career penalties, Holmstrom (1971) says that:

The catch is that they only do it for individuals with socially acceptable reasons. And domestic responsibilities have not been one of these reasons ... there is a difference between how different career interruptions are defined ... in the present study, half the women had interrupted careers—usually because of child rearing. And half the men had interrupted careers—typically for military duty . . . these interruptions have, at least up to now, been perceived very differently by employers and school officials. In a curious paradox of human values men have been criticized only slightly for career interruptions in which their task was to kill off other members of the human race; but women have been severely criticized for taking time away from their profession in order to raise the next generation. (p. 521)

The academic woman who is the mother of small children feels "the greatest pressures both for scholarly publication and for domestic perform- ance . . . in the years between the ages of twenty-eight and thirty-five" (Graham, 1972: 272). Even minimal devotion to her children's needs may curtail her scholarly productivity in the critical five to seven years within which a tenure decision is usually made for a new assistant professor.

Many women avoid the dual pressures of family and career by entering the labor force later than men, or they work before they have children and resume work once the children are in school. This solution has adverse effects on women as workers.

As a result of discontinuous work patterns, many women never accrue seniority, are not employed on a regular basis, and are never entitled to full fringe benefits. Many women do not progress beyond the lowest entry positions. The gap in earnings between men and women increases with age, because women as a group have not acquired as much work experience as men, and people with less experience are simply not worth as much to employers (U.S. Department of Labor, 1973a: 104–105).

Women in professions, who make the choice of withdrawing for several years, miss out on the long period of socialization which takes place during the first years on the job. A 40-year-old woman may still be somewhat of a novice, and she is much more likely to be an outsider than a man of that age (White, 1972). In occupations where sponsorship and referrals are crucial for the individual's career, a period of withdrawal adds to the problems women face in finding a spot in the essential social networks (Epstein, 1970a; Hall, 1946; Williams, 1950).

Age discrimination takes an extra toll, particularly for women seeking jobs which can be filled by younger, physically more attractive women (Bell, 1970). While age discrimination has been prohibited by an act of Congress (U.S. Department of Labor, 1969b), such cases will probably be tested pain- fully by those few people angry, resourceful, and willing enough to be "troublemakers."

Very simply, many women fail to plan for the years when their family responsibilities lessen. Inadequately prepared by education or experience, they suddenly find themselves in competition with alert young people, full of energy and the latest learning.

SOCIAL CLASS.   It is important to consider social-class factors in thinking about women's work plans and behavior. The attractiveness of "marriage as a career" can vary. For example, when Rose (1951) concluded that college women were not preparing for the careers they said they intended to pursue, he noted that women from poorer homes were the exception to the findings. They were taking preparatory steps for careers to a far greater extent than women who were better off financially.

Interviews with 79 future female physicians, lawyers, teachers, and nurses (Levine, 1968), revealed differences in work plans by career field, and to some extent by social class. More of the women planning to enter the men's fields had higher "commitment to work" scores than women planning to enter nursing and teaching (91% vs. 35%.) However, within the latter group there was a strong correlation between social class and work commitment. The lower the social class, the greater the number of uninterrupted years the women planned to spend at work. Interviews revealed that the women from upper-class backgrounds viewed marital and familial activities as more attractive than future work as nurses and teachers. Women from lower-class backgrounds had, in their own lifetime and through their own efforts, moved far from their social origins, and they were not about to jeopardize their achievements (Levine, 1968).

RACE.   Racially (and ethnically) based experiences can play an important part in women's work orientations and behavior. Black women comprise 90% of the minority women in our country. Their labor force participation and occupational distribution patterns differ from those of white women. Minority women, in general, are more likely to be working in every age group, to work when they have small children, to be heads of their families, to be living in poverty, to expect to work, and to be in poorer paying and harder jobs than white women (Murray, 1970; Parnes et al., 1970: 135–138; U.S. Department of Labor, 1971b, 1972a).

White American women are predominantly employed in clerical work, teaching, nursing, health services, and sales work. In contrast, in 1974, 11% of all employed minority women were engaged in domestic work, down from 33% in 1964 but still over three and a half times the proportion of white women (U.S. Bureau of the Census, 1975: 74).

Earnings.   In 1974 the median income of full-time, year-round white female workers was $7,021, compared to $6,371 for black women (U.S. Bureau of the Census, 1975).

EDUCATIONAL ATTAINMENT.   In our economy, a worker's income is directly related to educational attainment (see Table 6.2). The proportion of women graduating from high school was greater than for men in

TABLE 6.2
Educational Attainment of Civilian Labor Force, March 1974

	Percentage completing:	
	4 years high school	*4+ years college*
White males	36.5%	17.2%
Nonwhite males	31.5	9.5
White females	45.2	13.3
Nonwhite females	37.4	9.2

Source: U.S. Department of Labor, *Manpower Report of the President, 1975* (Washington, D.C.: U.S. Government Printing Office, 1975), pp. 265–266.

1974, but smaller at every level thereafter. Fewer women than men obtained college and postcollege educations, and this held true within minority groups as well.

SEX AS A STIMULUS.   Discrimination takes many forms. Even when women do acquire the education, work hard, and earn good incomes, they may stimulate negative reactions from unexpected quarters. Rossi (1970a) found that "Ambitious women who aspire to careers on what has been masculine turf must have thick skins and the utmost inner security to withstand what they so often experience, subtle and overt forms of punishment rather than encouragement and support" (p. 924). Some men find they cannot really relate to women who work, unless those women are employed in jobs whose status is clearly inferior to theirs. Women are fine as assistants, wonderful if they are sexually available, but for whatever complex reasons, such men find women colleagues deeply disturbing. Cheerfully admitting to being a "male chauvinist pig" is still considered a socially acceptable reason for a variety of otherwise inexcusable behaviors (see Levine, 1975).

But it is not always men who make working women uncomfortable. Indeed, if there were no male fellow workers to offer friendship, sponsorship, guidance, referrals—in short, to include women in the social network—women who work with men might find working life impossible. Sometimes career difficulties are caused by fear and jealousy from other women. These reactions seem based on the assumption that since women are dependent on men, they must exchange their services and assistance to men for that support. Therefore, any woman who is working with men must be manipulating the men through her "feminine wiles" or gaining a competitive edge, compared to other women, because as a working colleague she can and does "talk shop" and shares that shop.

Wives sometimes get concerned about their husbands' women colleagues. Newspaper headlines (Holles, 1974) on this subject read:

No TIME FOR HANKY-PANKY ON BEAT:
WIVES OF NEW ORLEANS PATROLMEN ASSURED BY POLICEWOMAN

and

FIREMEN'S WIVES FIGHT FOR CHAUVINISM ON JOB

The "office wife" is sometimes unhappy about women in formerly all-male jobs. A young woman who spent a summer working as an intern in a governmental office recently told me that she found that while the men were relaxed and collegial in their relationships with her, the office secretary, a woman of her own age, reacted bitterly toward her. The secretary kept information from the intern, criticized her work, and called her by her first name, while she called men by their titles and last names. The secretary continually tried to show the boss how much sexier *she* was compared to the intern.

Indeed, sexual attraction can be a problem in work settings (Caplow, 1954: 237–238). Women in medical and law schools reported that men "neutralized the girls' sexual nature, making them into sisters, into toys, into harmless objects" (Levine, 1975).

Lewis's (1975) work on letters of reference for academic positions shows the importance of working women's appearance and behavior, both of which are assessed along with scholarly performance and potential. The letters reveal that marital status, good looks, compliant behavior, sociability, graciousness, and intense career interest are all factors which may be counted as assets or liabilities, depending on the writer's viewpoint. In many settings, youth and physical attractiveness are competitive assets in obtaining jobs. However, for positions thought to require more serious, responsible persons, women who are older, married, or less sexually attractive may be the only ones considered (Safilios-Rothschild, 1972).

In many cases, women unconsciously, or perhaps very consciously, utilize well-practiced techniques of pleasing men in order to advance their careers. Women are inundated almost from birth with advice and exhortations on the importance of being sexually attractive to men (but *not* sexually skilled, of course). Many women rather cynically elicit favorable responses from men. The responses may augment the women's own independent capabilities, but it is unlikely in competitive fields that male sponsorship can substitute for proven ability on a woman's part.

As the number of women in a variety of jobs increases, these problems should resolve themselves (Levine, 1975). "Sex is here to stay" as Caroline Bird says, "but its future is in private life not in the office" (Bird, 1971: 18).

Results of Socialization

What then are the consequences of socialization for women as workers? A woman is told in many ways that there are really two scales of achievement—one for men and one for women. If she achieves at all in the working world, that is good enough, for a woman. But the *real* scale is the one that measures men's achievements.

Perhaps this double message results in a blunting of aspiration levels at a very deep, often unconscious level. Women often fail to value themselves not only by accepting inequitable pay, but by *not* acting as though their *own* education and early work experiences are capital investments with rewards to be gained at later times. In fact, many spend the very years when they have minimal familial responsibilities investing their energy in a young husband's potential by working to help put him through school. The payoff in later years is often lost opportunities.

Some women do not want to work outside the home if they are un-trained and inexperienced. Many of them feel defensive about pressures from a number of sources which tell them if they do not have paying jobs when their children are teen-agers, they are failures. On the other hand, since housework is officially accorded no economic value, many women also tend not to value it, and not to value themselves if that is their chief occupation (Kreps, 1971: ch. 4, 5; Gove & Tudor, 1973).

The uncertainty of the marital partner, making contingency planning necessary, the fear of discrimination and its actual occurrence, the differing socialization of men and women, and the need to take time off for family responsibilities all result in a different attitude toward work on the part of men and women. The latter tend to see their work as a job and not as part of a long-term career to be carefully developed (Theodore, 1971: 1–35).

Women are not found at the highest level, or even at the second and third levels of publicly acknowledged accomplishments in proportions re-flecting their numbers in the population, in the labor force, or in the ranks of well-educated people. In our nation of some 210 million persons, the number of women who serve in the President's Cabinet, the Supreme Court, and Congress, combined with governors, holders of seats on a stock ex-change, top-level union leaders, university presidents, and Nobel Prize winners could scarcely fill a guest list for a medium-sized cocktail party. The women mayors, deans and academic department chairmen, tenured associ-ate and full professors, civil service employees at GS–13 levels or higher, judges, lawyers, doctors, engineers, architects, school superintendents, company managers, and ship captains could easily convene in a moderate-sized resort hotel (see U.S. Congress, House, 1970: 23 ff).

This section concludes on a rather dismal note, in part because the discussion has compared women to men. However, there are many sources for change in women's status, and they will be the subject of the next section.

THE SOURCES OF CHANGE

To review briefly, there are pervasive cultural ideas about women and their adult roles which persist despite the equalitarian ideology characteristic of our industrial society (Wilensky, 1968). Expressed in laws and buttressed by traditional practices, these ideas so modify and influence women's behavior that they do not achieve as highly as men in occupational or educational endeavors. However, our society is in the midst of great social transitions. Women's participation in the labor force is one element in these transitions, influencing and influenced by changes in the economic and occupational structures, the civil rights and "liberation" movements of the late fifties and sixties, and changes in sexual relationships and familial dynamics. All these elements are the sources of new or changed laws and practices, reflecting new and changed attitudes about women and their roles.

Of primary importance have been the massive changes in the economy related to increasingly complex levels of technology, which have resulted in increased opportunity or demand for women to work in a variety of jobs. As the 19th-century economy changed from an agricultural to an industrial base, women entered factory work, then white-collar clerical and sales positions (Baker, 1964). During the 20th century, there has been a shift of the occupational structure from industry to the service sectors. By 1957, the majority of the labor force was employed in white-collar positions, and by 1972, 68% of the nonagricultural jobs were in service establishments (Wolfbein, 1964; U.S. Bureau of the Census, 1972c: Table 36, p. 225).

The increased demand for labor has occurred in the very occupations—chiefly clerical—that have been dominated by women from the beginning of those occupations.[8] Women have responded to the demand even while maintaining marital and familial responsibilities.

Concomitant with the labor force shift to white-collar occupations there has been an increase in the educational level of members of the labor force. Recent decades have seen a rapid expansion of positions requiring high-level academic credentials (Wolfbein, 1964; Taeuber & Taeuber, 1971). As a consequence, women have been explicitly and formally encouraged by the government and industry to prepare themselves educationally for high-level positions. During the 1950s and 1960s editorial commentary; conferences with representatives from business, government agencies, and women's colleges (e.g., Mattfeld & Van Aken, 1965); and myriad governmental bulletins on the underutilization of womanpower have all proclaimed the need for highly trained personnel (see Campbell, 1973).

Together with the needs of an expanding economy, and in part as a consequence of it, the Civil Rights movement gained strength rapidly in the late 1950s. This movement—or set of related movements—provided a climate for questioning all status relationships, afforded some women with experience in organized expressions of disaffection, and also provided pressures which resulted in some key legislation affecting working women.

Finally, at least three important factors are changing sexual and familial relationships. People have gained important control over reproduction through the increasing availability of contraceptives and abortions, women are contributing an increasing share to the family income, and domestic responsibilities have been eased considerably by the goods and services provided by the expanding technology.

Women have thus responded to the demand or opportunity to be in the labor force: the "facilitators" of this response are the smaller families and lighter domestic work, and the "motivators" (Hoffman, 1963a, 1974) are their need and desire to make money to enable them to purchase for themselves and their families necessities formerly produced at home, and material goods, services, experiences, and entertainments which are now seen as necessities.

It is against this backdrop that we can ask how cultural attitudes might change in regard to working women, and how they might continue to change if current trends continue. There should also be changes resulting from organized efforts at change, efforts which stem from the increasing numbers of women in the labor force.

GENERAL SOURCES OF CHANGE

Changes in the Family and Socialization

FINANCIAL SUPPORT.   Let us examine again the assumption that women are supported by men. First, an increasing number of women are not totally dependent on a husband's support. In March 1972, the Census Bureau reported that the long-term decline in the median age at first marriage had been reversing since 1960. In 12 years the median age of women at first marriage had increased by one half year. Thus the percent of single people has increased in the past decade. In the age group 20 to 24 there has been an increase from 53 to 57% of single men and from 28.4 to 36.4% of single women. The number of divorced women per 1,000 married persons with "spouse present" also increased, from 42 to 66, between 1960 and 1972. For men the figure went from 28 to 38 (U.S. Bureau of the Census, 1972b: 2, 4). In addition, there were nearly 8 million families headed by women in 1974 (U.S. Department of Labor, 1975: 71).[9]

All the women who are living with men are not totally supported by them, for wives contributed a good share of the income in a very large number of the 44 million husband-wife families in the United States in 1970. In fact, there was a positive correlation between the level of family income and the percentage of families with both spouses working, from the lowest income level to the $15,000 to $24,999 bracket. In the latter income group, both husband and wife worked in 60% of the families. Above that level the proportion with both spouses working dropped to 42%. When 1971 figures were compared to those of 1959, there had been an overall increase of working wives in the husband-wife families, from 36% to 47%. The wives' median contribution to family income remained stable over those years—between 25 and 30% at all income levels (Cymrot & Mallan, 1974: 13, 18, & 21). Minority wives who worked in 1970 contributed a median of 31% to family income, and for white wives the median contribution was 26% (U.S. Department of Labor, 1972a).

STATUS WITHIN FAMILY. Blood's (1965) review of literature and his own empirical studies have led him to conclude that a significant change is taking place within families as a consequence of working women's contributions. He anticipates that a new phase in American family life may well be starting.

> Employment emancipates women from domination by their husbands and secondarily raises their daughters from inferiority to their brothers (echoing the rising status of their mothers). The employment of women affects the power structure of the family by equalizing the resources of husband and wife. A working wife's husband listens to her more, and she listens to herself more. She expresses herself and has more opinions. Instead of looking up into her husband's eyes and worshipping him, she levels with him, compromising on the issue at hand. Thus her power increases and, relatively speaking, the husband's falls. (p. 46)

LIFESTYLE, HOUSEHOLD ACTIVITIES. The research on "family power structures" has been criticized by Safilios-Rothschild for its lack of conceptual and methodological sophistication (Safilios-Rothschild, 1971). However, it is obvious that changes are taking place in families with working wives and mothers. Barth and Watson, using data from the "One in 10,000 Sample" of the 1960 Census, found that a wife's employment, her level of employment, and her income had an important effect on family lifestyle. Lifestyle included the presence and number of children, home ownership, and husbands in school, among other indicators (Barth & Watson, 1967).

Other research indicates that not only does woman become man's partner as she shares his economic activities, but other traditional activities are reallocated as well. Household work and child-rearing activities are more frequently undertaken by husbands in homes where wives work, even though the wife is still chiefly responsible for household responsibilities, as the husband is for family support (e.g. Blood, 1963: 285; Hoffman, 1963b: 215; Chafe, 1972: 222).

In the millions of homes where women are contributing a good share of the income, we must assume that the husbands' reactions to their wives' working range from tolerance to enthusiasm. These men are sharing activities with working spouses who are relieving their support burden. One might also assume that a strong interest in such matters as equal pay, maternity provisions, and the easing of tax burdens for child care would be found in these families.

ROLE MODEL.   Changes in family patterns of activity mean changes in family role models for sons and daughters. There should be modifications not only in the general assumption that women are supported by men, but also in the idea that women's chief adult role is child care and housework.

When Douvan (1963) studied the effect of maternal employment on adolescent development, she found that the daughters of working mothers chose them as their adult ideal more often than the daughters of nonworking mothers. Adolescent daughters of working mothers were also more likely to hold jobs. These findings held in both working-class and middle-class homes (see Nye & Hoffman, 1963: Sec. II).

From his research, Blood (1965) has concluded that in families where the mother is employed, sons share in the household tasks more and daughters tend to earn money more than in families where mothers do not work. (Hartley 1972: 122) found that the sex-role perceptions of 150 boys and girls aged 5, 8, and 11 were significantly related to the presence of a working mother. Boys included nondomestic work in women's roles when their mothers worked. Girls with working mothers were more likely to plan to work and to indicate a choice of nontraditional vocations than girls whose mothers did not work. The differences were statistically significant.

Young adults are remaining free of familial responsibilities for longer periods of time. Among young adults who are married, birth expectations are declining. In 1967, 44% of wives aged 18 to 24 expected to have two or fewer children. By 1972, the percentage had increased to 70 for this age group. In 1965, the average number of children already born to women in the age group 25 to 29 was 2.1. In 1973 an average of 1.5 births had occurred among women in that age group. The Census Bureau noted that the 1973 rates for married women in the 15–24 age range resembles the 1940 data, which "reflected the reaction of young couples to the severe economic depression of the 1930s" (U.S. Bureau of the Census, 1973c: 1–3). In the present case, the causes are undoubtedly quite different, reflecting greater control of reproduction and wider choice of activities of all sorts for both men and women.

Education

We have noted the negative correlation between family size and the probability of a married woman working. The attainment of higher levels of education is also related to small family size, and educational attainment levels have risen rapidly during recent decades. The rise is important when we consider sources of cultural change. It is a truism that the educational level of both sexes is related closely to life changes, lifestyles, and flexibility of attitudes about myriad things, including men's and women's roles.

SOME COLLEGE EDUCATION. In a preceding section it was pointed out that women do not complete postsecondary schooling to the same extent as men.[10] In fact, the percentage of women enrolled in college and earning degrees at all levels in 1970 was less than the level shown by the 1930 census. However, let us consider numbers and not percentages for the moment. When we say that in 1930, 43% of the college students were women, and compare that with the 1969–70 figure of 41% we must keep in mind that we are comparing 481,000 people to 3,507,000 people.[11] There should be enhanced possibilities of general cultural changes as a consequence of the presence in the adult population of over 33 million people who have completed at least one year of college—18 million men and 15 million women (U.S. Bureau of the Census, 1972a).

CONSEQUENCES OF INCREASED EDUCATION. The more education a woman has, the more likely she is to work, and that correlation has become stronger over the past two decades (U.S. Department of Labor, 1969c: 10). This trend reflects the general availability of upper-level jobs as unskilled jobs become less available. Also it is probable that a large percentage of well-educated women will find themselves employed below their level of preparation, thus making it even more important for them to enter a wider variety of jobs (Bergmann & Adelman, 1973).

The more education a woman has, the more likely she is to work, and the more work experiences a woman has prior to childbearing, the more likely she is to continue to work later. The more education a woman has, the more likely she is to convey a positive orientation toward work to her daughter (Blood, 1965; Levine, 1968). And, as Melder (1965) pointed out in discussing 19th-century feminists, while all of the educated are not rebels, the rebels are always educated—rebels who are willing and able to challenge stereotypes and conventional lifestyles.

What is the meaning of work to the woman herself? Working does more for women than simply change their status in the family. They derive psychic benefits from work as well (Hoffman, 1974). Many women view work as an activity outside the home, which is acceptable because it is nurturant to provide an income for the family, but there is more than that involved. Women work

> ... for greater personal autonomy in spending, for status inside and outside the family, to occupy themselves in an interesting way, to meet people, to have the excitement of being in a contest for advancement, to reduce the amount of housework they do, and to get away from spending all day with their children. The jobs most women have now tend to fulfill these desires to a less satisfactory extent than the jobs men have but they frequently fulfill them better than staying at home would. (Bergmann & Adelman, 1973: 512)

Work also provides an opportunity for women to get out of the house. The lack of enthusiasm many women have for housework has been documented (Bernard, 1973; Gove & Tudor, 1973). Lopata (1971) found that housewives who perceived their work as challenging and interesting expanded their activities and the focus of their attention beyond the routines of the daily tasks in the home.

Many women cannot engage in other activities because they do not have the financial resources unless they work for pay. In such instances, paid work may then become an activity of interest. Hartley (1972) reports that the nonworking mothers she interviewed detested housework far more than did mothers with a job. Household tasks might not be hated so much if they were rewarded. As Kreps (1971) points out, the "activity which is rewarded with a paycheck is likely to be valued more highly in our society"[12] (p. 75).

Hoffman's (1974) research led her to conclude that working mothers have a greater sense of competence and less traditional ideas about women's roles than do nonworking mothers of comparable age, number of children, education, and income. The cause-effect relationship is difficult to distinguish, but the correlation is quite evident. She cites studies which conclude that working women report a need to achieve outside the home, desire a variety of activities, and want to meet people (Eyde, 1968; Sobol, 1963).

Researchers who are themselves well-educated professionals often fail to appreciate that jobs they might not personally choose can have important meanings and values for other people. Workers might prefer better jobs, but the jobs they hold also change their lives and feelings about themselves, and *not* necessarily for the worse. Sexton (1971) describes the importance of a job to working class women: "Jobs mean freedom, independence, excitement for women. More than that, jobs mean equality, or a route to it" (p. 39).

Whether it is called the power of the purse (de Beauvoir, 1968), or a lessening of financial uncertainty (Bergmann & Adelman, 1973), the feeling of security and independence that comes with the earned paycheck is of great importance to many women. The playwright Anita Loos summed it up well when asked by reporters if diamonds are still a girl's best friend: "No! Today a job is!"

More Women Will Be Working More

When we consider the increasing numbers of educated women and men, together with deferred marriages, declining birth rates, and the intricate meaning that work has for women, the reasonable prediction would seem to be that more women will be working in the future, a trend that researchers predict will continue (Taeuber & Taeuber, 1971: 987). Furthermore, there should be continued movement toward "new career concepts" (White, 1972) or "hybrid models" of sex equality (Rossi, 1972b) where work and family activities are accorded equal respect and status by men and women.

Recent reports show little difference by sex in college aspirations of high school graduates (U.S. Bureau of the Census, 1973b). Interviews with women college seniors (Baird, 1973) and an examination of the "rising expectations" of college women (Luria, 1974) indicate that changes in attitudes are taking place—attitudes about future life roles and future plans for work.[13] Chafe, a historian who has analyzed the changes in women's status between 1920 and 1970, states that "important shifts in behavior have taken place and it seems that the changes bear directly on some of the root causes of sexual inequality: the definition of male and female spheres, the role models we provide our children, the permissible horizons available to men and women."History," Chafe concludes, "is on the side of continued change in women's status" (Chafe, 1972: 252–253).

THE WOMEN'S MOVEMENT AND CHANGE

The slow forces of history are being pushed along these days by organized activities undertaken chiefly by women, but supported by men as well. The "new" or "reborn" feminist movement (Carden, 1974; Hole & Levine, 1973) is diverse in membership, appeal, and methods. But the central purpose of every group and sympathizer associated with the movement is to challenge women's legal status, economic inequities, traditional roles, and the cultural stereotypes of women. In short, there is a major challenge to what we have called the cultural attitudes, laws, and practices affecting working women (Freeman, 1973, 1975).

The current feminist movement benefits from the social climate, the cultural ideology, a core of people eager to change social conditions, articulate leadership, explicit goals, plans of action, the support of influential persons not gaining direct advantages from change, plus a large group of persons who could be aroused to awareness of the real injustices women are subjected to.

The wide-scale 19th-century feminist movement was correlated with, and partly responsible for, great improvements in women's status, education, and physical freedom, as well as a rapid expansion of women's activities in all phases of society. After passage of the woman's suffrage amendment in 1920, there was a diminution of activity in the "Woman's movement." Despite the important constitutional legacy and the establishment of agencies such as the Women's Bureau in the federal government (Koontz, 1970), organizations whose chief concerns were women's issues were rare.[14]

The Woman's movement, then, was dormant for several decades. However, women were increasing their activities in the labor force during this dormant period, even though by the 1950s millions of families had taken advantage of readily available and relatively inexpensive suburban housing, the baby boom was in full swing, and the mass media described fulsomely the new emphasis on family life in America. In the meantime, the 1950s were also the beginning of a long period of national concern for the development of scientists, mathematicians, and a host of other highly trained workers, particularly after Sputnik was launched by the U.S.S.R. in 1957. There were exhortations to revamp methods of schooling, and the search for "untapped sources of brain power" became of interest to government and industry. A statement by President Lyndon Johnson typifies this concern during the late fifties and early sixties:

> In the next decade alone we will need . . . 1 million additional specialists in the health services; 800,000 additional science and engineering technicians; 700,-000 scientists and engineers and 4½ million State and local government employees . . . . that requirement cannot be met by men alone; and unless we begin now to open more and more professions to our women, and unless we begin now to train our women to enter these professions, then the needs of our Nation just are not going to be met. (U.S. Congress, House, 1971: Part 1, p. 467)

During the period of economic expansion from 1940 to 1960, when the number of women at work doubled, the greatest increase occurred among better-educated women. Between 1952 and 1968 women with high school education or better were employed at a rate higher than those with less than a high school education (U.S. Department of Labor, 1969c: 10). By 1962, 36% of the women who had completed high school were employed, as were 53% of the women who had completed college, and over 70% of those with five or more years of college (Chafe, 1972: 219; Oppenheimer, 1974).

Not only were the greatest increases in employment occurring among better educated women, but they were increasingly from middle-class homes.

> In households where the husband earned from $7,000 to $10,000 a year, the rate of female participation in the job market rose from 7 percent in 1950 to 25

percent in 1960. . . . Of the wives twenty to forty-four years old with no children under eighteen, the women whose husbands earned $4,000—10,000 a year worked in almost exactly the same proportion as those whose husbands earned $1,000—4,000. . . . By 1964, a larger proportion of wives worked when their husbands received $7,500–10,000 (42 percent) than when their spouses earned under $3,000 (37 percent) and by 1970 60 percent of all non-farm wives in families with incomes over $10,000 were employed. (Chafe, 1972: 218–219)

The median age of women workers was still rising: from 37 years in 1950 to 41 in 1960, higher than in any previous time. In the decade after 1951, the percentage of married women at work increased over 33% (Oppenheimer, 1970: 14). By 1963, almost one third of the married women were working, and 40% of them were by 1970.[15] In short, Chafe (1972: 219) found, "not only was the revolution in female employment continuing; it was also spearheaded by the same middle-class wives and mothers who allegedly had found new contentment in domesticity."

As an expression of governmental interest in women's issues, John F. Kennedy established the President's Commission on the Status of Women in 1961. Eleanor Roosevelt chaired this federal commission, the first to formally address "women's issues."[16] The Commission Report on American Women issued in October 1963 was the result of an intensive review of the laws affecting women and women's general status in American society. It focused on civil and political rights and women's employment as well as other areas and proposed specific employment standards. In two areas, Commission recommendations were swiftly enacted. In 1962, a Presidential directive was issued reversing a legal interpretation dating from 1870 which had barred women from high-level civil service positions. In 1963 the Equal Pay Act was passed, forbidding employers to discriminate in paying wages on the basis of sex.[17]

By the time the President's Commission disbanded early in 1963, a number of state Commissions on the Status of Women had been formed. By 1967, every state had such a commission. In November 1963, President Kennedy established two new high-level committees, the Inter-departmental Committee on the Status of Women and the Citizen's Advisory Council. By June 1964, these two groups had sponsored the First National Conference of State Commissions on the Status of Women, which emphasized women as an "untapped resource."

One month later, the 1964 Civil Rights Act was approved by Congress. Title VII of this act "prohibits discrimination based on race, color, religion, national origin or sex by private employers, employment agencies and unions. . . ." (Hole & Levine, 1973: 30). The Equal Employment Opportunity Commission (EEOC) was established to administer Title VII.[18] In 1965, Executive Order 11246 was passed, prohibiting federal contractors and subcontractors from discriminating on the basis of race, color, religion, and national origin. In 1967 "sex" was added to the Executive Order, now numbered 11375, or "Executive Order 11246 as amended." In the intervening two years, women's groups had lobbied persuasively for the addition of the important word. Where had these active groups come from?

Over the years little public attention was paid to the efforts of the few organizations interested in women's issues. When attention finally came, it was directed toward a new group of feminists. What had happened? First of all:

> The passage of Title VII in 1964 added a sense of excitement and reality to the issue of "women's equality" and precipitated a psychological shift of emphasis from the idea of "women as an untapped resource" to "women as a discriminated against class." After Title VII went into effect in 1965, the lack of strict enforcement of the sex provision added another element: anger—perhaps the most important element in the creation of any social movement. (Hole & Levine, 1973: 81)

The anger was the result of the extreme frustration experienced by well-educated women who were increasingly concerned by the Equal Employment Opportunity Commission's poor record in taking sex discrimination seriously (Scott, 1971). In June 1966, the third National Conference of State Commissions on the Status of Women convened in Washington. Here these interested people decided to form a new action group—"a civil rights movement for women"—to be named NOW, the National Organization for Women.

Incorporated in June 1966 with 300 members, most of whom were women, NOW determined to press for equality in laws, education, and employment and to improve the image of women. In short, their stated purpose was to change the culture. In subsequent years NOW has become involved in almost every aspect of feminist activity; it has been a strong political lobby and has provided a basic philosophy of up-to-date feminism.

NOW's first president, Betty Friedan, served until 1970. She played a sociologically interesting part in the new feminist movement, authoring *The Feminine Mystique* (1964), which became an immediate and controversial best seller. It articulated for millions of women their feelings that they were not engaged in activities highly valued in our society. For those who were housewives, staying home, particularly in suburban environments, with young children, their boredom and guilt were described to a T. The book evidently spoke as well for women who were working in jobs below their educational expectations, for low salaries, and who had problems with child care.

Not only were women's dissatisfactions articulated, but the blame for women's position was placed on the forces of cultural expectations. Friedan spoke of the "chains in the mind" of women, chains forged by adherence to the admonitions of educators, advertisers, and social scientists, admonitions that domesticity, motherhood, and sexuality were all that a mature and well-balanced woman could want of life. In addition, Friedan offered life plans for women based on holding demanding jobs, and she proposed structural changes, among them a GI Bill for women to enable them to return to school.

Thus she developed an ideology or rationale and a program for personal and social change. Later, as president of NOW and one of its driving forces, she helped establish an organization to put the ideas into practice. Therefore, she performed two leadership functions in the founding of a social movement: *inspirational,* in arousing the feelings and articulating the grievances of a large group of people, and *organizational,* in founding a social group which could set goals, use specific means of attaining the goals, and provide for continuity beyond the effective time of the original leader.

As a new group, NOW's members covered a wide spectrum of interest and orientations. Some of the members formed other groups, such as WEAL, the Women's Equity Action League, which has pressed for legal changes in the areas of women's employment, education, and taxes (Scott & Komisar, 1971). Today there are thousands of women involved in women's liberation groups which had their origins in the mid-1960s among women working for civil rights, for peace, and in college student movements. It is significant that their membership is heavily drawn from college students and other young women, that their major focus is the arousing of consciousness and their guiding vision the implementation of broad social changes.

Organized groups interested in ending discriminatory practices affecting women are now so numerous among women's units in professional organizations (see "Women's Units in 67 Organizations," 1973) that they have formed a federation to coordinate their efforts.[19] Many older, more established women's organizations have given feminist issues prominence since the new outpouring of concern and energy began. The YWCA, for example, and the League of Women Voters are now specifically interested in new feminist causes.

There is a newly organized Black Feminist group (*The Spokeswoman,* September 15, 1973, p. 1), and there is a recently organized National Coalition of Trade Union Women, with 3,000 delegates from 58 trade unions (Shanahan, 1974), who want to focus on affirmative action and other bread-and-butter issues affecting women workers. A strong trade union group could be an important and powerful force for improving working conditions through bargaining and legislation.

While there is resistance to the demands of organized groups, there is also great support, if not specifically for organized feminist groups, then for their goals. Such support comes from sympathizers who do not necessarily belong to any group.

The barrage of articles in popular magazines, the press, and traditional women's magazines—*Ladies Home Journal, Good Housekeeping, True Romance*—as well as the success of the magazine *Ms,* indicate popular interest in women's new efforts at changing their status. More specifically, general support for the goals of the new feminism has been indicated by a recent survey conducted by the Roper survey organization. Of the women questioned, 57% gave responses that indicated they support efforts to improve their status. In nationwide public opinion surveys (Harris, 1972) there has been a steady increase in the percentages of men and women responding favorably to the idea of raising women's status. Roper is quoted as commenting that "it demonstrates that the general drive toward sexual equality is now a mainstream movement" (Klemesrud, 1974).

The new wave of feminist activity has been described as being middle class—a description often offered in deprecatory tones. Indeed it seems to be true that the movement *is* middle class in its origins, members' backgrounds, and its goals and methods (Carden, 1974). The part of the movement which arose among college students is also a middle-class phenomenon. Sewell and Shah's (1967) work, for example, shows that women college students tend to come from social-class backgrounds which are even higher than those of college men. Other studies have shown that student activists in general come from liberal, middle-class backgrounds.

In the labor force the greatest change has been the increasing proportion of middle-class women entering middle-class jobs. It may well be that a shift in self-identification has played an important part in this change; that is, when enough middle-class women began to identify *themselves* as jobholders, as workers or future workers, and began to resent inequitable treatment, the potential emerged for organized efforts at social change. Women have always worked, but unlike wet nurses whose own babies starved, unlike migratory workers, unlike factory employees hanging out laundry at eleven o'clock at night, this affected group has the economic base, the voice, and the knowledge of how to effect change. When leaders arose, they used their social networks. They knew how to get attention from the mass media, how to organize meetings, raise money, lobby, and press lawsuits. As mature groups of women, they have displayed their determination and ability to doggedly pursue each specific issue, using and improving the new legal instruments in ways which will touch and change the lives of all women, in all classes.

FINAL COMMENTARY

Women, the victims of cultural lag, are themselves helping to change the body of beliefs, values, and norms which influence them. Some women are working for changes in an organized fashion and clearly identify themselves as change agents. Many other women are creating changes as members of the labor force where they share the goals of equal opportunity, treatment, and rewards, but may eschew the label of "women's libbers." Some women who have achieved high status in their occupations are finding it increasingly possible to help other women as a consequence of the changes in opinion which have already occurred.

The changes have not, and will not, come about easily, for vested interests are not given up cheerfully by individuals or social organizations. An example of resistance is the reaction by the forces opposed to the Equal Rights Amendment, which warn women that they are about to be forced to assume the obligations as well as the privileges of equality (Degler, 1964). The fate of the Equal Rights Amendment may well be a test of the strength of the organized forces backing it, and a measure of the overall changes in attitudes. If the ERA is ratified, changes in the legal system will be felt in every quarter.[20]

Profound changes are now occurring in family activities and in socialization processes relative to work. These changes are affecting middle-aged couples as well as the attitudes and plans of young men and women. Our currt family form may be relatively recent in a historical sense (Aries, 1962), and we can expect men and women will continue to develop new combinations of family and work activities.

An understanding of the consequences of past demographic changes provides a good basis for predicting human behavior. Migratory patterns; sex, age, and dependency ratios; fertility and mortality rates can be used by perceptive scholars to anticipate future roles and statuses of women. Legal changes, their effects on everyday life, and the political struggles around massive normative shifts could also be the subject of many research undertakings. Whether such studies will be undertaken by substantial numbers of social scientists is an interesting question. It is ironically amusing to observe how stubbornly social scientists cling to outmoded theories in the face of massive contrary evidence. Studies of social stratification, social mobility, and occupational aspirations are examples of areas where researchers blithely ignore the female half of the population, which comprises almost half the labor force (for some exceptions, see Barth & Watson, 1967; Haug, 1973; Watson & Barth, 1964).

All the processes affecting women and men take place within an overall background provided by our technology and economy. The current world situation is one where starvation threatens a good proportion of humanity; where Middle Eastern sheiks are aware of their oil treasures and have the organized determination to protect their interest; where war or the threat of war hangs over some portion of the globe at all times. The direction of our technology and economy is linked to these considerations. If, for example, the Western countries were to decide to develop their own sources of energy, there would be a new emphasis on educating people to their highest level of intellectual potential. Women would be urged to enter scientific and professional positions at all levels. Solutions would then be found for familial responsibilities. With declining school populations, the school age could be lowered, filling empty rooms in school buildings by converting them to nursery schools and group day-care centers. The "oversupply" of teachers could be diverted through retraining to care for and teach the new school population. In other words, if there is a need for working women, structural arrangements can be readily changed, and accommodations can be made in pension plans, tenure arrangements, working hours, maternity compensation and other considerations, as well as child-care arrangements.

It is important to understand that discriminatory attitudes and behavior do not occur in isolation. They are integrally woven into our entire social fabric. The complexity of the problem has implications for social scientists who try to understand and interpret social forms and processes, and for activists eager to achieve changes in those forms and processes. An empirically grounded understanding of women's work status could enrich and alter theories of status relations and of social change, illuminating the dynamic interplay between marcocosmic social changes and the microcosmic processes of primary groups.

Those of us who are interested in improving the status of women must not celebrate victories prematurely, for the complexity and size of the problem is becoming clear. Nor should we become prematurely discouraged, for we must recognize that it will take a long period of hard work, perhaps over generations, to forge a society where women and men can combine work and family activities and where true equality between the sexes can become a reality.

NOTES

1. A direct relationship exists between educational level and the probability of women working. Astin (1969: 57) reported that 91% of the 1,500 women doctorates she surveyed were working in 1965. The Women's Bureau described the situation in 1970:

> Of all women 18 years of age and over in the population who had completed less than 8 years of schooling, only 1 out of 4 (23 percent) was in the labor force in 1970, but half of those who had completed high school and almost 3 out of 4 (71 percent) of those who had 5 years or more of college were workers. (U.S. Department of Labor, 1971c: 3)

2. This is not to say that male workers were receiving princely sums. In the early 20th century, when $700 a year was considered a minimal amount adequate to raise a family, the situation has been described thus:

> At the top were the "aristocrats" of labor, the railroad engineers and conductors, the glass blowers, and some of the steel-mill employees and members of the building trades. These men earned anything from $1,500 to $2,000 a year—a very good wage at the existing level of prices. *At the bottom were those*

adult male workers, numbering between one-fourth and one-third of the total employed in factories and mines, who were paid less than $10.00 a week; and also a majority of women workers engaged in industry or trade who received less than $6.00 a week." (Pelling, 1960: 120; emphasis added)

3. In 1900, the life expectancy for men was about 46 years; in 1965, it was about 67 years. For women, the increase was from about 48 years to about 74 years in the same period (see Taeuber & Taeuber, 1971: 500).

4. The "labor force" concept dates from 1940, and there are problems in comparability with previous censuses (U.S. Bureau of the Census, 1943; Kaplan & Casey, 1958). Some experts have argued that the very large increase in women workers from 1900 to recent decades is more apparent than real. Jaffe (1956: 563) compared working women living in cities in 1910 and 1950 to "circumvent the problem of agricultural workers," who were often uncounted, unpaid family members. He concluded that the increases in employed women are smaller than is usually reported.

Smuts (1960), as previously cited, felt that attitudes about working women might have helped to create an underenumeration at an earlier time. In addition, he concluded that

the increase in reported numbers . . . reflects the broadening of census definitions, improvement in census organization and procedure, growing awareness on the part of enumerators that many women do work, increased willingness of respondents to report women's work and the shift of working women from self-employment and homework to wage and salary employment outside the home. (p. 78)

Oppenheimer (1970: 5), however, states that even if the 1900 and 1940 figures are overstated, "there is no doubt whatsoever that the female work rate has gone up considerably since 1940."

The figures for women's employment may well be somewhat inaccurate even since 1940, for the labor force categories do not include intermittent, seasonal, or unpaid workers, and women in particular may be in these categories. However, the phenomenon we are certainly witnessing is that more and more women are working for pay in occupations and for periods of time which are enumerated.

5. From 1960 to 1970, the number of men in the labor force increased by 9% (from 43.3 to 47.7 million), and the number of women increased by 38% (from 21.1 to over 29 million) (U.S. Bureau of the Census, 1963: Table 21, and 1973c: Table 43).

6. It is not within the scope of this chapter to discuss the differences in the quality and types of education received by men and women with the same level of education. For example, vocational education is strongly sex related. Of the 6.4 million women and girls in vocational programs in 1972, 49% studied home economics and 29% were in clerical training. Few were in educational tracks which could prepare them to enter highly paid, skilled crafts (Roby, 1975). For a brief discussion of sex bias in guidance counseling, see Safilios-Rothschild (1974: 31–33).

7. Furthermore, even emotionally supportive husbands who also help out with household tasks do not as a rule provide the same sorts of help to a working woman that many women have traditionally provided to husbands: "A successful woman

preacher, [Anna Garlin Spencer], was asked 'What special obstacles have you met as a woman in the ministry?' 'Not one,' she answered, 'except the lack of a minister's wife.' " (A. F. Scott, 1971: 76; see Rossi, 1972b).

8. In fact, Oppenheimer (1970) argues that the growth of white-collar occupations, coupled with a drop in the available supply of single women of working age, accounts for the tremendous increase in married women and mothers in the labor force since 1940. For a brief review of women's work between 1920 and 1970, see East (1975).

9. One in three of these families lived in poverty in 1971, compared to 1 in 14 families headed by men, and the poverty threshold that year was but $3,968 for a family of four (U.S. Department of Labor, 1971b).

10. The long history of barriers to higher education for women as well as to their academic employment were stunningly reported in 1970 in testimony before the congressional committee considering discrimination in employment (U.S. Congress, House, 1971: Parts 1 and 2; also see Astin & Bayer, 1973; Flexner, 1959; Lewis, 1975; Roby, 1973).

11. Over a period of time the increase in educational level in the United States has been remarkable. In 1930, 6 people out of 100 were college graduates; by 1968, 22 out of 100 were. It is true that 19 out of 100 in 1968 were women, while 26 were men. However, the greatest proportional decline in advanced degrees for women occurred between 1940 and 1960, chiefly as a consequence of the large number of World War II veterans with the GI bill. That decline has reversed, and the *rate* of increase since 1960 has been greater for women in earning bachelor's degrees than for men (U.S. Department of Labor, 1969c: 5). The proportion of secondary degrees earned by women has been increasing and is expected to continue to do so. In 1960–61, women earned 36% of bachelor's and first professional degrees. By 1970, they earned 41.9%, and it is anticipated that by 1980–81 they will earn 46.5% of these degrees (U.S. Department of Health, Education, and Welfare, 1971). In 1972, 20% of the entering class of medical students was women, up from 13.5% in 1971. For law students, the percentages has increased from 4.6% in 1967 to 12% in 1972 (Citizen's Advisory Council, 1973: 7).

12. Housework is an occupation with tasks classified as light manual labor. The rewards for the woman doing her own work are supposed to be chiefly intrinsic, related to the satisfaction of doing the job well. Other than housewives, only professionals, scientists, and creative artists are assumed to derive their major rewards from doing the work, and these groups of workers are paid well when they are employed. Only housework performed by someone other than the housewife is rewarded by payment for domestic service, and that payment is notoriously low. The chief extrinsic reward for the housewife is her economic support, whose level is unrelated to the performance of her household tasks. Women who are best supported, in fact, usually need to do the least household work. Given free choice in the labor market, few workers would appear for a job with such uncertain rewards. The recent report on *Work in America* (U.S. Department of Health, Education, and Welfare, 1973) proposes that housewives be considered active labor participants, since estimates of the economic value of housework go as high as $6,417 yearly (U.S. Department of Health, Education, and Welfare, 1975).

13. Men's changing attitudes may encourage women's working more than some women think. A recent study of groups of college students elicited statements about what they most liked and disliked about being male or female. In some groups, knowing that they could depend upon a man for support was best liked by up to 50% of the women. Yet, up to 50% of the men stated that the least liked part of being a man was knowing that women depend on them for support (Morris, 1974).

Kreps (1971: 103), cites a study by Steinmann (1969) of 1,200 women and 600 men in which the men's stated concept of the ideal woman was close to the ideal the women said they aspire to. The women, however, thought the men's ideal woman was more passive than the one the men said they preferred!

14. For many years, the National Federation of Business and Professional Women's Clubs pressed in a number of ways for women's rights. The National Women's Party has lobbied diligently for passage of an equal rights amendment from 1923 to the present day (Hole & Levine, 1973; Nelson, 1974, 1975). For decades the issues had a widespread appeal comparable to that of vegetarians running for President.

15. The Banks's statement about the prelude to the feminist movement in Victorian England seems appropriate, despite the difference in location and century: "An ostentatious and expensive life of domestic leisure could hardly be mistaken for equality with men, at a time when ambition in a career and living productively in general were being stressed as virtues for the young men of the middle classes" (Banks & Banks, 1972: 11).

16. See Hole and Levine (1973) for the political background which led to establishing the commission. Much of the discussion in this chapter of the background of the reborn feminist movement and the material on NOW are drawn from Section I of their book *Rebirth of Feminism*.

17. For the complex relationship between the Equal Pay Act of 1963 and the 1964 Civil Rights Act, see Hole and Levine (1973: 1–77) and Kanowitz (1971).

18. There was little enforcement power in the original act; it has been amended and expanded since its inception. The relationship to state protective legislation has been the subject of conflict which is still ongoing. Kanowitz has advocated extending the beneficial limitations on working conditions to men, and in the case of hours of work, enacting statutes that would "permit virtually unlimited overtime at the discretion of the worker—male or female—but would prohibit employers from discharging employees for refusing to work overtime" (Kanowitz, 1971: xiii).

19. The Federation of Organizations for Professional Women, 1918 R Street, Washington, D.C. 20009. The first three such organizations in the academic disciplines appeared in 1969, in political science, psychology, and sociology (Hole & Levine 1971: 342).

20. The proposed Equal Rights Amendment to the Constitution reads: "Equality of rights under the law shall not be denied or abridged by the United States or by any State on account of sex." For discussions of the amendment see Brown, Emerson, Falk, and Freedman (1971); Citizen's Advisory Council on the Status of Women materials (1970a, 1970b, 1972a, 1972b, 1973); and Kanowitz (1971). Also see U.S. Congress, Senate (1970) for a wealth of material.

REFERENCES

Addams, Jane. "Woman's Conscience and Social Amelioration." In Charles Stelzle (ed.), *Social Applications of Religion*. New York: Methodist Book Concern, 1908.

Alberts, Robert C. "Catch 65." *New York Times Magazine*, August 4, 1974, pp. 11–28.

Angrist, Shirley. "The Study of Sex Roles." In Judith M. Bardwick (ed.), *Readings on the Psychology of Women*. New York: Harper & Row, 1972.

Aries, Phillipe. *Centuries of Childhood: A Social History of Family Life*. New York: Random House, 1962.

Astin, Helen. *The Woman Doctorate in America*. New York: Russell Sage Foundation, 1969.

Astin, Helen, & Alan E. Bayer. "Sex Discrimination in Academe." In Alice S. Rossi and Ann Calderwood (eds.), *Academic Women on the Move*. New York: Russell Sage Foundation, 1973.

Bailyn, Lotte. "Career and Family Orientations of Husbands and Wives in Relation to Marital Happiness." In Judith Bardwick (ed.), *Readings on the Psychology of Women*. New York: Harper & Row, 1972.

Baird, Leonard. *The Graduates*. Princeton, N.J.: Educational Testing Services, 1973.

Baker, Elizabeth F. *Technology and Woman's Work*. New York: Columbia University Press, 1964.

Banks, J. A., and Banks, Olive. *Feminism and Family Planning in Victorian England*. New York: Schocken Books, 1972.

Barnes, Gilbert Hobbs. *The Anti-Slavery Impulse: 1830 to 1844*. New York: Harcourt, Brace & World, 1933.

Barth, Ernest A. T., and Watson, Walter B. "Social Stratification and the Family in Mass Society." *Social Forces* 45 (March 1967): 392–402.

Beard, Mary R. *Woman as Force in History*. New York: Collier Books, 1962.

Bell, Inge Powell. "The Double Standard." *Trans-action*, 8 (November 1970): 75–80.

Bem, Sandra L., & Daryl J. Bem. "Case Study of a Nonconscious Ideology: Training the Woman to Know Her Place." In D. J. Bem, *Beliefs, Attitudes and Human Affairs*. Belmont, Calif.: Brooks/Cole Publishing Co., 1970.

Bergmann, Barbara R., and Irma Adelman. "The 1973 Report of the President's Council of Economic Advisers: The Economic Role of Women." *The American Economic Review* 63 (September 1973): 509–514.

Berkin, Carol Ruth. "Within the Conjurer's Circle: Women in Colonial America." *University Programs Modular Studies*. Morristown, N.J.: General Learning Press, 1974.

Bernard, Jessie. *The Future of Marriage*. New York: World Publishing Co., Bantam Books, 1973.

Bird, Caroline. "Androgyny?" from *Born Female*. New York: David McKay Co., 1968. Reprinted in Anne Firor Scott (ed.), *The American Woman: Who Was She?* Englewood Cliffs, N.J.: Prentice-Hall, 1971.

Blood, Robert O. "The Husband-Wife Relationship." In F. Ivan Nye & Lois W. Hoffman (eds.), *The Employed Mother in America*. Chicago: Rand McNally Co., 1963.

Blood, Robert O. "Long Range Causes and Consequences of the Employment of Married Women." *Journal of Marriage and the Family* 27 (February 1965): 43–47.

Boone, Gladys. *The Women's Trade Union Leagues in Great Britain and the United States*. New York: Columbia University Press, 1942.

Brooks, Thomas R. *Toil and Trouble: A History of American Labor*. New York: Dell Publishing Co., 1964.

Brown, Barbara A., Thomas I. Emerson, Gail Falk, and Ann E. Freedman. "The Equal Rights Amendment: A Constitutional Basis for Equal Rights for Women." *Yale Law Journal* 80 (April 1971): 871–985.

Brozan, Nadine. "Part-Time Workers—Making Inroads into a Full-Time World." *The New York Times*, October 16, 1973, p. 44.

Bullough, Vern L. *The Subordinate Sex: A History of Attitudes toward Women*. Baltimore: Penguin Books, 1974.

Campbell, Jean W. "Women Drop Back In: Educational Innovation in the Sixties." In Alice S. Rossi & Ann Calderwood (eds.), *Academic Women on the Move*. New York: Russell Sage Foundation, 1973.

Caplow, Theodore. *The Sociology of Work*. New York: McGraw-Hill Book Co., 1954.

Carden, Maren Lockwood. *The New Feminist Movement*. New York: Russell Sage Foundation, 1974.

"Case Summaries: The duty of Fair Representation." *Women's Rights Law Reporter* 1 (Spring 1973): 65–70.

Chafe, William H. *The American Woman: Her Changing Social, Economic and Political Roles, 1920–1970*. New York: Oxford University Press, 1972.

Citizen's Advisory Council on the Status of Women. "The Equal Rights Amendment—What It Will and Won't Do." U.S. Department of Labor, August 1970. (a)

Citizen's Advisory Council on the Status of Women. "The Proposed Equal Rights Amendment to the United States Constitution." U.S. Department of Labor, March 1970. (b)

Citizen's Advisory Council on the Status of Women. "The Equal Rights Amendment and Alimony and Child Support Laws." U.S. Department of Labor, August 1972. (a)

Citizen's Advisory Council on the Status of Women. "Only Equal Rights Amendment Will Promptly End Prison Sentence Discrimination Because of Sex." U.S. Department of Labor, February 1972. (b)

Citizen's Advisory Council on the Status of Women. *Women in 1972*. Washington, D.C.: United States Government Printing Office, 1973.

Cook, Alice. "Women and American Trade Unions." *Annals of the American Academy of Political Science* 375 (January 1968): 124–132.

Cymrot, Donald, & Lucy B. Mallan. *Wife's Earnings as a Source of Family Income.* U.S. Department of Health, Education, and Welfare, Pub. No. (SSA) 74–11701. Washington, D.C.: U.S. Government Printing Office, 1974.

Davis, Allen F. *Spearheads for Reform: The Social Settlements of the Progressive Movement, 1890–1914.* New York: Oxford University Press, 1967.

De Beauvoir, Simone. *The Second Sex.* New York: Alfred A. Knopf, Modern Library ed., 1968.

Degler, Carl. "The Changing Place of Women in America." *Daedalus* 93 (Spring 1964): 653–70.

Dewey, Lucretia. "Women in Labor Unions." *Monthly Labor Review* 94 (February 1971): 42–48.

Dorr, Rheta Childe. "The Home Lives of Factory Women." In Anne Firor Scott (ed.), *The American Woman: Who Was She?* Englewood Cliffs, N.J.: Prentice-Hall, 1971.

Douvan, Elizabeth. "Employment and the Adolescent." In F. Ivan Nye & Lois Wladis Hoffman, *The Employed Mother in America.* Chicago: Rand McNally & Co., 1963.

Douvan, Elizabeth. "Sex Differences in Adolescent Character Processes." In Judith M. Bardwick (ed.), *Readings on the Psychology of Women.* New York: Harper & Row, 1972.

East, Catherine. *Expectations and Results.* Department of State, Citizens Advisory Council on the Status of Women. Washington, D.C.: U.S. Government Printing Office, 1975.

Epstein, Cynthia. "Encountering the Male Establishment: Sex-Status Limits on Women's Careers in the Professions." *American Journal of Sociology* 75 (May 1970): 965–982. (a)

Epstein, Cynthia. *Woman's Place: Options and Limits in Professional Careers.* Berkeley: University of California Press, 1970. (b)

Eyde, L. O. "Work Motivation of Women College Graduates: Five Year Follow-up." *Journal of Counseling Psychology* 15 (1968): 199–202.

Falk, Gail. "Women and Unions: A Historical View." *Women's Rights Law Reporter* 1 (Spring 1973): 54–65.

Feldman, Saul. "Impediment or Stimulant? Marital Status and Graduate Education." *American Journal of Sociology* 78 (January 1973): 982–994.

Flexner, Eleanor. *Century of Struggle: The Woman's Rights Movement in the United States.* Cambridge: Harvard University Press, 1959.

Freeman, Jo. "The Legal Basis of the Sexual Caste System." Symposium issue, *Valparaiso University Law Review* 5 (1971): 203–236.

Freeman, Jo. "Women on the Move: The Roots of Revolt." In Alice S. Rossi & Ann Calderwood (eds.), *Academic Women on the Move.* New York: Russell Sage Foundation, 1973.

Freeman, Jo. *The Politics of Women's Liberation.* New York: David McKay Co., 1975.

Friedan, Betty. *The Feminine Mystique.* New York: Dell Publishing Co., 1964.

Garson, Barbara. "They're Trying to Molest our Kids." *The Village Voice,* August 16, 1974. .

Gilman, Charlotte Perkins. *Women and Economics,* with an introduction by Cal Degler. (Copyright of original book, 1898). New York, Harper & Row, 1966.

"Good Cause Refusal to Work." *Women's Rights Law Reporter* 2 (April 1974): 29.

Gove, Walter R., & Jeannette F. Tudor. "Adult Sex Roles and Mental Illness." *American Journal of Sociology* 78 (January 1973): 812–835.

Graham, Patricia Albjerg. "Women in Academe." In Constantina Safilios-Rothschild (ed.), *Toward a Sociology of Women.* Toronto: Xerox College Publishing, 1972.

Gross, Edward. "Plus ca change . . .? The Sexual Structure of Occupations over Time." *Social Problems* 16 (Fall 1968): 198–208.

Hall, Oswald. "The Informal Organization of the Medical Profession." *Canadian Journal of Economics and Political Science* 12 (February 1946): 30–44.

Harris, Louis, and Associates. *The 1972 Virginia Slims American Women's Opinion Poll.* Virginia Slims, 100 Park Ave., New York 10017 (1972).

Hartley, Ruth E. "Some Implications of Current Changes in Sex Role Patterns." In Judith M. Bardwick (ed.), *Readings on the Psychology of Women.* New York: Harper & Row, 1972.

Haug, Marie. "Social Class Measurement and Women's Occupational Roles." *Social Forces,* 52 (September 1973): 86–98.

Hedges, Janice N. "Women Workers and Manpower Demands in the 1970's." *Monthly Labor Review* 93 (June 1970): 19–29.

Hoffman, Lois. "The Decision to Work." In F. Ivan Nye & Lois Wladis Hoffman (eds.), *The Employed Mother in America.* Chicago: Rand McNally & Co., 1963 (a)

Hoffman, Lois. "Parental Power Relations and the Division of Household Tasks." In F. Ivan Nye & Lois Wladis Hoffman (eds.), *The Employed Mother in America.* Chicago: Rand McNally & Co., 1963 (b)

Hoffman, Lois. "Psychological Factors." In L. W. Hoffman & F. I. Nye, *Working Mothers: An Evaluative Review of the Consequences for Wife, Husband and Child.* San Francisco: Jossey-Bass Publishers, 1974.

Hole, Judith, & Ellen Levine. *Rebirth of Feminism.* New York: Quadrangle Books, 1973.

Holles, Everett R. "Firemen's Wives Fight for Chauvinism on Job." *The New York Times,* July 28, 1974, p. 46.

Holmstrom, Lynda Lytle. "Career Patterns of Married Couples." In Athena Theodore (ed.), *The Professional Woman.* Cambridge: Schenkman Publishing Co., 1971.

Holmstrom, Lynda Lytle. *The Two-Career Family.* Cambridge: Schenkman Publishing Co., 1972.

Hoskins, Dalmer, & Lenore E. Bixby. *Women and Social Security: Law and Policy in*

Five Countries. U.S. Department of Health, Education, and Welfare, Pub. No. (SSA) 73–11800. Washington, D.C.: U.S. Government Printing Office, 1973.

Jaffe, A. J. "Trends in the Participation of Women in the Working Force." *Monthly Labor Review* 79 (May 1956): 559–565.

Jordan, Joan. "Comment: Working Women and the Equal Rights Amendment." *Trans-action* 8 (November–December 1970): 16–20.

Kanowitz, Leo. *Women and the Law*. Albuquerque: University of New Mexico Press, 1971.

Kaplan, David L., & M. Claire Casey. *Occupational Trends in the United States, 1900 to 1950*. U.S. Bureau of the Census, Working Paper No. 5. Washington, D.C.: United States Government Printing Office, 1958.

Kashket, Eva Ruth, Mary Louise Robbins, Loretta Leive, & Alice Huang. "Status of Women Microbiologists." *Science* 183 (February 8, 1974): 488–494.

Klein, Viola. *The Feminine Character: History of an Ideology*. London: Routledge and Kegan Paul, 1971.

Klemesrud, Judy. "Survey Shows 57% of Women in U.S. Support Rights Drive." *International Herald Tribune*, October 4, 1974.

Koontz, Elizabeth. "Women at Work: The Women's Bureau Looks to the Future." *Monthly Labor Review* 93 (June 1970): 3–9.

Kraditor, Aileen S. *The Ideas of the Woman Suffrage Movement, 1890–1920*. New York: Columbia University Press, 1965.

Kreps, Juanita. *Sex in the Market Place: American Women at Work*. Baltimore: Johns Hopkins Press, 1971.

Lear, John. "Study Shows Working Wives are Busier than Heads of State." *Buffalo Courier-Express*, November 18, 1973, p. 81.

Lerner, Gerda (ed.). *Black Women in White America: A Documentary History*. New York: Random House, 1973.

Levine, Adeline. "Marital and Occupational Plans of Women in Professional Schools: Law, Medicine, Nursing, Teaching." Unpublished Ph.D. dissertation, Yale University, 1968.

Levine, Adeline. "Forging a Feminine Identity: Women in Four Professional Schools." *American Journal of Psycho-analysis* 35 (1975): 63–67.

Levine, Murray, & Adeline Levine. *A Social History of Helping Services: Clinic, Court, School and Community*. Englewood Cliffs, N.J.: Prentice-Hall, 1970.

Lewis, Lionel S. *"Scaling the Ivory Tower: Merit and Its Limits in Academic Careers*. Baltimore: Johns Hopkins University Press, 1975.

Long, Larry. "Women's Labor Force Participation and the Residential Mobility of Families." *Social Forces*, 52 (March 1974): 342–348.

Lopata, Helen Znaniecki. *Occupation Housewife*. New York: Oxford University Press, 1971.

Lopate, Carol. *Women in Medicine*. Baltimore: Johns Hopkins University Press, 1968.

Luria, Zella. "Recent Women College Graduates: A Study of Rising Expectations." *American Journal of Ortho-psychiatry* 44 (April 1974): 312–326.

Mahoney, Thomas A. "Factors Determining the Labor Force Participation of Married Women." *Industrial and Labor Relations Review* 14 (1961): 563–577.

Mattfeld, Jacquelyn A., & Carol G. Van Aken (eds.). *Women and the Scientific Professions.* Cambridge: M.I.T. Press, 1965.

Melder, Keith. "The Beginnings of the Women's Rights Movement in the United States, 1800–1840." Unpublished doctoral diss., Yale University, 1965.

Morris, Monica. "I Enjoy Being a Girl: The Persistence of Stereotypic Views of Sex Roles." Paper presented at the meetings of the American Sociological Association, Montreal, August 1974.

Murray, Pauli. "Discrimination against Negro/Black Women." In U.S. Congress, House, Committee on Education and Labor, *To Prohibit Discrimination Against Women.* 91st Cong., 2nd Sess. Washington, D.C.: U.S. Government Printing Office, 1970.

Nelson, Marjory. "The Role of the Working Woman in the Early Development of the Equal Rights Amendment." Unpublished manuscript, Department of Sociology, State University of New York, Buffalo, 1974.

Nelson, Marjory. "Ladies in the Streets." Unpublished Ph.D. diss., State University of New York, Buffalo, 1975.

New York Civil Liberties Union. "Suit Challenges Policy against Women." *Civil Liberties in New York* 21 (February 1974): 8.

Nye, F. Ivan, & Lois Wladis Hoffman. *The Employed Mother in America.* Chicago: Rand McNally & Co., 1963.

O'Neill, William. *The Woman Movement: Feminism in the United States and England.* New York: Barnes & Noble, 1969.

O'Neill, William. *Everyone Was Brave: A History of Feminism in America.* Chicago: Quadrangle Books, 1971.

Oppenheimer, Valerie Kincaid. *The Female Labor Force in the United States.* Berkeley, Calif.: Institute of International Studies, 1970.

Oppenhiemer, Valerie Kincaid. "Rising Educational Attainment, Declining Fertility and the Inadequacies of the Female Labor Market." In Charles F. Westoff and Robert Parke, Jr. (eds.), *Demographic and Social Aspects of Population Growth.* Commission on Population Growth and the American Future, Vol. I. New York: The New American Library, 1972.

Oppenheimer, Valerie K. "The Sociology of Women's Economic Role in the Family: Parsons Revisited and Revised." Paper presented at the meeting of the American Sociological Association, Montreal, August 1974.

Parnes, Herbert, John R. Shea, Ruth S. Spitz, Frederick Zeller, & Associates. *Dual Careers: A Longitudinal Study of Labor Market Experiences of Women.* U.S. Department of Labor, Manpower Research Monograph No. 21. Washington, D.C.: U.S. Government Printing Office, 1970.

Parrish, John B. "Women in Professional Training." *Monthly Labor Review* 97 (May 1974): 41–43.

Pelling, Henry. *American Labor.* Chicago: University of Chicago Press, 1960.

Pilpel, Harriet, & Minna P. Peyser. "Know Your Rights: What a Working Wife Should Know about Her Legal Rights." U.S. Department of Labor, Women's Bureau, Leaflet 39, 1965.

Poloma, Margaret M., & Neal T. Garland. "The Myth of the Egalitarian Family: Familial Roles and the Professionally Employed Wife." In Athena Theodore (ed.), *The Professional Woman.* Cambridge, Mass.: Schenkman Publishing Co., 1971.

Porter, Sylvia. "New Federal Credit Law—What's in It For You?" *Buffalo Evening News,* September 22, 1975, Section 2, p. 21.

Raphael, Edna. "Working Women and Their Membership in Labor Unions." *Monthly Labor Review,* May 1974, pp. 27–33.

Ridley, Jeanne Clare. "The Effects of Population Change on the Roles and Status of Women: Perspective and Speculation." In Constantina Safilios-Rothschild (ed.), *Toward a Sociology of Women.* Lexington, Mass.: Xerox College Publishing, 1972.

Roby, Pamela. "Institutional Barriers to Women Students in Higher Education." In Alice S. Rossi & Ann Calderwood (eds.), *Academic Women on the Move.* New York: Russell Sage Foundation, 1973.

Roby, Pamela. "Vocational Education and Women." Unpublished manuscript, Community Studies, University of California, Santa Cruz, 1975.

Rose, Arnold, M. "The Adequacy of Women's Expectations for Adult Roles." *Social Forces* 30 (October 1951): 69–77.

Ross, Susan Deller. "Sex Discrimination and Protective Labor Legislation." In U.S. Congress, Senate, Committee on the Judiciary, *To Amend the Constitution so as to Provide Equal Rights for Men and Women.* 91st Cong., 2nd Sess. Washington, D.C.: U.S. Government Printing Office, 1970.

Rossi, Alice. "Statement and Resolutions of the Women's Caucus." *American Sociologist,* February 1970, pp. 63–64.

Rossi, Alice. "Discrimination and Demography Restrict Opportunities for Academic Women." In U.S. Congress, House, Committee on Education and Labor, *To Prohibit Discrimination Against Women.* 91st Cong., 2nd Sess. Washington, D.C.: U.S. Government Printing Office, 1971. (a)

Rossi, Alice. "Women in the Seventies: Problems and Possibilities." In U.S. Congress, House, Committee on Education and Labor, *To Prohibit Discrimination Against Women.* 91st Cong., 2nd Sess. Washington, D.C.: U.S. Government Printing Office, 1971. (b)

Rossi, Alice. "The Roots of Ambivalence in American Women." In Judith M. Bardwick (ed.), *Readings on the Psychology of Women.* New York: Harper & Row, 1972. (a)

Rossi, Alice. "Sex Equality: The Beginnings of Ideology." In Constantina Safilios-Rothschild (ed.), *Toward a Sociology of Women.* Lexington, Mass.: Xerox Publishing Co., 1972. (b)

Safilios-Rothschild, Constantina. "The Study of Family Power Structure: A Review, 1960–1969." In Carlfred B. Broderick (ed.), *A Decade of Family Research and Action.* Minneapolis, Minn.: National Council on Family Relations, 1971.

Safilios-Rothschild, Constantina. "Women in Deviant Occupations: Discussion." In Safilios-Rothschild, *Toward a Sociology of Women*. Lexington, Mass.: Xerox College Publishing, 1972.

Safilios-Rothschild, Constantina. *Women and Social Policy*. Englewood Cliffs, N.J.: Prentice-Hall, 1974.

Scott, Ann. "Feminism vs. the Feds." *Issues in Industrial Society* 2 (1971): 32–46.

Scott, Ann, and Komisar, Lucy. *. . . And Justice for All*. National Organization for Women, Chicago, 1971.

Scott, Anne Firor (ed.). *The American Woman, Who Was She?* Englewood Cliffs, N.J.: Prentice-Hall, 1971.

Seigel, Max. "Widower Upheld on U.S. Benefits." *The New York Times*, June 20, 1975, p. 1.

Sewell, William H., & Vimal P. Shah. "Socioeconomic Status, Intelligence and the Attainment of Higher Education." *Sociology of Education* 40 (Winter 1967): 1–23.

Sexton, Patricia Cayo. "The Life of a Working Housewife." In Anne Firor Scott (ed.), *The American Woman: Who Was She?* Englewood Cliffs, N.J., Prentice-Hall, 1971.

Shack, Barbara. "Women's Rights Report." *Civil Liberties in New York* 12 (June 1974): 2.

Shanahan, Eileen. "3,000 Delegates of Chicago Meeting Organize a National Coalition of Labor Union Women." *The New York Times*, March 25, 1974, p. 27.

Sinclair, Andrew. *The Emancipation of the American Woman*. New York: Harper & Row, 1965.

Smuts, Robert W. "The Female Labor Force: A Case Study in the Interpretation of Historical Statistics." *American Statistical Association Journal*, 55 (March 1960): 71–79.

Smuts, Robert W. *Women and Work in America*. New York: Schocken Books, 1971.

Sobol, Marion G. "Commitment to Work." In F. Ivan Nye & Lois Wladis Hoffman (eds.), *The Employed Mother in America*. Chicago: Rand McNally & Co., 1963.

Sokoloff, Natalie J. "A Description and Analysis of the Economic Position of Women in American Society." Paper presented at the meeting of the American Sociological Association, August 1974.

Sommers, Dixie. "Occupational Rankings for Men and Women by Earnings." *Monthly Labor Review* 97 (August 1974): 34–51.

The Spokeswoman. "National Black Feminist Organization Established." Vol. 4 (September 15, 1973), p. 1.

The Spokeswoman. "Trade Union Women Meet in Chicago." Vol. 4 (April 15, 1974), p. 1.

The Spokeswoman. "Union Women and NOW Hit U.S. Steel." Vol. 4 (April 15, 1974), p. 4.

The Spokeswoman. "Government Sells Out Women and Minorities." Vol. 4 (May 15, 1974), pp. 1–3.

The Spokeswoman. "Husbands Denied Life Insurance Coverage." 4 (June 15, 1974), p. 4.

The Spokeswoman. "High Court Rules States May Deny Pregnant Women Disability Benefits." Vol. 5 (July 15, 1974), p. 1.

The Spokeswoman. "Employment Briefs." Vol. 5 (September 15, 1974), p. 4.

The Spokeswoman. "Supreme Court Upholds Women's Jury Rights." Vol. 5 (February 15, 1975), p. 4.

The Spokeswoman. "Supreme Court Extends Equal Rights to Widowers." Vol. 5 (April 15, 1975), p. 2.

Spruill, Julia Cherry. "Women's Life and Work in the Southern Colonies." New York: W. W. Norton & Co., 1972.

Steinfels, Margaret O'Brien. "Who's Minding the Children? The History and Politics of Day Care in America." New York: Simon & Schuster, 1973.

Steinmann, Anne. "The Ambivalent Woman." *New Generation* 51 (Fall 1969), pp. 32–48. Reprinted in Juanita Kreps, *Sex in the Market Place.* Baltimore: Johns Hopkins Press, 1971.

Sullerot, Evelyne. *Woman, Societyd Change.* New York: McGraw-Hill Book Co., 1971.

"Summary of Actions Taken by the Supreme Court." *The New York Times,* October 7, 1975, p. 14.

Sweet, James. *Women in the Labor Force.* New York: Seminar Press, 1973.

Taeuber, Irene B., & Taeuber, Conrad. *People of the United States in the 20th Century.* U.S. Bureau of the Census monograph. Washington, D.C.: U.S. Government Printing Office, 1971.

Teacher's Insurance and Annuity Association. "Retirement Benefits for Men and Women." *The Participant* (July 1973).

Theodore, Athena (ed.). *The Professional Woman.* Cambridge, Mass.: Schenkman Publishing Co., 1971.

U.S. Bureau of the Census. *Comparative Occupation Statistics for the United States, 1890 to 1940.* Washington, D.C.: U.S. Government Printing Office, 1943.

U.S. Bureau of the Census. "Occupational Characteristics." *Census of Population: 1960, Subject Reports.* Final Report PC (2)–7A. Washington, D.C.: U.S. Government Printing Office, 1963.

U.S. Bureau of the Census. "Educational Attainment: March 1972." *Current Population Reports,* Series P–20, No. 243. Washington, D.C.: U.S. Government Printing Office, 1972. (a)

U.S. Bureau the Census. "Marital Status and Living Arrangements: March 1972." *Current Population Reports,* Series P–20, No. 242. Washington, D.C.: U.S. Government Printing Office, 1972. (b)

U.S. Bureau of the Census. *Statistical Abstract of the United States, 1972.* Washington, D.C.: U.S. Government Printing Office, 1972. (c)

U.S. Bureau of the Census. "Birth Expectations of American Wives: June 1973." *Current Population Reports,* Series P–20, No. 254. Washington, D.C.: U.S. Government Printing Office, 1973. (a)

U.S. Bureau of the Census. "College Plans of High School Seniors: October 1972." *Current Population Reports,* Series P–20, No. 252. Washington, D.C.: U.S. Government Printing Office, 1973. (b)

U.S. Bureau of the Census. "Occupational Characteristics." *Census of Population: 1970, Subject Reports.* Final Report PC(2)–7A. Washington, D.C.: U.S. Government Printing Office, 1973. (c)

U.S. Bureau of the Census. "Social and Economic Status of the Black Population in the United States, 1974." *Current Population Reports,* Series P–23, No. 54. Washington, D.C.: U.S. Government Printing Office, 1975.

U.S. Commission on Civil Rights. "Sexism and Racism: Feminist Perspectives." *Civil Rights Digest,* Vol. 6 (Spring 1974), entire issue.

U.S. Congress, House, Committee on Education and Labor. *To Prohibit Discrimination against Women,* Hearings on Section 805, HR 16098, 91st Cong., 2nd Sess. Parts 1 and 2. Washington, D.C.: U.S. Government Printing Office, 1970.

U.S. Congress, Senate, Committee on the Judiciary. *To Amend the Constitution so as to Provide Equal Rights for Men and Women.* Hearings on S.J. Res. 61, 91st Cong., 2nd Sess. Washington, D.C.: U.S. Government Printing Office, 1970.

U.S. Department of Health, Education, and Welfare. *Projections of Educational Statistics to 1980–81.* Washington, D.C.: U.S. Government Printing Office, 1971.

U.S. Department of Health, Education, and Welfare. *Work in America: Report of a Special Task Force to the Secretary of Health, Education, and Welfare.* Cambridge: M.I.T. Press, 1973.

U.S. Department of Health, Education, and Welfare. *Economic Value of a Housewife.* Social Security Administration, Research and Statistics Note 9. Washington, D.C.: U.S. Government Printing Office, 1975.

U.S. Department of Labor. *1969 Handbook on Women Workers.* Women's Bureau, Bulletin 294. Washington, D.C.: U.S. Government Printing Office, 1969. (a)

U.S. Department of Labor. *How You Can Help Reduce Barriers to the Employment of Mature Women.* Women's Bureau. Washington, D.C.: U.S. Government Printing Office, 1969. (b)

U.S. Department of Labor. *Trends in Educational Attainments of Women.* Women's Bureau. Washington, D.C.: U.S. Government Printing Office, 1969. (c)

U.S. Department of Labor. *Automation and Women Workers.* Women's Bureau. Washington, D.C.: U.S. Government Printing Office, 1970.

U.S. Department of Labor. *Day Care Services: Industry's Involvement.* Women's Bureau, Bulletin 296. Washington, D.C.: U.S. Government Printing Office, 1971. (a)

U.S. Department of Labor. *Fact Sheet on the American Family in Poverty.* Women's Bureau. Revised. Washington, D.C.: U.S. Government Printing Office, 1971. (b)

U.S. Department of Labor. *Women Workers Today.* Women's Bureau. Washington, D.C.: U.S. Government Printing Office, 1971. (c)

U.S. Department of Labor. *Facts on Women Workers of Minority Races.* Women's Bureau. Washington, D.C.: U.S. Government Printing Office, 1972. (a)

U.S. Department of Labor. *Plans for Widening Women's Educational Opportunities.* Women's Bureau. Washington, D.C.: U.S. Government Printing Office, 1972. (b)

U.S. Department of Labor. *The Economic Role of Women.* Women's Bureau. Reprinted from *Economic Report of the President,* 1973. Washington, D.C.: U.S. Government Printing Office, 1973. (a)

U.S. Department of Labor. *Twenty Facts on Women Workers.* Women's Bureau. Washington, D.C.: U.S. Government Printing Office, 1973. (b)

U.S. Department of Labor. *Highlights of Women's Employment and Education: Employment in 1973.* Women's Bureau. Revised. Washington, D.C.: U.S. Government Printing Office, 1974. (a)

U.S. Department of Labor. *Twenty Facts on Women Workers.* Women's Bureau. Washington, D.C.: U.S. Government Printing Office, 1974. (b)

U.S. Department of Labor. *Why Women Work.* Women's Bureau. Revised. Washington, D.C.: U.S. Government Printing Office, 1974. (c)

U.S. Department of Labor. *Manpower Report of the President, 1975.* Washington, D.C.: U.S. Government Printing Office, 1975.

Waldman, Elizabeth. "Changes in the Labor Force Activity of Women." *Monthly Labor Review* 93 (June 1970), pp. 10–18.

Waldman, Elizabeth, & Beverly J. McEaddy. "Where Women Work: An Analysis by Industry and Occupation." *Monthly Labor Review* 97 (May 1974): 3–13.

Waldman, Elizabeth, & Robert Whitmore. "Children of Working Mothers, March 1973." *Monthly Labor Review* 97 (May 1974): 50–58.

Wallace, Walter. "The Perspective of College Women." In Wallace, *Student Culture.* Chicago: Aldine Publishing Co., 1966.

Watson, W. B., & E. A. Barth. "Questionable Assumptions in the Theory of Social Stratification." *Pacific Sociological Review* 7 (Spring 1964): 10–16.

Weaver, Warren. "Court Upsets Pregnant Teacher Curbs." *The New York Times,* January 21, 1974.

Wells, Jean. *Facts about Women's Absenteeism and Labor Turnover.* U.S. Department of Labor, Women's Bureau. Washington, D.C.: U.S. Government Printing Office, 1969.

White, Martha S. "Psychological and Social Barriers to Women in Science." In Constantina Safilios-Rothschild (ed.), *Toward a Sociology of Women.* Lexington, Mass.: Xerox College Publishing, 1972.

Wilensky, Harold L. "Women's Work, Economic Growth, Ideology, Structure." *Industrial Relations* 7 (May 1968): 235–248.

Williams, Josephine. "The Woman Physicians Dilemma." *Journal of Social Issues,* 6 (1950): 38–44.

Wolfbein, Seymour. "Labor Trends, Manpower and Automation." In Henry Borow (ed.), *Man in a World at Work.* Boston: Houghton Mifflin Co., 1964.

"Women's Units in 67 Organizations." *Chronicle of Higher Education,* October 26, 1973, p. 9.

CHAPTER 7

The "temporary minority": Workers after age 45

Leonard D Cain

THE MINORITY STATUS OF OLDER WORKERS

In the 1840s, as the Abolition movement intensified its attack upon the institution of slavery, a poem called "Sugar Estate" was published in *The National Anti-Slavery Standard* for January 5, 1842. In the following excerpt, an overseer of the workers in a sugar mill responds to a question about older workers:

> But where, you ask me, are the poor *old* slaves?
> Where should they be, of course, but in their graves?
> We do not send them there before their time,
> But let them die, when they are past their prime.
> Men who are worked by night as well as day,
> Some how or other, live not to be gray;
> Sink from exhaustion—sicken—droop and die,
> And leave the count another batch to buy.
> You cannot think how soon the want of sleep
> Breaks down their strength: 'tis well they are so cheap!
> Four hours of rest in time of crop—for five
> Or six long months, and few indeed will thrive.
> With twenty hours of unremitting toil,
> Twelve in the field, and eight in doors to boil

Or grind the cane; believe me few grow old.
But life is cheap, and sugar, sir, is gold.

Surely, there has been progress in protecting older workers since the time of this poet, but in 1970 the publication of *Toward an Industrial Gerontology* (edited by Harold Sheppard) provided new strength and direction to a field of study and action which has as its avowed purpose the upgrading of the minoritylike status of older workers in America. Norman Sprague's article in that work provided the rationale for the movement: "Industrial gerontology begins when age *per se* becomes a handicap to employment. Age discrimination in employment may start at 35 or 40 in some industries and occupations, and begins to take on major dimensions at age 45" (Sprague, 1970: v).

Industrial gerontology has been launched in the wake of successful political efforts to provide comprehensive national legislation to protect the rights of middle-aged and older workers, at least until they reach the age of 65. Key provisions of the Age Discrimination in Employment Act (ADEA) of 1967 are found in Section 623 of the act and are summarized by H. Roy Kaplan in Chapter 8.

A somewhat more elaborate rationale for an industrial gerontology than that advanced by Sprague is presented in Charles Odell's article in the same work, as follows:

> We know that older workers are valued on the job as long as they can hold the job but once they lose out they have problems in getting new employment. We know that employers do tend to prefer younger people when they are hiring, but that this preference is more clearly associated with the costs of pensions, insurance, workmen's compensation and other fringe benefits than it is with adverse attitudes about the productivity and performance of older workers. . . . We know that rational hiring and selection methods and techniques such as aptitude tests, personality tests and other so-called scientific selection techniques tend to screen out most older workers not because they are good predictors of job success, but because they have been standardized on young people. . . .
>
> We know that anti-discrimination laws are not particularly effective in increasing job opportunities for middle-aged and older workers. (Odell, 1970: 14)

Here, then, are the kinds of employment practices and attitudes which led to the enactment of ADEA in 1967 and which continue to call for special monitoring and action in the 1970s. But unresolved as yet are the frequency and the intensity of discriminatory practices which relegate at least some older workers to a status comparable to that of members of ethnic minority groups.

BUREAUCRATIZATION AND THE STATUS OF OLDER WORKERS

Although present data cannot provide complete answers, an analysis of certain characteristics of the labor market may increase our understanding, if it does not supply answers. Shortly after World War II, Ludwig von Mises (1946: 97–100) declared:

> It is evident that youth is the first victim of the trend toward bureaucratization. The young men are deprived of any opportunity to shape their own fate. . . . The youth depends entirely on the kind disposition of the old men. The rising generation is at the mercy of the aged.

If von Mises was accurate in noting a "trend toward bureaucratization" in the mid-1940s, his description is even more accurate of the 1970s. Increasing numbers of workers of all ages are dependent on large-scale organizations for jobs and job protection. Over 90% of our nonagricultural work force is employed in bureaucratic organizations, and 4% of all these organizations account for approximately 60% of all employment (Tausky, 1970: 3–4). However, von Mises's conclusion that bureaucratization inevitably leads to a gerontocracy in the work force was of doubtful validity even in the 1940s, and it certainly can be challenged today.[1] There is, to be sure, a certain plausibility to the von Mises hypothesis. Members of the labor force in a bureaucracy typically obtain tenure, or permanent employment status, after successful completion of a probationary period of employment. Seniority rights result in the accrual of special protections and privileges to older workers. Eligibility for promotion based on years of service, or years in rank, provides a pattern in bureaucratic careers which leads to increased wages and authority for those in middle and old age (up to retirement).

However, few if any benefits accrue to an older worker in most bureaucratic systems solely on the basis of chronological age. Length of service, often in one agency, is usually crucial. Older workers often achieve a preferred status with seniority. There is usually a high correlation between age and length of service, but such is not always the case. When a worker is forced to change jobs in midcareer, for whatever reasons, job security and seniority are extremely difficult to reestablish. A U.S. Department of Labor report (1965) found that "Length of service (seniority status) and age are synonymous only on the average, and in this instance the deviations from the average on the low side create part of the older worker problem" (p. 56).

In the midst of continuing bureaucratization and probably because of it, the elderly in general and some older workers in particular experience a severe loss of economic status and, often, of prestige. The entire gerontological movement, designed to enhance the status of older members of the society, is vivid evidence that, for whatever reasons, the reordering of work assignments through bureaucratization has not, contrary to von Mises, produced an economic gerontocracy.

Ordinarily, in considering an issue related to bureaucracy, turning to the insights of Max Weber provides analysis, if not resolution, of the issue. However, in the matters of the association of age with authority and of the rights of older workers, Weber (1946: 202) is, at best, ambiguous. He states, for example, that "the position of the official is held for life, at least in public bureaucracies; . . . *tenure for life* is presupposed. . . ." In the paragraph immediately following, however, he indicates that officials receive "old age security provided by a pension." He failed to consider the implications of compulsory retirement, currently a standard policy in many American bureaucracies, upon the assignment to statuses in a bureaucracy; he failed to consider the consequences of collapse of an organization, the closing of a department, or the removal of a plant to a new location; and he failed to evaluate the relative importance of formal education as contrasted with experience in obtaining promotions or new employment (Weber, 1947: 331–335).

From these deficiences there emerges one of the anomalies of Weber's analysis of bureaucracy, and a major issue in the consideration of the minority status of the older worker as well. Weber's concept of "office," together with the hierachical relationship among offices, produced the conclusion that the office dominates the individual who may occupy the office, and the rationale for bureaucratic organization resides, to a great extent, in the emphasis on the office rather than the holder of the office (Weber, 1947: 332). Yet the officeholders "tend to increase their power still further by the knowledge growing out of experience in the service. . . . [T]hey acquire . . . a special knowledge of facts and have available a store of documentary material peculiar to themselves" (Weber, 1947: 339).

Taken alone, the above quote, by emphasizing the indispensability of some older workers because of their distinctive, apparently difficult-to-transmit knowledge, tends to support the von Mises hypothesis. However, Weber elsewhere introduced ideas which provide counterinterpretations. One idea is that the controlling agents of bureaucracies are themselves not part of the bureaucracy. Rather, ultimate authority is superimposed from without; criteria other than proficiency within the bureaucracy are instrumental in filling the positions of top authority (Weber, 1947: 335).

The wavering continues, and the complication in understanding the roles and the rights of older workers increases, as one reads further: "A very strong development of the 'right to the office' naturally makes it more difficult to staff [the office] with regard to technical efficiency, for such a development decreases the career opportunities of ambitious [younger?] candidates for office" (Weber, 1946: 203).

The confusion resulting from the often sharp contrast between the logical conclusion that bureaucratization protects older workers and the empirical observation that many older workers suffer reduction to minority-group status cannot be resolved fully here, although this confusion does provide a context for exploring the empirical evidence for the conclusion that older workers are relegated to minority-group status merely because of their age.

Two quite separable issues are evident in considering work opportunities for older people. One issue centers on abrupt removal of workers from the labor force through compulsory retirement, typically at age 65. The second issue focuses on difficulties of workers in the age span 45–64 years who, apparently because of age, experience difficulty in obtaining reemployment and other economic opportunities more readily available to those who are younger.

With compulsory retirement, a minority-group status of sorts is heaped instantaneously upon the older person. Labor unions, governmental agencies, and employers, with full support of law and contracts, conspire to withdraw rights available to younger workers by supporting compulsory retirement policies ("Age Discrimination in Employment," 1958).

As recently as November 1975, the U.S. Supreme Court affirmed a federal court ruling which upheld a Louisiana state law which requires civil service employees to retire at age 65 [see *Cannon* v. *Guste*, 423 U.S. 918 (1975); also see Powledge, 1975]. However, in May 1975, the Court agreed for the first time to render its own decision on the question in a case involving the mandatory retirement of a Massachusetts state police officer at age 50 [*Murgia* v. *Massachusetts Board of Retirement*, 376 F. Supp. 753, D. Mass. (1974), certiorari granted, 43 U.S.L.W. 3609, U.S. (May 20, 1975); also see Botelho, Cain, & Friedman, 1975].

There are continuing controversies over justice for the individual worker and the general consequences to productivity and the economy which result from current retirement policies (Palmore, 1973). Whether or not efforts to alleviate losses resulting from retirement—such as social security payments, pension benefits, Medicare, various tax exemptions, and special services—promote equity in the face of the loss of equality in the labor force is debatable (Cain, 1974a, 1974b).

In addition, the emergence in recent years of various early-retirement options, to be imposed either by the employer alone or through an agreement between the employer and employee, adds a new dimension to the minority status of older workers. In contrast to the so-called "regular early retirement" option, which allows a worker to retire at an earlier age than the one specified, but with a reduced monthly benefit, recent negotiations between management and labor have provided procedures whereby a worker may be forced to retire well before normal retirement age, albeit typically with benefits considerably higher than those provided by the so-called regular plans. This strategy has been adopted in a few industries to assist involuntarily separated workers to make adjustments to a status which otherwise would simply be labeled unemployment. In a 1965 report of the U.S. Department of Labor, it was noted that:

> The major significance of these provisions for older workers is that they tend to increase pressures for early retirement and to force workers into an unfavorable employment situation. Moreover, pressures for early retirement further solidify the resistance to hiring older workers. The employer who assumes the expense of an accelerated early retirement program is unlikely to be interested in hiring older workers. (p. 35)

It is widely known that in order to receive full social security benefits a retiree may not earn more than a minimum income, even though contributions were made to social security throughout her or his working life.[2] It is less widely known that serious restrictions are placed on many retirees by those who maintain control over private pension programs. Labor unions, as a means of providing maximum job opportunities for younger workers, and employers, as a means of discouraging retired employees from going to work for a competing firm, may insist upon constraints on the retiree who may be tempted to resume working. A recent survey of pension plans found that plans which represented 40% of the workers under review incorporated some form of restrictions on postretirement employment (Davis, 1973: 45).

The question of how to, at the same time, gain optimum use of manpower for efficiency and safety and grant justice to aging workers is very difficult to answer but necessary to pose. F. Le Gros Clark was among the first to detail the dimensions of this problem. In a 1960 book, *Growing Old in a Mechanized World,* Clark asked:

> How will the contemporary revolution in manufacturing methods begin to affect the employment prospects of older men? . . .
>
> The problem arises mainly from the technical and economic inability of modern industry to use all the labour that has become "marginal" simply by reason of age. For most men senescence, when it overtakes them is a gradual though irreversible process. No doubt substantial numbers of men are more or less chronic invalids by their middle and late sixties. But industrial surveys have suggested that considerably larger numbers merely pass into a kind of transitional stage; their health may be relatively unimpaired, but they can no longer carry out their normal tasks in a completely satisfactory manner. They are plainly growing old. These are men who must soon, it is believed, constitute one of the great problems of an industrial society. (p. 9)

MAINTAINING EMPLOYMENT WHILE GROWING OLDER

The gerontological movement is confronting, with at least partial success, the problem identified by Clark. The major emphasis has been to promote postemployment services and protections of many kinds. Another emphasis, still unfulfilled, is the abolition of all compulsory retirement strictures based on chronological age, and the substitution of some form of functional age evaluation combined with voluntary withdrawal from the labor force by the worker.[3]

Although the minority status of the retired worker is no doubt partly the result of arbitrary and compulsory retirement policies, which is a significant topic itself,[4] the thrust of this chapter is to examine the second issue posed above, that of reduced job opportunities for the middle-aged and aging who choose to remain in the labor force.

A recent report from the Oregon Bureau of Labor (1972) declared:

> Middle age, as a barrier to equal opportunity, has its own characteristic dimension: potentially, once in the 45–65 age group, we are all exposed to the ways society acts and reacts in regard to middle age. If we are employed or seek employment, we all become members of a "temporary minority" as we move through that phase in our lives. While racial characteristics or ethnic backgrounds determine minority status, with all the consequences for some Americans all the time, middle age may make every American experience "minority status" at some time. (p. 1)

The report by the Secretary of Labor to the Congress, *The Older American Worker: Age Discrimination in Employment* (U.S. Department of Labor, 1965), also labeled workers in the 45–64 span of years a "minority group":

> [A] nation which already worships the whole idea of youth must approach any problem involving older people with conscious realization of the special obligation a majority assumes with respect to "minority group" interests. This 45–64 age group is, to be sure, one minority group in which we all seek, sometimes desperately, eventual membership. Discrimination against older workers remains, nevertheless, a problem which must be met by a majority who are not themselves adversely affected by it and may even be its temporary beneficiaries. (p. 3)

Secretary of Labor W. Willard Wirtz continued: "The 'discrimination' older workers have most to fear . . . is not from any employer malice, or unthinking majority, but from the ruthless play of wholly impersonal forces—most of them part of what is properly, if sometime too casually, called 'progress' " (p. 3).

Not all of those who have studied the opportunities available to older workers accept the diagnosis that "wholly impersonal forces" are to blame for this form of discrimination. Harold Sheppard (1970) charges "age-ism":

> Just as "racism" may be an endemic part of American culture, in that many whites act on an unquestioned belief that Negroes are inherently inferior, it

may also be that "age-ism" is just as influential, in that a belief in the inevitable differences and changes through the process of aging in the area of work permeates the actions of Americans in their dealings with older workers—not just those in their 70's, but also those in their 40's and 50's. (p. 17)

How accurate is the hypothesis that a worker, by the mere fact of becoming 45 years old, is forced into a "temporary minority" status? What kinds of workers become most vulnerable to loss of income and to reduction of employability? What social factors contribute to these losses? What remedies have been adopted or proposed?

If unemployment rates alone are considered, it appears as though older workers are actually in a favored category. Information from Table 7.1

TABLE 7.1
Unemployed Persons, by Age and Sex, November 1963 and November 1973

Age	Male				Female			
	Number (000), 1963	Unemployed (%), 1963	Number (000), 1973	Unemployed (%), 1973	Number (000), 1963	Unemployed (%), 1963	Number (000), 1973	Unemployed (%), 1973
Total ...	2,253	4.7%	2,025	3.7%	1,682	6.6%	2,031	5.7%
16–19 .	441	16.3	666	14.8	376	17.4	581	15.1
20–24 .	329	7.4	447	6.3	281	9.2	400	7.0
25–34 .	433	4.4	336	2.9	291	6.7	463	6.0
35–44 .	361	3.2	165	1.6	307	5.4	243	3.9
45–54 .	287	2.9	185	1.8	219	3.8	206	3.1
55–64 .	268	3.9	166	2.4	128	3.8	107	2.6
65+ ...	91	4.4	62	3.3	46	3.6	30	2.8

Source: Adapted from U.S. Department of Labor, Employment and Earnings 10 (December 1963): Table A–4, p. 3, and 20 (December 1973): Table A–8, p. 28.

indicates that males 45 and over have a lower unemployment rate than the average of the total working-age population. For females, those 45 and over have the lowest rates of unemployment of all age categories. On the surface it would appear difficult to make a case for minority status of older workers on the basis of these rates of unemployment.

The picture changes somewhat, however, when evidence from Table 7.2 is examined. A partial explanation for low unemployment rates among older persons (as of November 1973) may be that a sizable number simply with-

TABLE 7.2
Participation in the Labor Force, by Age and Sex, November 1973

Age	Males		Females	
	Labor Force (000)	Participation Rate (%)	Labor Force (000)	Participation Rate (%)
Total	56,543	79.1%	35,625	45.8%
16–19	4,875	59.2	3,853	48.1
20–24	8,030	86.2	5,744	62.1
25–34	13,702	96.1	7,757	53.2
35–44	10,575	96.3	6,278	54.5
45–54	10,476	93.0	6,744	55.2
55–59	4,152	86.2	2,532	47.1
60–64	2,840	68.2	1,645	34.0
65+	1,891	22.4	1,072	9.0

Source: Adapted from *Employment and Earnings* 20 (December 1973): Table A–4, p. 24.

draw from participation in the labor force. Whereas participation among males aged 25–55 is well above 90%, it declines steadily thereafter. For females there is a similar pattern, although attention is called to the higher participation of those 45–54 than those 25–44.

The picture changes still further when Table 7.3 is reviewed. In November 1973, variation by age groups in the periods of unemployment was evident. Males who were out of work in the 25–34 age group averaged 12.5 weeks of unemployment; those in the 35–44 age group, 11.6 weeks; the 45–54 age group, 15 weeks; and the 55–64 group, 15.3 weeks. Similarly, among younger female workers, the average duration of unemployment was 8.1 weeks for those 25–34 and 8.8 weeks for those 35–44, whereas the duration was 13.2 weeks for those 45–54 and 14.7 weeks for those 55–64.

Before reviewing some recent scholarly efforts which address particular aspects of the hypothesis that minority status accrues to a worker upon reaching middle age (say, 45), there is need to identify some rather obvious exceptions. After all, bureaucratization, as von Mises's position suggests, does typically provide some basic protections for many older workers. The policy of *tenure* is widespread in large-scale organizations. Ordinarily, after the probationary period, which may vary from a few months to several years, a worker achieves permanent status as an employee and may thereafter be removed from his office only "with cause" (or the attainment of a compulsory retirement age).

In addition, the policy of *seniority* typically protects the older worker from layoffs, unwanted transfers, and demotion. Of course, because many

TABLE 7.3
Unemployed Persons by Age, Sex, and Duration, November 1973

Sex and Age	Total Unemployed	Duration of Unemployment by Number (000)				Percent in Age Group Unemployed 15 weeks +	Average Duration of Unemployment (weeks)
		5 weeks	5–14 weeks	15–26 weeks	27 weeks +		
Males							
Total	2,025	1,048	585	214	178	19.4%	10.6
16–19	666	366	234	46	19	9.8	7.4
20–24	447	229	137	47	33	17.9	10.0
25–34	336	162	77	58	38	28.8	12.5
35–44	165	97	25	25	18	26.3	11.6
45–54	185	87	49	17	31	26.0	15.0
55–64	166	72	52	11	32	25.6	15.3
65+	62	35	10	9	7	—	12.0
Females							
Total	2,031	1,159	574	177	120	14.7	8.5
16–19	581	381	147	36	16	9.1	6.5
20–24	400	240	105	40	15	13.8	7.5
25–34	463	258	139	40	26	14.3	8.1
35–44	243	134	75	19	15	13.9	8.8
45–54	206	89	67	25	25	24.3	13.2
55–64	107	40	33	16	18	31.8	14.7
65+	30	17	7	2	4	—	9.3

Source: Adapted from Employment and Earnings 20 (December 1973): Table A–17, p. 32.

tenure and seniority rules pertain to local areas or to segments of large-scale organizations, relocation of a plant or the reorganizing of an agency can make an older worker vulnerable to insecurity.

Furthermore, there is need to consider the historical context in which the label "temporary minority" is affixed. Actually, the status of the older worker until rather recent times has been somewhat blurred. Undoubtedly, many workers formerly "died with their boots on" and thus did not suffer unemployment or reduced job status. For those plagued with the so-called culture of poverty, work has provided little economic security at any time in the life-span. In an agricultural economy the older person often has an opportunity to reduce work responsibilities gradually, without necessarily losing prestige or the sense of belonging.

SOME VIEWS ON THE FUTURE MINORITY STATUS OF OLDER WORKERS

Closely related to the historical context is the issue of future prospects for the older worker. Whether an evolving job market will yet provide equity, and whether new awareness and new fair-employment practices legislation will overcome second-class citizenship for older workers, is problematic. But a review of some projections is in order.

Dunlop (1966) has identified several factors which contribute to a minority status for the current cohort of older and retired workers, whom he designates as the "transition generation." However, he is somewhat optimistic that at least some of the sources of inequity are disappearing rapidly:

> Many will have retired without benefits or with low benefits under private pension plans only recently adopted . . . . The generation that entered employment since the mid-fifties faces much more generous pension opportunities on retirement than their fathers a generation earlier. The transition generation of retirees can well claim a disadvantage relative to their sons. (p. 14)

The prospects for equity are enhanced, Dunlop concluded, because of a declining need for physical strength and exertion to fulfill job requirements. As arduous tasks in mining, construction, and manufacturing decline, maintenance, clerical, technical, and professional occupations are expanding. These changes are especially congenial to older women, who have been liberated from family responsibilities and are available for work. Projections for the percentage of women aged 55–59 in the work force indicate an increase from 45.9% in 1964 to 56.2% by 1980 (Dunlop, 1966: 16).

Dunlop identified two major obstacles to equity for older workers: the rising level of educational requirements for emerging jobs, and the personal and social costs to older workers in accommodating to occupational and geographical mobility so often required in today's job market. Regarding educational requirements, he wrote:

> Some idea of the intergenerational differences in formal educational attainment is seen in the fact that the median years of school completed in March, 1964, for those 65 and over was 8.4 years as compared to 12.4 years for those in the 25–29 age bracket, a four year difference . . . . It is projected that in 1975, 37.3 percent of the labor force 65 and over will have had four years of high school while in the age bracket 25–34 years the figure will be 73.4 percent (double the percent for the elderly); in 1975 9.4 percent of those 65 and over will be college graduates as compared to 18.9 percent in the age group 25 to 34. This perpetual lag of the older worker in educational attainment may not be new but it may raise more serious problems of adaptation in a day of increasing emphasis upon educational requirements for more jobs. (p. 18)

In 1974, workers 45 years and older comprised 34% of the U.S. work force. Although the percentage of men aged 45–54 in the labor force held firm at approximately 20% since the end of World War II (1947–1974), and the percentage of men aged 55–64 dropped only slightly during that period, middle-aged and older women were added to the labor force in larger numbers. In 1947 only 28% of women 45 and older were in the labor force; by 1974 their numbers reached 33% (U.S. Department of Labor, 1975: 206). Today, only 15% of workers 64 and over find paid work (Powledge, 1975). Eckstein (1966: 76–78) notes the complexities of assessing the minority status of older workers but acknowledges that certain types of older workers face distinctive problems, such as lowered mobility and job displacement due to plant closings, relocations, and automation.

Eckstein blamed the vulnerability of the older worker to unemployment of long duration on a combination of objective factors and arbitrary discrimination by employers. His objective factors include: the education disadvantages of older workers as opposed to younger ones, new job requirements generally favorable to younger workers resulting from changing technology, and the requirements in some jobs for attributes of health or strength most easily found in the young. At the same time, many employers (at least prior to fair-employment practices legislation, which makes discrimination in employment because of age illegal) have established arbitrary hiring restrictions against those 45 and older, regardless of ability, health, or experience. Reasons cited by employers for age discrimination include:

> . . . physical capability; a policy of promotion-from-within and accompanying restriction of hiring to younger ages and to entry jobs; ability to hire younger workers for less money and concern that older workers' earnings expectations are too high; pension plans and, to a much less extent, costs of health and life insurance; lack of skills, experience, or education requirements; limited work

expectancy; training costs and lower productivity; lack of adaptability; and
desired age balance in the work force. (Eckstein, 1966: 79)

It remains very difficult to distinguish between those factors that have some
degree of legitimacy and those that are based on ignorance of ability of older
workers or on calculated policies inimical to equity and the public interest.

It is not clear to what extent the minority-group status of older workers
is endemic to an urban, industrial civilization, and to what extent the vulnerability of older workers to loss of status and earning power reflects a
transitional stage. However, it would appear that the diminution of work
responsibility with aging on a farm; the reduction of responsibility in a small,
family-operated business; or the trailing off of work load of a skilled
craftsman are all sharply different from the experience of abrupt dismissal
from a job in middle age, with a long wait for reemployment, or compulsory
retirement, with an abrupt reduction in pay. The minority status of certain
classes of older workers is likely to be overcome only if public policies are
adopted and assiduously enforced to minimize the impact on older workers
of continuing automation, factory relocation, and development of new
production techniques.

THE ECONOMIC SITUATION OF OLDER WORKERS

Kreps (1971) has observed that "analysis in the variation in the annual
income of a particular family as it moves through the life cycle is meager . . . .
Information on the family's needs at different stages is similarly scant" (p.
85). However, certain cross-sectional data do provide some insights into the
comparative status of older workers. Table 7.4 reports the estimated annual

TABLE 7.4
Average Annual Money Income, after Taxes,
by Age and Occupation, 1960–1961

Age	Occupation					
	Self-Employed	Profes-sional	Clerical	Skilled	Semi-skilled	Unskilled
Under 25	$4,528	$4,990	$4,459	$4,676	$4,602	$3,426
25–34	7,645	7,240	5,704	5,993	5,351	4,495
35–44	9,466	9,159	6,675	6,993	6,042	4,882
45–54	9,429	10,772	6,804	7,232	6,136	4,521
55–64	8,100	9,156	5,851	6,730	5,760	4,180

Source: U.S. Department of Labor, Bureau of Labor Statistics, *Survey of Consumer Expenditures:
Consumer Expenditures and Income, Urban United States,* Report 237–238, supplement 2, Part A
(Washington, D.C.: U.S. Government Printing Office, 1964), pp. 30–34.

money income (after taxes) of workers in six classifications, from 1960–61 data. Note that in every classification the older worker (55–64) earned less income than the middle-aged worker (35–44, 45–54). It also needs to be pointed out that in every instance except the "unskilled" category, the older worker earned more than the younger worker (25–34); however, the younger worker can anticipate a rising income and plan accordingly, whereas the older worker experiences not only a declining income but imminent retirement and its further reduction of income.

A major inadequacy of these cross-sectional data is that they do not convey that the older, retired worker of today received a lower income when he was younger than the contemporary young worker receives today. Thus, opportunity to build equity in real property or in an insurance policy, or to accumulate a savings account, has been lower for older than for younger cohorts of workers. Since most projections of income continue to indicate that successive cohorts of workers will attain increasingly higher salaries, there is, in a sense, a built-in second-class role for older workers, at least unless some countermeasures to redistribute income are developed.

Miller's (1965) study of annual increase in income at successive stages of the life cycle casts additional light on income status (see Table 7.5). Using income data from 1949 and 1959 for three consecutive ten-year age cohorts, he found that the 25–34-year-old cohort of 1949 had, ten years later, the highest percentage increase in annual income—the result of both experience and general economic growth. The 35–44-year-old cohort also experienced an increase in salary over the ten-year period, both because of experience and general growth, although to a lesser extent than the younger cohort. In contrast, the oldest cohort, those 45–54 in 1949, experienced an actual decrease in income associated with experience and the smallest total annual increase in salary. For example, whereas the average young worker in 1949 with four years or more of college experienced an annual salary increase of 12.7% between the ages of 30 and 40, and the "middle aged" experienced an annual increase of 3.5% between ages 40 and 50, the older worker had an increase of only 1.2% per year, and that resulted exclusively from general economic growth, not experience (Miller, 1965).

HIRING DISCRIMINATION AGAINST OLDER WORKERS

A survey of employment practices of employers toward older workers which was conducted in 1964 by the United States Employment Service (U.S. Department of Labor, 1965) reveals the extent of discrimination. The 454 employers surveyed were located in five cities in states without age-related fair-employment practices legislation. The cities were: Baltimore; Indianapolis; Kansas City, Missouri; Memphis; and Salt Lake City. As Table 7.6 shows, during 1964 only 8.6% of all new workers hired by employers in this

TABLE 7.5
Components of Change in Mean Income for Selected Cohorts of Males, 1949 and 1959

Extent of Education	Annual Rate of Increase in Income (percentage)								
	Between Ages 25–34 and 35–44			Between Ages 35–44 and 45–54			Between Ages 45–54 and 55–64		
	Total	Experience Related	Economic Growth Related	Total	Experience Related	Economic Growth Related	Total	Experience Related	Economic Growth Related
Less than 8 years	5.5%	1.8%	3.7%	3.3%	0.8%	2.5%	1.9%	−0.6%	2.5%
8 years	5.3	1.9	3.4	3.3	0.7	2.6	1.8	−0.7	2.5
1–3 years high school	5.9	2.1	3.8	3.7	0.9	2.8	2.4	−0.6	3.0
4 years high school	6.3	2.4	3.9	3.8	1.7	2.1	1.8	−0.3	2.1
1–3 years college	9.1	4.6	4.5	4.4	1.4	3.0	2.9	−0.9	3.8
4+ years college	12.7	7.6	5.1	3.5	1.5	2.0	1.2	−0.6	1.8

Note: Components of change are experience and growth. The first reflects income differential related to years in the work force, the second the differential related to general economic growth.

Source: Herman P. Miller, "Lifetime Income and Economic Growth," *American Economic Review* 55 (September 1965): 842–843.

TABLE 7.6

Percent of New Hires Compared to Percent of Unemployed, Workers under and over 45 Years of Age

Age Span	Percent of New Hires	Percent of All Unemployed Persons
Under 45 years	91.3%	73.1%
45 years and over	8.6	26.9
45 to 54 years	6.3	14.0
55 to 64 years	2.0	9.9
65 years and over	.3	3.0

Source: Adapted from U.S. Department of Labor: *The Older American Worker: Age Discrimination in Employment* (Washington, D.C.: U.S. Government Printing Office, 1965), p. 5.

survey were 45 years or older, although this age group made up 26.9% of the unemployed (U.S. Department of Labor, 1965: 3–5).

During the 1955–65 decade there was an increase in the magnitude of discrimination against the older job seeker. In 1955 a survey of hiring practices by employers in seven cities, conducted by the Bureau of Employment Security, found that approximately 20% of all people hired were workers over 45, and a not strictly comparable study by the U.S. Employment Service of 1962 hiring practices found that 10.6% of all hires were of older applicants (U.S. Department of Labor, 1965: 5). The 1964 survey of 454 firms by the U.S. Employment Service (discussed above in connection with Table 7.6) solicited the employers' reasons for refusal or reluctance to hire older workers. Table 7.7 indicates that physical demand upon the worker was by far the most frequently cited reason, followed by policies of promotion from within the ranks of the already employed, earnings, pension plan costs and provisions, and lack of skills or experience of older applicants.

The study confirmed that there is a widespread belief among employers that workers, upon entering middle age (the forties, maybe fifties), become less capable of carrying on occupational duties because of physical or mental deterioration. Most of the employers revealed that their basis for decisions on this matter are related more to "experience" and "observation" than to objective standards or measurements of performance. Another physical factor which reduced employment opportunities for those over 45 or so was the inability (actual or presumed by the employer) of older applicants to pass required physical examinations. Examinations have become more prevalent with the supposed progressive step of adding fringe benefits for health insurance for workers. Since the exams themselves are costly, the employers' belief that only a small percentage of older applicants would pass apparently

TABLE 7.7
Employers' Reasons for Upper Age Restrictions and for Limited Hiring of Older Workers

Reason for Age Discrimination Stated by Employer	Percent Distribution of Number of Times Reason Cited by Employer
Physical requirements	34.2%
Job requirements	25.1
Company standards	9.1
Policy of promotion from within	8.1
Earnings required for older workers	7.3
Pension plan costs and provisions	6.7
Lack of skills and experience	6.3
Limited work-life expectancy	5.1
Few applicants apply	5.0
Educational requirements	4.2
Other reasons	23.1

Source: Adapted from U.S. Department of Labor, *The Older American Worker*, p. 10.

has led to exclusion of their consideration for employment altogether (U.S. Department of Labor, 1965: 11–12). Ironically, gains by labor in a fringe benefit such as insurance assist the ensconced employee but add more burdens to the temporarily unattached worker who may be unemployed for reasons not at all of his own making.

Similarly, the policy of promotion from within the ranks of those already employed by a firm, which has widespread endorsement by management and labor, has adverse consequences for the older unemployed person, mainly by restricting the number of middle- and upper-level jobs available to outsiders, regardless of their qualifications (U.S. Department of Labor, 1965: 12). If jobs are available at all, they are at lower ranks and pay scales, and older job seekers frequently balk at cuts in rank and pay (Sobel & Wilcock, 1963).

Gross statistics on unemployment typically do not distinguish between workers in the "structured" and in the "unstructured" labor market, between those workers who have been protected by rules of contract between or within large-scale organizations and, those who are more itinerant or independent of such rules. Probably many of the prejudices and discriminatory practices are associated with those in the unstructured sector. Crucial to an understanding of the minority status of the older worker is apparently the ever-present prospect that a structured situation may become unstructured, through no fault of the workers. Numerous studies reveal that when a plant closes its operation or moves to a distant location, thus reducing the enforceability of protective rules, it is the dismissed older worker who is the most likely victim of long-term unemployment or of rehiring at less pay and less authority.

The pioneer study of the impact of the shutdown of a Packard Motor Company plant in the 1950s is a classic illustration of these discriminatory results (Sheppard, Ferman, & Faber, 1960). Wilcock and Franke (1963), in a study of workers in several communities[5] where plants were shut down in the prosperous period of the late 1950s, also confirmed this observation about older workers. "In all five cities, long-term unemployment was more prevalent among workers aged 45 and over than among those younger ... " (p. 55). They found that although employers generally praised the competency and performance of older workers, a number of factors, including "increased insurance and pension costs, promotion-from-within policies, declining physical and mental abilities, [and] slow recovery from illness or injury" (pp. 55–56), were given as reasons for avoiding the hiring of older, unemployed workers. From interviews with workers, Wilcox and Franke learned that the older the unemployed interviewee, the more likely he was to mention that his age was a barrier to reemployment. Whereas only 17% of the long-term unemployed under age 45 mentioned age as a barrier, 51% of those 45 to 54, and 71% of those 55 and over, referred to their age (p. 99).

A similar study by Stern (1972) on a plant closure in the mid-1960s involving 1,800 workers revealed that the salary after reemployment was typically lower than the preclosure salary, and that the older the reemployed worker, the larger the loss in salary: "Each individual year of age tended to depress annual earning by about $60 [and] each additional year of seniority depressed annual earnings by $63" (p. 11).

There are variables in addition to age which contribute to minority status. Some of these, especially race and sex, are reviewed elsewhere in this book. But results of a comprehensive survey of prospects for older workers are worth noting in these regards:

> The picture that emerges [for older workers] is one of developing problems for all males in the 55–64 and 65 and over age categories, and especially for non-white workers .... Declining participation rates in the 45–54 age group indicate that many men dropped out of the labor force entirely rather than continue searching for work. Older women workers were able to find work more readily than older men, and their participation rates, both white and non-white, rose between 1948 and 1966 except for non-white women aged 65 and over. (Adams, 1969: 11–12)

One basic conclusion that emerges from our partial review of the growing body of literature on research into the status of older workers is that mere statistical reports are not adequate in reaching an understanding of the vulnerable status of the older worker. This conclusion is supported, for example, by a summary statement in a Manpower Research Monograph, *The Pre-Retirement Years:*

> Were the labor market situation of all other segments of the population at least as favorable as that of [American male workers 45–59 years of age], the manpower problems of society would be considerably less serious than they are. Their labor force participation is very high. . . . Unemployment is quite low. . . . Those who are employed are, by and large, in better jobs than the average of all males. . . . [T]wo thirds regard their current occupational assignment to be the best of their career. . . . [Yet] there are very real problems among this group of males. . . . [A] large majority of those out of the labor force appear to be there not by choice. . . . [T]he low rates of unemployment that exist in a given week grossly understate the amount of unemployment experienced during a year. . . . Also unemployment tends to be visited upon the same men repeatedly. (U.S. Department of Labor, 1970: 238–239)

In the face of ambiguous, possibly contradictory evidence about the extent and causes of barriers to equal treatment of older workers, Adams has attempted to provide a summary of contributing factors. Some factors are related to the conditions of labor markets, others to the qualifications, skills and levels of energy to be found among older workers, and still others to the erratic growth and decline of job opportunities in particular regions, occupations, and industries. Unfavorable attitudes on the part of employers toward hiring older workers continue to prevail, even though there is an abundance of evidence which confirms the competency of older workers. Adams also noted that women workers continue to be substituted for older male workers to lower costs and increase productivity. Those younger workers who are mobile and flexible adapt better to the dynamism of job redistribution than older, less mobile workers (Adams, 1969: 74–75).

CONCLUDING THOUGHTS ON THE MINORITY STATUS OF OLDER WORKERS

It is necessary to qualify the hypothesis that workers, upon becoming 45 years of age, automatically enter the status of "minority." Some older workers clearly suffer the same sort of deprivation and discrimination as have racial and ethnic minorities. Among those workers who are protected by seniority, permanent status, and other rules, many, if not all, remain vulnerable to abrupt loss of job because of economic conditions and technological changes in their work. The hypothesis needs to be questioned further, however, since older men and women face different treatments. Inconclusive evidence hints that older women may be favored both over older men and younger women. This situation demands further exploration.

It is also difficult to advance and support solutions to the vulnerability of older workers. It is clearly too simple to propose that society should stop discriminating, stop supporting age-ism. Indeed, many employers need to be educated about positive attributes of older workers, and possibly threatened with harsh penalties for discriminating. Continuing experiments in redesigning jobs for older workers and retraining them for those jobs, and in redrafting laws and policies regarding pensions, as well as a new awareness of the consequences of shutting down or relocating plants, are very much needed. In the meantime, improved financial support for the unemployed, more effective counseling programs, and the removal of the stigma from those who have been involuntarily displaced from the labor force will help alleviate the problems faced by middle-aged and older workers.

NOTES

1. The relationship between bureaucracy and gerontocracy was examined in an earlier paper by Cain (1957).

2. The maximum amount a social security beneficiary could earn in 1976 was $2,760. For every $2 earned above this, $1 in benefits is lost.

3. Justice William H. Rehnquist of the U.S. Supreme Court, in a dissenting opinion to the decision in *Cleveland Board of Education* v. *La Fleur*, 94 S.Ct. 791 (1974), declared:

> The Court will have to strain valiantly in order to avoid having today's opinion lead to the invalidation of mandatory retirement statuses for governmental employees. In that event . . . governmental bodies will be remitted to the task, thankless both for them and for the employees involved, of individual determinations of physical impairment or senility. (Cain, 1976)

4. In fact, the aged already have been identified as occupying a minority status (Rose & Peterson, 1965).

5. East St. Louis, Illinois; Columbus, Ohio; Fargo, North Dakota; Peoria, Illinois; and Oklahoma City.

REFERENCES

Adams, Leonard P. "Employment Prospects for Older Workers." In National Council on the Aging, *Employment of the Middle-Aged Worker.* New York, 1969.

"Age Discrimination in Employment: Legislative and Collective Bargaining Solutions." *Northwestern University Law Review* 53 (March–April 1958): 96–108.

Botelho, Bruce M., Leonard D Cain, & Stephen M. Friedman. "Mandatory Retirement: The Law, the Courts, and the Broader Social Context." *Willamette Law Journal* 11 (Summer 1975): 398–416.

Cain, Leonard D "Age, Authority, and Bureaucratization." Paper presented at the meeting of the Pacific Sociological Association, Eugene, Oregon, April 19, 1957. Abstract in *Research Studies of the State College of Washington* 25 (June 1957).

Cain, Leonard D "The Growing Importance of Legal Age in Determining the Status of the Elderly." *The Gerontologist* 14 (April 1974): 167–174. (a)

Cain, Leonard D "Political Factors in the Emerging Legal Age Status of the Elderly." *The Annals of the American Academy of Political & Social Sciences,* 415 (September 1974): 70–79. (b)

Cain, Leonard D "Aging and the Law." In Robert Binstock and Ethel Shanas (eds.), *The Handbook of Aging and the Social Sciences.* New York: Van Nostrand Reinhold, 1976.

Clark, F. Le Gros. *Growing Old in a Mechanized World.* London: Nuffield Foundation, 1960.

Davis, Harry E. "Pension Provisions Affecting the Employment of Older Workers." *Monthly Labor Review* 96 (April 1973): 41–45.

Dunlop, John T. "Technological Change and Manpower Policy—The Older Worker." In Juanita M. Kreps (ed.), *Technology, Manpower, and Retirement Policy.* Cleveland: World Publishing Co., 1966.

Eckstein, Otto. "Economic Growth, Employment, and Manpower Policy." In Juanita M. Kreps (ed.), *Technology, Manpower, and Retirement Policy.* Cleveland: World Publishing Co., 1966.

Freed, Mayer G., & Edwina Dowell. "The Age Discrimination in Employment Act of 1967." 29 U.S.C.§ 623 (a),(b),(c). *Clearinghouse Review* 6 (August–September), 1972.

Kreps, Juanita M. *Lifetime Allocation of Work and Income: Essays in the Economics of Aging.* Durham, N.C.: Duke University Press, 1971.

Miller, Herman P. "Lifetime Income and Economic Growth." *American Economic Review* 55 (September 1965): 842–843.

Odell, Charles E. "Industrial Gerontology in the Employment Service." In Harold E. Sheppard, *Toward an Industrial Gerontology: An Introduction to a New Field of Applied Research and Service.* Cambridge, Mass.: Schenkman Press, 1970.

Oregon Bureau of Labor. *Up against the Middle-Age Barrier: A Report on an Inquiry into the Employment Problems of Oregonians between 45 and 65.* Salem, 1972.

Palmore, Erdman. "Compulsory vs. Flexible Retirement: Issues and Facts." *The Gerontologist* 12 (Winter 1973): 343–348.

Powledge, Tabitha M. "Retirement: One of the Hardest Jobs in America." *The New York Times,* December 21, 1975, Sec. E, p. 14.

Rose, Arnold, & Warren Peterson (eds.). *Older People and Their Social World: The Subculture of Aging.* Philadelphia: F. A. Davis, 1965.

Sheppard, Harold. "Introduction" to Solomon Barkin's "Retraining and Job Design." In Sheppard (ed.), *Toward an Industrial Gerontology.* Cambridge, Mass.: Schenkman Press, 1970.

Sheppard, Harold L., Louis A. Ferman, & Seymour Faber. *Too Old to Work, Too Young to Retire: Case Study of Permanent Plant Closure.* U.S. Congress, Senate, Special Committee on Unemployment Problems, 86th Cong. Washington, D.C.: U.S. Government Printing Office, 1960.

Sobel, Irving, and Richard Wilcock. "Job Placement Services for Older Workers in the United States." *International Labour Review* 88 (August 1963): 129–156.

Sprague, Norman. "Introduction." In Harold L. Sheppard (ed.), *Toward an Industrial Gerontology: An Introduction to a New Field of Applied Research and Service.* Cambridge, Mass.: Schenkman Press, 1970.

Stern, James L. "Consequences of Plant Closure." *Journal of Human Resources* 7 (Winter 1972): 11.

Tausky, Curt. *Work Organizations: Major Theoretical Perspectives.* Itasca, Ill.: F. E. Peacock, Publishers, 1970.

U.S. Department of Labor. *The Older American Worker: Age Discrimination in Employment* (research materials). Report of the Secretary of Labor to Congress, June 1965. Washington, D.C.: U.S. Government Printing Office, 1965.

U.S. Department of Labor. *The Pre-Retirement Years: a Longitudinal Study of the Labor Market Experience of Men.* Vol. 1. Manpower Research Monograph, No. 15. Washington, D.C.: U.S. Government Printing Office, 1970.

U.S. Department of Labor. *Manpower Report of the President, 1975.* Washington, D.C.: U.S. Government Printing Office, 1975.

Von Mises, Ludwig. *Bureaucracy.* New Haven, Conn.: Yale University Press, 1946.

Weber, Max. *From Max Weber: Essays in Sociology.* Trans. Hans H. Gerth & C. Wright Mills. New York: Oxford University Press, 1946.

Weber, Max. *The Theory of Social and Economic Organization.* Trans. A. M. Henderson & Talcott Parsons. New York: Oxford University Press, 1947.

Wilcock, Richard C., & Walter H. Franke. *Unwanted Workers: Permanent Layoffs and Long-Term Unemployment.* New York: Free Press, 1963.

CHAPTER 8

The road ahead:
Prospects for equality
in the world of work

H. Roy Kaplan

OCCUPATIONAL AND ECONOMIC DISPARITIES BETWEEN MAJORITY AND MINORITIES

Disparities among whites, Spanish Americans, blacks, and men versus women in income and the quality of employment still exist. For example, despite the economic need of women to work and the inroads they have made into male-dominated occupations (on this point see Hedges & Bemis, 1974: 14), there remains a considerable wage differential between male and female workers. Nearly two thirds of full-time employed women workers earned less than $7,000 in 1972, while more than three fourths of full-time male workers earned *more* than $7,000 that year (U.S. Department of Labor, 1975: 62). This earnings differential has persisted over the past two decades, even when adjusted for hours of work and levels of education. One recent analysis of 1970 census data of approximately 400 selected occupations indicated that men earned more than women in every occupational category except public kindergarten teachers. Even the most lucrative women's jobs

Note: The author wishes to thank Professors Patricia Hollander and David Kochery, and Deborah Brodnick of the State University of New York at Buffalo for their helpful comments on an earlier draft of this chapter.

had half the median earnings of the top-ranking men's occupations. The bottom *decile* for men's occupations, $687 to $4,354, encompasses nearly all the occupations in the *bottom half* of the rankings of women (Sommers, 1974: 34–51). In March 1974, the average earnings in private industry for all workers was about $4 per hour, but in occupations with a predominance of women, the average compensation was about $3 per hour (U.S. Department of Labor, 1975: 63). The five largest occupations for women, which encompass over 25% of their employment, are secretaries, salesclerks in retail trade, bookkeepers, public elementary schoolteachers, and waitresses. Although women's earnings rose 4.8% as compared to men's from 1959 to 1969 (Fuchs, 1974: 23), there is still a 40% differential between male and female earnings and substantial income differences in most occupations, as Table 8.1 indicates.

TABLE 8.1
Median Incomes of Full-Time Women Workers
by Occupation, 1972

Major Occupation Group	Median Income	Percent of Men's Income
Professional and technical workers	$8,796	68%
Nonfarm managers and administrators	7,306	53
Clerical workers	6,039	63
Sales workers	4,575	40
Operatives, including transportation	5,021	58
Service workers (except private household)	4,606	59
Private household	2,365	*
Nonfarm laborers	4,755	63

* Percent not shown where median income of men is based on fewer than 75,000 individuals.

Source: U.S. Department of Labor, *Manpower Report of the President, 1975* (Washington, D.C.: U.S. Government Printing Office, 1975), p. 63.

Further evidence of occupational discrimination comes from a longitudinal study of women in the labor force aged 30–44. More of these women retrogressed than progressed in their careers, and black women were more downwardly mobile than whites (U.S. Department of Labor, 1970: 161–163). While there has been an influx of women into professional training which promises to place them in higher-level jobs, data indicate that between 1948 and 1970 the proportion of women receiving such degrees grew less rapidly than that of men, and the gap is *widening* (Parrish, 1974: 40). This situation is affecting women's ability to compete with men for the more prestigious professional positions, since they are not moving into those degree areas as fast as men, nor do they hold as many professional positions in the labor force as they did in prior times (Blitz, 1974: 34).

There is also evidence indicating the existence of substantial occupational and income differentials between whites and nonwhites. The data in Table 8.2 show that white workers control an inordinate share of professional and other white-collar jobs. It is also noteworthy that Spanish-Americans have a better position in the labor force than blacks (and a lower unemployment rate—8.2% in the fourth quarter of 1974, compared to 12.5%).

TABLE 8.2
Employment of White, Black, and Spanish-Speaking Workers, by Occupation Group, 1974 (percent distribution)

Occupation Group	Total	White	Black[1]	Spanish-speaking
Total				
Number (000)	85,936	76,620	8,112	3,609
Percent	100.0%	100.0%	100.0%	100.0%
White-collar workers	48.6%	50.6%	28.9%	31.5%
Professional and technical	14.4	14.8	8.8	7.0
Managers and administrators,				
except farm	10.4	11.2	3.4	5.7
Sales workers	6.3	6.8	1.9	3.9
Clerical workers	17.5	17.8	14.8	15.3
Blue-collar workers	34.7%	33.9%	42.1%	47.6%
Craft and kindred	13.4	13.8	9.5	12.4
Operatives	16.2	15.5	23.2	26.7
Nonfarm laborers	5.1	4.6	9.4	8.5
Service workers	13.2%	12.0%	26.3%	16.5%
Farm workers	3.5%	3.6%	2.8%	4.5%

Note: Detail may not add to totals because of rounding.
1. Data refer to black workers only.
Source: *Manpower Report of the President, 1975,* p. 35.

Contrary to the popular myth that depicts Spanish-Americans as rural inhabitants and farm workers, in 1974 83% lived in metropolitan areas, compared to 68% of the total white population in 1974. Over 1.2 million

Spanish-American families live in central cities (U.S. Bureau of the Census, 1975: 1).

Although they do not face the color barrier that blacks do, Spanish-Americans are discriminated against in the labor market, and their competitive position is diminished by their relative lack of skills compared to other white workers, by their lower educational level, and by the language barrier.[1] Of the three major groups of Spanish-Americans, Cubans are in the best position economically, and Puerto Ricans are in the worst, having family incomes below those of blacks. The earnings of Cuban men came to 80% of all white men's earnings in Florida in 1969 ($7,200), while those of Mexican-American men were about three fourths of all white men's earnings in the Southwest ($6,000 vs. $8,100), and Puerto Rican men earned two thirds of what other white men earned in the Middle Atlantic states ($5,500 vs. $8,300) (Ryscavage & Mellor, 1973: 6). A recent report by Kal Wagenheim for the Puerto Rican Migration Division indicated that incomes of Puerto Rican families on the mainland averaged only 57.9% of other white families, down from 64.6% in 1959. The number of mainland Puerto Ricans living in poverty increased from 29% to 32.2% from 1969 to 1971 (Bureau of National Affairs, Fair Employment Practices Bulletin, June 26, 1975: 6).

There are also considerable wage differentials between Spanish-American men and other white men in higher-status occupations and professions, regardless of locality. Spanish-American workers are concentrated in the poorest-paying occupations offering the least opportunity for advancement, such as food-service workers, freight-services handlers, cashiers, and cleaning-service workers. In April 1970, 19% of all employed Spanish-American men were in the 10 lowest-paying occupations, compared to 10% of all employed white men. Puerto Ricans were again the most disadvantaged, with approximately 60% working as operatives, laborers, and service workers (Ryscavage & Mellor, 1973: 6). A comparison of the median earnings by occupation for whites and Spanish-Americans is presented in Table 8.3. There was a concentration of people of Spanish origin in low-paying occupations. In 1973 (see Table 8.4), men of Spanish origin 14 years and older had median incomes of about $6,200 compared with a median income of about $8,100 for all men in the population. Only 5% of men of Spanish origin had incomes over $15,000 in 1973, compared to 17% of all men in the population. Spanish-American women fared even worse, having median incomes of $2,652. One third of Spanish-American women earned less than $2,000. The median incomes of Mexican-American and Puerto Rican men were similar, but Puerto Rican women earned considerably more than Mexican-American women—about 25% of Puerto Rican women had incomes under $2,000 in 1973, compared to 50% of the Mexican-American women. In 1973 there were 470,000 (about 20%) Spanish-American families living below the poverty level. Of the 411,000 Spanish-American families

TABLE 8.3
Median Earnings of Men and Women 16 Years Old and Over, by Occupation, for Whites and Persons of Spanish Heritage, Selected States, 1970

Sex and Occupation	In Five Southwestern States			In Three Middle-Atlantic States			In Florida		
	White	Spanish-American[1]	Spanish as a Percent of White	White	Spanish-American[2]	Spanish as a Percent of White	White	Spanish-American[3]	Spanish as a Percent of White
Men									
Total experienced labor force	$ 8,069	$5,963	74%	$ 8,270	$5,474	66%	$ 7,169	$5,621	78%
Professional, managerial, and kindred workers	11,482	9,195	80	11,874	7,441	63	10,010	8,425	84
Craftsmen, foremen, and kindred workers	8,471	7,125	84	8,569	6,274	73	7,378	6,226	84
Operatives	6,987	5,959	85	7,220	5,239	73	5,691	4,991	88
Laborers, except farm	4,513	4,523	100	5,799	5,005	86	3,411	3,965	116
Farmers and farm managers	5,373	4,663	87	5,344	4,468	84	5,595	8,022	143
Farm laborers, except unpaid and farm foremen	3,333	3,123	94	2,987	2,807	94	3,495	2,706	77
Women									
Total experienced labor force	3,868	3,065	79	4,054	3,868	95	3,553	3,222	91
Clerical and kindred workers	4,411	3,847	81	4,577	4,478	98	3,964	3,761	95
Operatives	3,480	3,151	91	3,721	3,594	97	3,101	3,139	101

1. Persons of Spanish language or surname, primarily Mexican-Americans.
2. Persons of Puerto Rican birth or parentage.
3. Persons of Spanish language, primarily Cubans.
Source: Paul M. Ryscavage and Earl F. Mellor, "The Economic Situation of Spanish Americans," Monthly Labor Review 96 (April 1973): 6.

TABLE 8.4
Income in 1973 of All Persons and of Persons of Spanish Origin, 14 Years Old and over, by Type of Spanish Origin and Sex

Income	Total Population		Spanish Origin								
			Total		Mexican		Puerto Rican		Other[1]	
	Male	Female	Male	Female	Male	Female	Male	Female	Male	Female
Total										
Persons 14 years and over (000)	75,040	82,244	3,282	3,575	1,967	2,022	425	526	889	1,027
Persons 14 years or older with income (000)	69,387	57,029	2,867	2,154	1,723	1,177	364	295	780	681
$1 to $999 or less	8.4%	21.0%	9.3%	21.0%	11.0%	25.4%	8.2%	10.5%	6.3%	17.9%
$1,000 to $1,999	6.4	17.7	7.2	18.0	7.5	19.0	6.6	13.2	6.8	18.4
$2,000 to $2,999	6.6	13.4	7.3	15.9	7.9	17.7	6.0	15.6	6.4	13.1
$3,000 to $3,999	5.6	10.1	6.7	12.1	7.5	11.5	5.5	18.3	5.4	10.3
$4,000 to $4,999	5.8	8.4	8.3	10.3	9.0	9.1	9.3	13.6	6.3	11.2
$5,000 to $6,999	11.2	12.8	18.7	12.9	17.4	10.6	23.6	18.3	19.2	14.5
$7,000 to $7,999	5.5	4.5	8.0	3.3	6.8	2.8	11.8	3.1	8.7	4.4
$8,000 to $9,999	11.1	5.8	12.3	3.8	12.8	2.2	10.2	4.7	12.1	6.2
$10,000 to $14,999	22.3	4.8	16.8	2.1	16.0	1.5	13.5	2.7	20.0	2.9
$15,000 to $24,999	12.9	1.1	4.5	0.4	3.5	0.1	4.4	0.3	6.8	1.0
$25,000 and over	4.0	0.2	0.9	0.1	0.5	0.1	0.8	*	1.9	0.1
Median income of persons with income	$8,056	$2,796	$6,200	$2,652	$5,789	$2,270	$6,197	$3,593	$6,949	$3,067

*Zero or rounds to zero.

1. Includes Cuban, Central or South American, and other Spanish origin.

Source: U.S. Bureau of the Census, "Persons of Spanish Origin in the United States: March 1974," *Current Population Reports,* Series P-20, No. 280 (Washington, D.C.: U.S. Government Printing Office, 1975), Table 24, p. 44.

headed by women, nearly 50% were below the income level of $2,000 (U.S. Bureau of the Census, 1975: 7–8).

The occupational distribution of Spanish-Americans in the labor force in 1974 was similar to that of blacks and inferior to all other whites. While half of all white workers were employed in white-collar jobs in 1974, less than one third (31.5%) of Spanish-Americans were. Spanish-Americans occupy fewer (7%) of the highest paying and most prestigious jobs (i.e., professional and technical positions) than whites (14.8%) or blacks (8.8%). Spanish-Americans are more likely to be working as operatives in unskilled or semiskilled jobs such as produce packers, laundry workers, manufacturing checkers, and garbage workers than the general employed population is—28% vs. 16%. Mexican-Americans are much less likely to be employed in professional and technical fields than Cubans, Central and South Americans, and other persons of Spanish origin (U.S. Bureau of the Census, 1975: 7).

OPTIMISTIC SIGNS ON THE LEGISLATIVE FRONT

Legislation passed in the past two decades has sought to create equal employment opportunities. This section reviews some of the most important legislation.

The Equal Pay Act of 1963[2]

In 1963 the Equal Pay Act was passed to equalize earnings between the sexes when they do work of equivalent skill, effort, and responsibility in similar working conditions. A subsequent federal court decision held that the jobs of men and women need only be "substantially equal" to merit equal pay, and later amendments extended the act's coverage to executive, administrative, professional, federal, state, and local government employees (U.S. Department of Labor, 1975: 67).

Civil Rights Act of 1964—Title VII[3]

Title VII of the 1964 Civil Rights Act prohibited employers from discriminating in hiring, firing, promotion, job assignments, compensation, training, or other "terms, conditions, or privileges of employment." It also established the Equal Employment Opportunity Commission (EEOC), which has responsibility for enforcing the employment provisions in cases against private employers of 15 or more people and labor unions representing 15 or more members. Charges filed against state and local agencies go through EEOC, and enforcement authority is vested in the Department of Justice. Charges against the federal government go through civil service channels. In 1972 the EEOC issued new guidelines strengthening provisions in the act against sex-related job discrimination.

Prior to 1972 the EEOC could enter suits under the principle of *amicus curiae,* as a friend of the court. This procedure allowed the commission to introduce arguments or evidence on behalf of other parties and to assist the court through the presentation of pertinent material. Since 1972 amendments to Title VII, known as the Equal Employment Opportunity Act, have permitted the EEOC to initiate enforcement litigation in its own name when conciliation fails and enabled it to intervene as a party in private suits (Equal Employment Opportunity Commission, 1975: 19–23).

Title IX of the Education Amendments of 1972[4]

The regulation for Title IX of the Education Amendments took effect on July 21, 1975. Title IX will have far-reaching ramifications in education and employment for women if actively enforced. It stipulates that, on the basis of sex, no one shall be excluded from participation in, denied the benefits of, or subjected to discrimination in any educational program or activity receiving federal financial assistance. Sex discrimination is barred from preschool to postgraduate education in academic, extracurricular, and research activities, and from occupational training and other educational programs operated by organizations or agencies receiving or benefiting from federal aid. Recipients of federal aid must evaluate current policies and practices to determine whether they comply with Title IX and take remedial steps to end discrimination.

Sex discrimination is also barred in admissions to public institutions, and sex quotas are forbidden. Efforts must be made to recruit comparable numbers of each sex, except when special efforts are made to remedy the effects of past discrimination. The regulation also prohibits sex discrimination in employment, recruitment, and hiring in any educational program or activity which receives or benefits from federal financial aid. Institutions are barred from entering into union, employment agency, or fringe-benefit agreements which subject individuals to discrimination. Sex discrimination is prohibited from inclusion in employment criteria, advertising and recruitment, hiring and firing, promotions, tenure, training, leaves, and fringe benefits. Discrimination complaints must be filed with the Department of Health, Education, and Welfare within 180 days of the date of discrimination (Project on the Status and Education of Women, 1975).

Age Discrimination in Employment Act, 1967[5]

In 1967 Congress passed amendments to the Fair Labor Standards Act of 1938[6] to protect workers 45 and older from job discrimination in employment and representation in unions. The act seeks to prohibit the establishment of arbitrary age limits affecting the terms of employment and continued employment, and to promote the employment of older workers based on their ability rather than their age (see U.S. Congress, Senate, 1967). The law was also designed to promote the employment of older workers and to help employers and workers combat the problems arising from the impact of age on employment. Older workers were defined as people aged 40–65. The law applies to employers and unions having and representing 25 or more persons. The act makes it unlawful for an employer to refuse to hire or to discharge or discriminate against an individual because of age with respect to wages and conditions of employment. Labor organizations cannot exclude or expel from their membership or discriminate against individuals because of age. It is also unlawful to use printed or published notices or ads indicating a preference, limitations, or specifications on the basis of age (Lundquist, 1968: 48–50).

The Retirement Income Security Act, 1974[7]

The Retirement Income Security Act was passed in 1974 in an effort to reform the pension system in the United States. Among other things, special standards for vesting of pensions were altered, along with unrealistic age and service requirements for pension eligibility. Workers were guaranteed pensions in cases where their plans were terminated by establishing a Pension Benefit Guaranty Corporation in the Department of Labor. Portability, or the right of workers to take accrued pension credits with them to their new jobs, was also improved. The effect of these regulations will also guard against improper manipulation of pension funds for private purposes. The Treasury Department is responsible for judging conformity to plan provisions, operations, and standards for participation, vesting, and funding. The Department of Labor is responsibile for enforcing various facets of the law, including fiduciary standards. For a review of the law and a short history leading to its passage, see Henle and Schmitt (1974: 3–12).

SOME SIGNIFICANT COURT DECISIONS BREAKING DOWN JOB DISCRIMINATION BARRIERS

In the years since the passage of these laws there have been many significant court decisions upholding and extending the rights of women, older workers, and minorities to achieve job parity and equal pay and opportunities. This section focuses on a brief review of some of the important decisions. As with labor force statistics, court rulings are always changing. It is therefore important to focus on the direction decisions have been taking; consequently, the next section will present some decisions negating some of the advances that have been made.

Decisions Affecting Women

Women have been making some progress in achieving equal pay and treatment by employers. Recent court rulings have held that under Title VII of the Civil Rights Act of 1964 and the 1972 Equal Employment Opportunity Act, pregnancies must be treated as any other temporary disability, entitling women to receive wages and sick benefits while on leave. See the discussion of *Wetzel* v. *Liberty Mutual Insurance Co.* [372 F. Supp. 1146 (W.D. Pa., 1974)], in "Significant Decisions in Labor Cases" (May 1974: 76–77), and *Vineyard* v. *Hollister Elementary School District,* "Significant Decisions in Labor Cases," (February 1975: 78–79.)

In *Cleveland Board of Education* v. *La Fleur* [414 U.S. 632, 39 L.E.2d 52, 94 S.Ct. 791 (1974)] the Supreme Court held that a school board's mandatory maternity-leave rule, which required a teacher to quit her job several months before the birth of her child and prohibited her from returning to work until three months after the birth, violated the due process clause of the 14th Amendment because women have different capacities to work and to resume employment after childbirth. In *Turner* v. *Department of Employment Security* [96 S.Ct. 249 (1975)], the court indicated that some arbitrary state policies concerning pregnancies are unconstitutional because they, too, violate the due process clause ("Significant Decisions in Labor Cases," January 1976: 64–65).

Another court decision, *Brennan* v. *J. M. Fields, Inc.* [488 F2d 443 (5th Circuit 1973)] sought to redress inequities in pay to women supervisors who had been receiving lower wages than men performing the same jobs. A suit was also won in 1972 charging General Electric with paying women less than men for comparable work in 21 job categories; as a result, 350 women won higher wages, $300,000 in back pay, and new job posting and upgrading procedures in the plant. The adjusted wage rates were supposed to yield an additional $250,000 a year for them ("Developments in Industrial Relations," September 1973: 89).[8]

Title VII of the Civil Rights Act of 1964 also prohibits advertising for jobs in sex-designated categories. In a 1973 case, *Pittsburgh Press Co.* v. *The Pittsburgh Commission on Human Rights* [413 U.S. 376, 37 L.Ed.2d 669, 93 S.Ct. 2553, reh. den. 414 U.S. 881 (1973)], the Supreme Court extended the prohibition of sex bias in advertising to the publication of such material by any person, including a newspaper ("Significant Decisions in Labor Cases," September 1973: 81–83).

The most publicized victory over job discrimination came in January 1973, when the American Telephone and Telegraph Company entered into a consent decree with the EEOC, the Department of Justice, and the Department of Labor under Title VII and the Equal Pay Act, and agreed to pay $15 million in back wages to 15,000 nonmanagerial employees (13,000 of them women) and to increase job opportunities for women and minorities.

At the time discussions began on the case in 1970, 60% of AT&T's employees were female, but women accounted for nearly 100% of the company's secretaries, operators, and service representatives. Only 1% of its craft workers and operatives were women. Although 41% of the company's managers were female, most (94%) were located in first-level positions. While minorities accounted for 12% of the company's employees, they occupied only 7% of the skilled-craft positions and fewer managerial jobs (U.S. Commission on Civil Rights, 1975: 550).

The task force working on the case received over 100,000 pages of data from AT&T designed to prove it did not discriminate, and it compiled 30,000 pages of reports and documentation of its own. EEOC estimates that it took 13.5 person-years to assemble the information. The agreement cost AT&T $45 million in the first year of implementation (Equal Employment Opportunity Commission, 1975: 25). The National Organization of Women (NOW) termed the settlement "chickenfeed," contending an equitable amount would have been $4 billion ("Developments in Industrial Relations," March 1973: 69–70). For a chronology of the events and terms of the settlement, see U.S. Commission on Civil Rights (1975: 549–555). Under a supplemental agreement covering managerial employees, the company consented to increase hiring and promotional opportunities for women and minorities and implemented a change in wage policies estimated to cost $23 million. AT&T agreed to pay $7 million in back pay to managerial workers, over half of whom were women who had been promoted to managerial positions but were receiving less money than men ("Developments in Industrial Relations," August 1974: 87).

Racial Discrimination Decisions

Decisions affecting racial discrimination in employment have been handed down by many courts throughout the country in recent years. As with voting rights, important decisions have been made barring the establishment of discriminatory tests. At times, the methods of discrimination are subtle, as when tests and job interviews are utilized to disqualify applicants. In a landmark decision in *Griggs* v. *Duke Power Co.* [401 U.S. 424 L.Ed.2d 158, 91 S.Ct. 849 (1971)], the Supreme Court declared such tests must "measure the person for the job and not the person in the abstract" (401 U.S. at 436). Tests may not be used for hiring or promotions unless they can be demonstrated to be related to job performance. Henceforth, such tests may not be used as a ruse to exclude certain groups from employment ("Significant Decisions in Labor Cases," June 1971: 79–80).

Such practices as listing arrest and conviction records have been shown to have a racially exclusionary effect on blacks. Following the Griggs decision, courts have ruled it is also discriminatory to refuse to consider job applicants who have been convicted of crimes other than minor traffic violations, unless a reasonable business purpose for the requirement can be shown.[9]

In 1973 a U.S. district court awarded punitive damages of $4.25 million to black workers and unsuccessful job applicants who had been persistently discriminated against by Detroit Edison and two local labor unions. Among other things, the company was found to discriminate against job applicants by using interviews and ability tests that did not comply with EEOC guidelines and were deliberately designed to prevent blacks from obtaining employment.[10]

In 1974 a federal district court ordered the Georgia Power Company to pay $2.1 million in back wages and benefits to employees victimized by job discrimination. Most of the money went to 360 black workers who had been systematically assigned to jobs as janitors and mail clerks and denied promotions. The company was ordered to retroactively rectify inequities in pensions and to increase the proportion of black employees from 9% to 17%, within five years ("Developments in Industrial Relations," April 1974: 75–76).

In a recent ruling in *Albermarle Paper Co.* v. *Moody* and *Halifax Local No. 425, United Papermakers & Paperworkers* v. *Moody* [95 S.Ct. 2362 (June 25, 1975)], the Supreme Court held that workers who have been discriminated against in the past are entitled to back pay, despite an employer's show of good faith in obeying the law. In a 7–1 decision, the Court held that the power to grant back pay might induce employers "to shun practices of doubtful legality," leading them to alter offending employment practices before the courts are called on to resolve the issue. The decision also clarified the EEOC test validation guidelines and standards for employment tests and reaffirmed the *Griggs* v. *Duke Power Co.* principle ("Significant Decisions in Labor Cases," October 1975: 57–58).

The problem of obtaining compliance to Title VII by employers and unions has been a vexing one. Despite numerous successful suits, there remains a persistent resistance to end sex and racial discrimination.

The struggle for equal job opportunities is not confined to the private sector. There have been serious charges of job bias directed toward government at all levels. The amendments of 1972 to Title VII therefore extended the ban on job discrimination to most federal and District of Columbia civil servants. Recognizing that the government has enormous potential to redress inequities in the labor force, a Presidential Executive Order (No. 11246) was issued in 1965 which requires that contracts for federally assisted construction work contain fair-employment provisions and assurances that contractors will take affirmative action to avoid sex and racial discrimination ("Significant Decisions in Labor Cases," September 1971: 64).

In 1969 the Department of Labor began to implement this order in a five-county area of Philadelphia. The Department was aware of union pressure on contractors to hire employees exclusively through union hiring halls—a process which has traditionally excluded blacks from construction trades. The Department, therefore, issued regulations on June 27, 1969, which required bidders to submit "acceptable affirmative action" programs which demonstrated a commitment to employ blacks in accordance with "specific goals of minority manpower utilization." The goals were formally established during public hearings in Philadelphia and were to be achieved in the area's trades ("Significant Decisions," September 1971: 65). The contractors subsequently challenged the constitutionality of the order. In 1971, in *Contractors Association of Eastern Pennsylvania* v. *Secretary of Labor* [311 F.Supp. 1002 E.D. Pa. (1970): aff'd. 442 F.2d 159; cert. denied U.S. 854 (1971)], a federal court of appeals upheld the order, thereby lending legitimacy to the plan, which was to be used as a model for breaking down racial barriers in the construction trades throughout the country.

The intransigent position of unions on integrating their membership has been a particularly difficult problem to overcome, especially in the skilled construction trades. Analyses of membership in construction unions in 1969 and 1971 reveal a very low proportion of minority-group members. Although some gains in membership occurred, they were in unions that already had high minority-group representation—laborers, roofers, and trowel trades. This group of unions comprised less than one fourth of the total construction union membership but accounted for three fourths of black and one half of Spanish-American union members. In the higher-paying, more skilled construction trades, minority-group membership is low. Blacks held 5.4% of the skilled jobs in all industries in 1971, but their membership in the mechanical trades was below this. About half the locals in the mechanical trades had *no* black members that year. There was an increase in the number of minority-group members in apprenticeship programs—a finding which led one researcher to forecast greater minority group representation in coming years (Hammerman, 1972: 17–26; 1973: 43–46).

One method used by the government to increase minority participation in construction trades has been to advocate Philadelphia-type plans, which establish racial quotas of workers. In 1974 a federal court of appeals in New York upheld a district court's order directing a union to take affirmative action through apprenticeship and membership programs to meet a racial goal set for 1977.[11]

Challenge to Seniority

Even after the precedents establishing goals for minority group membership in unions had brought the power of the federal government to bear on the construction industry to implement affirmative action programs, the war against discrimination in unions had not been won. As the U.S. economy entered its worst post–World War II recession in 1974, it became disturbingly clear that many of the previous efforts for increasing the opportunities of women and racial minorities were being undone by the entrenched principle of seniority. The hopes and aspirations of many people had been raised, but the recession was wreaking havoc with the economy and causing cutbacks in production. In an effort to cope with rising inflation and decreased spending, employers began laying off thousands of workers. Some of the first people to go were the ones with the least seniority—women and racial minorities who had most recently begun to achieve a semblance of job parity through affirmative action programs.[12]

Two significant decisions have recently been rendered in the steel industry which, pending appeal, may fundamentally alter the seniority system in that industry. In *United States* v. *Bethlehem Steel Corporation* [446 F.2d 652, 2nd Circuit (1971)] a federal court ruled that the seniority system locked women and minorities into undersirable dead-end jobs. To remedy this inequity, dual seniority systems were established in the Lackawanna plant of Bethlehem Steel Corporation. Black employees were allowed to use continuous plant service as the basis of seniority, rather than the traditional measure of service in a particular job or unit which was still applied to white employees at the plant. Problems arose over the application of the two systems. One analyst contends the plan is unworkable, and few minority-group members have availed themselves of the opportunity to transfer to other jobs. This reticence has occurred despite the court's decree that rates of pay achieved by nonwhite employees must be retained when they transfer to jobs which might begin at lower wages (Matera, 1975: 43–46).

A subsequent case, concerning seniority and discrimination in the U.S. Steel Corporation in an Alabama plant, was *U.S.* v. *U.S. Steel Corporation* [371 F.Supp. 1045, N.D. Ala. (1973)]. This put the steel industry on notice that a thorough reorganization of the seniority system was in order. Then on April 15, 1974, EEOC and the Departments of Labor and Justice filed two consent decrees with nine steel companies and the United Steelworkers of America.[13] The affected companies produce nearly three fourths of the steel in the United States and employ 347,679 workers, including 52,545 blacks, 7,646 Spanish-surnamed, and 10,175 women (U.S. Commission on Civil Rights, July 1975: 556). The government contended that women and minorities were relegated to lower-paying dead-end jobs, denied opportunities for training, and evaluated more stringently than white males. Employees who had been discriminated against between January 1, 1968, and April 12, 1974, were awarded $31 million in back pay. The settlement provides that females be hired to fill 20% of all vacancies in clerical and technical jobs, and minority-group members and women are to fill 25% of the vacancies in supervisory positions or management training. Employees are now able to transfer to other jobs throughout the plant while retaining their previous salary, regardless of the scale in the new position. More importantly, seniority is to be determined by the length of service at *each plant* instead of in a specific unit or department in a plant (U.S. Commission on Civil Rights, 1975: 558).

A more direct threat to the job progress of women and minorities came from actions by the Jersey Central Power and Light Company. Because of the recession the company decided to reduce its work force; but this would have destroyed recent gains of women and minorities from an existing affirmative action program if prior agreements with seven local unions regarding layoffs of workers on the basis of seniority were honored. In its decision in *Jersey Central Power and Light Co.* v. *Local Unions, Brotherhood of Electrical Workers* [508 F.2d 687, 3rd Circuit (1975)], the court held that adherence to the traditional union practice of laying off persons with least seniority would unalterably frustrate the goals of the affirmative action program. The court declared that the EEOC agreement on affirmative action with the company took precedence over the union's seniority agreement. It directed that three separate seniority lists be compiled for minorities, women and other workers and that layoffs be made from each of the groups so that women and minority-group members "constitute essentially the same proportion of the total work force as they did" prior to the layoffs ("Significant Decisions," February 1975: 77–78). On May 24, 1976 the judgment was vacated by the Supreme Court and the case was remanded to the United States Court of Appeals for the Third Circuit for further consideration, in light of *Franks* v. *Bowman Trans. Co.*

In *Franks* v. *Bowman Trans. Co.* (U.S. Sup.Ct., March 24, 1976, 12 FEP Cases 549), the Supreme Court ruled that retroactive seniority should be awarded to people who can prove that they were rejected in violation of Title VII. The Court ruled that such victims of hiring bias must be granted seniority, pension, and other benefits retroactive to the time they were initially turned down. Although this decision indicates the Court's intent to uphold the "make whole" provision of Title VII, the burden of proof still rests with the plaintiff(s), and this can be a formidable task.[14]

Discrimination against older workers is, in many ways, less overt and therefore more difficult to establish. Nevertheless, a federal district court in New Jersey recently awarded $750,000 to the widow of an employee of the Exxon Research and Engineering Company who had been involuntarily retired at the age of 60 (*Rogers* v. *Exxon Research and Engineering Co.*, D.C.–N.J., No. 681—70). Mrs. Gladys Rogers brought the action, alleging that her husband had been transferred to a job which required him to be on his feet several hours a day, which ultimately forced him to resign. It was contended that this was a management strategy to make him resign ("Developments in Industrial Relations," April 1975: 79). This award was later reduced to $200,000.

Two Steps Forward, One Step Back

All court decisions have not worked in favor of redressing the inequities in the world of work. Many key legal issues have not yet been resolved, and gains in some areas have been balanced by losses in others. Indeed, there have been some curious reversals of established principles by courts in various parts of the country. Although four federal appeals courts have ruled that it is a violation of Title VII to deny female employees protection for pregnancy-related disabilities,[15] the Supreme Court ruled in *Geduldig* v. *Aiello* [417 U.S. 484, 41 L.Ed2 256, 94 S.Ct. 2485 (1974)] that women who experience normal pregnancies could not obtain benefits from their state (in this case, California). The major factor influencing the justices' decisions was the cost of providing such benefits. Justice Stewart concluded "There is nothing in the Constitution . . . that requires the State to subordinate or compromise its legitimate interests solely to create a more comprehensive social insurance program than it already has." ("Significant Decisions," October 1974: 70).[16] Then, on December 7, 1976, the U.S. Supreme Court held (*General Electric Co. v. Gilbert,* 74-1489, 74-1590) that employers may exclude pregnancy from sickness and accident disability insurance plans.

Perhaps a greater blow to antidiscrimination forces (and to environmentalists and consumer advocates as well) came in a 1974 Supreme Court decision in *Eisen, etc.* v. *Carlisle and Jacquelin et al.* [417 U.S. 156, 40 L.Ed 2 732, 94 S.Ct. 2140 (1974)] which held that all identifiable members of a class in future class-action suits must be notified through reasonable efforts. In effect, this limits the number of such cases, because few plaintiffs are able or willing to expend the money or effort necessary to notify all class members.

Litigation in civil rights suits can be time-consuming, and time can sometimes go against plaintiffs. In a recent appellate court decision in *Brown* v. *General Services Administration, Communications Division* [507 F.2d 1300, 2nd Cir. (1974)] a strict interpretation of the law was adhered to when the discrimination claim of a plaintiff was denied because he had not filed his action within the 30-day period stipulated for such suits ("Significant Decisions," March 1975: 66–67). A somewhat bizarre exaggeration of the time it takes to decide job discrimination cases recently came to light through the efforts of the NAACP's Legal Defense Fund. A federal judge in Georgia, Alexander A. Lawrence, heard arguments in the case of black employees alleging discrimination in promotion and seniority at the Seaboard Coast Line Railroad. When, two and a half years later, he had not yet made a decision, the Legal Defense Fund asked an appeals court for an order directing him to render a decision. This motion was denied, and fund lawyers took their case to the Supreme Court. If Judge Lawrence should decide the employees were victims of discrimination, a new trial will be necessary to determine damages in the case, and Lawrence will be the presiding judge (*Time*, July 28, 1975, p. 60).

Despite recent consent decrees and court decisions compelling reform in management practices regarding hiring, promotions, and seniority, some employers are slow in redressing the inequities within their companies. Such delays may be caused by the complexity and persistence of sex and racial discrimination which have become institutionalized within the labor force. It may also reflect management's reticence to confront unions and white male employees on the critical issues of seniority, promotions, and wages. In the present structure of organizations and jobs, the liberation of some workers necessarily means the relinquishing of power, privileges, and security by others. There are just so many pieces of the pie to be distributed to employees, and a reorganization of these areas will mean some workers who traditionally have received large servings will have to tighten their belts.

Although management may not welcome public exposure of its dirty linen, and the official opprobrium which might follow possible sanctions and financial damages awarded to wronged employees, these penalties are not always sufficient to foment change. Although AT&T made substantial settlements with employees after its 1973 consent decree, the company was forced to reach a supplemental agreement with several government agencies in 1975 and to pay an *additional* $2.5 million in compensation and penalties for failing to fully comply with its prior agreement ("Developments in Industrial Relations," July 1975: 59). Institutionalized discrimination is apparently impervious to prodding, even when large financial damages are awarded.

Unions, particularly trade unions, have also continued to resist integration in their apprentice programs. As with some corporations, initial court orders have frequently been ignored or incompletely complied with. The case of *United States* v. *Wood, Wire and Metal Lathers, Local 46* [471 F.2d. 408, 2nd Circuit (1972), cert. den. 412 U.S. 939 (1972)] illustrates the strength of trade union resistance to integration. The Department of Justice charged the union with excluding blacks and replacing them on jobs with union members and other white persons in its jurisdiction of New York City and certain adjacent counties. Shortly before the trial in 1968, the local entered into a consent decree with the Department and agreed to eliminate discrimination and provide equal employment opportunities. Two and a half years later the government returned to court [328 F.Supp. 429, S.D. N.Y. (1971)] and charged that the union was still discriminating. The court held the union in contempt for violating the consent decree, noting:

> There is a deep-rooted and pervasive practice in this union of handing out jobs on the basis of union membership, kinship, friendship and, generally

"pull." The specific tactics, practices, devices, and arrangements . . . have amounted in practical fact to varying modes of implementing this central pattern of unlawful criteria. The hirings at the site, the bypassing of the lists, and use of the hiring hall, when it was used at all, as a formality rather than as a place of legitimate and nondiscriminatory distribution of work—all reflected the basic evil of preferring Local 46 members, relatives, friends, or friends of friends in job referrals. And since the membership of this local has for so long been almost exclusively white, the result could have been forecast: the jobs, and especially the more desirable jobs, have gone disproportionately to whites rather than blacks (328 F.Supp. at 436).

The court then gave an appointed administrator two months to develop a set of rules and procedures for work distribution; ordered the union to compensate permit holders who had been victimized by discriminatory practices; and ordered the union to pay $5,000 for costs incurred by the Department of Justice in developing the case. A discussion of this case is in "Significant Decisions" (September 1971: 66–67).

As previously noted, the Philadelphia Plan was inaugurated in 1969 to combat the entrenched discrimination in building trades. Other plans to increase the flow of nonwhites into building trades were also implemented in major cities such as Chicago and New York. In 1973, New York's Mayor John Lindsay terminated his city's plan after 18 apparently unsuccessful months. The program's aim had been to employ 800 minority group workers in specific building trades. Deputy Mayor Edward K. Hamilton reported that 537 minority trainees had been placed, but the U.S. Commission on Civil Rights reported that only 34 trainees had achieved full union status ("Developments in Industrial Relations," March 1973: 71).

In January 1974 the Department of Labor ended its support of the Chicago Plan—a voluntary attempt to increase the number of minorities in an equal employment opportunity program—because of the inability of the concerned parties and the Department to develop skilled construction jobs in that area. In its place the Department imposed affirmative action requirements on contractors bidding on projects receiving federal funds. Thus Chicago joined Philadelphia, Camden, Washington, Atlanta, St. Louis, and San Francisco, where the Department of Labor had imposed similar requirements ("Developments in Industrial Relations," January 1974: 78–79).

An indication that the Supreme Court was not inclined to interfere with state policies concerning mandatory retirements came in *Canon* v. *Guste* (Sup.Ct., No. 75–134, November 3, 1975). In this case the Court ruled, without issuing an opinion, that a Louisiana statute requiring state civil service employees to retire at 65 did not violate the due process or equal protection clauses of the 14th Amendment. Then, on June 25, 1976, the Court went further and held in *Murgia* v. *Massachusetts Board of Retirement*

[376 F. Supp. 753 (D. Mass. 1974), Cert. granted, 43 U.S.L.W. 3609 (U.S. May 20, 1975)] that civil servants can be forced to retire when they reach a specified age limit even if they are still able to perform their duties. The case revolved around the complaint of a Massachusetts state policeman who was forced to retire under a Massachusetts state law which requires state police to retire at age 50. The Court ruled that manadatory retirement laws do not violate the equal protection clause of the 14th Amendment if they have a reasonable basis (in this case, the assumption that older policemen are less able to perform their work roles). The lawsuit was brought by Robert Murgia, a lieutenant colonel with more than 20 years of service. He was forced to retire despite uncontested medical evidence that he was able to perform his duties. (*Buffalo Evening News,* UPI Dispatch, June 25, 1976, p. 5).

THE FEDERAL ENFORCEMENT EFFORT:
HALTING AND INCONSISTENT

On the surface, the imposition of employment requirements seemed like a positive move by the Department of Labor to break down barriers to equal employment. However, recent developments cast some doubt on the ability, sincerity, and willingness of the Department to carry out its orders. Although the 1972 amendments to Title VII gave the EEOC the power to take court action on behalf of victims of unlawful employment discrimination, it must first seek to remedy the situation through conciliation. The first legal test of its authority, in *EEOC* v. *Container Corp. of America* [352 F.Supp. 262, M.D. Fla. (1972)] established this procedure. In the court's words:

> ... The act provides that, if a charge is filed with or by the Commission, notice must be served on the offending employer or union (the respondent) and the EEOC must investigate the charges. If it determines that no reasonable cause exists to support the charge, the respondent is so notified and the charge dismissed. If, however, the Commission finds reasonable cause to support the charge, it must notify the respondent and attempt to eliminate the problem through conciliation. If the Commission is unable to secure a satisfactory agreement within thirty days, suit may be brought. Finally, in the event the Commission does not commence an action within one hundred eighty days, it must notify the aggrieved party who has ninety days to file suit.
> This court views each of the deliberate steps in this statutory scheme—charge, notice, investigation, reasonable cause, conciliation—as intended by Congress to be a condition precedent to the next succeeding step and ultimately legal action. ... The language of the action is mandatory as to each step and the Commission must complete each step before moving to the next (352 F.Supp. at 264–65).

This procedure deprives the EEOC of an opportunity to obtain swift redress of grievances and ensures more lengthy periods of mediation and litigation.

Subsequent events indicate that EEOC may not have been too disappointed with this decision. In an attempt to avoid excessive layoffs of workers with low seniority, the Equal Employment Opportunity Coordinating Council developed guidelines for employers to utilize programs of work sharing, reduced work weeks, elimination of overtime, reverse seniority, and the promotion of early retirement. The Council devoted two years to the formulation of the guidelines and was expected to vote on them in the middle of 1975. The decision was deferred instead, largely at the behest of the EEOC, which favored further discussion among Council members ("Developments in Industrial Relations," June 1975: 64).[17]

Recent reports indicate that EEOC has been less than enthusiastic about pursuing its enforcement obligations. Part of the reason for this is its huge backlog of cases—98,000 as of June 30, 1975. But a massive analysis, *The Federal Civil Rights Enforcement Effort,* by the U.S. Commission on Civil Rights (1975) found more serious structural and procedural shortcomings in the EEOC. Although the Commission concluded that EEOC guidelines on discrimination were the broadest of any federal agency, it criticized the ambiguity of authority and roles of EEOC administrative heads. The Commission was also critical of EEOC staffing "far below its authorized level," which has resulted in long delays in filing lawsuits. The huge backlog of charges has made the median period of time required for the resolution of a complaint 32 months. The quality of investigative work done by the EEOC staff was judged inferior, with insufficient record keeping resulting in large numbers of suits being rejected or referred for further investigation. The Commission contended that, as of March 1974, EEOC attorneys were handling only 20% of their prescribed caseloads. Despite EEOC's authority to bring civil suits, it had filed only 290 direct lawsuits as of March 1975, and too few of the suits have focused on important industry leaders. In March 1974, EEOC obtained exclusive power to bring suits alleging patterns or practices of discrimination. One year later EEOC had filed only one such suit, a situation which the Commission termed "deplorable."

Although EEOC compiles data on the racial, ethnic, and sex makeup of the labor force under its jurisdiction, the Commission noted that it makes inadequate use of this information, thereby hindering the enforcement process. EEOC was also scored for not taking a more direct role in processing charges filed against state and local governments and employment agencies. Through a program of voluntary compliance, EEOC sought to obtain 61 affirmative action agreements, but the Commission found only one had been obtained and that agreement was "highly deficient" even by EEOC's standards (U.S. Commission on Civil Rights, 1975: 643–646).

A secret Civil Service Commission report made public by Representative John E. Moss (D.–Calif.) also revealed serious internal deficiencies in EEOC and a lack of commitment to equal employment goals *within* the agency. Civil Service Commission investigators found EEOC's internal complaint file in "chaotic condition." In 1973 there were 63 open complaints, and 36 were more than 180 days old. The report criticized EEOC management for violating its own procedures on communicating with employees about affirmative action and not following its own merit promotion plans. Furthermore, it was determined that career ladders were not clearly defined, and employees were not receiving equal promotional opportunities (Bureau of National Affairs, Fair Employment Practices Bulletin No. 268, May 29, 1975: 4).

A caustic review of the Civil Service Commission by the U.S. Commission on Civil Rights (1975) reveals that it, too, has been less than enthusiastic in promoting equal employment opportunities among the civilian personnel of the federal government, which employs about 4% of the labor force in the United States. The Civil Service Commission is responsible for ensuring that federal employment practices are nondiscriminatory. However, the CSC contends that it does not have to adhere to Title VII EEOC guidelines, which apply to all other employers; nor does it have to follow affirmative action principles applicable to federal contractors (p. 619). The Commission on Civil Rights contended that CSC has failed to demonstrate that many of its employee selection standards related to minorities and women are associated with job performance. Instead of using EEOC guidelines, CSC has adopted weaker criteria for demonstrating job relatedness of examination and testing procedures. The CSC Professional and Administrative Career Examination, which is designed to screen applicants for important professional and administrative positions, has not been empirically demonstrated to be related to job performance, and it has not been shown to be racially or sexually unbiased, in the judgment of the U.S. Commission on Civil Rights (p. 620).

Despite the conclusions of a General Accounting Office study in 1973, which showed that the ranking of candidates on the basis of biographical information is not related to job performance, CSC has not yet conducted an analysis to refute this claim nor the charge that this procedure is discriminatory. The Civil Rights Commission (1975) also maintained that giving veterans preference in the ranking procedure discriminates against women.

The Civil Rights Commission also charged that CSC complaint procedures vis-à-vis employment discrimination are still deficient, despite Congressional criticism of them in 1972, and these procedures "deny Federal employees a full and fair consideration of their employment discrimination grievances" (p. 621). CSC statistics reveal serious underutilization of minorities and women in federal agencies, yet CSC has not issued adequate instructions for remedying this situation. In agencies found to have voluntarily established timetables and goals for alleviating deficiencies, the objectives were so low that there was little likelihood of redressing the imbalance.

One agency established a hiring goal which *decreased* the percentage of the group whose employment the agency had intended to increase (p. 623). In fact, the Civil Rights Commission found, CSC prohibits agencies from using race, sex, or ethnicity as criteria for candidate selection, even when agencies are attempting to implement affirmative action goals (p. 621). The Commission concluded that CSC fails to require adequate reporting by agencies on affirmative action programs, and there is a general lack of enthusiasm in federal agencies for such reporting and elimination of systemic discrimination (p. 624).

The Commission on Civil Rights (1975) also criticized the Department of Labor for lax enforcement of the Equal Pay Act. Although it was passed in 1963 and was later broadened to cover larger numbers of workers in professional, technical, and administrative positions, and employees in state and local government, the number of officers having responsibility for investigating compliance to the act has not increased significantly since 1963 (p. 639). Among other shortcomings, the Commission cited inadequate efforts to monitor regional enforcement of the act, lack of a national enforcement program, ambiguous and misleading information furnished by the Department to employers concerning benefits and training programs, and deficient definitions of what constitutes a bona fide merit or seniority system. The Commission recognized a general lack of coordination between the Department of Labor field staff and the staffs of other agencies having jurisdiction. Compliance officers are required to report possible violations of other federal laws prohibiting sex discrimination, but the report notes the officers have consistently overlooked them. An examination of Equal Pay Act investigative files indicated that insufficient documentation is contained in them for litigative purposes (pp. 639–642).

The Office of Federal Contract Compliance (OFCC), located in the Department of Labor, likewise came under fire from the U.S. Commission on Civil Rights (1975). OFCC has responsibility for eliminating employment discrimination on the basis of race, sex, creed, color, and national origin by federal contractors, subcontractors, and construction contractors working on federally assisted construction projects under authority of Executive Order 11246 and amendments in Executive Order 11375 passed in 1967. OFCC has delegated the enforcement authority to 17 contracting federal agencies, while retaining general control. The Civil Rights Commission found OFCC's staff and budget to be inadequate to meet this task. In addition, its regulations requiring contractors to develop affirmative action programs were deemed deficient because of exemptions given to many facilities not directly engaged in work on federal projects and to contractors holding contracts of less than $10,000 (p. 632). Inadequate instructions on developing affirmative action goals and the reporting of information necessary to determine contractor compliance were also seen to be shortcomings of OFCC regulations for contractors. The Civil Rights study concluded that OFCC "has failed significantly in carrying out its responsibility for overseeing and guiding the contract compliance program covering supply and service contractors," and its agency compliance reviews of supply and service contractors were termed "fundamentally deficient" (p. 635).

Since 1969 there have been just two instances in which OFCC has assumed jurisdiction over contractors. These occurred after the compliance agency engaged in protracted negotiations with the contractors which resulted in deficient settlements, and after OFCC was notified by other federal agencies that the deficiences should be rectified. In the 10 years since the contract compliance program was initiated there has been widespread noncompliance, yet only nine companies have been debarred. The report noted that OFCC has never removed the entire compliance authority of an agency over contractors for violations of its regulations, even though there are "strong indications" compliance agencies such as the Department of Health, Education, and Welfare, the Department of the Treasury, and the General Services Administration "routinely commit violations" (U.S. Commission on Civil Rights, July 1975: 636–637). Furthermore, the report charged that OFCC "has obstructed efforts by other authorities to secure affirmative action commitments in the construction industry"; it has "consistently opposed efforts by compliance agencies to secure affirmative-action plans from construction contractors in nonplan areas, and it has issued regulations limiting the right of State and local governments to require goals of construction contractors in home town-plan areas, despite three court decisions upholding local requirements" (p. 636).

Lax enforcement of affirmative action programs has also been found to be rampant among federal nonconstruction contractors. A report done by the General Accounting Office (1975a) for a subcommittee of the Joint Economic Committee of Congress documents widespread flouting of Labor Department guidelines and only desultory interest in promoting equal employment opportunities. The potential for increasing the job status of women and minorities through positive affirmative action programs among federal nonconstruction contractors is great. In fiscal 1974 over $50 billion in federal contracts was awarded to nonconstruction contractors who employed 25 million people (p. 4). Nevertheless, the General Accounting Office (GAO) found the Department of Labor derelict in its administration of Executive Orders 11246 and 11375. Among the areas needing improvement cited were assessment of employment gains by women and minorities, and training and monitoring of compliance agencies (p. 7).

There are 13 compliance agencies appointed by the Labor Department which are responsible for enforcing the executive orders and Department guidelines.[18] Although reviews of the agencies were conducted in 1972 which resulted in recommendations for corrective action, GAO (1975a) noted that only 1 of the 13, NASA, has done comprehensive follow-up reviews (p. 12). Twelve of the agencies had not identified all the contractors they were responsible for. At least two compliance agencies, the Department of Defense and the General Services Administration, were found to be approving affirmative action programs that failed to meet Department of Labor guidelines. Most of the agencies were insufficiently reviewing the contractors they were responsible for, and some agencies were not conducting required preaward reviews. Some of the compliance agencies were also criticized for their reluctance to initiate enforcement actions and for taking too much time in their conciliations with contractors (p. 20). GAO found that only one contractor has ever had a contract terminated for noncompliance. In releasing the report Congressman Richard Bolling (D–Mo.), Chairman of the Subcommittee on Fiscal Policy of the Joint Economic Committee, summed up the situation: "In a program that is ten years old, the deficiencies uncovered by GAO boggle the mind. . . . We can't expect to make equal access to jobs a reality until the Federal Government puts its own house in order."

The lack of civil rights enforcement is not limited to the Department of Labor and compliance agencies. An earlier report of the U.S. Commission on Civil Rights (1974) took federal regulatory agencies to task for their weak efforts in eliminating employment discrimination in the industries they regulate. In evaluating the civil rights activities of the Federal Communications Commission, the Interstate Commerce Commission, the Civil Aeronautics Board, the Federal Power Commission, and the Securities and Exchange Commission, the Commission on Civil Rights noted that these agencies possess a huge potential for affirmative action in the labor force, since they regulate industries employing millions of workers. Unfortunately, their records in the area of civil rights are abysmal. Of all the agencies only the FCC, which is responsible for regulating the radio and television, cable television, and telephone and telegraph communications industries, had adopted rules prohibiting job discrimination by its licensees. But the Commission identified severe deficiences in FCC's enforcement of its rules, including (1) ambiguous reporting of the positions held by minorities and women in licensees' industries, (2) a lack of specificity in FCC guidelines for licensees' equal employment opportunity programs, (3) the low priority FCC gives to discrimination complaints, (4) the lack of an effective mechanism within the FCC to handle civil rights complaints, and (5) the refusal of the FCC to provide free legal counsel and services to needy parties wishing to challenge regulatory actions (pp. 222–225).

The Commission on Civil Rights 1974 report further maintained that "FCC's guidelines for equal employment opportunity programs are clearly not designed to bring about significant change in the employment practices of the broadcasting industry" (p. 13). Despite former Commissioner Nicholas Johnson's recommendations for improving the job status of women and minorities in the broadcasting industry, the Commission found, as of June 1974, that the FCC "had taken no action . . . to revise its criteria for identifying licensees with questionable employment patterns" (p. 23).

The movement toward civil rights enforcement was even slower in the Interstate Commerce Commission, the Civil Aeronautics Board, and the Federal Power Commission, which regulate surface and air transportation industries and public utilities. The Civil Rights Commission (1974) found a "severe underutilization of minorities and women" in the industries which they regulate in the public interest. Although this was an obvious deficiency, the regulatory agencies have done little to rectify the situation, preferring instead to delay changes, as in the ICC and CAB, or to defer action by contending that they lack authority to implement new equal employment guidelines, as has the FPC. Furthermore, the ICC and CAB have made their antidiscrimination efforts largely complaint oriented and have not implemented serious monitoring of civil rights compliance activities of their licensees. The Commission also charged the ICC with severely restricting minority entrepreneurship in the trucking industry (pp. 226–227).

While the securities industry has a blatantly poor record of underemployment and underutilization of women and minorities, the Civil Rights Commission (1974) charged that the Securities and Exchange Commission "has refused to adopt mandatory equal employment guidelines" for the industry (p. 228).

In its letter of transmission to the President, the Civil Rights Commission (1974) charged that, with the exception of the FCC,

> None of the agencies have acknowledged responsibility for dealing with . . . employment discrimination in the industries they regulate, ICC, CAB, FPC, and SEC appear to assume that their independent regulatory status allows them to stand above the national commitment to equal employment opportunity. This Commission finds their position neither legally nor morally justifiable. (p. 11)

A Government Accounting Office report (1975b) on the efforts of the Department of Health, Education, and Welfare to enforce affirmative action programs in colleges and universities was released in August 1975. A public college or university with 50 or more employees and a government contract of $50,000 or more was required to file an acceptable affirmative action program with HEW by May 19, 1973. Between 1,100 and 1,300 colleges and universities are subject to this regulation, but as of December 1975, only 31 had HEW–approved programs (Maeroff, 1975: 23), and HEW had not even identified all the institutions subject to the guidelines. One bizarre result of the lack of identification of eligible institutions was found in the Office of Civil Rights (OCR) of HEW. OCR received a sex discrimination complaint against a California college in November 1970 and attempted, but failed, to establish its jurisdiction at the institution. It therefore could not investigate the complaint. However, in March 1974, OCR was able to establish that the college had had a sufficiently large government contract at the time of the complaint, and its regional office in San Francisco notified the president of the college that the complaint would now be investigated. The lack of adequate information caused a delay of three years before an investigation was even begun (General Accounting Office, 1975b: 19).

GAO criticized HEW for its lack of progress in making colleges and universities submit adequate affirmative action programs and for its failure to issue show-cause notices and institute sanctions against institutions in cases of noncompliance. Furthermore, preaward reviews of contracts of $1 million or more are required by the Department of Labor, but HEW was not performing them. The Department was also criticized for negotiating and conciliating with colleges and universities over prolonged periods instead of demanding the submission of acceptable affirmative action programs within the specified time. OCR records revealed that the Dallas regional office of OCR rejected the affirmative action program of a large university in Oklahoma on April 16, 1973. On May 21 the university submitted a revised program, which was rejected on August 6, 1973. On September 6, 1973 the university submitted additional revisions, which were also rejected. The university still did not have an approved program as of December 9, 1974—nearly two years later, and it had not been issued a show-cause notice, nor were sanctions imposed (p. 9).

The record of commitment to equal employment opportunities by federal agencies can be characterized as a classic case of malfeasance, ineptitude, and inertia. After reviewing this lackluster performance, the U.S. Commission on Civil Rights (1975) concluded that the rate of change has been inadequate, and major problems of systemic discrimination continue to adversely affect minorities and women.

> The Federal effort to end this discrimination has not been equal to the task. It has been seriously hampered by lack of overall leadership and direction, deficiencies in existing laws, and the assignment of authority to a number of agencies which have issued inconsistent policies, and developed independent and uncoordinated compliance programs. (p. 619)

To remedy these deficiencies the Commission proposed the establishment of a National Employment Rights Board which would consolidate all federal equal employment enforcement responsibilities.

One of the problems in promoting equal employment opportunities and ensuring fair treatment of workers is the lack of strong, unencumbered laws. Just as the Civil Rights Commission felt that laws weakened by political compromises had fostered inadequacies in federal agencies, so too have compromises jeopardized the impact of the Retirement Income Security Act. There are still sizable segments of the labor force not covered by this act. Many workers do not receive pensions, because the act stipulates that an employee must participate at least ten years in a plan to become eligible for a pension. Yet, a recent report indicates that one fourth of the 81 million people in the labor force in January 1973 had been continuously employed at the same job for a year or less, and only 30% of men and 18% of women had been working in their current jobs for 11 years or more. In fact, the average job tenure of workers *declined* between January 1963 and January 1973, from 4.6 to 3.9 years. Although there were no significant differences in job tenure between whites and blacks, men had nearly twice the job tenure of women (4.6 years compared to 2.8 years) (Hayghe, 1974: 53–57).

Among persons covered by pensions, there are glaring differences in the benefits they receive by sex and race. In April 1972 only half (23 million) of the full-time workers in private wage and salary jobs were covered by a private pension or deferred profit-sharing plan. Forty-five percent more men were covered than women, and 25% more whites were covered than all other races. People in the highest wage and skill jobs obtained the benefits of pension coverage to a much greater extent than those in low wage and skill jobs. Even among covered workers, only a third had vested rights. Whites were more likely to be vested than nonwhites (33% versus 24%), more men had vested rights than women, and workers with high earnings were more likely to have such rights than people with low earnings (U.S. Department of Labor, 1973).

The need for pension coverage is acute. Only half the workers over 50 with 10 or more years of employment have vested pension rights (U.S. Department of Labor, 1973). A 1971 analysis of earnings replaced by Social Security and private pensions revealed that retired workers not covered by pensions were receiving a meager amount of money from Social Security. Workers whose taxable earnings exceeded $200 a month in their three best years were receiving a median replacement rate of only 30% of their previous income. The median 1974 replacement rate for retirees in 1970 was estimated to be 35% of their preretirement standard of living (Fox, 1974).

JOB DISCRIMINATION: REAL, PERCEIVED, OR NONEXISTENT?

The EEOC has recorded a consistent increase in the number of job discrimination charges it receives—from 8,800 in fiscal 1966 to 48,899 in fiscal 1973 (EEOC, 1975: 1). The increase in complaints may be attributable to a heightened awareness and sensitivity about equal employment opportunities among some segments of the population. Feelings of subjective job discrimination were also measured in two recent studies of the U.S. labor force (Quinn & Shepard, 1974). Between 1969 and 1973 there was an increase in reported sex discrimination, from 8% to 13%. Reporting the largest increases in sex discrimination were blacks, blue-collar workers, operatives and kindred workers, women in low-prestige positions, and women having less than a high school diploma (Staines, Quinn, & Shepard, 1976: 12). Women who attended but did not complete college reported more sex discrimination than any other occupational group.[19]

There is evidence indicating that women and other minorities are making some progress toward equal employment opportunities. For example, the Civil Service Commission reported that minorities accounted for 64% (approximately 12,000) of the increase in federal employment from May 1973 to May 1974. Blacks gained 9,314 jobs and held 14.6% of all federal nonpostal jobs, and persons of Spanish origin increased their proportions in federal jobs from 3.2% to 3.4%. However, minorities were still concentrated in lower-level jobs. They accounted for 46% of Grade 1 jobs and 30% of jobs in Grades 2 and 3 out of an 18-grade pay structure ("Developments in Industrial Relations," August 1975: 50).

In actuality, the progress toward securing equal job opportunities has been laboriously slow. The increase in the number of charges of discrimination may be attributable to a realization among affected groups about their rights and a new willingness to confront discrimination in the workplace. Much contemporary sex and racial discrimination is less overt than before. It is, nevertheless, deeply rooted in our social mores and is therefore highly resistant to change. Many of the victims of this discrimination do not protest because they have been socialized into accepting their inferior roles in the world of work, they have resigned themselves to their situation, or they are located in low-skilled, insecure jobs and they fear reprisals from co-workers and management if they make waves and rock the organizational boat.

Low-skill workers especially are faced with the uncomforting reality that they can be easily replaced. Many poorly educated workers may be unaware of their rights and the grievance procedures against employers for discriminatory practices—a situation which, as the U.S. Commission on Civil Rights (1974) noted, has not been improved by federal agencies. Even when workers might wish to file a complaint, they are often constrained by their economic situation. The prospect of recouping lost wages and back pay at some future time after an extended period of litigation does not help to pay one's bills in the present.

It takes a very courageous person to risk the minimal security already attained. A case in point was the recent strike by Mexican-American workers against the Farah Company in the Southwest. When 3,000 of 8,000 workers went on strike protesting company policies and working conditions and claiming the right to union representation, they were replaced by other Mexican-Americans from the area. Though these other workers sympathized with their goals, as did many of the workers who did not walk out, they could not afford the luxury of acting on their sympathies. Two thirds of the workers at the plants signed cards stating they wanted union representation (*AFL–CIO News*, March 2, 1974, p. 1). The strike and boycott of Farah products lasted 21 months. Willie Farah, the president of the company, vowed he would not allow a union in his plants. Then came a ruling against him by a National Labor Relations Board administrative judge, who stated that in the three and a half years of litigation before the NLRB and federal courts the company pursued a policy of "flouting the [National Labor Relations] Act and trampling on the rights of its employees as if there were no act, no board, and no Ten Commandments" ("Developments in Industrial Relations," April 1974: 73–74). Losses of $8.3 million in 1972 also gave Farah second thoughts, and he agreed to allow the Amalgamated Clothing Workers of America to represent the workers, most of whom were women. Although the union spent nearly $5 million to support the striking workers, it was not enough. Living conditions among the strikers deteriorated to the extent that a nationwide food and clothing drive to aid them was launched shortly before the settlement. Ultimately, the company agreed to rehire striking workers, but the pain and suffering they had to endure during their unemployment was an enormous burden for them and their families to bear.

Action, overt or covert, which denies people opportunities to achieve equal employment opportunities can be interpreted as hostile and punitive, for its consequences are the perpetuation of inferior socioeconomic status and the relegation of the affected individuals to states of relative deprivation and want. Sometimes, it is inaction or an uninformed public which perpetuates inequality. Although it is hoped that increasing the educational level of the population will lead to a breakdown of traditional sex and racial stereotypes and a more equalitarian society, a recent study sponsored by the Department of Labor of 901 male and 950 female college seniors in six Pennsylvania colleges is not encouraging. Most students thought men and women should have equal opportunities, but 82% said women lack physical strength, 43% believed they are more emotional than men, and 36% felt they have different thinking patterns. The students viewed these differences as impediments to sex equality, and a fifth of them contended that men and women are not really equal and should therefore have different jobs (Gottlieb, 1974: 13). Yankelovich (1974: 98) found similar naive beliefs in national samples of college and noncollege youths.

Confirmation of the pervasiveness of these negative attitudes comes from the recent backlash toward the Equal Rights Amendment. If ratified, it would guarantee equal rights to men and women and abolish preferential treatment for either sex. To date, 34 states have ratified the amendment. However, Illinois, a pivotal state, failed to do so in 1975, and following that nonratification, groups of women opposed to the amendment began working in earnest to have ratification rescinded in other states. On November 4, 1975, voters in New York and New Jersey rejected state equal rights amendments, adding impetus to the movement to scuttle the national ERA.[20] It is questionable whether the necessary 38 states will ratify by the deadline in 1979. Whether through fear, misinformation, or mistrust, the effect of nonratification would be to ensure the status quo and to deny a moral victory to the forces advocating equality and social change in the world of work.

THE POLITICAL INVISIBILITY OF THE DISADVANTAGED WORKER

Although much attention has been focused on the problem of increased unemployment in the mid 1970s, there is reason to believe that this is a transitory phenomenon. As the economic recession dissipates, so too will public enthusiasm for combating the problems of the unemployed, for the motivation to ameliorate the problem is the same as the cause—political. In an effort to curb double-digit inflation, the Nixon administration embarked on an economic program of tight money and selective fiscal restraint, which, among other things, precipitated a decreased commitment to promoting nonwhite membership in trade unions and to the phasing out and consolidation of federal job-training programs. Concomitantly, the level of unemployment was *intentionally* increased. In testimony before the Joint Economic Committeé, Kenneth Rush, Counselor to the President for Economic Policy, stated:

> We anticipate it [unemployment] will go up as a result of current policies to perhaps between 5-1/2 to 6 percent. And we consider that this is a price that we do not like to pay; it will be necessary to pay it in order to help get inflation under better control. (U.S. Congress, Joint Economic Committee, 1974: 41)

Of course, these estimates were wrong, but it is significant that the administration was willing to pursue a policy which intensified the social and economic suffering of one segment of the population for the sake of improving the lives of another. In a later statement, before the Joint Economic Committee, Senator William Proxmire (D–Wis.) expressed dismay upon hearing a member of the President's Council of Economic Advisors state that the administration was not actively developing programs to aid workers being displaced by its antiinflationary policies:

> I think we would have a far better chance in the Congress and with the public if we knew that we had a program that wasn't going to be inequitable, unfair, cruel, on so many hundreds of thousands of Americans. I think if the Government explored public employment with half the energy we are exploring outer space, we would have a pretty good program and we would have it ready right now. (U.S. Congress, Joint Economic Committee, 1974: 110)

Such a callous course of action could be selected by the administration because it was politically expedient to write off traditionally disadvantaged segments of society. The administration knew it could calculatingly inflict deprivation on the few with impunity because they lacked the power and presence to influence decision making. Not having received the support of the disadvantaged in previous elections, the administration risked nothing by a program which would further alienate them. When, however, unemployment began to rise past expected levels and stable working-class and white-collar workers became affected, federal machinery was brought to bear on the problem. Thousands of public service jobs were created under the Emergency Employment Act of 1971, the Comprehensive Employment and Training Act (CETA) of 1973, and the Emergency Jobs and Unemployment Assistance Act of 1974. Then, in May 1975, President Gerald Ford vetoed a bill which would have broadened the scope of the CETA program because it was "inflationary." Although he delivered a Labor Day message which pledged him to create jobs and cut unemployment, a Library of Congress study released a month before revealed that his vetoes in 1975 initially eliminated 1,810,500 jobs.[21] As long as the poor and discriminated-against persons in our society are perceived as being politically expendable, they will have to wage an uphill fight against systemic inequality and the indifferent forces which seek to preserve the status quo.

THE EFFECT OF AFFIRMATIVE ACTION PROGRAMS: CHAOS OR COMPLIANCE?

Although considerable emotional and legal arguments are used to justify affirmative action programs, we would be remiss if we did not attempt to develop management's perspective on the equity of the affirmative action effort. Management sometimes views the efforts of governmental agencies or civil rights groups to secure equal employment opportunities for women and minorities as further examples of interference in private enterprise, and it resents being simultaneously scrutinized by several agencies which may have conflicting and ambiguous objectives. In a speech before personnel managers at the Buffalo Urban League's annual Equal Opportunity Conference on November 14, 1975, Ernest R. Frazier, Director of Equal Opportunity Field Operations for the International Telephone and Telegraph Corporation, compared the federal affirmative action effort to a butcher indiscriminately hacking at a side of beef instead of a surgeon precisely excising diseased tissue. What Frazier and other personnel specialists are decrying is the morass of federal equal opportunity guidelines and regulations. Although they admit legislation is necessary to ensure the rights of deprived groups, they see severe inadequacies in the present laws and enforcement procedures. Particularly onerous in the federal equal opportunity effort are the myriad regulations and their continual revision and enlargement. This process, perhaps inevitable due to the dynamic quality of social legislation, blunts the thrust of the effort and creates an anomic situation for people responsible for implementing the program at the job level.

Many personnel managers find regulations to be vague and ambiguous and resent federal encroachment in their domains. While enforcement of equal-rights legislation is lax at the upper echelons of industry and government, people in the personnel field with smaller, less influential employers complain of harassment by field representatives of federal agencies, and they fear reprisals if they do not meet the requirements, however difficult and complicated they may be.

There is growing consternation among employers and supervisors over the disciplining or firing of women and minorities, who, it is feared, will claim they were discriminated against even though, in the eyes of management, the disciplinary action was justified. The litigation process in such cases is long and expensive, and it is especially burdensome on small employers. (Although there is evidence indicating that the cost and length of such litigation creates more hardships for plaintiffs, the employers and supervisors feel it is they who are wronged by the system.) Even if management should win, individuals alleging discrimination have recourse to extralegal methods of appeal, such as to human rights organizations, which are capable of bringing pressure to bear against employers and damaging their public image.

Consequently, employers and supervisors may eschew disciplining errant women and minority employees to avoid confrontations. This tactic is adopted at the expense of incurring the resentment of other workers who abhor such preferential treatment. The resentment may increase the hostility toward the individual in question and could result in generalized negative feelings to other members of the group. Such situations create a self-fulfilling prophecy. The negative stereotypes employers and supervisors have about the motivation and ability of women and minorities cause them to scrutinize their work more closely. Just as police patrols are concentrated in heavily populated black areas, leading, in part, to higher arrests among the more closely watched residents, so, too, women and minority employees may be excessively scrutinized and criticized. Management's fear of a confrontation may, on the other hand, predispose it to tolerate inferior work behavior, and perceptive disadvantaged workers may even exploit this situation, further reinforcing the stereotypes.

How widespread such inferior work is, we do not know. Such complaints may be a manifestation of latent racist anxieties, but the behavioral outcomes operate to the disadvantage of women and minorities. Fear of disciplining is counterproductive because it leads some employers to prolong their search for "qualified" minorities. Since employers do not wish to risk a confrontation if the employee proves to be incompetent, many deserving individuals may be passed over in the search for the superior candidate, who is often so highly sought after that she or he is impossible to hire. This situation is common in universities, where outstanding women and minority candidates are highly prized but are often gobbled up by a few elite schools. Obviously, the principles of merit should apply to all workers, with recognition that some employees may warrant preferential treatment for a short while to overcome disabilities and deficiencies which result from decades of neglect and discrimination.

It is not difficult to comprehend the animosity, jealousy, and hostility generated toward women and minorities who may be receiving preferential treatment. Such policies as programs of preferential hiring and promotion; tolerance of idiosyncratic work behavior, including tardiness and absenteeism; special training; adjustments in working conditions; and circumvention of traditional seniority systems hardly endear disadvantaged groups to their co-workers. Such treatment can be expected to heighten the hostility toward them and stiffen the resistance to job equality.[22] A glimpse of what the future may bring occurred in the spring of 1975 when black and white Detroit policemen fought one another after a federal court forbade the police department to lay off black and female officers (Bureau of National Affairs, Fair Employment Practices Bulletin No. 268, May 29, 1975: 2).

Negative feelings about affirmative action are often latent or expressed as murmured denunciations among supervisors and workers, but there is rising dissatisfaction, resentment, and hostility toward the government, the laws, and the groups which are supposed to be the recipients of affirmative action programs. As in the case of enforced school busing, the long-awaited backlash may be upon us. At times it seems as if the architects of the federal affirmative action effort could not have devised a more effective method of scuttling equal employment opportunity objectives.

A GLIMPSE INTO THE FUTURE?

Social change is a dynamic phenomenon, but the pace at which it progresses in the world of work depends on a number of interrelated factors which have been resistant to change. Although many immigrant ethnic groups have managed to make substantial gains in upward occupational mobility, so that we have seen a circulation of elites, a number of formidable obstacles to job equality face the groups discussed in this book. Many of them look and sound different from the white males who overwhelmingly occupy positions of power, prestige, and authority in our society. In a society such as ours, based upon competition rather than cooperation, a period of economic expansion is necessary to permit the relaxation of barriers to social and economic equality by men who feel economically threatened by aspiring groups. Pleas to relinquish power and economic advantages when times are good are far more palatable than they are when times are bad—when the relinquishing of advantages might jeopardize one's own security. In a society where people's preoccupations are predominantly oriented toward self-interest, it is not surprising that unions are reluctant to accept large numbers of minorities to compete with members for jobs; that managers and professionals feel threatened by the influx of aggressive, qualified women with higher aspirations; and that companies dump older workers to avoid paying them higher fringe benefits and pensions.

The seventies have brought with them the reality that the economic boom and expansionism of past decades may be over forever. We are slowly coming to realize that there is a growing shortage of natural resources, especially domestic energy reserves and raw materials necessary for manufacturing consumer goods. Traditional foreign suppliers of raw materials have raised the ante and even threaten to withhold resources for their own domestic purposes. In addition to the severe recession of the 1970s, there has been a dramatic decline in the amount of money allocated for investment capital—an expenditure vital to the long-run development of jobs.[23]

These events not only threaten to impede the expansion of the job market and the opportunities for minority occupational mobility in the short run, they also imply that the climate for qualitative social change in the world of work may remain unfavorable for the foreseeable future. Faced with rising competition for scarce resources from abroad and with challenges to power and privilege from disadvantaged workers at home, it is likely that efforts to equalize job opportunities will meet with continued, and perhaps increasing, intransigence by the entrenched white, male power structure.

Prognosticating about sociological events is hazardous, and one who indulges in it often jeopardizes one's credibility. The world of sociological phenomena is an imprecise world, fraught with contradictions, inconsistencies, and irrationality. People are not objects which can be manipulated, calibrated, and observed in the antiseptic conditions available to the natural scientist. Since human behavior is the product of many causes (what sociologists term multiple causality), and people have a propensity for doing the unexpected (the phenomenon referred to as human variability), the social sciences are inexact, just as their subjects are imperfect. Our predictions about future occurrences are, therefore, not always borne out by events.

Nevertheless, there are phenomena, which, when analyzed historically, lend themselves to future speculation. In an effort to develop some insight into the future we traced major legal and administrative decisions affecting discrimination in the workplace. Since our country is predicated on the rule of law, the attainment of job equality will depend on battles won or lost on the legal front. Our review indicates the journey toward equality in work will continue, but it will be long and arduous. Even though present laws and enforcement efforts are flawed, they are a beginning—an attempt to break the chain of poverty, discrimination, and inequality which has prevented the fulfillment of the promise of our nation: With liberty and justice for all.

NOTES

1. The educational attainment of Spanish-Americans is considerably below that of the general population. In March 1974, about 20% of Spanish-American men and women age 25 and over had completed less than five years of school, compared to 5% of men and 4% of women in the general population (U.S. Bureau of the Census, 1975: 6). There is considerable sentiment among Mexican-American educators that Mexican-Americans are being discriminated against in higher education. They account for only 1% of all graduate students, and there are only 50–60 Mexican-Americans with the doctor of philosophy degree in the United States. A forthcoming report to President Gerald Ford by a special assistant, Fernando C. de Baca, contends that a 330% increase in Mexican-American college and university enrollment is needed to ensure their adequate representation in higher education. There are widespread complaints by Mexican-Americans of insufficient and improper recruiting techniques, biased admission tests, policy barriers, and insufficient financial aid for Mexican-American students. See Watkins (1974: 1, 1975: 7).

2. 77 Stat. 56, 29 U.S.C. 206.

3. 78 Stat. 255, 42 U.S.C. 2000e et seq.

4. 86 Stat. 235, P.L. 92–318.

5. 80 Stat. 830, 29 U.S.C. 201 et seq.

6. 52 Stat. 1060, Ch. 676, 29 U.S.C. 201 et seq.

7. 88 Stat. 829, 29 U.S.C. 1001 et seq.

8. See also *Corning Glass Works* v. *Brennan* [417 U.S. 188, 41 L.Ed.2d 1, 94 S.Ct. 2223 (1974)].

9. See the discussion of *Green* v. *Missouri Pacific Railroad Co.* [381 F.Supp. 992, E.D. Mo. (1974)] in "Significant Decisions in Labor Cases" (October 1975: 58–59). Another case involving this issue, *Gregory* v. *Litton Systems, Inc.* [472 F. 2d 631, 9th Cir. (1972)], is briefly discussed in EEOC (1975: 21).

10. See the discussion of *Stamps v. Detroit Edison Co.* and *U.S.* v. *Detroit Edison Co.* [365 F.Supp. 87, E.D. Mich. (1973)], in "Developments in Industrial Relations" (January 1974: 70–72).

11. See the discussion of *United States* v. *Local 638, Enterprise Association of Steam, Hot Water, Hydraulic Sprinkler, Pneumatic Tube, Compressed Air, Ice Machine, Air Conditioning, General Pipefitters,* and *George Rios* v. *Enterprise Association Steamfitters Local Union 638* [360 F.Supp. 979, S.D. N.Y. (1973), modified 501 F.2d 622, 2d Cir. (1974)].

12. Although it is believed that the burden of layoffs was falling disproportionately on women and minorities, an April 15, 1975, memorandum prepared for the Secretary of Labor, John Dunlop, by the commissioner of the Bureau of Labor

Statistics, Julius Shiskin, indicated otherwise. Hardest hit were mature, experienced male workers with family responsibilities. Nevertheless, it is not comforting for women to know that their job losses since 1973 were up only 140% compared to the 150% loss experienced by males. Nor can blacks draw much security from knowing that their job losses in this period were only up 18%, and although they are "overrepresented among the job losers," their layoff proportion is about the same as it was in the second half of 1973. (See a summary of this memorandum in Bureau of National Affairs, Fair Employment Practices Bulletin No. 266, May 1, 1975: 2.)

13. The companies who signed the decrees were Allegheny-Ludlum Industries, Inc., Armco Steel Corporation, Bethlehem Steel Corporation, Jones and Laughlin Steel Corporation, National Steel Corporation, Republic Steel Corporation, United States Steel Corporation, Wheeling-Pittsburgh Steel Corporation, and Youngstown Sheet and Tube Company.

14. In the summer of 1975 a federal court of appeals judge in New Orleans declared that blacks laid off by the Continental Can Company because of low seniority were not victims of discrimination, and last hired–first fired provisions are legal. An appeal to the Supreme Court is anticipated ("Developments in Industrial Relations," September 1975: 64–65).

15. The four appeals courts' decisions occurred in Philadelphia (*Wetzel* v. *Liberty Mutual Insurance Co.*); New York (*CWA* v. *AT&T*); St. Louis (*Holthaus* v. *Compton & Sons, Inc.*); and Richmond (*Gilbert* v. *General Electric Co.*). The Supreme Court is expected to resolve the ambiguity when it rules on the Philadelphia case. For a summary of these decisions, see Bureau of National Affairs, Fair Employment Practices Bulletin No. 271, July 10, 1975: 6.

16. In a dissenting opinion, Justice Brennan observed:
In my view, by singling out for less favorable treatment, a gender-linked disability peculiar to women, the State has created a double standard for disability compensation: a limitation is imposed upon the disabilities for which women workers may recover, while men receive full compensation for all disabilities suffered, including those that affect only or primarily their sex. . . .
In effect, one set of rules is applied to females and another to males. Such dissimilar treatment of men and women . . . inevitably constitutes sex discrimination. ("Significant Decisions," October 1974: 70–71)

17. Council members include the Secretary of Labor, the Attorney General, the heads of the Civil Service Commission, the U.S. Commission on Civil Rights, and the EEOC. In its investigation of Federal civil rights enforcement, the U.S. Commission on Civil Rights noted the infrequency with which the Council met, its general inertia, and its lack of enforcement authority, and recommended that it be abolished (U.S. Commission on Civil Rights, 1975: 647–648 & 673).

18. These are the Agency for International Development; Atomic Energy Commission; Department of Agriculture; Department of Commerce; Department of Defense; Department of Health, Education, and Welfare; Department of the Interior; Department of the Treasury; Department of Transportation; General Services Administration; National Aeronautics and Space Administration; United States Postal Service; Veterans Administration.

19. During this same time period objective sex discrimination in jobs remained

the same. Women continued to earn an average of $3,000 less than they should have (Staines, Quinn, & Shepard, 1976). This was measured by predicting the income of women on the basis of six indices of income merit performance and comparing it with their actual earnings. Interestingly, reported racial discrimination decreased, although not significantly, during this time period, from 17 to 15 percent (Quinn & Shepard, 1974: 185).

20. The National Organization of Women (NOW) called for a national women's strike on October 29, 1975. Few women participated, and what was to be a day of consciousness raising passed relatively unnoticed. The failure of the strike may have been the result of a general lack of interest, but it is also likely that the economic necessity to report for work figured prominently in the decisions of women to engage in business as usual. There were also threats of reprisals from employers. Interestingly, a similar strike in Iceland the previous week literally ground the country to a halt.

21. Subsequent compromise legislation reduced the loss to 638,500 jobs.

22. In the most recent AT&T settlement the company agreed to "frontload," i.e., preferential hiring of women and minorities and promoting on the basis of a predetermined formula; and "affirmative action overrides," which entails circumventing traditional seniority systems to promote women and minorities (Bureau of National Affairs, Fair Employment Practices Bulletin No. 271, May 29, 1975: 6).

23. See the discussion of the ramifications of the decline of capital investment in *Time*, July 28, 1975, pp. 54–55.

REFERENCES

Blitz, Rudolph. "Women in the Professions, 1870–1970." *Monthly Labor Review* 97 (May 1974): 34–39.

"Developments in Industrial Relations: AT&T Settles Bias Claim." *Monthly Labor Review* 96 (March 1973): 69–70.

"Developments in Industrial Relations: New York Plan Dies." *Monthly Labor Review* 96 (March 1973): 71.

"Developments in Industrial Relations: Sex Bias Suit Filed." *Monthly Labor Review* 96 (September 1973): 89.

"Developments in Industrial Relations: Chicago Plan Voided." *Monthly Labor Review* 97 (January 1974): 78–79.

"Developments in Industrial Relations: Farah Settles Ending Long Strike." *Monthly Labor Review* 97 (April 1974): 73–74.

"Developments in Industrial Relations: Bias Found, Backpay Ordered." *Monthly Labor Review* 97 (April 1974): 75–76.

"Developments in Industrial Relations: Women Widen Job Rights." *Monthly Labor Review* 97 (August 1974): 87.

"Developments in Industrial Relations: Age Bias Award Totals $750,000." *Monthly Labor Review* 98 (April 1975): 79.

"Developments in Industrial Relations: U.S. Delays Bias Decision on Layoffs." *Monthly Labor Review* 98 (June 1975): 64.

"Developments in Industrial Relations: AT&T Backpay Award Increased." *Monthly Labor Review* 98 (July 1975): 59.

"Developments in Industrial Relations: Seniority Systems Upheld." *Monthly Labor Review* 98 (September 1975): 64–65.

"Developments in Industrial Relations: Minorities a Majority of New U.S. Hires." *Monthly Labor Review* 98 (August 1975): 50.

Equal Employment Opportunity Commission (EEOC). *Eighth Annual Report*. Washington, D.C.: U.S. Government Printing Office, 1975.

Fox, Alan. *Earnings Replacement from Social Security and Private Pensions: Newly Entitled Beneficiaries, 1970*. U.S. Department of Health, Education, and Welfare, Social Security Administration, Report No. 13. Washington, D.C.: U.S. Government Printing Office, 1974.

Fuchs, Victor R. "Women's Earnings: Recent Trends and Long-Run Prospects." *Monthly Labor Review* 97 (May 1974): 23–26.

General Accounting Office. *The Equal Employment Opportunity Program for Federal Nonconstruction Contractors Can be Improved*. Report for the Subcommittee on Fiscal Policy of the Joint Economic Committee, Congress of the United States. Washington, D.C.: U.S. Government Printing Office, 1975. (a)

General Accounting Office. *More Assurances Needed that Colleges and Universities with Government Contracts Provide Equal Employment Opportunity: Departments of Labor and Health, Education, and Welfare*. Washington, D.C.: U.S. Government Printing Office, 1975. (b)

General Accounting Office. *National Aeronautics and Space Administration's Equal Employment Opportunity Program Could be Improved*. Report to the Committee on Labor and Public Welfare, U.S. Senate. Washington, D.C.: U.S. Government Printing Office, 1975. (c)

Gottlieb, David. *Youth and the Meaning of Work*. U.S. Department of Labor, Manpower Research Monograph No. 32. Washington, D.C.: U.S. Government Printing Office, 1974.

Hammerman, Herbert. "Minority Workers in Construction Referral Unions." *Monthly Labor Review* 95 (May 1972): 17–26.

Hammerman, Herbert. "Minorities in Construction Referral Unions—Revisited." *Monthly Labor Review* 96 (May 1973): 43–46.

Hayghe, Howard. "Job Tenure of Workers, January 1973." *Monthly Labor Review* 97 (December 1974): 53–57.

Hedges, Janice Neipert, & Stephen E. Bemis. "Sex Stereotyping: Its Decline in Skilled Trades." *Monthly Labor Review* 97 (May 1974): 14–22.

Henle, Peter, & Raymond Schmitt. "Pension Reform: The Long, Hard Road to Enactment." *Monthly Labor Review* 97 (November 1974): 3–12.

Lundquist, Clarence T. "The Age Discrimination in Employment Act." *Monthly Labor Review* 91 (May 1968): 48–50.

Lyle, Jerolyn R. "Factors Affecting the Job Status of Workers with Spanish Surnames." *Monthly Labor Review* 96 (May 1973): 14–22.

Maeroff, Gene I. "Program to Spur College Hiring of Women and Minority Teachers Lags amid Continuing Controversy." *The New York Times*, December 28, 1975, Sec. L, p. 23.

Matera, Vincent L. "Consent Decree on Seniority in the Steel Industry." *Monthly Labor Review* 98 (March 1975): 43–46.

Parrish, John B. "Women in Professional Training." *Monthly Labor Review* 97 (May 1974): 41–43.

Project on the Status and Education of Women. *Summary of the Regulation for Title IX Education Amendments of 1972.* Washington, D.C.: Association of American Colleges, 1975.

Quinn, Robert P., & Linda J. Shepard. *The 1972–73 Quality of Employment Survey.* Report to the Employment Standards Administration, U.S. Department of Labor. Ann Arbor: University of Michigan, Institute for Social Research, 1974.

Ryscavage, Paul M., & Earl F. Mellor. "The Economic Situation of Spanish Americans." *Monthly Labor Review* 96 (April 1973): 3–9.

"Significant Decisions in Labor Cases: 'Measure the Person for the Job.'" *Monthly Labor Review* 94 (June 1971): 79–80.

"Significant Decisions in Labor Cases: The 'Philadelphia Plan' Is Valid." *Monthly Labor Review* 94 (September 1971): 64–66.

"Significant Decisions in Labor Cases: The Price of Racial Discrimination." *Monthly Labor Review* 94 (September 1971): 66–67.

"Significant Decisions in Labor Cases: Sex in Job Advertisements." *Monthly Labor Review* 96 (September 1973): 81–83.

"Significant Decisions in Labor Cases: A Stiff Price for Racial Bias." *Monthly Labor Review* 97 (April 1974): 75–76.

"Significant Decisions in Labor Cases: Pregnancy—A Disability?" *Monthly Labor Review* 97 (May 1974): 76–77.

"Significant Decisions in Labor Cases: Pregnancy and Disability Benefits." *Monthly Labor Review* 97 (October 1974): 69–71.

"Significant Decisions in Labor Cases: Affirmative Action and Layoffs." *Monthly Labor Review* 98 (February 1975): 77–78.

"Significant Decisions in Labor Cases: Pregnancy Leave under Title VII." *Monthly Labor Review*, 98 (February 1975): 78–79.

"Significant Decisions in Labor Cases: Federal Workers under Modified Title VII." *Monthly Labor Review*, 98 (March 1975): 66–67.

"Significant Decisions in Labor Cases: 'Good Faith' Discrimination and Backpay." *Monthly Labor Review* 98 (October 1975): 57–58.

"Significant Decisions in Labor Cases: Crime and Size as Bars to Employment." *Monthly Labor Review* 98 (October 1975): 58–59.

"Significant Decisions in Labor Cases: Due Process and Pregnancies." *Monthly Labor Review* 99 (January 1976): 64–65.

Sommers, Dixie. "Occupational Rankings for Men and Women by Earnings." *Monthly Labor Review* 97 (August 1974): 34–51.

Staines, Graham L., Robert P. Quinn, & Linda J. Shepard. "Trends in Occupational Sex Discrimination: 1969–1973." *Industrial Relations* 15 (February 1976): 88–98.

U.S. Bureau of the Census. "Persons of Spanish Origin in the United States: March 1974." *Current Population Reports*, Series P–20, No. 280. Washington, D.C.: U.S. Government Printing Office, 1975.

U.S. Commission on Civil Rights. *The Federal Civil Rights Enforcement Effort— 1974*, Vol. 1, *To Regulate in the Public Interest*. Washington, D.C.: U.S. Government Printing Office, 1974.

U.S. Commission on Civil Rights. *The Federal Civil Rights Enforcement Effort— 1974*, Vol. 5, *To Eliminate Employment Discrimination*. Washington, D.C.: U.S. Government Printing Office, 1975.

U.S. Congress, Joint Economic Committee. *Examination of the Economic Situation and Outlook*. Hearings, July 29, 30, and August 1, 2, 6, and 14. Washington, D.C.: U.S. Government Printing Office, 1974.

U.S. Congress, Senate. *Age Discrimination in Employment*. Hearings before the Subcommittee on Labor of the Committee on Labor and Public Welfare, March 15–17, 1967. Washington, D.C.: U.S. Government Printing Office, 1967.

U.S. Department of Labor. *Dual Careers*. Manpower Research Monograph No. 21. Washington, D.C.: U.S. Government Printing Office, 1970.

U.S. Department of Labor. *Coverage and Vesting of Full-Time Employees under Private Retirement Plans*. Bureau of Labor Statistics, Report No. 423. Washington, D.C.: U.S. Government Printing Office, 1973.

U.S. Department of Labor. *Manpower Report of the President, 1975*. Washington, D.C.: U.S. Government Printing Office, 1975.

Watkins, Beverly T. "Graduate Schools Unfair to Chicanos?" *Chronicle of Higher Education* 9 (December 16, 1974): 1.

Watkins, Beverly T. "Mexican-Americans Assail Barriers." *Chronicle of Higher Education* 10 (October 20, 1975): 7.

Yankelovich, Daniel. *The New Morality: A Profile of American Youth in the '70's*. New York: McGraw-Hill Book Co., 1974.

CHAPTER 9

Some reflections upon work and the work ethic in contemporary America

Sidney M. Willhelm

> . . . it is the experience of being powerless
> against men, not against nature, that generates
> the most desperate embitterment against existence.
> —*Friedrich W. Nietzsche*

There's trouble in the land of paradise. In the midst of plenty is the squalor of many. Never in all of history has there been a people so competent and willing to produce the bountifulness of blissful wealth as we Americans, yet more of us are becoming less involved in productive employment with the passing of each decade. Further, dissent and turmoil run rampant in an economy of unparalleled prosperity. Charles Dickens's introductory passage in *A Tale of Two Cities* conveys, in terms equal to the fervor of his day, the paradox of human plight in our own moment of affluence:

It was the best of times, it was the worst of times, it was the age of wisdom, it was the age of foolishness. . . . it was the season of light, it was the season of darkness, it was the spring of hope, it was the winter of despair, we had everything before us, we had nothing before us.

The calamities of a Golden Era are upon us. In the words of Charles R. Bowen (1966):

America is the richest nation in the history of mankind, and yet one-fifth of us live in poverty. We have a surplus of labor, capital and in the production ability of both our farms and factories, and yet we have vast unmet needs in our slums and depressed areas, in medical care, educational facilities, and in urban transportation. (p. 71)

The wealth we Americans generate is apparent in the astronomical expansion of our gross national product (GNP). Between 1944 and 1956, the U.S. GNP increased $100 billion, to $453 billion in 1957; between 1957 and 1969, it not only expanded, but the rate of increase was so rapid that, in constant dollars, it amounted to $728 billion in 1969—almost a threefold expansion over 1957. During the sixties, the GNP passed the trillion-dollar mark, and, for the years 1970–80, it is expected to exceed the 1969 figure by at least $500 billion, should the present rate of growth persist (Dale, 1971: 163). The recent magnitude of this wealth is difficult to comprehend when one considers that "the real output of goods and services in the United States has grown as much *since* 1950 as it grew in the *entire period* from the landing of the Pilgrims in 1620 up to 1950" (Dale, 1971: 163, emphasis added.). What Americans have produced since 1950 took 330 years for all previous generations to achieve! In 1970, the GNP for the world amounted to $3 trillion; to match the American living standard, the world's GNP would have to be $18 trillion (Polk, 1972: 9). Although comprising only 6% of the world's people, Americans consume about 50% of the world's production of goods; "we consume 12 times as much electricity, 50 times as much steel, 22 times as much coal, and 21 times as much oil as the rest of the world *combined*" (Chasteen, 1972: 5; emphasis supplied).

In spite of this conspicuous material luxury, the political system displays a degree of instability unknown since the revolutionary spirit of '76 and the bitterness of the Civil War era. John F. Kennedy, elected in 1960, was assassinated in 1963. Elected in 1964 by the largest plurality of voters in the nation's history, Lyndon B. Johnson abandoned all thoughts of seeking reelection in 1968. The wounding of Governor George Wallace eliminated all doubts about electing Richard M. Nixon and Spiro Agnew in 1972, but by 1973 Agnew had vanished, propelled out of the Vice-Presidency without so much as a slight rumor beforehand. In 1973, Gerald Ford was appointed Vice-President by then President Nixon, but by 1974 Ford had replaced his appointer, as President of the United States. In 1974, Nelson Rockefeller was appointed Vice-President by President Ford, but by November 1975, under severe political pressure from Ford's White House confidants, he had publicly removed himself as a potential Vice-Presidental nominee on the Republican ticket for the 1976 election, and, during 1975, several serious attempts were made to assassinate President Ford. If the fifties, as commonly labeled, were the "silent decade," the sixties and seventies could be said to have burst forth as the "explosive decades."

NEW KNOWLEDGE

> We have more information and less understanding
> than at any time in history.
> —*Robert Hutchins*

Robert Oppenheimer (cited by Perkins, 1962: 2), observed in 1959 that 9 of every 10 persons who had made a major scientific discovery still lived. Two thirds of the world's scientific knowledge has come forth since 1945; the pace is so rapid that "if the rate of progress which has been maintained ever since the time of Sir Isaac Newton continued for another 200 years, every man, woman and child on earth would be a scientist, and so would every horse, cow, dog and mule as well" (Bowden, 1967: 17). It is estimated that all Europe produced only 1,000 new book titles each year before 1500; at this pace, it would take an entire century to accumulate a 100,000-volume library consisting of newly published works. Four and a half centuries later, in 1950, Europe turned out 120,000 new titles *each* year, and by the midsixties the world output had reached 1,000 titles *per day* (Toffler, 1970: 30–31). In 1971, the United States published 25,526 new books (Pace, 1972: 30). During the course of a year, the U.S. government produces 3,000,000 reports and 450,000 articles, books, and papers; 60,000,000 pages of scientific and technical writings appear each year (Toffler, 1970: 31).

In science, 200 years elapsed between the discovery of the 11th and 12th chemical elements, yet after 1900 the rate accelerated so that one element was discovered every three years (Toffler, 1970: 31). In transportation, the camel caravan, the fastest means for transportation over long distance in 6000 B.C., averaged eight miles an hour—a record that remained unbroken until 3000 B.C., when the chariot mustered 20 mph. The first mail coach, established in England during 1784, averaged only 10 mph; the first steam locomotive reached 13 mph in 1825 and did not exceed 100 mph until the 1880s. Although centuries elapsed before the 100-mph record, it would be a mere 50 years later, in 1931, that airborne flights would exceed 400 mph (Toffler, 1970: 26). Just two decades later the pace had doubled, and by the 1960s rocket planes approximated 4,000 mph; in September 1974, the Air Force SR-ul "Blackbird" flew 33 miles a minute—three times the speed of sound and faster than the earth travels about the sun, so that it spanned the 5,645 miles between London and Los Angeles in 3 hours and 47 minutes. Space capsules circled the earth in the 1960s at 18,000 mph; by November 1973, the Pioneer–10 space craft zoomed millions of miles from the earth at a speed of 36,200 mph—10 miles per second! Prior to World War I, the average person throughout the world walked 1,300 miles each year; Americans walked 1,300 miles and rode another 350 by train, horse, or ship. In 1919, the typical American went 1,600 miles by mechanical vehicles; by the start of World War II, 4,000 miles; and, during the sixties, 9,000 miles by this means (Fuller, 1972: 24–25).

During the fifties, the Astro Division of Marquardt Corporation developed a memory device capable of storing *all information recorded during the past 10,000 years* (Clarke, 1960: 218). In 1972, the advanced scientific computer became available; this device could extract from its memory system 400 million words *per second* (Rensberger, 1972). A single laser beam is capable of transmitting all information being handled "by all the television stations, radio stations, teletypewriters and telephones in the world, operating at the same time" (*Current*, May 1960, p. 4). During the sixties, computers translated a foreign language into English at 2,400 words per minute; in February 1971, the Pentagon relied upon the IBM 360s to translate 52,000 words of English into Vietnamese *per minute*—in contrast to 8,325 words *per day* by human translation (*The New York Times*, March 19, 1976, p. 18).

Between 1700 and 1900, a time span of 200 years, knowledge throughout the world doubled; 50 years later it doubled again; a mere decade later, in 1960, another doubling occurred. The claim is now made that it takes only eight years to accomplish the same feat. Throughout the world, the production and application of knowledge are simultaneously generating new economic production, which in turn enhances the accumulation of tremendous wealth. "Both knowledge and the potentiality for creating wealth," the technological expert, John Diebold (1973: E13) contends, "may be more than 32 times greater than they are today by the time 1972's babies die." France, for example, expanded industrial output a mere 5% for the 29 years between 1910 and 1939; but between 1948 and 1965, a period of 17 years, its production rose in excess of 220% (Toffler, 1970: 24). Today's knowledge makes it possible for more people to live longer with higher living standards than has ever been the case in all of history.

Our sojourn on planet Earth has been a history of dark ages; we have been blind to our fate because knowledge provides the light for human destiny:

> . . . if [only] the past 50,000 years of man's existence were divided into lifetimes of approximately 62 years each, there have been about 800 such lifetimes. Of these 800, fully 650 were spent in caves. Only during the past 70 lifetimes has it been possible to communicate effectively from one lifetime to another—as writing made it possible to do so. Only during the past six lifetimes have masses of men ever seen a printed word. Only during the past four has it been possible to measure time with any precision. Only in the past two has anyone anywhere used an electric motor. And the overwhelming majority of all the material goods we use in daily life today have been developed within the present, the 800th, lifetime. (Toffler, 1970: 14)

In the void of darkness a people—and the person—endure a life of prolonged poverty. This is true in our own era, a moment in time when wealth is predicated upon knowledge applied to technology. Thus, to control technology is to control wealth; to control wealth is to control people and to determine the intensity of the human struggle to survive the rampancy of natural circumstances. Income inequality "creates," as Gabriel Kolko (1962: 111) says, "a visible class structure that determines the immediate existence as well as the longer-range life opportunities of each income class—from tonight's supper to the school a child will, or will not, attend."

People remain in the grips of nature's domain to the extent that knowledge remains unattainable. And what is so vital to the human condition in the modern world is that the knowledge of living flourishes, yet the disparity between the haves and the have-nots looms larger with the passing of each decade. Whereas knowledge previously generated wealth, today wealth is essential to take knowledge, through education, to the masses of uneducated people. Women, for example, are oppressed in part because, in increasing numbers, they are kept in a state of ignorance in a world that is increasingly better educated. According to a survey report by the United Nation's Education, Scientific and Cultural Organization (see Pace, 1975), 58% of the world's 426 million adult illiterates were women in 1960, a figure that climbed to 60% of 470 million for 1970, and 62% of 800 million in 1974.

Oppression flourishes because the extension of economic resources for the acquisition of knowledge is suppressed. In Venezuela, 12% of the nation's families own 50% of the GNP; in Colombia, 41% of the income goes to 5% of the population; one thousand persons take in 78% of the capital and thereby gain 90% of the GNP in Argentina; a mere handful of men—50 in number—control 69% of Guatemala's wealth and account for 66% of the GNP; and 12 Hondurans own 90% of the capital, to gain 90% of the national income (Williams, 1964: 68). Of the world's people, 70% have no more than 65 cents income a day, and their lack of technological development is self-evident in that they consume only 8% of the world's energy. By contrast, 30% average $8.21 per day, while absorbing 92% of the world's energy (Sterba, 1973). Wealth begets wealth: "The average income per head in 1970 in the nonindustrialised countries rose during the 1960's by about 40 dollars; in the industrialised countries by 650 dollars. By 1980 it has been estimated that the rise will be 100 dollars and 1,200 dollars respectively" (Omo-Fadaka, 1973: 6). The potential for political turmoil accelerates as greater wealth goes to the already rich nations, while the poor struggle to survive with meager funds.

CHRISTIAN THEOLOGY AND HUMAN LABOR

> In the sweat of thy face shalt thou eat bread.
> —*The Bible*

The Biblical account of Adam and Eve in the Garden of No Need conveys a theological foundation upon which the meaning of work might be constructed. The configuration informs us not only of the origin of human labor as a consequence of original sin, but also of the human's relation both to God and to nature, the basis of that relationship, and the quality of life under optimum economic conditions wherein life's needs are fulfilled without human effort.

No economic concerns beset Adam and Eve in the Garden, since there was no reason to grapple with questions of who got what, when, and how in the midst of plenty. That pair of human beings remained unblemished by the struggle to survive, and they held dominion over the earth and all living creatures. Superior to all—both Nature and human nature—was the Almighty; God ruled over all the universe. In spite of an abundance of material comfort, *domination* prevailed, and a definite power hierarchy existed: God, human beings, and Nature.

Just as apparent is the fact of uncertainty; the political system was highly problematic. Trouble in the Godly paradise developed along political lines when Adam and Eve violated God's command not to eat of the fruit of knowledge about good and evil. Human discretion to disobey testifies to the presence of an unstable hierarchy under the very best of economic conditions. A total acceptance of subordination to God's order meant human beings could thrive by commanding, in turn, all living creatures and consuming without hindrance from the Garden. To assure human compliance, God warned Adam and Eve of a frightful result—namely, death—should there be any disobedience by eating the forbidden fruit. Thus God could command but did not mandate human consent, and the human relation to God, and hence to Nature, could not be taken for granted but rested instead upon the force of authority. God relied upon the negative sanction of death to gain human subordination and the positive reward of paradise for conformity to the command. However—and significantly—God offered no justification to his human pair for his dominance and no explanation to justify his command not to devour the unauthorized fruit. God ruled by his sole possession of wisdom; by his knowledge of good and evil he held sway over the universe, and by *monopolizing* the wisdom of right and wrong, God sustained his distinctiveness from the human beings He created. If Adam and Eve were to partake of the forbidden fruit they would be transformed from mere images of God into gods themselves: "For God doth know," the serpent revealed to Eve, "that in the day ye eat thereof, then your eyes shall be opened, and ye shall be as gods, knowing good and evil" (Genesis 3:5).

The Garden of Eden thus provided optimum economic conditions where political strife flourished due to the presence of a hierarchy founded upon sheer domination. The economy of abundance did not generate political dissension but was rather the *reward* for human beings willing to accept, without justification, subordination to God's wisdom of knowing of good and evil. By eating of the forbidden fruit, Adam and Eve immediately became self-conscious and realized their biological differences and "they sewed fig leaves together" to hide the fact from themselves since "the eyes of them both were opened, and they knew that they were naked" (Genesis 3:7). Although God promised death for the disobedience, the actual penalty for gaining the knowledge only God once possessed was banishment from the Garden. By willfully partaking of God's privileged access to wisdom, human beings were compelled to take on God's responsibility of providing the necessities for life. No longer would human beings have full access to provisions without effort; the expulsion from Paradise meant the necessity for human labor, as well as the wisdom of knowing good and evil.

The Fall from Grace meant not only a paradise lost but a radical transformation of the political system. Economic pursuits supplanted political strife; work became mandatory, and, as a result, human beings entered into a struggle against Nature. Instead of ruling over Nature, humans became subject to it. In being forced to forsake the Garden, humans were relegated to a position below Nature and, as further punishment, woman was placed directly under the control of man. "Thy desire," God (Genesis 3:16) said unto woman, "shall be thy husband, and he shall rule over thee." In the stead of a strict political hierarchal system of God, human beings, and Nature came an entirely new arrangement: God, Nature, man, and woman. The animal kingdom would no longer be under the automatic control of humans; wild animals would have to be domesticated or destroyed. Nature's wilderness must be tamed by converting natural soil into cultivated gardens that would, hopefully, be as bountiful as the original Garden, albeit as the fruit of human labor. Just as God Himself labored intensely for six days to create Nature before resting on the seventh, so must human beings work diligently to revamp Nature under full human control to obtain the bliss of rest from Nature's spite and wrath.

With the faculty to establish right and wrong, Christians came to know the measure of the person in terms of labor; they transformed a sinful necessity—human labor—into a divine virtue. The 16th-century Calvinists drew heavily upon the Fall from Grace to construct their religious notions of human toil:

> The Calvinist conception of life and afterlife revealed a God who ruled the universe arbitrarily and without counsel or advice, or subjection to the pleas of those over whom he exercised his majestic authority. Calvinists responded to this not by resignation, suicide, or hedonism, but rather by an intensive search for signs of their election or damnation, signs of that over which they had no control whatsoever (Lyman & Scott, 1970: 17).

The accumulation of worldly goods through hard, industrious, diligent work became the sign of Godly approval. This Puritan ethic is the mainstay for *personal* integrity in keeping with God's approval; it becomes not only a badge of salvation but constructs the very character for a Godly life during the person's sojourn on earth. The individual's own moral progress is achieved by a deep devotion to gaining a livelihood and, by appropriate labor, to taming Nature as a source of sustenance; diligent labor to gain ascendancy over Nature extends the opportunity to gain human perfection. Thomas Jefferson articulated the Puritan work creed when setting forth, in his *Notes on Virginia*, the view that "those who *labor in the earth* are the *chosen* people of God, if ever he had a chosen people, whose breasts he has made his peculiar deposit for substantial and genuine virtue."

As people learned more about physical and biological processes, they reflected more upon the human fate in an ordered universe. Isaac Newton uncovered Nature's secrets of motion; Carolus Linnaeus, in the 1730s, sealed human beings *into* the animal kingdom by his catalog of organisms, and, about a century later, Charles Darwin announced the very origin of species through descent in accord with the principle of natural selection based upon adaptation to survive in the struggle for existence. The subordination of people to Nature is apparent in the *Commentaries* (1765–69) of Sir William Blackstone:

> This law of nature being coeval with mankind, and dictated by God himself, is of course superior in obligation to any other. It is binding over all the globe, in all countries and at all times: no human laws are of any validity, if contrary to this; and such of them as are valid derive all their forces and all their authority, mediately or immediately, from this original.

By 1775 Alexander Hamilton was proclaiming that "Good and wise men, in all ages . . . have supposed that the Deity, from the relations we stand in to Himself, and to each other, has constituted an eternal and immutable law, which is indispensably obligatory upon all mankind, prior to any human institution whatever. . . . " The Laws of Nature remained paramount over all people, in all ages, and in perfect accord with God himself; as the Puritan theologian John Preston preached, "God alters no law of Nature."

With insignificant technological development, the accumulation of wealth in America rested upon tilling the soil; production depended upon intense human labor to clear and work the virgin land, with limited reliance upon tools. In the era of preindustrial technology, success in earning a livelihood resulted from hard labor, beneficial weather conditions, and heaven's blessings. Under these circumstances God and Nature remain dominant over the ability of human beings to attain security. Human beings could demonstrate personal character by persistent labor, but ultimate success was contingent upon favorable natural conditions and a God to whom human beings might appeal for assurance to provide favorable farming weather.

During the 19th century dramatic advances were made in technological developments. The Industrial Revolution, a form of technology that substituted inanimate sources of energy in the stead of human energy, took hold in

America. Massive tooling systems drawing upon such technologically generated fuels as electricity, oil, steam, and coal (and, eventually, atomic power) replaced human muscles. Individual initiative, motivated by the Puritan ethic, could no longer be the central human effort in the act of production; rather, the social organization of work came to the fore. The assembly line of factory production, by *organizing* people whose contributions to productivity were contingent upon coordination of social activity in accord with the pace *set by machine operations*, epitomizes the industrial accomplishment in technological development. Under the preindustrial technology of farming, the pace of work was accommodated to *natural* rhythms—especially the seasons of the year and the natural light of day; hard, industrious, and faithful effort by the *individual* yielded not only dividends of wealth but the personal character and Heavenly approval which validated the Puritan ethic. Under industrial technology the tempo of life shifts from a natural base and into the social arena; productivity grows free of the seasons and the moments of daylight, since the physical qualities of nature recede when soil cultivation is abandoned in favor of technological inventions of human ingenuity.

Muscular work became the work of machines. This transfer, obviously, impairs the validity of work per se. How can human labor be exalted when machines do so much of the work? Human toil can no longer be highly prized with the onslaught of technology; rather, *productivity* of mass machine production becomes paramount. The measure of *worth* likewise shifts, from the industrious and energetic *individual* to the *efficiency* of the *equipment*. First expounded by some businessmen, the notion of efficiency was picked up during the 1880s by scientific and engineering journals; it was adapted and made famous by Frederick W. Taylor to fit *managerial* expectations, and the Harvard Business School, under the direction of Elton Mayo, rationalized the 20th-century American political economy under corporate control. The locus of rationality itself shifted from a human quality possessed by the person to a feature attributed to the *social organization* of work (i.e., the bureaucracy), as production shifted from preindustrial to industrial technology. Work was treated as the rational quality in production, not the individual. Alexander Hamilton, expressing the belief of his era, maintained that "He [i.e., God] endowed him [i.e., human beings] with rational faculties, by the help of which to discern and pursue such things as were consistent with his duty and interest; and invested him [i.e., human beings] with an inviolable right to personal liberty and personal safety." Freedom came from individuals' exercising rational thought, as intended by the Supreme Being. C. Wright Mills (1951) would observe, almost two centuries after Hamilton, that "Now rationality seems to have taken on a new form, to have its seat not in individual men, but in social institutions which by their bureaucratic planning and mathematical foresight usurp both freedom and rationality from the little individual men caught in them" (p. xvii). In short, all the human virtuous attributes—righteousness of work, rationality, personal character, Godly sanctity, the tempo of life—were either reallocated to machines and/or to the social organization of production or were abandoned entirely, while the individual gained nothing in the exchange. In fact, he or she became more machinelike, in that behavior on the job is expected to be as mechanical as the mechanized production in order to fulfill the *social*—and not the Godly—mandate demanding efficiency.

The technological displacement of the human endeavor to work for a living while living to work destroyed not only the agricultural economy but also all previous universals by which human conduct could be validated. With the appearance of industrialization the redemptive quality of work vanished, and with it the basis for human salvation founded upon Puritan theology. Furthermore, *Nature* was converted into *nature* as mechanical inventiveness remolded natural ingredients into goods for human consumption; economic production expanded by *applying*, rather than *abiding by*, the Laws of Nature. As earth became a composite of objects subject to transformation by technological know-how, drawing upon scientific understandings of natural phenomena, human destiny no longer yielded to the immutables of Nature, since industrial technology could be invoked to command Nature. And as humans seized control over Nature, God could not long remain in his exalted position, since there could be neither a naturalistic creed nor a religious faith affirming economic productivity specifically and human existence in general. The owners of technology accumulated vast sums of wealth not by the will of God or in accord with the Laws of Nature, but rather by the expropriation of nature. Laborers moved off the land, with its social life of the landed gentry, and into the city, to become employees in factories headed initially by captains of industry bent upon extracting fortunes not from "labor in the earth," as Jefferson proclaimed, but labor per se, and later by huge corporate conglomerates. Consequently, as Richard Henry Dana prophetically observed in 1853, "The whole modern system seems to me to be grounded on a false view of man . . . as acknowledging no God, nor the need of any. . . . There is a spirit of self-confidence in it, which, left to its natural tendencies, will inevitably bring a deeper and wider woe upon man than earth has ever yet known." The transcendental qualities that sanctified human dignity while enduring the calamities of Nature and a subordination to God's command have no relevancy upon the appearance of industrial technology. Their decimation invites feelings of futility, a sense of powerlessness, and a wanton disregard for the future. As Mills (1951) contended during the fifties:

> The uneasiness, the malaise of our time is due to this root fact: in our politics
> and economy, in family life and religion—in practically every sphere of our

existence—the certainties of the eighteenth and nineteenth centuries have disintegrated or been destroyed and, at the same time, no new sanctions or justifications for the new routines we live, and must live, have taken hold. So there is no acceptance and there is no rejection, no sweeping hope and no sweeping rebellion. There is no plan of life. (p. xvi)

The momentum of technological development has, by no means, ceased; rather, as noted above, it has accelerated. During the 1950s an entirely new technological configuration came into existence—automation, with its unique computerized feedback principle. The novelty of automation stems from the ability to design technology into a reciprocal relationship with the product being produced; electronic computers monitor and retrieve information during the process of production and thereupon instruct the equipment doing the work. By contrast, the industrial machinery operates in terms of built-in mechanical features with fixed, predetermined movements, so that it is operating independent of the substance it is processing. Computerized technology eliminates the decision-making process of machine handling which previously had been performed by the human operator. Just as industrial technology dislodges human energy, postindustrial technology, as automation is sometimes called, displaces reliance upon the mental faculties of human beings; the former dispenses with human muscles, the latter disposes of human thoughts. The feedback principle disengages human beings from the process by engaging what is being produced during the very process of production.

Automation enters as a truly revolutionary force. During the preindustrial era of American society, work was highly prized and considered so significant as to certify Godly approval. The Industrial Revolution transferred labor to the machine and created social organizations of work; the postindustrial technology eradicates not only labor but the worker as well. With automatic production there is no relevance for the work ethic but rather a conspicuous anxiety whenever someone does work; in the automated plant, manifestation of human effort can be a sure sign of trouble. Operators of automated production work only when something goes wrong; they are *activated* only when disruption develops, and, therefore, to see someone working is to know that production—not the person—is not working properly. Human work, therefore, is a response to chaos presented upon the breakdown of automatic equipment. Foremen no longer are hatchetmen "laying the law down" to get more work out of employees; in overseeing employees responsible for automatic productivity, the supervisor is elated to enter a work station and find no one is working. Work, rather than expressing Heavenly approval, becomes the equivalent of "sin," a waywardness in the productivity of machine production.

The foremost problem with labor today is people rather than getting work out of people. "The biggest trouble with industry," says a former president of International Harvester, "is that it is full of human beings" (see Bazelon, 1965: 315). Under preindustrial technology, work is a virtuous attribute of the person; under industrialization, work is coordinated with machines that set the pace and measure of productivity; under postindustrial technology, work is contemptuous, production purely technological, and opportunity for employment resides in the discretion of corporate executives rather than the initiative of individual employees.

Individual initiative and person striving to achieve greater economic rewards cannot withstand the efficiency of automatic equipment in an economy dominated by corporate conglomerates. As noted above, business leaders now lament the fact that industry is "full of people." With technological displacement motivated by management's efficiency, an employee's work ethic cannot possibly remain vital; the intent to eliminate workers in light of increasing technological sophistication takes priority over any person's desire to work. For the private economy, it is the managerial values that are the crucial incentives to set the pace of work opportunities, not the workers' values. And it is management, not employees, that holds and expresses great contempt toward human labor; productive initiative rests with the organizational abilities that management can muster to invest capital into automation. "Productivity," explains Henry Ford, chairman of the Ford Motor Company, "is a responsibility of management . . . . We can't blame lower productivity on the union or the workers. We've got to blame it on ourselves in the industry and our company. We're highly automated, and to increase productivity, we need additional capital" (quoted in Kelly, 1976: C–4).

In a speech before the Economic Club of New York in November 1975, Thomas A. Murphy, chairman of General Motors, urged American managers to resist vigorously labor demands for wage increases in excess of productivity gains. Regarding labor agreements made during 1974, he maintained that

> The historical test will be whether these agreements make even further commitments to cost without commensurate provisions for productivity improvement. If they do, history may read these agreements as fateful mortgages upon our economic future, because more cost without more productivity will only weaken America's [competitive] position in the world. We will risk a situation where American products will be priced out of the markets of the world, including our own domestic market. (Reuters News Service, 1975, p. 55)

But it is anachronistic to consider wage earners either as a major cost factor or as an impediment to competitive necessities of the market. It is not labor but technology that generates surplus wealth. For example, America's farm products, traditionally one of the most labor-intensive sectors of any nation's economy, are highly competitive in the world economy, in spite of the fact that world production remains highly dependent upon cheap human labor. The reasons are our technological acceleration for production, and the failure of American capital to establish its monopoly control over the agricultural market. A single American farm worker, according to a study conducted by the Department of Commerce in 1972 (see Wren, 1976), feeds 46 Americans on a very high diet, while his Soviet counterpart feeds only seven persons in the Soviet Union with a rate of consumption lower than in this country. In areas where technology is highly advanced and under oligarchical control, labor costs are not the essential ingredient in competitiveness on either the world or domestic market. The petroleum industry, for example, is an oligarchy that is highly automated; according to claims set forth by the Oil, Chemical and Atomic Workers International Union (OCAW), labor costs dwindle while executives acquire extraordinary pay increases:

> We found that oil executives got average salary raises of more than 21% last year [1973]. They got an average *increase* of more than $22 per hour. Their *raise* was almost four times *our total wages*.
>
> Despite their huge profits, the seven largest oil companies have been paying federal taxes at a rate of about five cents on the dollar. . . .
> In 1966, our average wage was $3.45 an hour. Today [1973], we get $3.27 an hour in 1966 dollars.
> Our productivity has increased 71% in the past fifteen years. But all the benefits of our increased productivity are going to the industry. They should be going to lower prices and fairer wages. (Lovel, 1974: 18)

Thus, management exhortations about wages being a major cost consideration, while the pay scale for executives leaps upward, reflect not the economics of production but a historic hostility toward labor per se, a class interest under the gloss of economic anxiety about worldwide business competition. The oil industry assured itself lower tax rates for 1973 by contributing illegal funds to sympathetic candidates during Congressional elections for 1972— thereby confirming the view (being developed here) that taxation is a political and not an economic issue.

Workers were once people who struggled against Nature to gain the necessities of life in an agricultural economy. They then entered into a commodity market of industrialization, where their labor competed against the law of supply and demand in response to market—rather than natural—conditions. With the introduction of automation, human labor competes against machines that destroy jobs for an oncoming generation and, simultaneously, the earned income so essential for purchasing goods and services and so vital for sustaining the economy of industrialization. The acceleration of production through automation means that fewer people will find employment in the private sphere of the economy. The loss of jobs means that people will not have the income for securing basic needs; a reduction in income brings a drop in demand for goods. The reduction in purchasing power brought on by unemployment—each percentage point of unemployment means a $55 billion drop in the nation's GNP (Wicker, 1976)—means that products turned out by automated plants cannot be bought. Thus surplus production and high unemployment invite economic chaos. What to do with nonproductive people in a society with a highly productive technology is the crucial issue for the people of wealth who stand at the helm of corporations geared for maximum profits.

During the fifties, mechanization spread into rural America, disrupting the traditional agricultural economy of hand labor. It supplanted the livelihoods of people engaged in subsistence farming with the social organization of corporations bent upon attaining a high rate of profit from investment in technology and not from labor. Through intensified planting, which relies heavily upon chemical fertilization, irrigation, and machinery, corporations assumed ownership of massive acreage and thereby displaced thousands of landowners and millions of farm workers. Simultaneously, production was expanded at an unprecedented rate. From 1950 to 1965, farm output increased 45%, while farm employment declined 45% (President's National Advisory Commission on Rural Poverty, as quoted in Piven & Cloward, 1971: 201). Surplus farm production (as in production generally) came to the fore, and, of course, a high rate of agricultural unemployment prevailed.

Farm mechanization took place virtually simultaneously with the appearance of automation, so that the technological displacement of the millions of rural workers could not be compensated for by employment in cities. As productivity becomes increasingly technological, people become superfluous for the making of profits. Without jobs, the work ethic becomes as meaningless to the economy as work itself; in an economy of technological production, work and working cannot be central in the lives of people. It has been claimed that Americans could, by 1990, sustain the GNP for 1970 on a 20-hour work week or choose to work 40 per week and retire at the age of 38 (*Parade*, December 27, 1970, p. 2).

The elimination of labor occurs while (as noted above) the GNP expands at record rates. According to the liberal economic theory formulated by John Maynard Keynes for assuring economic prosperity in an industrialized economy under corporate control, expanding productivity perforce means an expanding work force. Yet, automation breaks the intrinsic connection between technology and employment; more production does not expand employment opportunities. The steel industry, for example, employed 584,000 workers in turning out 131 million tons of steel in 1965; by 1971, it had completed its initial phase of automation and eliminated 65,000 workers, while keeping output at the level of 1965 (Flint, 1972). A new record in automobile sales was set in 1972—13.2 million—yet employment in the state of Michigan, where the industry is concentrated, dropped from 398,700 in late 1969 to 355,000 in 1972. General Motors is able to turn out 40% more automobiles without increasing employment over the labor needs of the conventional assembly line because of automatic equipment (Wargo, 1972). Tax manipulations, modification of interest rates, balanced and unbalanced government budgets, and other fiscal techniques in keeping with Keynesian economics cannot assure higher employment, in the light of automation and its labor-saving capacities. Measures to stimulate the economy of industrialization are inoperative for the postindustrial economy. It is not possible to lower unemployment by initiatives that update production which functions most efficiently by eradicating jobs.

CAPITAL AND STATE*

> All things have their place,
> knew we how to place them.
> —*G. Herbert*

The emergence of new technologies for production over the past century has meant not only new concepts of prosperity but also new expectations with respect to government itself. The dictum of laissez-faire capitalism flourished as the doctrine for business success when private entrepreneurs ruled the nation. The ideology called upon the market of supply and demand to generate economic pursuits; thus investment and production rested upon individuals willing to take substantial economic risks in the quest for wealth. As each individual sought personal gains by responding to consumer demands in a market uninhibited by government intervention, this philosophy maintained, the general welfare for all people would best be served. The public welfare, therefore, emerged as a consequence of individuals risking their own money in business enterprises. State involvement was not only unwarranted but highly suspect, since the open market provided all the economic requirements for assuring the most favorable opportunities for the economic growth so essential to attract investments in productive businesses. The conditions of work could not be entrusted to labor, and, in any case, as George F. Baer, who represented Wall Street interests at the turn of the century, noted, "The rights and interests of the laboring man will be protected and cared for—not by labor agitators, but by the Christian men to whom God in His infinite wisdom has given the control of the property interests in this country" (quoted in Bazelon, 1965: 10). For an agricultural economy surplus capital was scarce, and fiscal policies reflected this fact by stressing the necessity to adhere to an economic doctrine

---

* Capital and State are considered in this chapter as personifications and are therefore capitalized.

highly favorable for private investment in production and control over labor. The economics of laissez-faire for industrialization endorsed the work ethic which flourished when labor worked the earth; the employee was expected to display a complete willingness to work constantly during a 12-hour day, 6-day work week.

In sum, the doctrine of laissez-faire articulates a form of economic prosperity dependent upon the maximization of individual initiative in seeking greater economic gains by investment in property for production. Production necessitates the employment of people with a commitment to work without collective demands through union representation; labor receives its just reward through wages set by the owners of property. These wages, in turn, generate the income to purchase the goods of production, and consumption in terms of personal income establishes each person's living standard.

Toward the end of the 19th and into the 20th century, economic chaos interrupted the economic prosperity that laissez-faire was supposedly to achieve. Recession and depression marred all prospects, not only for keeping the economy on an even keel but also for assuring social tranquility. The economic pressures to keep wages as low as possible generated discontent and restrained the consumption essential for keeping production moving. The relentless thrust to maximize individual profits, regardless of the social consequences, impoverished the masses of the people, and the increasing disparity between the rich and the poor in the midst of economic uncertainty posed a danger to political stability and provided the fertile soil for seeding socialist ideologies. Business responded by turning to State to mediate economic differences between capital and labor and among businesses themselves. New legislation established regulatory bodies, such as the Interstate Commerce Commission and the Railroad Commission, and mandated rather modest reforms to improve working conditions and to allow for collective bargaining by labor unions.

Nonetheless, Capital's slight retreat from laissez-faire economics failed to bring economic stability; even though State intervention became a force within what would otherwise have been an open marketplace, the economy remained erratic throughout the first quarter of the 20th century. Finally, the acute economic disjunctures culminated in the Great Depression of the 1930s, and the huge industrial complex verged upon total collapse as many of the nation's productive enterprises ground to a halt. It was at this point that a new economic perspective took hold, since it became patently clear that economic policies geared so much to capital investment in production designed to reap profits had become obsolete. Although meeting with vigorous opposition from powerful business interests which were firmly committed to the unregulated market, the fiscal role of State nonetheless expanded, in accord with the new economics of Keynesian analysis, in order to revive profits. During the thirties, entirely new monetary policies which emphasized the stimulation of consumption as the key for rejuvenating the economy were implemented at the behest of the state. Deficit financing became, for the first time, an explicit device for generating demand for goods and services, as State spent in excess of income, became a major employer, financed a wide variety of welfare programs to assist the unemployed, and passed massive legislation which, with Constitutional endorsement through numerous Supreme Court decisions, was to regulate both business and labor.

Economic prosperity eluded the nation throughout the thirties, in spite of the new economic guidelines for replacing productive requirements with consumerism. Surplus production and high unemployment continued to impede the realization of anticipated economic growth. Full utilization of productive resources and full employment did not materialize until the advent of World War II, when *military needs* displaced *market demands* for absorbing surplus profit, surplus productivity, and surplus labor. Only by militarizing the economy under direct State control did economic prosperity reappear. The feat was accomplished, therefore, not in terms of either private capital investment or private employment but rather through the war-making powers of the state, which shifted production into meeting military technological requirements for armaments rather than fulfilling market demands, and took millions of men out of the labor force and put them into military uniforms. This sudden alteration of economic incentives from private enterprise to State control occurred at the expense of Capital. During the war years profits receded, from 7.5% of the GNP in 1941 to 3.9% in 1945; wages reached new heights upon the resumption of full employment (Baran & Sweezy, 1966: 153); and government deficits soared to finance the war effort.[1]

Although observers may realize that economic recovery finally returned because of the war, rather than because of Keynesian economics, very few acknowledge the more basic economic transformations resulting from a burgeoning State enterprise. The establishment of a permanent, massive State organization came about not to fulfill Capital's needs for profits but because of the most important technological breakthrough of the war: nuclear weaponry.[2] When nuclear technology developed within the social organization of government, State seized this source of energy as a means to perpetuate itself once World War II had ended. The Cold War era provided a rationale whereby State exerted its exclusive prerogative over nuclear energy to confront the Soviet Union, and its nuclear monopoly allowed for the emergence of a new objective, namely, "national interests." Thus, State pursued national interests, while Capital continued its advocacy for profits. What this means is that State no longer provides crucial economic services for Capital as its foremost raison d'etre; more importantly, it is organized to achieve its own interest and thereby becomes an interest group divorced from Capital. It is a configuration of power with a logic of its own and bearing its own economic imperatives independently of Capital. In short, the economics of Capital become secondary to the power needs of State as a social organization.

The establishment of State as a network of power for advancing national interests is essential to comprehend the flow of work, employment, and the work ethic. To begin with, State, as noted, is an organization of power; on the basis of economic standards, it is a *nonproductive* organization. Efficiency, the hallmark for Capital's profit, evades State. It is vain to judge State activities by traditional criteria set by Capital, since there is no marketplace for State, and national interests erase the profitability objective so crucial to Capital's success. Such State services as policing, education, foreign policies, social security, and so forth, are not susceptible to productivity measurements that have for so many generations been the standards guiding expenditures for work and the services provided to people. The Committee for Economic Development (1958: 17), one of Capital's most notable policy groups, asserts that "no satisfactory measure of output-per-man-hour of government employees can be computed. . . . " There is no compelling necessity to curtail costs within State, inasmuch as the government is immunized from economic risks in the traditional capitalistic sense of investment uncertainty. Cost overruns are commonplace both for military and civilian contracts between State and private businesses; the aerospace industry is notorious for exceeding initial cost estimates, and the building industry constantly exceeds contractual bids in constructing federal buildings.

Not only is State nonproductive, according to Capital's fiscal expectations, but also in respect to the economy in general. In most direct terms, State is a *highly destructive* organization simply because its very technological base is nonproductive. Nuclear power generates no wealth but instead, on the one hand, consumes tremendous economic resources that drain the economy of productive potential and, on the other, is the source for developing a technology of destruction—nuclear weapons—fully capable of eradicating entire societies. To date, nuclear energy remains uneconomical. Generation of electricity, the most widespread application of nondefense atomic power, far exceeds the initial cost estimates for utility companies. Each killowatt of plant capacity will skyrocket from $300 in 1972 to $1,135 by 1985, an expense well beyond the venture of profit making (see Wicker, 1975). Furthermore, the economics of production for private companies to produce electricity from nuclear fuel became feasible only through substantial financial backing provided by federal monies for research and, more importantly, for insurance guarantees in the event of a nuclear accident that could easily amount to $6 to $17 billion in damage claims (Wicker, 1975).

To sustain and expand its destructive technology, State-established economic policies give top priority to agencies within the government that flourish in keeping with the technology of destruction—the armed services, research organizations devoted to new weaponry, institutes for planning military strategies, colleges and universities willing to embrace the military effort through research, and so on. For the postwar years, 60% to 80% of the federal budget has been allocated to military specifications. This constitutes a new form of economic outlay which competes with Capital's investment in new production; by 1960, 9.2% of the nation's GNP was being allocated for military expenditures, in contrast to 5.5% invested by Capital for machinery and equipment (Melman, 1965: 69). "Profits retained by corporations and the sums set aside for capital consumption (machinery and buildings 'used up') are a measure of the fresh capital available to private U.S. management for investment," Seymour Melman (1974: 71) explains. He goes on:

> In 1939, for every dollar of this private corporate capital, the War and Navy Departments received thirty-five cents from the federal government. By 1971, for every dollar of this private corporate capital the budget of the Department of Defense alone received $1.06. That means that by 1971 the government-based managers of the U.S. military system had superceded the private firms of the American economy in control over capital. (Melman, 1974: 71)

Thus State increasingly designates capital investment, making it most difficult to uphold a private form of economy.

State's economic investments in its technology of destruction—militarized hardware—has, like Capital's investment in automated technology, nullified employment opportunities. The Public Interest Group, a Ralph Nader organization, maintained in 1974 that 20,000 civilian jobs could be created by state and local governments for every $1 billion spent by the military, and thus an $80-billion Pentagon budget brings in its wake an annual net reduction of 1,600,000 jobs (cited by Anderson, 1974a). Congressman Les Aspin maintains that while each $1 billion for defense generates 10,000 jobs, it would create 50,000 jobs for school construction, 76,000 for public housing construction, and 132,000 to provide public services. Aspin notes that 2 million additional people could be employed in public service and another 1.14 million in public housing—in contrast to the mere 160,000 jobs that a $15.7 billion increase in the 1975 military budget would produce (*Guardian*, March 19, 1975, p. 8). Thus, just as expenditures no longer nourish substantial employment opportunities among private firms which resort to postindustrial technology, so do massive economic allocations for the militarization of the economy fail to create substantial job opportunities. State's economic investment in destructive technology destroys the employment potentials that would otherwise come forth if State could break from its own national interests and seek to promote the person's living standard. No such reallocation will come, not because of Capital's vested economic interests in a militarized economy—inasmuch as the State economy destroys economic growth for Capital—but because State itself cannot flourish unless it preserves its monopoly over the technology of destruction.

While militarized technology diminishes full utilization of labor, State, as a nonproductive social organization, absorbs huge numbers of people who have been made redundant by the postindustrial corporate economy. During the fifties, private enterprise provided only one tenth of all the new jobs; the nonprofit sector of the economy (philanthropic organizations, private universities, hospitals, and so on) and governments at all levels accounted for 90% of all new employment. The nonprivate employers hired 15% of the working force in 1929; today they retain at least a third of the employed (Heilbroner, 1965: 52). The federal government employs approximately 3 million civilians; state government workers expanded from 1,057,000 in 1950 to 2,614,000 in 1969; and local government employees increased from 3,228,000 to 7,102,000 for the same time period (U.S. Department of Commerce, 1971: 91).

Furthermore, as State enlarges its nonproductive technology in militarizing the economy and Capital turns to automation for greater profits, more Americans become nonproductive, economically debilitated, and, therefore, dependent upon State welfare and legislation for sustaining incomes. In 1947, 1 of every 10 workers secured employment with government agencies at all levels; 25 years later, in 1972, 1 of every 6 nonmilitary persons was on the public payroll (Hanley, 1974). In July 1975, 31,369,000 Americans received social security benefits (Farrell, 1976). One in every seven Americans received a monthly paycheck from social security in 1975 (*Newsweek*, January 19, 1976, p. 37), and by the year 2000 another 10 million will be recipients—1 of every 6 persons (Bassett, 1975). In 1950, there were 12 employed people for each social security recipient; in 1960, the ratio dropped to 4:1; in 1974, the ratio stood at 2.5:1 (Anderson, 1974b); and by 2030, the ratio is expected to be 1:2 under existing standards (Bassett, 1975). In 1961, 7.2 million persons received welfare benefits, at a cost of $4.3 billion (*U.S. News and World Report*, August 9, 1971, p. 13); by 1972, more than 15 million were on the welfare rolls, with expenditures of $18.2 billion by all levels of government (Associated Press, 1972b). As of July 1, 1975, 59,596,052 persons—including all individuals on social security—were receiving funds from federal income-support programs at a cost of $121.9 billion (Farrell, 1976).

Moreover, millions of youths are currently removed from the work force by attending college. In the midseventies, approximately 10 million people were enrolled in the nation's colleges. Sociologist Abbott L. Ferris of Emory University reported in mid-1973 that at least 200,000 youths were simply roamers who had dropped out of employment altogether (United Press International, 1973). The magnitude of disengagement from gainful employment is all the more apparent when one realizes that as many as 35 to 45 million new jobs would have to be created, according to Albert G. Hart, professor of economics at Columbia University, if State were to pass legislation guaranteeing every adult American a legal right to employment (Wicker, 1976: 29).

In short, the postindustrial era generates an economy of uselessness; private enterprise increasingly produces goods while relying less and less upon people in light of its highly productive technology, and State, a nonproductive social organization, turns out numerous nonproductive programs in order to cope with the surplus population arising out of the displacement caused by Capital and its own militarized technology of destruction. State, due to its monopoly over nuclear technology, is a nonproductive organization for warfare on the one hand and, on the other, a nonproductive organization in market terms and in providing welfare to cope with surplus people. Under these circumstances, economic costs shift from a private concern into a public issue associated with budgetary policies expounded by State. While cost has always been a measure of labor, today, in an emerging State economy, it is more visible as a political issue that is to be resolved, for the most part, through administrative units such as the powerful Office of Management and Budget under the direct control of the White House. Cost, in other words, is no longer confined to labor in relation to technological production for maximizing private profits but is also the expense of financing the social organization of State rule. Whereas productivity itself once prevailed strictly in terms of human energy under preindustrial technology, that energy was transformed into technological efficiency under both industrial and postindustrial technology, and today it is simply no longer viable to the State economy. The expansion of the warfare-welfare State brings in its wake ever-increasing outlays of State expenditures for a greater number and variety of intents, such that, according to James O'Connor, "The evolution of the state budget as a crucial factor in [the] economic life [of the nation] has gone hand in hand with the development of a permanent state bureaucracy" (1973: 72).

Federal expenditures amount to one third of the nation's GNP. While many businesses accrue huge profits from contracts with the State, especially the defense industries, Capital, of course, intends to avoid taxation. The upper-income groups also exert tremendous pressure to have lower-income families pay for government expenses (see Stern, 1962). Wealth is becoming more concentrated, and corporations pay less into the federal coffers. A study conducted by the Congressional Joint Committee on Internal Revenue Taxation of America's 102 largest corporations reports a downward trend in federal taxes. It also found that the smaller corporations paid more than the larger ones (Liberation News Service, 1975: 4). Corporate tax payments to the federal Treasury dropped from 33.6% of corporate income in 1944 to 14.6% by 1974 (Sipser, 1975: 31); corporate tax, as a percent of all federal receipts, declined from 22.7% in 1967 to 14.6% during 1974, while, for the same time period, individual income and social security taxes, as a percentage of federal receipts, climbed from 63.4% to 76.5% (Liberation News Service, 1975: 4). Under President Ford's proposed budget for fiscal 1976, the percentage for corporations was to drop another 1.6%, i.e., to 13%.

A highly regressive tax has been placed upon earnings to finance the billions of dollars distributed under Social Security, so that those in the higher-income brackets pay substantially less relative to their annual salary than do lower-income people. In 1972, a person with an income of $9,000 paid, relative to income, five times as much as an individual earning $40,000 (Ribicoff, 1972). Moreover, there is no social security tax upon investment earnings, and thus a major source of revenue from the most wealthy escapes coverage.

The poorest 20% of America's families receive only 4% of the total income each year, while the top 20% gets 45%; one third of all wealth is owned by just 1% of the people. There are approximately two million corporations, yet a mere one tenth of 1% controls 55% of all corporate assets, and 1.1% controls 82% (Gans, 1972: 43). From 1947 to 1973, nonfarm weekly wages rose from $45.58 to $145.43—an increase of 219%—while corporate profits climbed from $25.6 billion to $105.1 billion—a rise of 311%. The average nonfarm weekly earnings, after tax deductions, increased during the same time period from $44.64 to $127.41, a rise of 185%, while corporate after-tax profits went from $20.2 billion to $72.9 billion—a 261% increase (Roberts, 1975: 25). Yet, by taking into account the loss of purchasing power because of inflation over these same years, the average weekly wage climbed 43%; "undistributed corporate profits after taxes, divided by the wholesale price index, that is, the *real* purchasing power of corporations, rose 77 percent" (Roberts, 1975: 25).

Increasingly, the fundamental economic variables of American society elude market controls. Now they reside under the direct jurisdiction of political-making, not profit-making, decisions; the power of State, rather than the play of market forces, contributes decisively to the nation's economic processes. State expenditures constitute such a high percentage of the GNP that State provides more yearly employment than private enterprise, and it is gaining an increasing percentage of the total labor force. State itself is a massive, nonproductive organization with dramatic impact upon supply, demand, wages, profits, investments, expenditures, employment, production, and so forth. Taxation is a fiscal policy exercised by State which has now become an important cost factor but is not affected by the market economy. Although the federal government does not compute taxes in determining the cost of living for American families, its taxes rose more rapidly than any other living cost during the recession year 1974. The Joint Economic Committee disclosed that "this is the first recession in history during which the tax burden on families and individuals has increased" (Knight News Service, 1975: 6). The market is increasingly more responsive to the ramifications of political processes now that fiscal policy is formulated in terms of political impact within Congress and through the Executive branches of government. The "very considerable displacement of the business world," the economist Robert L. Heilbroner (1965: 52) contends, "clearly points to a corresponding shift in the importance and influence of public officials in the determination of the course of national affairs." Power politics (rather than work and technology) become the foremost process for formulating economic policies. The economic well-being of millions of Americans and the profit taking for many corporations depend ultimately upon the effectiveness of their political maneuvering, instead of the traditional successes that were once forthcoming through hard work, prudent investment risks, greater technological productivity, sensitivity to market demands, and so forth.

The classical economics of America's agricultural past vouchsafed an abiding respect for hard work that was compromised by the growth of corporate organizations seeking to maximize human productivity through industrial technology. In the same way, new organizational demands emanating from State are producing a novel social context within which notions about work will be substantially modified. Work cannot be a central component of living, and employment cannot be the underpinning of people's livelihoods in a State economy that is dominated by warfare-welfare economic requirements instead of market demands under competitive Capital or the tight control of monopoly Capital.[3] Output for the private sector is established in terms of technological capabilities vis-à-vis profit-making results, but within State's organization of employment output is beyond economic computation, so that there are few opportunities for the person's work incentives to serve as motivation. State is a composite of political processes with economic consequences; it is under the reins of the powerful. Power struggles within State, and, indeed, State against Capital itself, are the overriding considerations among State rulers who set the pace for enterprising individuals, as business managers do for employees.[4] "Institutionally," Seymour Melman (1974) observes, "the state managers are dedicated to *maintaining and enlarging their decision power*" (p. 107, emphasis added). Power, not the work ethic, is the hallmark which grants personal acclaim to the achiever and permits him or her to make headway in State's hierarchy.

We are not proclaiming the total passing of either the Puritan ethic or the work ethic, however. The notion of earning a livelihood through diligent economic pursuits worthy of individual acclaim flourishes rather conspicuously, in spite of its demise in Capital's domain and State's organization of power. The millions of social security recipients, for example, reject notions of being "on the dole" and insist their benefits constitute an *earned* right financed through previous taxes upon their salaries; they contend that social security is a self-supporting retirement program for personal dignity in old age. Another area where great emphasis is placed upon the ethical qualities of labor is State welfare. Work remains central to the welfare system, inasmuch as a person qualifies if one is jobless. Should the person remain on the welfare roll for any great length of time, there is the risk of being viewed as a failure. One's sense of self-worth is being put to the test in terms of both the Puritan and work ethics; being on welfare by virtue of being out of work is considered a moral defect in the individual which justifies widespread contempt toward the welfare recipient. In 1890 General William Sherman righteously opposed government "hand-outs" for the surviving Indians: "Injuns must either work or starve. They have never worked. And they never will work" (Steiner, 1968: 127). Powerful government officials such as former President Nixon and President Ford have publicly condemned a bulging welfarism during their periods in office. While the cause is the deepening recession, they have strongly favored reduced federal expenditures and curtailment of social programs and have called for legislation that would compel people to accept work for wages lower than existing welfare benefits (see Piven & Cloward, 1971; Shabecoff, 1972: 1ff). People on welfare are perceived by such officials as twofold cheaters: (1) they are individuals who, by lacking the ethics of work, wish to live off public funds sustained by taxing "hard-working people"; and (2) they are part of a subsociety—an underclass—in which people thrive by cheating even the welfare rules in order to obtain unearned income. Within that context, any person on welfare becomes a suspect, a derelict in a society of workers.

The forceful application of the work ethic upon the unemployed, by placing blame for economic failure upon the victims, is a social control measure. Diligence in pursuit of personal achievement can no longer be a meaningful motivation for employment, but it is being made to apply to those who are not working! No personal characteristic of hard work can ever make the average American successful on the job; what makes getting a job worthwhile in America is that employed people receive the income so essential to social status and a decent living standard. As noted above, when production depends upon the effectiveness of technology, character building in terms of the Puritan ethic contributes little to the scales of pay that are negotiated through collective bargaining or accorded as nonunion wages. State employees are not paid relative to productivity generated by individual initiative, since in this case personal success is based upon striving in a labyrinth of political maneuvering. The condemnation of the unemployed for not working is made easier by invoking a rather irrelevant ethical standard; in fact, the jobless are doomed to contempt not because they are unemployed, but because they are economically irrelevant and powerless people. Economically debilitated people on welfare are being assessed by criteria that have become obsolete for the working population, precisely because they can be considered disposable people. No amount of empirical data that counter the brutality of judging welfare recipients by the work ethic (see Kaplan & Tausky, 1972) will be adequate to dislodge the practice, even though no more than 1% of the persons on welfare lists were able to work, according to a study conducted in 1967 which showed that a mere 50,000 out of the 7.3 million were "capable of being given job skills and training that will make them self-sufficient" (*The New York Times*, April 20, 1967). A Labor Department report contends:

> The figures also show that a larger proportion of blacks than of whites are job-oriented: Those employed plus those seeking work (unemployed) plus those wanting a job but not actually seeking one constitute 66 percent of the black population and 62 percent of the white population . . . the figures help dispose of the myth that blacks are less interested in jobs than whites. (Bureau of Labor Statistics Report 416, quoted in Perlo, 1975: 96)

Attempting to hold welfare recipients accountable to the ethics of work degrades the individuals by instilling a sense of their own failure so that responsibility for unemployment cannot be placed upon decision makers who rule over corporations and who are the heads of State and, simultaneously, sow the seeds of discontent among the employed for ventilation upon the unemployed. Debby D'Amico (1971) insists that

> We [whites] have hated black people. . . . By believing black people are inferior, we have kept the truth about ourselves from each other—that the people who have the power and money in America never intend to raise our incomes or those of black people, not because we aren't worthy, but because it would cut into their profits to do so. (p. 180)

Furthermore, defining welfare strictly as a system of public funding to the *unemployed* and the *poverty-stricken* allows greater opportunities for people of wealth to gain still more wealth. The designation of welfare as applying only to powerless and poor people conveniently permits distraction from the massive government "giveaways" to rich individuals and wealthy corporations. When State subsidizes wealthy people, there is seldom any characterization of the benefactors as exploiters of welfare programs which can be compared to the outrage expressed against welfare clients. However, the sums given to welfare people are miniscule by comparison with the amounts given to people of wealth and businesses just for doing nothing— the very accusation leveled against people on the welfare doles! In 1971 the federal government saved Lockheed Aircraft Corporation, the nation's largest defense contractor, from bankruptcy by guaranteeing to repay $250 million of its private bank loans. Just one program of welfare to the employed—the federal crop subsidization—cost more in 1970 than all federal, state, and local welfare-to-the unemployed programs combined. According to Casalino (1972: 33), in 1970 Tenneco, a monolithic corporation, received crop subsidies of over $1 million, and J. G. Boswell of California, one of the world's largest cotton growers, received $5 million. Casalino also noted that "in a recent year 500 large growers in California's Imperial Valley received $12 million in farm subsidies—or $24,000 each. Meanwhile 10,000 poor, landless residents of the Valley received less than $8 million in welfare payments—or $800 each" (p. 34).

Thus welfare, in terms of who receives the greatest amount, is clearly implemented for the rich, first to control the jobless, second, to gain still greater wealth for themselves at the expense of the less fortunate, and, third, to keep wages suppressed. "After three and a half decades and costs of billions of dollars," Dr. C. E. Bishop, agricultural economist and a vice-president of the University of South Carolina, has noted, "the Department of Agriculture's farm programs continue to widen the gap between the rich and the poor. They have helped create a class of wealthy landowners while bypassing the rural poor—and that means 40 per cent of the poor people in this country" (quoted in Robbins, 1970: 1). To assure billions in profit—$16 billion net out of $50 billion in sales—State enforces subsidies to regulate farm commodities but offers no program to ease the discomfort and economic sufferings of surplus people; extensive State research programs provide new machinery, new seeds, new fertilizers, new chemicals, new farming methods to enhance profits, but no new programs to enhance the living standards for unemployed farm laborers. In sum, welfare programs cannot provide adequate economic allocations to poverty-stricken people but are extremely successful in providing greater incomes for the well-to-do.

THE VICTIMS

> If [a thing] be useless, the labor
> contained in it is useless.
> —*Karl Marx*

The people made economically superfluous upon the loss of employment become, in the words of Baran and Sweezy (1966), "special victims," while "industrial workers are a diminishing minority of the American working class, and their organized cores in the basic industries have to a large extent been integrated into the system as consumers and ideologically conditioned members of the society" (p. 363). Thus workers grow more conservative and become solely concerned with preserving their own working conditions under the pressure of automation. Technological displacement and deeply embedded traditions of racism, sexism, and prejudice have combined to make for rather acute hardships for particular kinds of people in America, beyond the mere fact of economic exploitation. The economic disengagement brought about by the intensification of technological production in the private economy and technological dependency on the increasing militarization initiated by State poses greater hardships along class lines, as well as for a broad spectrum of social collectivities striving to cope with economic realities in spite of social degradation. The modernization of production has been used to displace workers who might otherwise, after long periods of strife against business domination, gain economic concessions such as higher wages, retirement benefits, and improved job conditions. For at the point where labor cost approaches the expense of investment in technology for production, business resorts to machinery and thereby reduces employment opportunities. State likewise invokes technology, not, however, to gain profits, but to expand upon its exotic technology of destruction, which (as analyzed above) eliminates considerable work opportunities for the laboring sector of the economy. What this means is that low-income people and socially stigmatized individuals are the groups who initially compete against technological efficiency. Each grouping of people discussed in the various chapters in this book must come to terms, in some manner, with the economic realities vis-à-vis labor costs to business and the political processes of power mandated by an emerging State economy.

Blacks

A study of 17 Arkansas counties revealed that cotton growers had only 483 cotton-picking machines in 1952, but by 1963 5,061 were in use. During the same period the black population for 15 of the 17 counties dropped, from 21,863 to 6,587 (Dillingham & Sly, 1966). Although black tenants averaged a pitiful yearly cash income of $800 in 1965, by 1966 90% of the Mississippi Delta cotton was being plucked by harvesters of steel, not human flesh. The *last* stronghold for black employment in southern agriculture is the tobacco field, where, in the midsixties, 1 million out of the 1.5 million black farm workers were concentrated. In 1971, the mechanical tobacco machine harvested the crop for at least four North Carolina farmers. Dr. Selz C. Mayo, head of Sociology and Anthropology at North Carolina State College, anticipates that the "four-legged, four-wheeled contraption of conveyor belts and hydraulic motors that moves down a row of tobacco plants and strips leaves from stalks almost as gently as a human hand" will soon displace 50,000 farm people in North Carolina alone: "The blacks will probably be totally out of North Carolina agriculture by the end of this decade, and certainly by the end of the next decade" (quoted in Stevens, 1971: 1). What is true for the state of North Carolina will also hold for the entire tobacco production throughout the South. When a small mechanical harvester picks an acre of cotton in six man-hours, rather than the 74 required by hand, the economic advantages supersede even those obtainable with poorly paid black fieldhands. One person operating a mechanical tobacco harvester does the amount of work accomplished by a field gang of eight pickers; with this labor-saving capability, the machine pays for itself in less than two years (Stevens, 1971).

A report by the Census Bureau and the Department of Agriculture (Associated Press, 1976) reveals a 1.2% reduction for the nation's farm population from 1970 to 1974; the number of blacks, however, decreased 9%—over eight times the general rate—during the same time period, declining from 938,000 to 655,000. Because of farming mechanization, along with chemical fertilizers and improved hybrid seeds, the nation's agricultural economy is no longer dependent upon a high per-acre human energy requirement. Productivity for farming, as was the case a century earlier for industry, now rests conspicuously upon efficient application of equipment.

About 80% of America's black population resides in cities, and four fifths of these live in all-black ghettos. The rural-to-urban migration has not "paved the way for integration," as Philip Hauser (1965: 863), a noted demographer, would have us believe, but has instead meant greater social and economic isolation. Employment opportunity for blacks is no greater in the city than in the country. The city would supposedly be less racist in that the requirements of industrialization should lead to people being judged on the basis of learned abilities, rather than on the nonrational ground of skin color. In such a case, well-educated and well-qualified blacks could anticipate rapid advancement in the urban environment. While this expectation was being voiced by a notable number of scholars (see Broom & Glenn, 1966: 187), unemployment statistics revealed that the black-white employment rates were virtually identical for unskilled and agricultural categories of work, while they were 2 to 1 in favor of whites for skilled and professional occupations (U.S. Bureau of the Census, 1961: Table 205).

America's technological economy could afford to keep blacks subjugated and segregated, out of sight in the ghetto. The nonwhite civilian labor force participation for black males 16 years and over stood at 80.1 in 1960, 74.7 in 1970, and 73.7 in 1972; the figures for white males were 82.6 in 1960, 79.7 in 1970, and 79.6 in 1972 (U.S. Department of Labor, 1972: Table E–4). During the sixties and into the seventies males of both races were less likely to participate in the labor force—yet the reduction was substantially greater for blacks than for whites, a drop of 6.4 percentage points for blacks and 3.0 for whites—a 2 to 1 ratio. By not entering the work force, blacks become invisible persons; by dropping out of employment they become totally irrelevant. Further, while official government computations show black unemployment at 14.1%, twice the white rate, in 1975 the Urban League's more accurate survey reported 30%, a figure more than twice the government computation (*The New York Times*, January 18, 1976, p. 37). *Newsweek*, in its February 19, 1973 issue, declared:

> The black unemployment rate runs persistently double the rate for whites, and in the worst-off ghettos it is frozen at Depression levels—18 per cent in Watts, 20 per cent in the Hunters Point slums of San Francisco, 25 per cent in Chicago's Woodlawn district. The ghettos have grown physically worse with neglect and simple aging—a deterioration everywhere visible . . . (p. 31).

The difference between black and white median family incomes in 1941 was less than $1,600; by 1964, it was more than $3,000; in 1969, the difference expanded to just over $3,600; in 1972, it stood at $4,585 (*The New York Times*, July 23, 1973, p. 1). From 1970 to 1973 the white median family income increased by $759, while the amount was a mere $84 for blacks—a 9 to 1 ratio (U.S. Bureau of the Census, 1975: 26). In 1968, black income was 60% of white; the figure climbed to 61% in 1970, but by 1972 it had dropped to 59% (*The New York Times*, July 23, 1973, p. 1); and in 1975 it dropped to 56% (*The New York Times*, January 18, 1976, p. 37). Between 1973 and 1975, the proportion of black families in the middle-income range dropped dramatically from one fourth to one fifth (*The New York Times*, 1976, p. 37).

The number of poor blacks increased 600,000 between 1969 and 1972, while white poverty declined 500,000 (Hill, 1973: Table 3). Although more whites (17.5 million and 67% of the total) than blacks (7.7 million and 33% of the total) were in poverty in 1970, only 1 out of 10 whites were so classified, while 1 out of 3 blacks persisted in poverty (Rosenthal, 1973b: 1). Although the official total poverty figure dropped from 40 million in 1959 to 25.5 million in 1970, the proportion of blacks among the poor expanded; in 1959, 28% of those classified as poor were black, and in 1970 the figure rose to 33% (Rosenthal, 1973b: 1). In 1972, 1.1 million persons pulled out of the poverty category—and all of these were entirely white, owing to a 10% increase in social security benefits (Thomas, 1973: 35).

The Aged

Margaret Mead views the aged as "a strangely isolated generation" which carries a dying culture (*Time* Magazine, 1971: 433). Millions of Americans survive at a moment in history when technology can keep them alive and simultaneously has made them obsolete. There is a daily net gain of 1,000 persons 65 years and older; half of the aged are 73 or older (Isenberg, 1973: 626). The marvels of medical technology, on the one hand, retain the breath of life, while, on the other, the productive technology of the nation sounds the death knell for persons 65 or over. Moreover, the aged are obstructions in the orderly lives of others; they are social outcasts to the younger generations preoccupied with economic realities and social strivings. A survey on aging undertaken by the *Los Angeles Times* in 1973 (see Isenberg, 1973) discovered "that older women associated it with loneliness, older men associated it with poverty, and youth associated it with death" (p. 627). A Harris survey of retired people showed 37% withdrew from the work force against their will; 43% with earnings less than $3,000 wanted to remain on the job; 50% of the blacks would have preferred to remain employed; and, in total, 4.4 million retired against their own desires (see Finlay, 1974: 5). Consequently, as Curtin (1973) notes, "The experiences of a lifetime disappear in the feeling of being useless and passed by" (p. 227). Under these circumstances, death itself holds no meaning; it "leaves only a sense of despair" which, in all likelihood, means that passing on must come as a relief.

Removing people from employment provides another avenue for ridding the economy of potential employees; only 16% of the people over 65 now remain in the work force (Isenberg, 1973: 626), as against 68% in 1890 (Eglit, 1975). Termination because of a birthdate is an arbitrary landmark, since more than a third of all retired males, 50% of the married females, and 75% of the unmarried prefer employment rather than retirement (Eglit, 1975). Yet, the profit-making sector can, at little cost, compel retirement in order to cope with surplus people. Retirement programs work to the advantage of capital formation without incurring any substantial liabilities. In 1973, private pension plans held $150 billion in trust, and another $10 billion was being added each year (Cook, 1973: 269); in 1945, they were $5.4 billion, and $52 billion in 1960 (Leinenweber, 1972: 31). These plans remain "the greatest aggregate of unregulated wealth in the nation" (Cook, 1973: 269). Management bears three fourths of the costs for pensions (Jensen, 1972: 42); two thirds of the funds are controlled by trust departments of banks, and four such banks manage almost half of the funds (Shannon, 1972: 35). In 1940, 4.1 million people were *covered* by a pension program; today, more than 30 million receive *coverage*. Nonetheless, between 30% to 50% will never gain any benefits whatsoever, according to the U.S. Department of Labor (*Time*, August 23, 1971, p. 56). The records of AT&T, one of the world's largest business conglomerates, revealed in 1972 that 188,453 employees had participated in the company's retirement program since 1950, yet only 32 had acquired any pension rights (Cook, 1973: 63). At best, only 1 out of 3 persons who are employees of companies providing retirement funds can anticipate some financial support—and the average amount is $1,080 yearly (Leinenweber, 1972: 30).

Pension programs, relegated to trust funds under the control of banks and with little employee benefits, are not intended to provide financial resources in old age. By holding retirement contributions in trusts, the business is making an investment for profits—not for its workers' retirement dreams. Consequently, destitution among the aged is not only extensive but increasing; more Americans are getting older, and more of the older Americans plummet into the ranks of poverty. A report from the Senate Special Committee on the Aging stated that in 1971 "the likelihood of being impoverished is more than twice as great for older Americans as it is for younger Americans. One out of every four persons 65 and older, in contrast to one in nine for younger individuals, lives in poverty" (Powell, 1971). People over 65 have an average weekly income of $48 (McCurry & Jerome, 1974). Social security benefits average $145 per month; they provide the sole source of income for over one third of all retired persons (McCurry & Jerome, 1974). People experiencing a history of long-standing unemployment during their productive years, such as among blacks and other minorities, will receive much lower social security benefits; should unemployment persist in the future as in 1975, then poverty will accelerate among the aged. By contrast, the state's retirement program for its nonproductive technological militia is economically untenable, not, however, for the recipients but for the public treasury; if present trends continue, retirement programs for military personnel will cost $341 billion by the end of the century, a sum over three times the 1975 Department of Defense budget (*The New York Times*, January 21, 1973, p. 43). Thus, just as military expenditures prove destructive for generating employment opportunities, so will the retirement program become a negative drain upon the economy.

Retirement financing beyond the individual's own economic resources has now become the responsibility of State; it is not a cost factor for Capital but is instead a political issue. It is another instance of economic disutility transforming economic questions into political issues under State's jurisdiction.

Women and the Family

Technological innovations have also affected the traditional productivity measure of American women—the birth rate. With widespread application of birth control techniques and abortion, women produce a substantially lower number of children. During 1974, the crude birth rate remained at the record low set in 1973—14.9—while the general fertility rate dropped to 68.5, as against the previous 1973 low of 69.2 (Associated Press, 1975). Contraceptive devices, medical improvements for abortions, and the growing likelihood of growing babies in laboratories rather than in females' bodies have inspired women's sense of liberation from the reins of nature; biology is no longer destiny. Just as technology maximizes production of material goods more efficiently and provides greater control for accomplishing preconceived results, so too does technology supplant female productivity vis-à-vis reproduction and, upon application, allow for more extensive control. Family planning, like economic planning, becomes feasible with technological displacement of biological dependency for human reproduction, much as in the case of economic reproduction. Moreover, with the responsibility of child rearing in the home coming to an end for what is now viewed as middle life, women seek to restructure their own lives just as retooling for modernization takes place in factory production.

If the work ethic actually established personal character and provided the basis for economic prudence which assured high economic rewards, then the American housewife would surely be at the very summit of achievement. According to estimates provided by the Chase Manhattan Bank, women devote 99.6 hours a week to domestic work (Benston, 1969). The Social Security Administration conservatively estimates the cash value for the woman's average work in the home during 1972 at $4,705 (Love, 1976). Nonetheless, the economic worth of domestic labor is not computed in the nation's GNP; it is designated "nonmarket," inasmuch as it lies outside the bookkeeping of commercial profits and beyond the tax powers of State.

Hard work without pay on the home front remains a persistent factor for American women. Working as an employee, however, has been a variable for them, reflecting fundamental economic facts in the market of supply and demand. Economic necessity, for example, compels black women to seek employment. When labor becomes scarce, greater numbers of women move into jobs, and upon contraction of the labor force, they are propelled right back into the home. Such was the case during World War II as women provided labor being drained by military needs and, upon the end of the war, were subsequently displaced by males returning from the war front.

Today, married women seek jobs in numbers far greater than a quarter of a century ago. In 1940, 1 of 10 entered the work force and, by the 1970s, 4 out of 10 held jobs (Gray, 1972: 821). There are 109.4 million females (51.2% of all Americans), 37.4 million of whom are in the work force; thus in 1974, 2 of every 5 workers were females (*U.S. News & World Report*, 1975: 56). The economics of livelihood appear to be the foremost circumstances for women seeking employment, as Adeline Levine demonstrated in Chapter 6 above.

In making their entry into the nation's work force, women do so at the points of least resistance; they are hired for the lower-paying jobs where the powerless concentrate. According to the U.S. Bureau of the Census, between 1960 and 1970, 11.9 million jobs were added to the work force, and 65.3% were filled by women (Rosenthal, 1973a: 1), yet the median earnings of women at full-time work have declined substantially relative to their male counterparts: 63% in 1956, 59% in 1964, and 57% in 1974 (*U.S. News & World Report*, 1975: 57). In 1954, full-time women workers earned 36% less than their male equivalents, but by 1974 they were earning 43% less (see Houston, 1975). Although the percentage of all professional jobs held by women edged upward by five percentage points (going from 36% to 41%) between 1964 and 1974 it still fell short of the 45% figure for 1940. Only 15% of the female work force, one half of whom are public school teachers (*U.S. News & World Report*, 1972: 57), hold professional employment. By contrast, 70% of the expansion for male employment between 1960 and 1970 was concentrated among the professional, managerial, and skilled-craft categories (Buffalo *Evening News*, November 17, 1975, p. 8).

In having to seek their initial jobs among occupations with low income yields, women must compete for limited job opportunities with other social categories of poor people; they vie with ethnic minorities which must find work in an increasingly competitive labor market. As a result, the poor split deeply in trying to cope with economic oppression through collective organizations. Middle-class women, who particularly seize a leadership role in rallying females to challenge the status quo, have considerable difficulty in reconciling their aims with lower-class ethnics who have suffered for many generations from acute racial animosities. Frances M. Beal (1970), a New York City coordinator for SNCC's Black Women's Liberation Committee, laments that

> . . . some [white woman's movement] groups come to the incorrect conclusion that their oppression is due simply to male chauvinism. They therefore have an extremely antimale tone to their dissertations. Black people are engaged in a life-and-death struggle and the main emphasis of black women must be to combat the capitalist, racist exploitation of black people. (p. 350)

Just as industrialization destroyed the home base for craftsmanship, so have modern technological developments changed the home life of all people, yet most decisively for women. With improved medical knowledge and technology, people are living longer but cannot live the same lives earlier generations did. Some members of both sexes are finding the solemn promise of matrimony, "unto death do us part," an odious oppression, now that death fails to show up and part the united couple. In the past the oath could be made in good faith, with a full awareness that death would be the way for parting. At the turn of the century an American female's life expectancy at birth was only 36 years; at present, the life expectancy for women is 75 years (*The New York Times*, February 9, 1975). The life expectancy for males was 67 years in 1974. Today, divorce reaches one of its peaks at just the moment in a woman's life when, three quarters of a century earlier, life itself would have been expected to have ended. To some it seems simply tedious—at best—to expect people to remain married for life. Five generations are now surviving at an increasing rate, and it is not uncommon to learn of 75-year wedding anniversaries. In 1970, 67% of the women interviewed by a Harris public opinion poll agreed that "for a woman to be truly happy, she needs to have a man around," and 27% disagreed. A mere five years later, in December 1975, Harris reported 52% of the women interviewed rejected the same notion, while 42% agreed (Harris, 1975). Between 1960 and 1972 the divorce rate increased 80% (Jacoby, 1974: 41). By 1973, 1 of every 3 marriages ended in divorce; from October 1974 to October 1975 there were over 1 million divorces (U.S. Department of Health, Education, and Welfare, 1975: 3).

Thus marriage may be seen by some as a form of cruel and unusual punishment. It is proving too much to expect people to remain devoted, with compatible interests, from early marriage through four, five, and six decades. In the course of a single lifetime, a couple must now endure the stresses and strains that challenged several generations in previous centuries. Moreover, divorce offers a real chance to challenge the inevitable permanence of aging by allowing older people to think of themselves as young and free once again; by destroying marriage, they assault aging itself. Long years of matrimony are a constant reminder of growing old. To repeat the marriage vows for a second time is a kind of fountain of youth to which they return; as Mircea Eliade (1959: 68) commented, rituals "reverse" time so as to revive in the present what transpired in the past. "When you are 48 and have five teenagers running around the house," a male divorcee explains, "you feel older than God's own dog. But now I'm 53 and free and I feel like a kid of 23. Since the divorce I've taken ballet lessons, gone to cooking school, and done some scuba diving" (Nordheimer, 1974). To do what the young do is to feel young; to do what we did in our youth is to feel young again. Thus divorce extends a fresh start, not to relive the past but to break away and begin anew.

Family life is also affected by abortion, which allows for lower reproductive rates. With the liberalization of abortion laws, women are resorting to removal of the fetus far more than in the past. In 1971 there were an estimated 1,500,000 abortions in the United States (*Time*, August 21, 1972, p. 34). This rejection comes at a time when Capital faces surplus labor and State confronts the costs of taking care of the ever-expanding number of rejects from the forces of production. Thus abortion serves to eliminate unwanted births just when labor contributes less to production than ever before. Apparently, the means of reproduction are to operate in response to economic needs. Capital now supports population control not only within the nation but abroad as well: surplus people become more difficult to control as technology dislodges labor from the act of production. It would have been inconceivable for State to permit abortion had there been a labor shortage in the economy; abortion, for instance, would not have been legalized when labor was at a premium during America's preindustrial era.

As, more and more, technology limits human reproduction, the family as a household unit cannot be expected to survive any more than private entrepreneurship. Ideological justifications for upholding the conjugal family can be expected to experience the same fate and pass away, much as laissez-faire capitalism disappeared with the rise of corporate capitalism. Just as the social organization of production was modified drastically upon the introduction of new technology, so too is family organization in America experiencing fundamental—if not fatal—alterations.

Artificial insemination is bringing economic and moral issues to the fore: Is artificial insemination adultery? If so, then is it by the donor or the doctor who administers the semen? Who is the father to the unborn child—the woman's husband or the donor? Upon divorce, could the husband be required to provide financial support for a child with no biological relation, or should the donor be sued for child support? Could the divorced husband exercise a visiting privilege? If the divorced husband is denied visitation rights because he is not the "real" father, then does the donor, as the "real" father, hold visitation rights? Could the offspring of an artificially inseminated birth be the husband's heir? If the husband dies while a woman carries an artifically conceived fetus, can the woman declare the pregnancy illegitimate and thereby jeopardize the unborn child's legal rights to the husband's estate? If a wife becomes pregnant through artificial insemination taken from her husband's sperm bank some 20 or 30 years following the spouse's death, what will be the rights of inheritance for the child, especially if the estate has already been distributed to the grown children of the deceased father? Can estates be settled as long as births are still possibilities decades after the husband's death? Does a widow have the right to allow insemination for another woman's pregnancy from her late husband's sperm bank, and, if so, can surviving relatives exert kinship and legal claims toward the child—and vice versa? Could various State agencies, such as social security, withdraw or refuse payments to children of artificial insemination? Can a welfare agency compel child support of a donor when a woman receiving aid to dependent children funds becomes pregnant through artificial insemination, just as it can demand the same of a male who is responsible for the pregnancy of a woman on welfare? Can a woman abort an artificially fertilized fetus without her husband's knowledge or approval because the husband is not the "real" father and the donor is unknown? What are the kinship affiliations going to be in light of all the variations resulting from artificial insemination?

The same questions might be raised, along with many additional issues, concerning the creation of a human fetus by implanting a wife's egg in another woman's body for artificial fertilization with the husband's sperm, or when a married woman's egg is placed in another woman's body for fertilization by a donor. Can the recipient be an unwed individual? Is the woman who carries the child entitled to compensation for her labors of reproduction, much as doctors are now paid for child delivery, and can she—or her spouse—assert other economic and legal claims with respect to giving birth to the child? Who is to be the mother or father of the child? How will the child become a relative to others connected with its conception and birth processes in light of all the variations extended through artificial inovulation? If a wife who is an alien in America allows an egg from her body to be fertilized by her alien husband and then implanted in a woman's body who is an American citizen, what is the citizenship status of the offspring—an American because of having been born from the womb of an American citizen, inasmuch as child birth does establish citizenship in America, or an alien because the providers of conception are alien persons? Most important, if a donor remains unknown, are we prepared to establish virtually endless ethical decisions through the mystification of conception?

Just as work is dispensable in the technology of production, so too can technology dispose entirely of work in human reproduction. Perhaps a future generation can come forth purely through chemical processes of laboratory reproduction; a human being can be biologically produced through technological production, as any other material item is a product of technology. If, initially, the technologically produced human is an infant, who will be responsible for socializing the child? Is there going to be a kinship system for the child? Can citizenship be conferred, since there will be no biological affiliations? Who will bear the costs for rearing such children? What kinds of ethics can be realistically enforced? If there are emotional needs for children during the period of socialization, will adults be forced to accept the children to whom they have no biological relationship?[5]

Operations altering a person's sex pose basic questions with regard to the work of reproduction for the traditional family in America. Technological advancements allow for changing one's sex. Should disputes involving sexism be resolved by introducing unisex people? What kind of work claims will a person assert on the basis of one's prior sex? Will a person continue to hold the same job after as before the operation? Will offspring have a right to declare a parent who has undergone such an operation legally dead and reject her or him as their parent—and with what consequences for claims to property? Could a divorced male who changes and becomes a female still be required to pay alimony? Does a male offspring commit incest by having intercourse with a female who was once his father?

Technological advances for the economics of production have always had serious implications for the family unit; the social organization of family life has undergone substantial and dramatic alterations as a consequence of innovations. Now, however, rather than reflecting only broader technological ramifications that have been responsible for bringing about basic modification in the family system, the forthcoming era of technology promises to be a direct assault upon the productivity of human reproduction. New technology is applicable not only in secondary terms, as in the past, but it is also being directed specifically at the traditional American family. The foregoing questions reflect this reality; upon closer observation, they are basically issues focusing upon the economics of ownership vis-à-vis offspring and property.

Thus, in many ways, as humans are dislodged from the labor of procreation by technological reproduction, there will be similar results as when humans become less involved with technological production vis-à-vis Capital and the social organization of State. Economic relations intrinsic to existing kinship ties—such as bearing the expenses of childrearing, estate inheritance, property claims made upon divorce—will most assuredly collapse; the question of what will become of people's lives upon technological displacement of human reproduction is just as real as when workers become redundant for the work force. The work ethic in a family context can hardly remain viable in the absence of household work, any more than in today's modern labor market. Still, individuals will be held accountable to the sexual morality and social ethics of the conjugal unit during the process of technological reproduction, in an attempt to sustain social control over superfluous people. The precedent is invoking the work ethic in efforts to regulate the social lives and economic opportunities of welfare people who have been made superfluous by the technology of production. What this means is that with the economic disengagement for the family which follows the advent of the new technology, the economic strife (made apparent by what is known as "woman's liberation") will again, as is true in the broader society, be supplanted by intense political struggles. This is so because it will become necessary to rely upon political processes to resolve the key issues posed by the disruption of economic and property rights with the introduction of technological change. New living arrangements in a household can emerge only by challenging existing laws that assure the legality of the conjugal relationship, and new judicial decisions will have to be rendered and new legislation approved to grapple with all the contentions concerning property rights.

The gay liberation movement is an initial response to the new dimensions that have reduced the birth rate. It is difficult to oppose the gay life by arguing the need for human reproduction now that children, at least to the degree that was once true, are not wanted. It is difficult to oppose the gay life by traditional sexual codes in light of the rapid collapse of the basic economic factors associated with the conjugal family. If the idealized conjugal family is upheld, in spite of the potential for change, the politics of discord will rise to the fore, and the tranquility of social life will be far less likely. Already, individuals who are creating new family forms that are taking shape in terms of the recent technology are being denied opportunities because the legal system is predicated upon traditional standards about family life. A case brought before the courts to challenge the legal right of a city to enforce zoning laws that ban communal living in a house by more than two unrelated persons reveals a firm ideological commitment to the status quo. "A quiet place where yards are wide, people few and motor vehicles restricted are legitimate guidelines in a land use project addressed to family needs. This goal is a permissible one." So wrote the noted civil-libertarian Justice of the Supreme Court, William O. Douglas (Associated Press, 1974: 11). In a sweeping political statement, Justice Douglas declared that states were entitled to legalize family preferences, involving social and economic discretions, and to enforce such intents through zoning laws: "It involves no 'fundamental' right guaranteed by the Constitution such as voting, the right of association, the right of access to the courts, or any rights of privacy." As Herbert Spencer (1966) noted in 1858, "The current assumption respecting family government, as respecting national government, is that the virtues are with the rulers and the vices with the ruled" (p. 87).

Can a person who undergoes a change in sex exert employment rights established by that person's original sexual identity? The Appellate Division of New Jersey's State Superior Court upheld the dismissal of a teacher who changed from male to female and subsequently lost tenure to a teaching position that was established prior to the operation; the court maintained that school officials had just cause to remove such a person because of the "potential for psychological harm to the students" (*New York Teacher*, March 3, 1974, p. 24). Still, the State Education Commissioner ruled that all pension rights established as a male could not be denied now that the teacher was a female, since her conduct did not involve "moral turpitude," even though she continued to reside with her previous wife and daughters following the sex change operation (Associated Press, 1972a).

If State exercises such discretionary powers, then it is clear that tremendous political confrontations will flourish in the event of technological reproduction. Senator Edward Kennedy forecast that "from a constitutional point of view, the frontiers of law for the next 20 to 25 years will be in these areas of bio-ethics" (*Newsweek*, January 12, 1976, p. 50). It will be the powers of State that will allow or disallow a smooth transition into new human relationships; it will be the powers of State to decide all the crucial matters which will arise in producing a new generation—how many there will be; major biological characteristics by manipulating the genetic system; whether or not there will be any kinship, whether or not property can be held, citizenship, and so on.

In short, technological transformation, both of production and reproduction, invites the substitution of political processes in the stead of economic processes with respect to the traditional household. State becomes the more powerful regulator of human lives rather than Capital, and rather than individuals.

Ethnics

Technological developments designed to advance profits will surely confront other social groupings, with the consequence of greater economic hardship for the workers. Although many Puerto Ricans residing on the mainland of the United States have dispersed within recent years from their traditional New York City concentration, their poverty has increased. In 1970, 56.8% of the Puerto Ricans lived in New York City, compared to 87.8% in 1940 and 69% in 1960, yet the percentage living in poverty rose from 29% in 1969 to 32.2% in 1971, and 24% drew upon some form of public assistance in 1971 (Kihss, 1975). In spite of greater geographical assimilation over the past 35 years, Puerto Ricans are not achieving assimilation into the highly sophisticated technological economy on a par with non–Puerto Rican whites. In 1959, the average Puerto Rican income was 64.6% that of non–Puerto Rican whites, yet by 1971 it had dropped to 57.9% (Kihss, 1975).

The rather modest improvements Chicano field workers gained through unionization during the late sixties and into the seventies, after years of struggle against powerful business and government interests, will most likely evaporate in the very near future; they simply will not be able to compete against the new agricultural technology now available for harvesting the farm crops upon which they depend for a livelihood. The mechanical tomato picker, costing $30,000 in 1975, handles up to 100 tons daily. In the western region of New York, where farm labor costs exceed the wage scale for Chicanos in the Southwest, the tomato machine picks a ton at a cost of $3.50 compared to $22 for each hand-picked ton (Buyer, 1975: 32). The higher pay and improved working conditions achieved through union representation by the Chicanos in California's vineyards invite farm owners to dispense with manual employees in favor of a vineyard picking machine that can harvest a row of grapes in 15 minutes instead of the two days that two workers take to complete the task (*Buffalo Evening News*, October 2, 1971, p. B–5). These machines can harvest an acre every hour and can operate up to 20 hours per day to produce 80 tons of grapes, whereas a worker can pick only during daylight hours and bring in only a ton per day (Palazzetti, 1972).

Researchers at a state university in California have produced a mechanical lettuce harvester that can quickly maneuver down a row of lettuce and select, through its automatic electronic sensory device, only ripe heads.

The power of State has also been brought to bear against the Chicano effort to win economic improvement. George Margois (1972) notes, for example, that in 1950 a

> . . . Congressional Committee investigating the first major strike of the California grape workers . . . vehemently denounced the National Farm Workers Union, and for almost twenty years thereafter served as a powerful legal aid for agribusiness to stifle unionization. . . . Department of Defense purchases of grapes rose 800 per cent during the strike. . . .

Most destitute among America's oppressed minorities is the American Indian, who, since at least the 19th century, has been prevented from access to opportunities for meaningful economic acquisition. Official computations in federal reports reveal that nearly 40% of the Indian population lived below the established poverty line in 1969, as against 13.7% for the total population (Delaney, 1973).

CONCLUSION

> Experience should teach us to be most on guard
> to protect liberty when the government's
> purposes are beneficial.
> —*Justice Louis D. Brandeis*

The most significant development with respect to the nature of work and working in American society since the end of World War II has been the emergence of a powerful State fully capable not only of exerting the force of authority but also of establishing economic prerogatives for the conduct of national policies. State, with its goal of advancing national security, mandates the creation of a technology of destruction which deeconomizes economic productivity. The qualities of production become less significant in defining the character of Americans, and the concern is not with work, a work ethic, or profits, once State becomes dominant. The pride of nationhood, loyalty to the nation, trust in government, belief in country, and other *national* qualities supplant traditional notions associated with work as the dominant themes sounded both by political leaders and business executives. Alienation carries with it political undertones. It is not just the state of mind of workers toward their work; alienation is as much a measure of lack of political identification with the national government as it is toward the world of work; it invites instability for the political as well as the economic process.

State, with its numerous agencies of social control, has become so dominant that integrity no longer applies to character-building qualities of motivation articulated by the Puritan ethic for economic productivity. Rather, it is associated with national capabilities that are considered essential to assure the accomplishment of State's national security interests. By investing heavily in a technology of destruction upon which so much trust must be generated among the people, work can hardly maintain its preeminence within American society. When political crises compete with economic crises, willingness to die on the battlefield, rather than dedication to work on the job, is the means to regain a sense of purpose and to revitalize national identity, rather than the individual's character. "We are so cynical," former President Richard Nixon said during the course of an interview, "so disbelieving—it may take the shock of an invasion—in Korea or in Thailand. If American lives are threatened, we may regain our sense of belief in our country and our need for strength" (*Buffalo Evening News*, November 18,

1975, p. 4). Consequently, wealth itself is less significant and is secondary to political and military qualities that are being required by State. "What's wrong with being the second wealthiest country for a while?" Nixon asked during the same interview, "We as a country have to provide [military] strength and leadership." The country, Nixon is declaring, must be powerful on military terms even if this means the dimunition of economic productivity. This stands in contrast to the heyday of Capital, when President Calvin Coolidge could unblushingly proclaim: "The business of America is business." As late as the 1950s, Charles E. Wilson, Secretary of Defense and former head of General Motors, asserted that "What is good for General Motors is good for the country."

State is a vast enterprise which increasingly proclaims its authority and in so doing becomes counterproductive, according to the economic principles laid down by Capital. It undertakes vast economic investment in areas such as defense spending that defy cost estimates; it responds to powerful interests with little regard for cost-effectiveness (e.g., subsidization of unproductive private businesses such as shipbuilding, corporate agricultural firms, and defense contractors); it provides welfare for tremendous numbers of people considered uneconomical for the private sphere and therefore beyond the bounds of "sound" business precepts in receiving State support. In other areas of responsibility, State is held accountable to commercial principles and, if economically successful, stands to be condemned for competing with private enterprise. Government is expected, on the one hand, to avoid economic losses in providing mail service, electricity from TVA, and welfare through social security, and, on the other hand, if it attains economic returns in such activities, it will be accused of unfair competition with private enterprise. Under these circumstances, State is destined to be a nonproductive entity. Therefore, it is immensely difficult to expect the work ethic to flourish among employees hired to provide services through the nonproductive social organization of State. Employment responsibilities within State are specified by the job and cannot rest upon the character-building qualities of persons for motivation. Even pride in one's work is an anachronism within State's parameters; at best, one achieves self-approval as a "professional"—taking pride in one's technical resourcefulness, agility, and expertise, but not in diligent work. In our society, professionalism comes as close to approximating the self-indulgence of the work ethic as can be expressed under the contemporary conditions of technological development. Indeed, even the criminal articulates self-acclaim and notions of superiority in being a "professional" rather than an inept and unsophisticated crook.[6]

The key issue in America is not work but people. As technological innovations expand productivity and displace people from the work force of private enterprise; as the technology of destruction for defense under State

eliminates the creation of jobs; as political processes assume a more commanding reign over economic forces; and as a nonproductive State enterprise consumes greater amounts of economic resources—then survival for
those who are superfluous and who are powerless is brought into question.
As people become economically disposable and are unable to command
political leverage, they stand on the threshold of either destitution or liquidation. This is particularly so of the ethnic and racial minorities with a long
tradition of economic oppression in America—blacks, Chicanos, Indians,
and Puerto Ricans. The evidence, as noted above, points to a worsening of
economic opportunity for these minorities with the passage of time. Walter
Lippman prophetically wrote in his news column for September 29, 1963
that it was probable that

> . . . while the Negroes will prevail in regard to the first wave of their grievances,
> the removal of the badges of slavery, no substantial improvement of their
> general economic condition is likely to come soon. For this will require the
> conquest of dire poverty, and the country is not now ready for such an under-
> taking.

Jacobs and Landau (1971: 256) contend that the Mexican-Americans "have
gradually shifted from rural to urban life, from subsistence farming to the
welfare doles."

The aged, too, become meshed into the economy of uselessness: Isenberg (1973) declares, "old age has all those parts—poverty, loneliness, the
prospect of death—plus what is probably the worst part of all: uselessness. A
feeling of being shelved by a society which no longer needs you, although
you still need that society" (p. 627). Women are most likely to follow the
pattern of nonwhite ethnics in America and the aged—initially gaining
modest concessions through collective efforts, only, with the passage of time,
to descend once again. Juliet Mitchell (1971) assesses women's future status in
America:

> Today automation promises the *technical* possibility of abolishing completely
> the physical differential between man and woman in production, but under
> capitalist relations of production, the *social* possibility of this abolition is per-
> manently threatened, and can easily be turned into its opposite, the actual
> dimunition of woman's role in production as the labor force contracts.

She goes on to say that "under capitalism, automation could possibly
lead to an ever-growing structural unemployment which would expel
women—the latest and least integrated recruits to the labor force and
ideologically the most expendable for a bourgeois society—from production
after only a brief interlude in it" (1971b: 252).

The economic repercussions resulting from technological forces
applied for profit and to facilitate the affairs of State came quickly, and the

response along ethnic and sexual lines appeared suddenly. To meet the challenges, some concessions were made so that initially the minorities could boast of certain gains. Nonetheless: "In some peculiar form of regression," William J. Ronan (1971) believes, "we seem content to seek expiation—not by ridding ourselves of problems, but by indulging them ritually and transferring the whole mess to communally agreed-upon villains." Unfortunately, and unbeknown to Ronan and most Americans, the "villains" are turning out to be the very victims of social oppression; blame for economic difficulties and social dissatisfaction is being placed upon those who suffer most from economic dislocations and political ineffectiveness. A goodly number of social analysts, commentators, and scholars have come forth with forewarnings that the economic demise of our social identities portends the very genuine possibility of extermination.

BLACKS.   "When the decade of the 1970's began," Samuel F. Yette (1971) asserts, "the United States government was officially—but unconstitutionally—in the midst of two wars: (1) a war of 'attrition' (genocide) against the colonized colored people of Indochina, and (2) an expeditionary 'law and order' campaign (repression-selective genocide) against the colonized colored people of the United States." (p. 15; see also Willhelm, 1971).

INDIANS.   "Assimilate or starve!" Joe Muskrat, a regional director for the U.S. Civil Rights Commission, said in the *Civil Rights Digest* for October 1972 that this "has been the choice offered the American Indian by the dominant society. . . . When it has not been genocidal, the traditional approach to the American Indian has been to seek his assimilation into the larger society, an attitude based on the feeling of cultural superiority" (quoted in Delaney, 1973: 14).

CHICANOS.   John Womack, Jr. (1972) maintains that "regular Americans" have treated the 'Mexicans,' the 'Spanish-speaking,' the 'Spanish-surnamed,' and now the 'Mexican Americans,' as intruders in this country, whom they could always 'send back to Mexico' " (p. 16). Consequently, as Jacobs and Landau (1971) conclude, "the newly awakened Mexican-Americans now know that the conflict between Anglos and the Mexicans goes back to their earliest encounters. The result was that the Spanish-speaking people became victims of a kind of cultural imperialism that promised them equality but practiced a form of genocide" (p. 227).

WOMEN.   "In the eyes of man," writes one of the most astute scholars of woman's contribution to civilization, Elizabeth Gould Davis (1972), "there are two kinds of women: the sex object, and 'the other.' The class of the sex object . . . of women men have a tolerance. . . . 'The other,' the class of the non-sex-object, includes all unmarried women over forty, nearly all intellectual women, and above all, all women who are primarily male-oriented. To the masculist these women have no human rights, no reason for existence. They are expendable. They are allowed to exist only if they accept their inferiority in a 'womanly' way, . . . expecting neither justice nor consideration . . ." (p. 327).

If economic resources are allocated to advance profits and the power of State, then we must come to recognize that human vitality and, indeed, existence are incidental to the foremost concerns that have come to dominate the nation. "If we are not prepared to make the investment in human resources that is required," Philip M. Hauser, professor of sociology at the University of Chicago and a former president of the American Sociological Association, anticipates, "we will be forced to increase our investment in the Police, National Guard, and the Army. And possibly—it can happen here— we may be forced to resort to concentration camps and even genocide" (*Washington Afro-American,* September 7, 1968, p. 1). Economic allocations that deviate from production and state activities deemed "essential," especially for sustaining social control over foreign and domestic affairs, are unwanted costs; "investment in human resources" is treated as a "burden." George Wald (1974: 23) of Harvard, winner of the Nobel Prize in Physiology of Medicine for 1967, in his address at the 20th World Conference against Atomic and Hydrogen Bombs in Tokyo on August 2, 1974, stated: "With the increasing mechanization, increasing numbers of persons have become not only unemployed but superfluous. There is no use for them in the free-market economy. They are wanted neither as workers nor customers. They are not wanted at all. Their existence is a burden . . . ." Wald also noted:

> In his report to the World Bank in September, 1970, its president, Robert McNamara, former Ford [Motor Company] executive and Secretary of Defense, spoke of such persons as "marginal men." He estimated that in 1970 there were 500 million of them—twice the population of the United States— and that by 1980 there would be one billion, and by 1990, two billion. That would be half the world population.

Canada, a nation once receptive to immigrants, now closes its frontiers; it relies upon postindustrial technology for production: "As a sparsely settled developing country, Canada historically welcomed immigrants and even solicited them. They were badly needed to boost the country's labor force. Today, however, to an industrial nation, faced with more and more job-destroying automation, immigrants, unless highly skilled, soon become a burden" (Waltz, 1972). Intolerance breeds hostility among the discarded for being unwanted and unable, in spite of strong personal desires, to work, to secure employment. Hostility is bred as well among wealthy and powerful people, who have come to fear the potential of revolutionary demands and open rebellion from among the dispossessed. For example, in late 1974, the City Council of Hartford, Connecticut, debated a resolution calling for the erection of a fence around the city's black and Puerto Rican ghetto in order to contain a growing discontent (*Guardian*, November 6, 1974, p. 2).

The distresses of unemployment are apparently not confined to the unemployed, Capital's ruling interests, and/or State's managerial elites. Peter D. Hart, a national pollster, has found Americans in general "willing to go a lot farther than any of their leaders have been willing to take them" in formulating more drastic economic policies. According to the poll Hart made during 1975, a 41% plurality advocated major economic changes, as many as two thirds preferred to work for an employee-owned company, and 56% stated a willingness to vote for a presidential candidate who proposed that major businesses be owned and managed by employees themselves (United Press International, 1975).

We must realize that the appearance of the fantastically productive technology of automation, with its potential to do away with human labor, introduces a radically new economy, one where there is an abundance of productivity and a surplus of useless people. The point was made, at the beginning of this chapter, that in the midst of affluence, where labor is not appropriated, political processes come to the fore; in the Garden of abundance, a power hierarchy established dominion: God, humans, and Nature. Today, we have secured human command over Nature through technological controls and, hence, to make our reentry into the Garden of Eden it will be necessary to supplant economic with political processes. To triumph over Nature is to reorder the political system, since the power to command Nature is the very resource with which to exert power over humans. The emergence of a technological order makes our relationship to the means of production less significant and, simultaneously, our access to the political processes all the more vital if the necessities of life are to be provided as though we reside in the Garden of Eden. Finally, and unlike God in command over humans in the Garden, we must come to acknowledge and share with others the knowledge of right and wrong in order to share with one another an equitable distribution of technological wealth.

In the past, when we had no more than the primitiveness of preindustrial technology, human destiny resided in the whims of Nature; control over our lives depended much upon natural conditions, especially weather and terrain. Today, with the full bloom of technological sophistication, we feel powerless not because of an uncontrollable Nature but because of a sense of futility regarding our ability to grasp control over events. The effort to subdue Nature required the harnessing of energy to technology; to seize command of social realities seemingly beyond our grasp will require socially organized effort through political power. Today, we cite economic variables, not the perplexities of Nature, as the base of our anxieties. Typical is the lamentation of the economist James Tobin of Yale, a former member of the President's Council of Economic Advisers during the Kennedy Administration:

> The complacency of the media, the public and the politicians about the depression of the 1970's is very disheartening. Every [percentage] point of unemployment is a loss of Gross National Product of about $55 billion a year. At five percent unemployment, which we bettered as recently as 1973, the country would be producing $180 billion more per year.... (quoted in Wicker, 1976: 29)

Yet there is not only complacency but actual attempts, especially at the behest of government agencies, to manipulate poverty rather than acknowledge the necessity to manipulate wealth in behalf of the needy. For example, official government figures reveal 24.3 million poor people in 1974, in contrast to 40 million in 1959—leaving a rather vivid impression of a dramatic reduction in the number of poverty-stricken people. However, the reduction has been achieved *purely through statistical manipulation of family income data*. In 1959, the "poverty level" was set at 54% of the average median family income; in 1974, it was established by taking 40% of the average median family income. If the original 54% of 1959 were still used to compute the extent of people in poverty, instead of 40%, there would have been 46 million poor Americans in 1974—an *increase* of 21.7 million rather than the official *decrease* of 15.7 million![7] State simply manipulates poverty to manipulate the lives of people and, in the process, endeavors to reject the real-life experiences of Americans. This is no more than tyranny, as James Baldwin (Mead & Baldwin, 1971) has so well stated: "What I am trying to get at is that the American terror of the world, of reality, the American attempt to deny and manipulate experience, I have always equated with the American terror of dealing with me as a human being, dealing with Sambo" (p. 84). In other words, poverty is now a political and not an economic definition; State has the power to designate who is and who is not among the poor.

The rise of State power over the economy and the affairs of our lives is devoid of established morality. The victory over Nature will indeed be a hollow triumph if we the people must succumb to the will of State rule not intent upon human development but instead devoted to the fulfillment of the omnipotent national interest as the overriding consideration transcending the well-being of the citizenry.

NOTES

1. Profits also dropped during the Vietnam War; between 1960 and 1963, after-tax profits jumped 71%, while for the war period 1966–69 they rose only 9.2% (*I. F. Stone's Bi-Weekly*, May 4, 1970, p. 3). For an alternative explanation to the one presented here, see Alan Nasser (1976: 10–11).

2. Only a very broad outline can be presented here to account for the emergence of State as a post–World War II phenomenon; a more detailed analysis is to be found in my forthcoming article, "The Rise of State Rule: An Exploratory and Interpretative Essay," in *Catalyst*.

3. For a discussion of competitive and monopoly Capital, see O'Connor (1973).

4. See my forthcoming article, "The Rise of State Rule," for greater elaboration upon this point.

5. For an excellent article raising many of these same issues, see Albert Rosenfeld (1970).

6. This is why former President Nixon, with complete honesty, pathetically answered "I am not a crook" in response to all the accusations of impropriety that eventually forced him from the office; he considered himself a professional politician and therefore above all the blunders and the bunglings surrounding the Watergate scandals.

7. These figures come from an 82-page report prepared by the Campaign for Human Development, a Catholic organization, as published in *The Militant*, January 16, 1976, p. 2.

REFERENCES

Anderson, Jack. "Washington Merry-Go-Round," syndicated column. *Galveston Daily News*, June 14, 1974, p. 4–A. (a)

Anderson, Jack. "Washington Merry-Go-Round," syndicated column. *Buffalo Courier-Express*, November 17, 1974, p. 26. (b)

Associated Press. "New Jersey Upholds Teacher's Dismissal in Sex-Change Case." *Buffalo Evening News*, April 12, 1972. (a)

Associated Press. "Welfare Growth Hits 5-year Low in 1972." *Buffalo Evening News*, October 18, 1972, p. 46. (b)

Associated Press. "High Court Upholds Zoning to Exclude Communal Living." *Buffalo Evening News*, April 2, 1974, p. 11.

Associated Press. "Total Fertility Rate Dips to Record Low Despite Birth Rise." *The New York Times*, May 26, 1975, p. 15.

Associated Press. "A Decline in Blacks and Young People Is Found on Farms." *The New York Times*, January 10, 1976, p. 28.

Baran, Paul A., & Paul M. Sweezy. *Monopoly Capital*. New York: Monthly Review Press, 1966.

Bassett, Preston C. "Social Security's Weak Underpinning." *The New York Times*, December 14, 1975, p. E–14.

Bazelon, David T. *The Paper Economy*. New York: Vintage Books, 1965.

Beal, Frances M. "Double Jeopardy: To Be Black and Female." In Robin Morgan (ed.), *Sisterhood Is Powerful*. New York: Vintage Books, 1970.

Benston, Margaret. "The Political Economy of Women's Liberation." *Monthly Review* 24 (1969): 17.

Bowden, Lord. "How Much Science Can We Afford?" *The Nation* 204 (January 2, 1967): 17–21.

Bowen, Charles R. "Automation: The Paradoxes of Abundance." In William W. Brickman & Stanley Lehrer (eds.), *Automation, Education, and Human Values*. New York: School and Society, 1966.

Broom, Leonard, & Norval Glenn. *Transformation of the Negro American*. New York: Harper & Row, 1966.

Buffalo Evening News. "Income Gap Between Sexes Widens in 20-year Period." November 17, 1975, p. 8.

Buyer, Bob. "WNY Processors Cannot Handle Tomato Surplus; Market Glutted." *Buffalo Evening News*, September 10, 1975, p. 32.

Casalino, Larry. "This Land Is Their Land." *Ramparts* 11 (July 1972): 31–36.

Chasteen, Edgar R. *The Case for Compulsory Birth Control*. Englewood Cliffs, N.J.: Prentice-Hall, 1972.

Clarke, Arthur C. *Profiles of the Future*. New York: Harper & Row, 1960.

Committee for Economic Development. *Economic Growth in the U.S.: Its Past and Future*. New York, 1958.

Cook, Fred J. "The Case of the Disappearing Pension." *New York Times Magazine*, March 19, 1972, p. 31 ff.

Cook, Fred J. "Chicanery in Private Pensions." *The Nation* 216 (February 26, 1973): 268–272.

Curtin, Sharon R. *Nobody Ever Died of Old Age*. Boston: Atlantic–Little, Brown, 1973.

Dale, Edwin L., Jr.   "The Economics of Pollution." In Paul K. Anderson, *Omega*. Dubuque: William C. Brown Co., Publishers, 1971.

D'Amico, Debby. "To My White Working-Class Sisters." In *Liberation Now!* New York, Dell Publishing Co., 1971.

Davis, Elizabeth Gould. *The First Sex*. Baltimore, Md.: Penguin Books, 1972.

Delaney, Paul. "Census Statistics Indicate Indians Are the Poorest Minority Group." *The New York Times*, July 17, 1973, p. 14.

Diebold, John. "The World and Doomsday Fads." *The New York Times*, February 25, 1973, p. E13.

Dillingham, Harry C., & David F. Sly. "The Mechanical Cotton-Picker, Negro Migration, and the Integration Movement." *Human Organization* 25 (Winter 1966): 344–351.

Eglit, Howard. "The Green in the Green Pastures is Brown." *The New York Times*, August 2, 1975, p. 21.

Eliade, Mircea. *The Sacred and the Profane*. Trans. Willard R. Trask. New York: Harcourt, Brace, 1959.

Farrell, William F. "Welfare Reforms Near a Standstill." *The New York Times*, January 18, 1976, p. 1.

Finlay, George. "Ford Refuses Housing Aid for Rural Poor." *Guardian*, December, 1974, p. 5.

Flint, Jerry M. "Big Industries Not Likely to Cut Down Jobless." *The New York Times*, January 20, 1972, p. 1 ff.

Fuller, R. Buckminister. *Education Automation*. New York: Doubleday, 1972.

Gans, Herbert J. "The New Egalitarianism." *Saturday Review* 55 (May 6, 1972): 43–46.

Gray, Betty MacMorran. "Money and Marriage: The Usable Truth." *The Nation* 214 (June 26, 1972): 820–821.

Hanley, Harles. "Public Employment Still Growing; So Is Its Political Clout." *Buffalo Evening News*, August 12, 1974, p. 8.

Harris, Louis. "Women's Status: Figures Getting Better All the Time." *Buffalo Evening News*, December 11, 1975, p. 50.

Hauser, Philip. "Demographic Factors in the Integration of the Negro." *Daedalus* 94 (Fall 1965): 847–877.

Heilbroner, Robert. *The Limits of American Capitalism*. New York: Harper & Row, 1965.

Hill, Robert B. *Benign Neglect Revisited: The Illusion of Black Progress*. Washington, D.C.: National Urban League, 1973.

Houston, Jack. "Gap Continues to Widen in Men's, Women's Pay." *Buffalo Evening News*, December, 1975, p. 67.

Isenberg, Barbara. "Senior Power: Aging in America." *The Nation*, 216 (May 14, 1973): 626–628.

Jacobs, Paul, & Saul Landau. *To Serve the Devil*. New York: Vintage Books, 1971.

Jacoby, Susan. "49 Million Singles Can't All Be Right." *New York Times Magazine*, February 17, 1974, p. 13 ff.

Jensen, Michael C. "America's Pension System: A \$135 Billion Question." *Saturday Review* 55 (April 8, 1972): 42–44.

Kaplan, H. Roy, & Curt Tausky. "Work and the Welfare Cadillac: The Function of and Commitment to Work among the Hard-Core Unemployed." *Social Problems* 19 (Spring 1972): 469–483.

Kelly, Ed. "Basic Bargaining: Money vs. 'Productivity.' " *Buffalo Evening News*, January 24, 1976, p. C–4.

Kihss, Peter. "Job Study Issued on Puerto Ricans." *The New York Times*, June 1, 1975, p. 37.

Knight News Service. *Buffalo Evening News*, February 10, 1975, p. 6.

Kolko, Gabriel. *Wealth and Power in America*. New York: Frederick A. Praeger, 1962.

Leinenweber, Charles. "The Great American Pension Machine." *Ramparts* 10 (June 1972): 29–36.

Liberation News Service. "Monopoly Corporations Escape Taxes." *Guardian*, December 31, 1975, p. 4.

Love, Keith. "How Do You Put a Price Tag on a Housewife's Work?" *The New York Times*, January 13, 1976, p. 39.

Lovel, Frank. "Union Exposes Oil Trust Profiteering and Lies." *Militant*, January 17, 1974, p. 18.

Lyman, Stanford M., & Marvin B. Scott. *A Sociology of the Absurd*. New York: Appleton-Century-Crofts, 1970.

McCurry, Dan, & Alan Jerome. "Chicago Elderly Fight Back." *Guardian*, June 24, 1974, p. 6.

Margois, George. "Letter to the Editor." *The New York Times*, August 12, 1972.

Mead, Margaret, and James Baldwin. *Rap on Race*. Philadelphia: Lippincott, 1971.

Melman, Seymour. *Our Depleted Society*. New York: Holt, Rinehart, & Winston, 1965.

Melman, Seymour. *The Permanent War Economy*. New York: Simon & Schuster, 1974.

Mills, C. Wright. *White Collar*. New York: Oxford University Press, 1951.

Mitchell, Juliet. "Women: The Longest Revolution." In *Liberation Now!* New York: Dell Publishing Co., 1971 (a), and in Arlene S. Skolnick and Jerome H. Skolnick (eds.), *Family in Transition*. Boston: Little, Brown, 1971 (b).

Nasser, Alan. "The Twilight of Capitalism: Contours of the Emerging Epoch." *Insurgent Sociologist* 6 (Winter 1976): 5–28.

Nordheimer, Jon. "He Feels 'Like a Kid' Again, but His 'American Family' Is in Ruins." *The New York Times*, March 1, 1974, p. 34.

O'Connor, James. *The Fiscal Crisis of the State*. New York: St. Martin's Press, 1973.

Omo-Fadaka, Jimoh. "Exploding the Myth of Aid." *Resurgence* 4 (November–December 1973): 6.

Pace, Eric. "Authors Decry Snags in Marketing." *The New York Times*, December 27, 1972.

Pace, Eric. "Illiteracy among World's Women Rising Steadily." *The New York Times*, September 4, 1975, p. 12.

Palazzetti, Agnes. "Mechanical Grape Harvesters Work Day, Night in Chautauqua." *Buffalo Evening News*, October 9, 1972, p. 13.

Perkins, G. Homes. "The Architect and the City." In Marcus Whiffen (ed.), *The Architect and the City*. Cambridge, Mass.: M.I.T. Press, 1962.

Perlo, Victor. *Economics of Racism*. New York: International Publishers, 1975.

Piven, Frances Fox, & Richard A. Cloward. *Regulating the Poor*. New York: Vintage Books, 1971.

Polk, Peggy. "Economists Seek to Close Huge Income Gap among Nation." *Buffalo Courier-Express* March 5, 1972, p. 9.

Powell, Roland. "4.7 Million Elderly Now Living in Poverty, Senate Panel Finds." *Buffalo Evening News*, November 26, 1971.

Rensberger, Boyce. "'Super Computer' to Aid Climate Studies." *The New York Times*, February 7, 1972.

Reuters News Service. "Trim Labor's Cost, GM's Murphy Urges Industry." *Buffalo Evening News*, November 13, 1975, p. 55.

Ribicoff, Abraham. "The Alienation of the American Worker." *Saturday Review* 55 (April 22, 1972): 33.

Robbins, William. "Farm Policy Helps Make the Rural Rich Richer." *The New York Times,* April 5, 1970, pp. 1, 56.

Roberts, Dick. "Galbraith's 'Money': Fact & Fiction." *Militant,* December 19, 1975, p. 25.

Roberts, Steven V. "But Why the Epidemic? It Could Be as Simple as 'Making Do Won't Do.' " *The New York Times,* January 5, 1974, p. 16.

Ronan, William J. "The New Urban Witchcraft." *The New York Times,* March 24, 1971.

Rosenfeld, Albert. "Will Man Direct His Own Evolution?" In Leo J. Ryan (ed.), *USA/From Where We Stand.* Belmont, Calif.: Fearon Publishers, 1970.

Rosenthal, Jack. "Two-Thirds of Job Gains in '60's Made by Women." *The New York Times,* February 12, 1973, p. 1 ff. (a)

Rosenthal, Jack. "Poor in Nation Rise by 5%, Reversing 10-year Trend." *The New York Times,* May, 1973, p. 1. (b)

Shabecoff, Philip. "H.E.W. Study Finds Job Discontent Is Hurting Nation." *The New York Times,* December 22, 1972, p. 1 ff.

Shannon, William V. "Great Pension Issue." *The New York Times,* September 10, 1972, p. 35.

Sipser, I. Philip. "Looking into Corporate Power." *The New York Times,* August 22, 1975, p. 31.

Spencer, Herbert. *Essays on Education.* New York: Dutton, 1966 (orginally published, 1858).

Steiner, Stan. *The New Indians.* New York: Harper & Row, 1968.

Sterba, James P. "The U.S. Now Contributes Less, Others More, But to No Avail." *The New York Times,* December 23, 1973, p. E3.

Stern, Philip. *The Great Treasury Raid.* New York: Signet Books, 1962.

Stevens, William K. "Tobacco Farming Enters Machine Age." *New York Times,* October 4, 1971 p. 1 ff.

Thomas, Clayton. "Inflation Is Cruel to the Already Poor." *The New York Times,* July 5, 1973, p. 35.

Time Magazine. "The Old in the Country of the Young." In Arlene S. Skolnick & Jerome H. Skolnick (eds.), *Family in Transition.* Boston: Little, Brown, 1971.

Toffler, Alvin. *Future Shock.* New York: Bantam Books, 1970.

United Press International. " 'Easy Riders' May Be Learning Life." *Buffalo Evening News,* April 20, 1973.

United Press International. "Crisis of Confidence Looms in America, Pollster Warns." *Buffalo Evening News,* October 31, 1975, p. 7.

U.S. Bureau of the Census. "Detailed Characteristics." *Census of the Population: 1960, U.S. Summary.* Washington, D.C.: U.S. Government Printing Office, 1961.

U.S. Bureau of the Census. "Population Profile of the United States." *Current Population Reports,* Series P–20, No. 279. Washington, D.C.: U.S. Government Printing Office, 1975.

U.S. Department of Commerce. *Pocket Data Book, USA.* Washington, D.C.: U.S. Government Printing Office, 1971.

U.S. Department of Labor. *Manpower Report of the President, 1972*. Washington, D.C.: U.S. Government Printing Office, 1972.

U.S. Department of Health, Education, and Welfare. *Births, Marriages, Divorces, and Deaths for October, 1975*. National Center for Health Statistics, Monthly Vital Statistics Report, No. 24. December 29, 1975.

U.S. News & World Report. "A Close-up of Women in U.S. . . . and Ways their Status is Changing." December 8, 1975, pp. 56–57.

U.S. News and World Report. "Crackdown on Welfare Payments." (August 9, 1971): 13–16.

Wald, George. " 'It is Too Late for Declarations, for Popular Appeals.' " *New York Times*, August 17, 1974, p. 23.

Waltz, Jay. "Canada, with 6% Jobless, May Curb Immigration." *The New York Times*, July 19, 1972.

Wargo, James. "Car Sales Soar, but Increase in Related Jobs is Myth." *Buffalo Evening News*, September 20, 1972.

Wicker, Tom. "Reactors and Risks." *The New York Times*, December 12, 1975, p. 41.

Wicker, Tom. "The First Priority Is Jobs." *The New York Times*, January 16, 1976, p. 29.

Willhelm, Sidney M. *Who Needs the Negro?* Garden City, N.Y.: Doubleday Anchor Books, 1971.

Williams, William Appleton. *The Great Evasion*. Chicago: Quadrangle Books, 1964.

Womack, John, Jr. "The Chicanos." *New York Review of Books* 19 (August 31, 1972): 12–18.

Wren, Christopher S. "Not Only Drought Hurts Soviet Crops." *The New York Times*, January 25, 1976, p. 31.

Yette, Samuel F. *The Choice: The Issue of Survival in America*. New York: G. P. Putnam, 1971.

Name Index

Subject Index

THE BOOK MANUFACTURE

American Minorities and Economic Opportunity was set in linotype at Weimer Typesetting Company, Inc., Indianapolis, and was printed and bound at Kingsport Press. Cover design was by John D. Firestone & Associates, Canal Winchester, Ohio. The paper is Glatfelter Offset. The type is Baskerville with English Bold display.